EDINBURGH STUDIES IN LAW
VOLUME 9

Law Making and the Scottish Parliament

The Early Years

Edited by
Elaine E Sutherland, Kay E Goodall,
Gavin F M Little and Fraser P Davidson
all of
The School of Law,
University of Stirling

D1615496

EDINBURGH
University Press

EDINBURGH STUDIES IN LAW

Series Editor: Elspeth Reid (University of Edinburgh)

Volumes in the series:

Elspeth Reid and David L Carey Miller (eds), *A Mixed Legal System in Transition: T B Smith and the Progress of Scots Law* (2005)

Hector MacQueen and Reinhard Zimmermann (eds), *European Contract Law: Scots and South African Perspectives* (2006)

John W Cairns and Paul du Plessis (eds), *Beyond Dogmatics: Law and Society in the Roman World* (2007)

William M Gordon, *Roman Law, Scots Law and Legal History* (2007)

Kenneth G C Reid, Marius J de Wall and Reinhard Zimmerman, *Exploring the Law of Succession: Studies National, Historical and Comparative* (2007)

Vernon Valentine Palmer and Elspeth Christie Reid (eds), *Mixed Jurisdictions Compared: Private Law in Louisiana and Scotland* (2009)

J W Cairns and Paul du Plessis (eds), *The Creation of the* Ius Commune: *From* Casus *to* Regula (2010)

James Chalmers, Fiona Leverick and Lindsay Farmer (eds), *Essays in Criminal Law in Honour of Sir Gerald Gordon* (2010)

Neil Walker (ed), *MacCormick's Scotland* (2012)

First published in hardback in 2011

This paperback edition 2014

Edinburgh University Press Ltd
The Tun – Holyrood Road
12 (2f) Jackson's Entry
Edinburgh EH8 8PJ
www.euppublishing.com

Typeset in New Caledonia by Koinonia, Manchester, and
printed and bound in Great Britain by CPI Group (UK) Ltd, Croydon CR0 4YY

A CIP record for this book is available from the British Library

ISBN 978 0 7486 4019 5 (hardback)
ISBN 978 0 7486 9676 5 (paperback)
ISBN 978 0 7486 9736 6 (webready PDF)
ISBN 978 0 7486 8766 4 (epub)

Contents

THE SCOTTISH PARLIAMENT – ITS GENESIS AND OPERATION

RIGHTS AND SOCIETY

PUBLIC ADMINISTRATION AND SERVICES

JUSTICE AND LEGAL SYSTEM

ECONOMY AND ENVIRONMENT

Preface to the Paperback Edition

We are delighted that *Law Making and the Scottish Parliament: The Early Years* is being published in a paperback edition, making it more accessible to a wider audience with an interest in Scotland's evolving constitutional status and what it means for the legal process and the law.

There have, of course, been dramatic developments since the publication of the hardback edition in 2010. The Scotland Act 2012 and the forthcoming 2014 Scottish independence referendum herald the prospect of further constitutional change, irrespective of whether or not Scots choose to remain within the United Kingdom. Widespread reform of the court system has brought further – and sometimes controversial – changes to the legal process. Members of the Scottish Parliament have continued to reform specific aspects of substantive law. That said, the purpose of this paperback edition is the same as its hardback predecessor: "to offer critical analysis of the first ten years of law making by the Scottish Parliament in a number of key areas, putting it in its wider policy and socio-legal context."

It is no accident that this edition appears in the run up to the independence referendum which has so heightened interest in Scotland's future both at home and abroad. Understanding the past – including the recent past – is an essential precondition to moving forward. Whatever happens in the referendum, it is our hope that this volume will contribute to that process.

Elaine E Sutherland
Kay E Goodall
Gavin F M Little
Fraser P Davidson
Stirling Law School
February 2014

Preface

As the tenth anniversary of the new Scottish Parliament approached, we believed the time was ripe to offer some assessment of the Parliament's contribution to various areas of Scots law. This volume is the result.

Of course, it is never as simple as that. First, there was the matter of selecting contributors for the individual chapters. Approaches were made to the bravest and the best from the wealth of talent found amongst Scotland's legal academics and practitioners: each was asked to pass judgment on the progress made by legislators, offering critical analysis of the Parliament's contribution in his or her field of expertise.

We would like to offer our profound thanks to the contributors who made time in their busy schedules to rise to the challenge, strove to meet our editorial guidelines and to do so timeously.

We were most gratified when the project was greeted with enthusiasm by the Edinburgh Legal Education Trust and we are indebted to the trustees and to Elspeth Reid for her insight and unfailing courtesy and efficiency in helping to steer us through the Trust's approval process in order that the volume could appear in the Edinburgh Studies in Law Series. Thereafter, the proposal was considered and accepted by Edinburgh University Press and we are grateful to Sarah Edwards, Eddie Clark and their colleagues for their assistance with editing and production.

Contributors have endeavoured to state the law as at 31 December 2009 and, on occasion, it has been possible to incorporate more recent developments.

Elaine E Sutherland
Kay E Goodall
Gavin F M Little
Fraser P Davidson
Stirling
November 2010

List of Contributors

DAVID CABRELLI joined the School of Law at the University of Edinburgh as a lecturer in commercial law in 2007, having lectured previously at the University of Dundee. Prior to becoming an academic, David worked as a solicitor practising in commercial and company law.

TRUDI CRAGGS is a partner in the firm of Dundas and Wilson CS LLP where she specialises in planning and transport law. She is co-author of *Scottish Roads Law*. Trudi advises a range of public sector transport authorities.

STUART CROSS is a Senior Lecturer in the School of Law at the University of Dundee. He moved to Dundee after fourteen years in private practice as a solicitor in Edinburgh and Glasgow.

FRASER DAVIDSON joined Stirling Law School in 2005 having previously been Head of the School of Law and Alexander Stone Professor of Commercial Law at the University of Glasgow.

ROBERT DUNBAR is a Reader in Law and Celtic at the University of Aberdeen. He is an expert of the Council of Europe and a Senior Non-Resident Research Associate of the European Centre for Minority Issues. A fluent Gaelic-speaker, he is a member of Bòrd na Gàidhlig and MG Alba.

ANN FAULDS is a partner in the firm of Dundas and Wilson CS LLP where she specialises in planning and transport law. She is co-author of *Scottish Roads Law* and she annotated the Transport (Scotland) Act 2001. Ann is a Member of the Institute of Highways and Transportation and a Legal Associate of the Royal Town Planning Institute.

PAMELA FERGUSON holds the Chair in Scots law at the University of Dundee. She has been an academic for twenty years, having previously been employed in the Crown Office and Procurator Fiscal Service.

KAY GOODALL is a Senior Lecturer and Director of Research at Stirling Law School. She came to Stirling from the University of Glasgow in 2007, having taught at Glasgow since 1998.

GAVIN LITTLE is a Professor of Law at the University of Stirling. His main areas of research interest are Scots public law and environmental law. He is currently writing a book on the Administration of the Modern Scottish Legal System for the Scottish Universities Law Institute.

CLAIRE MCDIARMID has been teaching criminal law at the University of Strathclyde since 1999. She is currently a senior lecturer. From 1996 to 2006 she was also a member of the children's panel for the City of Glasgow.

FRANCIS MCMANUS joined the Edinburgh Napier University School of Law in 1991, having previously been a lecturer in environmental health at the same university.

AIDAN O'NEILL is a Queen's Counsel, practising primarily in human rights and constitutional law. He is an Honorary Fellow and Chairman of the Edinburgh Centre for Constitutional Law, University of Edinburgh. He has been a Visiting Professor in the Woodrow Wilson School of Public and International Affairs, and Senior Research Scholar and Fellow in Law and Public Affairs, Princeton University.

ALAN PAGE is Professor of Public Law at the University of Dundee. His books include *The Executive in the Constitution* (1999) (with Terence Daintith), *Investor Protection* (1992) (with Bob Ferguson) and *Legislation* (2nd edn, 1990) (with David Miers). He is currently completing a book on Constitutional Law for the Scottish Universities Law Institute.

COLIN T REID is Professor of Environmental Law at the University of Dundee, after previously working at the University of Aberdeen. He is a founder member of the UK Environmental Law Association and founding Convener of the Environmental Law Section of the Society of Legal Scholars.

ROBERT RENNIE has held the Chair of Conveyancing at the University of Glasgow since 1992. He is also a partner in the legal firm of Harper Macleod

PETER ROBSON has been Professor of Social Welfare Law at the University of Strathclyde since 1992. He was until recently Chairman of SHELTER and is currently Chair of Weslo Housing Management, a registered social landlord in West Lothian.

JANYS M SCOTT has been a member of the Faculty of Advocates since 1992. She was appointed Queen's Counsel in 2007.

ELAINE E SUTHERLAND began her academic career at the University of Edinburgh, later moving to the University of Glasgow. She joined the Law School at Stirling University in 2006 as Professor of Child and Family Law and has been a Professor of Law at Lewis and Clark Law School, Portland, Oregon since 1999.

Table of Cases

Table of Westminster Statutes

Table of Scottish Parliament Statutes

Table of Westminster Statutory Instruments

Table of Scottish Statutory Instruments

The Scottish Parliament
– Its Genesis and Operation

1 Law Making and the Scottish Parliament: The Early Years in Context

The Editors

The creation of the Scottish Parliament under the Scotland Act 1998[1] was without doubt a momentous political, constitutional and social happening in Scotland. The *zeitgeist* was captured at the first meeting of the Parliament in May 1999 by Dr Winnie Ewing, its most senior member, when she declared that "The Scottish Parliament, which adjourned on 25 March 1707, is hereby reconvened".[2] Although the constitutional actuality of the new Scottish Parliament, which exercises law-making competence subject to the statutory authority of the UK Parliament,[3] is very different from that of the Scottish Parliament of 1707, which was the legislature of an independent nation state, the spring of 1999 was undoubtedly the beginning of a new political and constitutional era for the people of Scotland.

The objective of this collection of essays is to offer critical analysis of the first ten years of law making by the Scottish Parliament in a number of key areas, putting it into its wider policy and socio-legal context. As is inevitably the case in a collection of essays, individual topics are addressed on a subject-by-subject basis and, while a certain amount of the content is necessarily narrative in nature, the bulk of the content is critical and analytical. Each chapter is written by a leading expert in his or her field. Contributors were invited to subject the key legislative themes in their own areas to rigorous critical

---

1 Hereafter "the Scotland Act".

2 Scottish Parliament, *Official Report*, 12 May 1999, vol 1, col 5, available at: *http://scottish. parliament.uk/business/officialReports*.

3 The Scottish Parliament and its law-making powers are, in formal terms, creations of an Act of the UK Parliament: see the Scotland Act 1998 ss 1, 28-35. This point was stressed by Lord Rodger in *Whaley v Lord Watson* 2000 SC 340 at 348. The Parliament has a statutorily restricted law-making power, or legislative competence, for Scotland in the areas which have been devolved to it by the UK Parliament: see Scotland Act 1998 s 29. In substantive terms, its legislative competence extends to a number of key areas of domestic policy, such as law and order, health, education and the environment. The Scotland Act does not, however, itemise the areas in which the Parliament may legislate. Rather, it specifies those areas of law making, such as the constitution, foreign affairs, defence, and fiscal, economic and monetary policy, which are "reserved" to the UK Parliament – everything else is presumed to be devolved: see the Scotland Act 1998 Sch 5.

analysis and also, in this context, to consider whether the Parliament has achieved what had been hoped for when it was established by the Scotland Act. Although the book does not seek to provide comprehensive coverage of all of the legislation of the Scottish Parliament, a number of significant issues emerge from the individual chapters, which are grouped loosely under five headings: the genesis and operation of the Parliament; rights and society; public administration and services; justice and legal system; and economy and environment.

While care must be taken when extrapolating general themes from a selective collection of essays, it is nonetheless striking that the overall thesis which emerges from the majority of the individual discussions is that of optimism tempered by experience. The picture is, however, complex and nuanced, for a number of the contributors also express admiration for the Parliament's legislative skill and respect for its achievements. In particular, as Robert Rennie's study of property law, Gavin Little's chapter on the reform of the judiciary, Stuart Cross's analysis of charities and David Cabrelli's discussion of arbitration indicate, there are important areas where careful technical revision and well debated, thoughtful legislation have significantly improved legal provision for Scotland. Indeed, in their first ten years, MSPs have, for the most part, proved themselves to be industrious, effective and competent law makers, enacting often weighty and complex legislation in a wide range of areas. Moreover, as Ann Faulds and Trudi Craggs explore in their chapter on transport, they have not been afraid to review and change the ways in which they legislate in the light of experience. And, as Alan Page points out in his analysis of the law-making process, very much more legislation has been passed by the Parliament than was envisaged originally. He describes this as an "explosion" of law making, and argues that legislating has emerged as one of the key defining activities of the new Parliament. But, thus far at least, it is fair to say that there has been relatively little in the way of the legislative pyrotechnics that were envisaged by some when the Parliament first sat in its temporary lodgings on the Mound in Edinburgh in May 1999.

Perhaps this is unsurprising, for the argument that the Parliament would be an engine of radical legislative change in devolved areas was always unconvincing. Neither the Scottish Constitutional Convention's campaign for a Scottish Parliament[4] nor the Labour government's 1997 White Paper on Scottish devolution[5] promised sweeping legal reform in Scotland. Rather,

---

4 See the Scottish Constitutional Convention, *A Claim of Right for Scotland* (1988); *Towards Scotland's Parliament* (1990); and *Scotland's Parliament, Scotland's Right* (1995).
5 *Scotland's Parliament* (Cmnd 3658: 1997).

they were premised on the importance of meeting the political and social need for Scotland to have a legislature which could rectify the so-called "democratic deficit" which had become apparent during the 1980s and 1990s. The experience of successive UK Conservative governments, with low levels of parliamentary representation in Scotland, passing radical and unpopular legislation[6] in "domestic" policy areas, which had historically and administratively been semi-autonomous,[7] had created a powerful consensus between the Labour and Liberal Democrat parties. Along with Scottish trade unions, local authorities and churches, they established the Scottish Constitutional Convention.[8] It argued that the Scottish people had the fundamental right to decide on their own constitution within the UK and, after the election of the UK Labour government in 1997 and the subsequent referendum on Scottish devolution,[9] the Scotland Act implemented this consensus. Viewed from this perspective, the law-making power of the Scottish Parliament over key domestic policy areas therefore represents an expression of Scottish national consciousness and identity within the Union, and provides a constitutional "safety-valve" in the event of future UK governments having low representation and support in Scotland, an issue which continues to resonate in the aftermath of the May 2010 UK general election. The existence of the Parliament as a political, constitutional and legal fact is also a statement of belief that Scotland, as one of the two founding nations of the UK,[10] with its own distinct culture, legal system, domestic administration,[11] education system, local government, national churches and history as an independent kingdom, ought, as a matter of political principle and national self-respect, to be making its own law, albeit inside the UK.

6 For example, the introduction in 1988 of the community charge, colloquially known as the "poll tax", to reform Scottish local government finance. See C Himsworth and N Walker, *The Scottish Community Charge* (1989).

7 That is, those areas of law and policy which prior to devolution had been the responsibility of the Secretary of State for Scotland: for example, justice and criminal law, health, education, the environment, local government, transport, and the legal system.

8 For discussion of the role of the Scottish Constitutional Convention in the campaign for the Scottish Parliament, see T M Devine, *The Scottish Nation 1700-2000* (1999) 609-617. The SNP and the Conservatives excluded themselves from the Convention.

9 In the 11 September 1997 referendum on Scottish devolution, 74.3% of those voting agreed that there should be a Scottish Parliament, with 63.5% agreeing that the Scottish Parliament should have tax-varying powers. The SNP, which supports independence rather than devolution, joined with Labour and the Liberal Democrats in the referendum campaign: only the Conservatives were opposed to the establishment of the Parliament.

10 The United Kingdom of Great Britain came into existence when the Union with England Act was passed by the Scottish Parliament in 1707 and the Union with Scotland Act was passed by the English Parliament in 1706.

11 That is, prior to devolution, the Scottish Office.

Seen in historical context, therefore, the primary political driver for the creation of the legislative power of the Scottish Parliament was not that the law in Scotland required wholesale, radical reform. Devolution was not a legal "year zero" and the new Scottish Parliament inherited a body of developed statutory provision from Westminster which was neither appreciably better nor worse than that which had been enacted for the rest of the UK. Indeed, as Fraser Davidson's chapter on the law of evidence and Frank McManus's discussion of local government demonstrate, some areas had received significant attention from Westminster, and the Scottish Parliament's legislative contribution was largely a continuation of what had gone before. And, as Robert Rennie and Elaine Sutherland discuss, although there were important technical aspects of Scots private law that were in need of modernisation and more thorough consideration than the Westminster timetable had allowed, there was little in terms of the actual substance of the law that passengers on a proverbial Sauchiehall Street omnibus would have thought to be either monstrously unjust or otherwise seriously objectionable.

Moreover, as a matter of *realpolitik*, neither the majority Labour/Liberal Democrat coalitions nor the current SNP minority administration in the Parliament have had a mandate from the Scottish electorate to enact radical legislation. Members of the Scottish Parliament are elected to implement their party manifestos, and all but one of the four main political parties in the Scottish Parliament operate within the context of UK-wide party structures.[12] Party discipline and the operation of proportional representation mean that the Scottish Parliament's law making often reflects the political priorities of Westminster-based parties, albeit with a devolved Scottish twist. Thus, a number of the chapters in the collection are concerned with legislative reforms which the Parliament implemented at the same time as similar measures were being passed at Westminster. And although the Scotland Act devolved very important areas of domestic law making to the Parliament, it is prohibited under the provisions of the Scotland Act from legislating in areas reserved to the UK Parliament and it must, of course, comply with EU law, the European Convention on Human Rights and international conventions to which the UK is party.[13] In addition, as Colin Reid points out in his chapter, in areas of devolved law making such as the environment, much legislation – as is also the case at Westminster and throughout the EU – has its origin in Brussels.

12 Scottish Labour is part of the British Labour Party; the Scottish Conservative and Unionist Party is part of the British Conservative Party; and the Scottish Liberal Democrats are one of the three parties within the federal structure of the Liberal Democrats. Self-evidently, the Scottish National Party, which campaigns for Scottish independence, is not part of a UK-wide party structure.
13 Scotland Act 1998 s 29.

There were also, however, important ambitions for the ways in which the new Parliament should operate. The Constitutional Convention had envisaged that it would not be a mere replica of Westminster sitting in Edinburgh – a view that was shared by the Consultative Steering Group on the Scottish Parliament, the body established by the UK government shortly after the 1997 referendum to consider how the Parliament should work.[14] The Group articulated four key principles, which still resonate:[15] first, the Parliament should embody and reflect the sharing of political power between the Scottish people, MSPs and the Scottish government; second, the Scottish government[16] should be accountable to the Parliament, and both the Parliament and government should be accountable to the Scottish people; third, the Parliament should be accessible, open and responsive, and it should develop procedures which enable the Scottish people to participate in developing, considering and scrutinising policy and legislation; and fourth, the Parliament should in its operation and appointments seek to promote equal opportunities for all.[17]

It is the third principle which is of most relevance to the Parliament's law-making functions, and which expresses the hope that the Parliament would prove to be more responsive to the needs of the people and less remote and formal than Westminster. The 2008 interim report of the Calman Commission on Scottish Devolution, which was established by the Parliament,[18] reviewed its transparency and openness and its "greater democratic scrutiny of public life in Scotland and of legislative proposals" before concluding, perhaps somewhat self-servingly, that devolution had been a "remarkable success".[19] But without doubting the view that the Parliament is indeed more open, responsive and egalitarian than the UK Parliament – although when set in the context of the recent Westminster expenses scandal this may not

---

14 See the Scottish Constitutional Convention, *Scotland's Parliament: Scotland's Right* (1995) 24; and *Report of the Consultative Steering Group on the Scottish Parliament* (1998) section 2.

15 For example, as in the recent interim report of the Commission on Scottish Devolution, chaired by Sir Kenneth Calman, *Serving Scotland Better: Scotland and the United Kingdom in the 21st Century* (2009).

16 The first two administrations (1999-2003 and 2003-2007) were dominated by the Labour party and styled themselves "the Scottish Executive", the term used in the Scotland Act 1998. When the Scottish Nationalist Party formed the third (minority) administration, in 2007, it changed the designation to "the Scottish Government".

17 C M G Himsworth and C M O'Neill, *Scotland's Constitution: Law and Practice* (2009) 59.

18 Unusually, the Commission was established as a result of co-operation between the opposition parties in the Parliament, in the wake of, and in opposition to, the establishment by the minority SNP government in 2007 of its "National Conversation".

19 Commission on Scottish Devolution, *The Future of Scottish Devolution within the Union: a First Report*, (2008) para 4.6.

be thought too difficult – the essays in this collection often suggest that while the Parliament has certainly established itself as a permanent constitutional fixture, there is little room for complacency.

Thus, Alan Page argues that, although the structure of the Parliament is distinctive and aspects of its procedure are more open and inclusive than the Westminster equivalent, the executive dominates the legislative process as much as it does at Westminster. Moreover, in her evaluation of child and family law, Elaine Sutherland contends that, although there has been wide consultation on legislative reform, the public petitions procedure has failed to live up to expectations, and politically controversial measures such as same-sex relationships were all too often passed by the Labour/Liberal Democrat coalition to Westminster under legislative consent procedures, in what amounts to a failure of political leadership. In the juvenile justice context, Claire McDiarmid notes that, while the Labour/Liberal Democrat coalition indulged in punitive youth crime rhetoric, in contrast to the SNP administration's emphasis on welfare issues, neither government has actually legislated very much in the field. Rob Dunbar's chapter on culture also argues that when the Parliament has engaged with particular issues in legislation it has often achieved much, but that the leadership and overall vision of the Scottish political class have been disappointing. The view that there has been a somewhat passive and even supine approach to law making by MSPs is shared by a number of contributors. Echoing Alan Page's point that the Parliament's processes are executive dominated, Aidan O'Neill's study of human rights and people and society makes trenchant criticisms of the Parliament's failure to monitor and challenge the Scottish government. A further theme which emerges from Pamela Ferguson's discussion of criminal law, Colin Reid's chapter on environment and sustainable development, Janys Scott's study of education and Peter Robson's analysis of housing is that, although the past ten years have seen a glut of law making, reform has been implemented in a largely piecemeal, fragmented fashion. In this too, the Parliament would seem to have followed in Westminster's ad hoc footsteps.

The purpose of an introduction is, however, to introduce and not to summarise. There is much richness and insight in each of the chapters, which cover a wide and eclectic range of the Parliament's first ten years of law making: they should be read and enjoyed and not pre-empted here. With this in mind, we close this introduction by expressing the hope that, given the ongoing development of the Scottish Parliament's political authority and the range and importance of its legislation, this book is the first of many studies into the Parliament's contribution to law making.

2 A Parliament that is Different? The Law-Making Process in the Scottish Parliament

Alan Page°

A. INTRODUCTION

Law making has emerged as one of the defining activities of the Scottish Parliament. In the ten years since devolution the Parliament has passed almost 150 Acts, on subjects ranging from criminal law to evidence, from

---

° Professor of Public Law at the University of Dundee.

local government to planning, and from mental health to family law. In doing so it has confounded the expectations of those who thought that law making would not feature prominently among the new Parliament's activities:

> So passionate were some of the expectations of devolution that some respectable voices argued that little or no devolved legislation would be needed. A nation that had voted decisively in favour of devolution would require precious little legislative governance.[1]

Had it been suggested at the outset that in its first two sessions (1999-2007) the Parliament would pass no fewer than 128 Bills, the likelihood is that the suggestion would have been dismissed as absurd. In the third session the pace of law making has slowed, but the Parliament is still passing more Bills than the first Presiding Officer and others anticipated it would once the Westminster "backlog" of legislative business had been cleared.[2]

In this chapter we concentrate not on the substance of the laws that have been made but rather on the process by which they have been made. We take a deliberately wide view of the legislative process, looking at what happens before a Bill is introduced, when the conventional wisdom asserts "all executive policy and most legislation is conceived, drafted and all but enacted",[3] as well as at what happens once it embarks on the parliamentary stages of the process. We begin, however, by looking at the expectations that were held of the process.

B. A PARLIAMENT THAT IS DIFFERENT?

The Scottish Parliament was not meant to be the "Scottish Westminster", a "legislative sausage machine" churning out laws on the Westminster model.[4] It was meant to be "different". One respect in which the Parliament is different is that its powers are limited in a way in which – as a matter of strict constitutional theory, at least – those of Westminster are not; it is part of "that wider family of Parliaments", as the Lord President noted in *Whaley v Lord Watson*, which, though modelled in some respects on Westminster, "owe their existence and powers to statute and are in various ways subject

---

1 J McCluskie, "New approaches to UK legislative drafting: the view from Scotland" (2004) 25 *StatLR* 136 at 138-139.
2 "I think in the fullness of time that backlog will have been cleared and I hope that we will have a little longer at each stage of the legislation than we have now": House of Lords Select Committee on the Constitution, *Devolution: Inter-Institutional Relations in the United Kingdom, Evidence Complete to 10 July 2002*, HL (2001-02) 147, question 754.
3 *Report of the Commission of Inquiry into Industrial and Commercial Representation* (1972) 5.
4 Scottish Parliament, *Official Report*, col 2211 (5 September 2001), David McLetchie.

to the law and to the courts which act to uphold the law".[5] This is not the only respect in which the Parliament was meant to be different. It was also meant to be different in the less tangible sense of not replicating what were commonly regarded as the worst features of the Westminster system. For the Scottish Constitutional Convention the hope was that the coming of a Scottish Parliament would usher in a way of politics that was "radically different from the rituals of Westminster: more participative, more creative, less needlessly confrontational".[6]

What being "not like Westminster"[7] might mean for the exercise of the Parliament's legislative function was not widely discussed before devolution. For the Consultative Steering Group, which was set up to recommend the procedures the Parliament might adopt, the "key" principles, later elevated to "founding" principles, were "power-sharing" and "access and participation".[8] The former was seen as requiring opportunities for members and committees as well as the government to legislate; it also meant enabling outside groups and individuals to participate in the making of legislation through an "effective consultative process". The latter was likewise seen as requiring "genuine" consultation. It is by no means clear, however, that this is radically different or even slightly different from Westminster. Private Members' legislation has been a feature of Westminster law making for so long that it is difficult to conceive the circumstances in which a government might once more lay claim to a monopoly of the legislative initiative. In addition, the importance of pre-legislative consultation with affected interests is widely acknowledged even if the reality may not always match up to the ideal.

A clearer insight into what "radically different" might mean is suggested by King's distinction between "power-sharing" and "power-hoarding" constitutional archetypes.[9] Power-sharing constitutions are characterised by the fragmentation of political power, bargaining, negotiation and deal making, and a culture which stresses the values of accommodation and consensus over exclusion and conflict. Power-hoarding constitutions, on the other hand, are characterised by the concentration of political power in the hands of government, the relative absence of competing centres of autonomous political power, and a political culture that legitimises and reinforces

---

5 *Whaley v Lord Watson* 2000 SC 340 at 349.
6 *Scotland's Parliament, Scotland's Right* (1995) 9.
7 The phrase is Winetrobe's: see B Winetrobe, *Realising the Vision: A Parliament with a Purpose* (2001) 12.
8 *Shaping Scotland's Parliament* (1998), section 2, paras 17-18, and section 3.5. There were two other founding principles: "accountability" and "equal opportunities".
9 A King, *Does the United Kingdom Still Have a Constitution?* (2001) 7-9.

the hoarding of political power; its guiding normative principle is "winner takes all".[10]

It comes as no surprise to learn that King's chosen example of a power-hoarding constitution should be the United Kingdom. The Scottish Constitutional Convention might therefore be understood to have rejected the traditional "winner takes all" approach to the exercise of political power in favour of genuine power-sharing or a consensus-seeking one.

There is an obvious correlation between the concepts of power sharing and power hoarding and more traditional ideas of parliamentary and executive law making. Under the United Kingdom constitution the law-making power belongs to Parliament – to the Queen in Parliament, strictly speaking – but the conventional wisdom is that legislation is more an executive than a parliamentary function,[11] which wisdom would seem to fit rather well with the idea of the constitution as a power-hoarding constitution; a feature of power-hoarding constitutions is that parliaments are essentially weak institutions.[12] Pursuing the idea of a Scottish Parliament that is different, we might look therefore for a Parliament that plays a more significant role in the legislative process than has traditionally been the case at Westminster. Such indeed seems to have been the goal of some commentators at the time of devolution. Crick and Millar thus looked forward to a system in which the executive "need not and should not have such total domination over the legislative process as has evolved at Westminster".[13]

What has emerged, however, is a process in which Westminster assumptions about the exercise of legislative power continue to hold sway, and which is therefore much closer to the Westminster model than the Constitutional Convention and others arguably had in mind. Coalition governments with comfortable working majorities in the Parliament's first two sessions partly account for this – possession of a parliamentary majority is treated as bringing with it the right to pursue a legislative programme – but a minority government since 2007 has not so far resulted in any real change in the pattern established in those years. Lacking an overall majority, the Nationalist government is legislating less, but, as has been observed, there has been "no rush by the opposition parties to fill the legislative void. They remain comfortable with the Westminster model of law-making and an opportunity for a greater share of the spoils come the next election".[14]

10 King, *Does the United Kingdom* (n 9) 10.
11 D Miers and A Page, *Legislation*, 2nd edn (1990) 4-7.
12 King, *Does the United Kingdom* (n 9) 9.
13 B Crick and D Millar, *To Make the Parliament of Scotland a Model for Democracy* (1991) 5.
14 J Johnston, "The legislative process: the Parliament in practice", in C Jeffery and J Mitchell, *The*

C. THE LEGISLATIVE INITIATIVE

Bills may be introduced by the Scottish government, by individual MSPs or by committees, the latter in a departure from the Westminster pattern. As the Consultative Steering Group anticipated, most of the legislation enacted has been promoted by the Scottish government.[15] Government Bills account for fifty of the sixty-two Bills enacted in the first session, fifty-three of the sixty-six enacted in the second session, and seventeen of the twenty-one enacted so far in the third session. In its report on the application of the founding principles in the first session, the Parliament's Procedures Committee was quick to defend the "substantial volume of Executive inspired law" as not necessarily at odds with the principle of power sharing.[16] It accepted that the bulk of legislation would continue to be initiated by the government, but it envisaged the proportion of non-government Bills increasing, and thought it vital that this process be encouraged by the allocation of sufficient resources, including the allocation of committee and plenary time:

> we do not believe that the small number of Committee Bills passed to date is a cause for concern, but we do think that it would be reasonable to expect the number of Committee Bills and Members' Bills to rise in future years.[17]

Far from increasing, however, as the Committee thought it reasonable to expect, the number of Members' Bills and Committee Bills fell sharply in the second session – from eleven to four. Nor, despite a minority government, has there been an increase in the current session – four non-government Bills have been enacted so far (see below).

D. THE LEGISLATIVE MACHINERY OF DEVOLVED GOVERNMENT

The Scottish government started out with no machinery for planning or managing a legislative programme.[18] This gap was filled over the course of the first session:

> Procedurally, within the Executive, a growing realisation of the amount of legislation it was promoting, of the extent to which legislation could be used to obtain political and practical results and of its centrality to governmental and

---

Scottish Parliament 1999-2009: The First Decade (2009) 29 at 35.

15 *Shaping Scotland's Parliament* (n 8) section 3.5, para 5.

16 *The Founding Principles of the Scottish Parliament* (3rd report, 2003) para 49.

17 *The Founding Principles of the Scottish Parliament* (n 16) paras 713-714.

18 For the UK machinery, see T Daintith and A Page, *The Executive in the Constitution: Structure, Autonomy and Internal Control* (1999) 241-246.

parliamentary business, has brought about increasingly sophisticated internal procedures for the planning, monitoring and progress-chasing of the Executive's legislative programme and of the individual Bills in it.[19]

At the heart of the government's legislative machinery is the Cabinet Sub-Committee on Legislation (CSCL) made up of the Deputy First Minister and Cabinet Secretary for Health and Wellbeing, the Minister for Parliamentary Business and the Lord Advocate. Before the Committee was set up in early 2002, regular reports on the progress of the legislative programme were made to the Cabinet by the Minister for Parliament, as he was then styled, but the legislative programme came to be regarded as sufficiently important to warrant its own machinery. The Committee's current terms of reference are to:

- monitor the management of the government's current legislative programme and submit regular progress reports to the Cabinet;
- keep under regular review the government's priorities for future legislation and recommend future legislative programmes to Cabinet;
- consider proposals for significant changes in the policy content of Bills following approval by the Cabinet of that policy content;
- consider proposals for Members' Bills, Committee Bills, and Private Bills and make a recommendation on the position to be taken by the government on each proposal;
- approve proposals for the Parliament to be invited to give consent, by means of a legislative consent motion, to the inclusion in UK Bills of legislation relating to devolved matters; and keep the operation of the Sewel convention under review;
- consider other matters relating to the management of the government's legislative programme, monitor the position of the government's programme of subordinate legislation; and
- monitor the transposition of EU obligations and infraction cases.

Where the Committee considers proposed changes to the policy content of a Bill or the subject-matter of a proposed non-government Bill or legislative consent motion to be of such significance or sensitivity as to require Cabinet consideration (or where it is unable to agree on a course of action), the matter is referred to the Cabinet for decision together with the Committee's recommendation (where appropriate). In other cases the Committee takes a final decision on behalf of the Cabinet.

---

19 McCluskie, "New approaches" (n 1) at 139-140.

E. THE LEGISLATIVE PROGRAMME

The Westminster tradition is one of single-party government. The Holyrood tradition, by contrast, looks set to be one of coalition or minority government; in this respect, at least, it differs from the power-hoarding archetype. Coalition government requires agreement between the partners to the coalition over the legislative programme. The key discussions in the first two sessions took place beforehand when the core of the programme was worked out in negotiation between the coalition partners as part of the process of putting the coalition together. The resulting agreement, which in legislative terms became much more detailed with the growth in importance of legislation to the coalition,[20] formed the basis of a more detailed "rolling" legislative programme, which was regularly reviewed and updated by ministers and departments throughout the life of the coalition.

A single-party minority government, on the other hand, is not constrained by the wishes of a coalition partner in framing its legislative programme. But, as Mitchell points out, minority governments "must engage in *majority building* whether in the form of explicit, formalised, comprehensive policy agreements with long-term duration on the one hand or shifting coalitions to create new majorities issue by issue, Bill by Bill, even clause by clause", if they are to have any prospect of realising of their legislative ambitions (witness the current government's abandonment of its plans to abolish the council tax) and indeed of securing parliamentary approval for their spending plans.[21]

(1) An annual programme

The Holyrood session is a four-year session: there is no annual cut-off as there is at Westminster. The idea was that a four-year session would allow more time for "proper scrutiny" and would avoid important Bills being "lost" at the end of the parliamentary year.[22] The Consultative Steering Group anticipated that in the absence of an annual cut-off, the government would announce a legislative programme for the four-year session, which it would be free to

---

20 Compare *Making it Work Together: A Programme for Government* (September 1999) with *A Partnership for a Better Scotland* (May 2003). As Seyd points out, a detailed agreement may be to the detriment of the Parliament: the more detailed the initial government "road map" – in the form of the coalition agreement – the less leeway there is for the government to be responsive to initiatives taken by backbench committees. What may be a valid instrument for coalition government may be less beneficial for a proactive legislature: *Coalition Government in Scotland and Wales* (2004) 12.

21 J Mitchell, "The narcissism of small differences: Scotland and Westminster" (2010) 63(1) *Parliamentary Affairs* 98 at 113; as Mitchell points out, this willingness to engage with Parliament is unlikely to survive a government with a parliamentary majority.

22 *Shaping Scotland's Parliament* (n 8), section 3.5, para 22.

revise in response to changing circumstances, and that it would inform the Parliament annually of its planned timetable for bringing forward legislation.[23] Following Westminster, however, the practice of the government in the first two sessions was to announce an annual legislative programme. This practice has been continued by the current government with programme statements in September each year.[24]

For some observers the government's pursuit of an annual legislative programme in the first two sessions suggested a desire to obtain legislation as quickly as possible rather than to realise the potential benefits of a devolved legislative process in terms of increased participation, more effective scrutiny and, ultimately, "better" legislation. Speed is, of course, a prime power-hoarding virtue, undue haste its corresponding vice.[25] In evidence to the Procedures Committee, the first Presiding Officer argued that the Parliament:

> has failed to adapt full to the concept of a four-year legislative term. In general the Parliament, in particular the Executive, still works to an annual cycle, aiming to complete the bulk of the legislative work by each summer recess. This leads to unnecessary pressure on the Parliamentary timetable at that time. It has also led to complaints from civil society about insufficient consultation time in between the different stages of Bills.[26]

However, the absence of legislative "sudden death", as practised at Westminster, does not mean that legislation does not generate its own pressures for delivery – from politicians who may be impatient for results and hence critical of what may seem an unnecessarily complex and time-consuming process. During the first two sessions an annual programme was seen from a government standpoint as a useful discipline, providing an opportunity to take stock of what had been achieved in the year just ended and what was planned for the next year. The government was prepared to use the flexibility afforded by the lack of annual cut-off where difficulties were encountered, but it was adamant that this flexibility must not be "abused" by taking longer than "expected" over the preparation and enactment of legislation.

---

23 *Shaping Scotland's Parliament* (n 8), section 3.4, para 2, and section 3.5, para 23.
24 See, most recently, *Towards A More Successful Scotland: The Government's Programme for Scotland 2009-2010* (2009).
25 King, *Does the United Kingdom* (n 9) 11.
26 Quoted in *The Founding Principles of the Scottish Parliament* (n 16) para 333.

F. THE PRE-PARLIAMENTARY STAGES

(1) Policy formation and consultation

The Consultative Steering Group's proposals were based on a concern that individuals and organisations found it difficult to inform and influence the policy-making process:

> in the case of legislation it was felt that the opportunity to influence legislation was limited after it had been introduced; and that the consultation process leading up to the introduction was ineffective, in part because the detailed content of the legislation was often not known until a Bill was introduced to Parliament.[27]

What was sought, therefore, was a more participative approach to policy making, with a clearly defined policy development stage. "A formal, well-structured, well-understood process would not only deliver a scrutiny stage pre-Introduction, but would also allow individuals and groups to influence the policy making process at a much earlier stage than at present."[28] The CSG insisted:

> Consultation in the form of inviting comments on specific legislative proposals would not meet our aspiration for a participative policy development process ... What is desired is an earlier involvement of relevant bodies from the outset – identifying issues which need to be addressed, contributing to the policy-making process and the preparation of legislation.[29]

The Consultative Steering Group's goal of a more participative policy development process was not to be realised.[30] Instead, the government continued to consult on legislative proposals in much the same way as it had done before devolution. Its approach to consultation is nevertheless generally well regarded despite its more or less unchanged nature – in its report on the application of the founding principles in the first session, the Parliament's Procedures Committee described it as "commendable".[31]

---

27 *Shaping Scotland's Parliament* (n 8), section 2, para 18. The criticisms reported by the CSG echoed those of the Hansard Commission: "the overwhelming impression from the evidence is that many of those most directly affected are deeply dissatisfied with the extent, nature, timing and conduct of consultation on bills as presently practised": *Making the Law* (1992) para 113.

28 *Shaping Scotland's Parliament* (n 8), section 3.5.3.

29 *Shaping Scotland's Parliament* (n 8), section 3.5, para 4.

30 A weakness of leaving the Parliament to work out the details of its own procedures, which was the devolution White Paper's preferred approach, is that these procedures offer affected interests little in the way of formal procedural safeguards. Compare, for example, the requirements governing the making of subordinate legislation under the Human Rights Act or the Regulatory Reform Act.

31 *The Founding Principles of the Scottish Parliament* (n 16) para 952. For the government's approach, see *Scottish Executive: Consultation Good Practice Guidance* (2004). The government originally set itself a target of two rounds of consultation on each Bill. The policy memoranda

Under the Consultative Steering Group's proposals, consultation would be undertaken by the government itself, with the process being overseen by the relevant subject committee of the Parliament. Committees themselves would not engage in consultation, although they might do so if they considered the government consultation inadequate. They would also be involved in deciding who should be consulted and kept informed of progress.[32] Rather than content themselves with checking on the sufficiency of government consultation, however, committees have preferred to conduct their own consultation. This had led to complaints from the government in the first two sessions that they were being "standoffish" and a "bit precious", in not responding to government consultations, and to complaints from affected interests of consultation overload.[33]

Committees have usually waited until a Bill has been formally introduced before carrying out their own consultation. They have not become involved in pre-legislative scrutiny of Bills published in draft of the kind that has become more common at Westminster in recent years. The Procedures Committee, in the second session, recognised that pre-legislative scrutiny as practised at Westminster "can offer a real opportunity to make a constructive contribution to the shape of the eventual legislation", but felt that this must inevitably be at the risk of compromising a committee's independence, or the perception of it, at later stages: "It is difficult for a committee that sees itself as a partner in the law-making process also to be seen as a detached and critical scrutineer."[34] In the Committee's view, it was for committees to decide how best to subject legislative proposals to scrutiny; committees should be free to embark on pre-legislative scrutiny "where they wish to and have the time – but neither should it be expected as a normal part of the legislative process".[35]

---

which accompany Bills should show the extent of consultation, but the distinction between an extended but single consultation process and separate rounds is seldom clear cut.

32 *Shaping Scotland's Parliament* (n 8), section 3.5, paras 5-6. It is clear from the reference in the next paragraph to committees concentrating on proposals which have already been the subject of participative involvement of interested parties that the CSG did not envisage committees duplicating government consultation.

33 *The Founding Principles of the Scottish Parliament* (n 16) para 977.

34 *Timescales and Stages of Bills* (7th Report 2004) paras 105 and 107.

35 *Timescales and Stages of Bills* (n 34) para 107. The Committee took the same non-prescriptive approach to the question of the publication of Bills in draft, arguing that it was for the government to decide, according to the particular circumstances, where publication in draft could make a useful contribution to consultation and policy development (para 111). The government's original intention was that all Bills would be published for consultation, as part of the proposed second round of consultation, but publication in draft has been the exception rather than the rule. In the first session only a quarter (13 out of 50) of government Bills were published for consultation; McCluskie put the number at "rather fewer than half" (McCluskie, "New approaches" (n 1) at 141).

There is, of course, no certainty that a power-hoarding government would welcome attempts by committees to become involved at an earlier stage in the legislative process, other than by making their views known as part of the consultation process, but it may be that by not becoming involved in pre-legislative scrutiny, committees are passing up the opportunity to shape legislation before it has assumed its final form.[36]

(2) Drafting

The Office of the Scottish Parliamentary Counsel (OSPC) is responsible for the drafting of Scottish Bills. Since devolution the establishment of the Office has more than doubled. As in Whitehall, the task of drafter is conceived as being to ensure that draft legislation is prepared on time, and that it is effective, both in the sense of being capable of withstanding parliamentary scrutiny – "bills are made to pass as razors are made to sell"[37] which may result in oddities like "statutory rights" in the Land Reform (Scotland) Act 2003[38] – and in the sense of being capable of withstanding judicial scrutiny.

> The principal concern in drafting a Bill is to achieve the intended legal effect. Normally this involves making provision that is as clear, certain and unambiguous as possible, leaving minimal scope for the courts to determine what legal effect the provision has ... Considerations other than achieving the intended legal effect, including comprehensibility and accessibility of language, are necessarily secondary.[39]

Necessarily secondary but not unimportant: OSPC's main aim is "to draft Government Bills to be introduced in the Scottish Parliament in a way which ensures that the resultant Acts of the Scottish Parliament deliver Ministers' policy effectively in language that is easy to understand". OSPC is also committed to drafting legislation in plain language. "The aim is to produce clear, precise and accessible law".[40] At an early stage it was decided that OSPC was not responsible for ensuring the *vires* of Scottish legislation (see below).

It is for the Scottish Parliament to determine how its legislation is expressed,[41] but Scottish Bills are very similar to Westminster Bills in terms of

---

36 On Westminster, see J Smookler, "Making a difference? The effectiveness of pre-legislative scrutiny" (2006) 59 *Parliamentary Affairs* 522.
37 For the origins of the phrase, see G Engle, "'Bills are made to pass as razors are made to sell': practical constraints in the preparation of legislation" (1983) 4 *StatLRev* 7.
38 McCluskie, "New approaches" (n 1) at 141-142.
39 The Scottish Parliament, *Guidance on Public Bills*, 3rd edn (2007) Annex B.
40 See OSPC at: *http://www.scotland.gov.uk/About/Directorates/Safer-Stronger/OSPC*. Following a reference to the Scottish Law Commission, the Office has prepared a booklet on plain-language drafting: *Plain Language and Legislation* (2006).
41 *Guidance on Public Bills* (n 39) Annex B.

layout, structure and the conventions of legislative drafting. This is primarily because Acts of the Scottish Parliament are conceived as fitting into a single UK statute book, with no room for differences in, for example, statutory interpretation. The view taken at the outset was that:

> however profound and far-reaching the constitutional and governmental changes to be brought about by devolution, there would be no benefit in bringing about any departure or exception from the homogeneity and continuity of British statutes ... Our devolved legislation should ... slip easily into the warp and weft of pre-devolution Scottish legislation and of GB and UK legislation whether pre- or post-devolution. In particular, it should be drafted so as to be consistent with those parts of *post*-devolution Westminster legislation which, by reason either of being on non-devolved topics or being enacted by Westminster in pursuance of its continuing legislative sovereignty, applies to Scotland.[42]

For the drafter, the homogeneity of the existing statute book is one of the main virtues of legislation in the UK, making it easy, for example, to apply the provisions of an earlier Act for the purposes of a later one, and facilitating the substantial textual amendment of earlier Acts by later ones.[43]

There is thus considerable similarity between pre- and post-devolution Scottish legislation, which even extends to the inclusion of the word "Scotland" in the short titles of Acts of the Scottish Parliament despite the fact that the Scottish Parliament has no power to legislate other than for or in relation to Scotland.[44] The style of Scottish legislation is nevertheless changing. When he was First Scottish Parliamentary Counsel, John McCluskie suggested that Scotland was moving "towards a body of devolved statute law which is expressed in a larger number of shorter simpler legal propositions".[45] He also suggested that Scottish legislation often seemed shorter and simpler than English legislation on the same subject-matter, a feature which he attributed in part to the fact that resources available for its preparation were much fewer than in England and Wales.

(3) Scrutiny of legislative competence

The vulnerability of Acts of the Scottish Parliament to judicial review means that the exercise of the Parliament's legislative powers is dominated by questions of legislative competence to a much greater extent than is the case

42 McCluskie, "New approaches" (n 1) at 137-138.
43 McCluskie, "New approaches" (n 1) at 143.
44 Clive describes the practice as "absurd": "Law-making in Scotland: from APS to ASP" (1999) 3 *EdinLR* 131 at 136.
45 McCluskie, "New approaches" (n 1) at 143. A view echoed by Lord Hope, for whom there is "a simplicity of style and tightness of language that would certainly have appealed to Sir William Dale": "What a second chamber can do for legislative scrutiny' (2004) 25 *StatLRev* 3 at 7.

at Westminster. As Angiolini explains, the effect of the "overarching constitutional framework" within which the Parliament and government operate is:

> to raise the profile of law much higher than at Westminster. I do not say that Minis-
> ters at Westminster are careless about the law. The combination of European law
> and human rights law and the reserved matters in Sch 5 makes the legal issue –
> the issue of competence – much more of an immediate concern to the Scottish
> Ministers and administrators than is the case south of the Border.[46]

As the government's chief legal adviser it falls to the Lord Advocate to clear
Executive Bills for introduction. A government Bill must be accompanied by
a ministerial statement certifying that it is within the legislative competence
of the Parliament,[47] and a minister cannot make a statement on legislative
competence without the Law Officers' clearance.

The Lord Advocate's role is not confined to questions of *vires*. What began
as a concern with legislative competence broadened early on in the life of
the coalition into a more general concern with the proper management of
the legislative programme, i.e. with ensuring that Bills are ready on time
and that they are of an appropriate quality. A "Bill management" meeting is
mandatory before a Bill can be formally announced or introduced to Parliament. The purpose of a meeting, which usually takes place after drafting
instructions have been submitted to OSPC, is to allow the Law Officers and
the Minister for Parliamentary Business to assess in discussion with the lead
minister a Bill's readiness. As well as an opportunity to make this assessment,
the meeting also provides early notice of any questions of competence that
may arise. So favourably was this "project management" approach to legislation viewed when it was first introduced that the government was said to be
considering its extension to subordinate legislation, in particular to subordinate legislation made in the implementation of EU obligations, but this did
not happen.

A statement on legislative competence by itself is singularly uninforma-
tive: all that it states is that, in the minister's view, the provisions of the Bill in
question "would be within the legislative competence of the Scottish Parliament". The lack of information has attracted criticism:

> It is not good enough that ministers assert in a one-line submission to the Scottish
> Parliament that a bill is compatible with ECHR. It should be incumbent on the
> executive to produce a full statement with a rigorous analysis, explaining the
> ECHR implications of its legislative proposals.[48]

46 "Legislation, litigation and prosecution: the role of a Scottish Law Officer" [2003] *JR* 220 at 223.
47 Scotland Act 1998 s 31(1).
48 Lord James Douglas Hamilton, *The Scotsman*, 1 December 2001.

This is not something the government has volunteered, but neither has there been any attempt, possibly because the machinery is lacking, to scrutinise the basis of statements in the manner of the Human Rights Committee at Westminster.[49] The evidentiary basis for the statement itself is not an especially onerous one. All that is required is that the minister be more satisfied than not, rather than satisfied beyond all reasonable doubt, that the Bill is within the legislative competence of the Scottish Parliament.

A Bill must also be accompanied by a statement from the Presiding Officer stating whether or not in his view the provisions of the Bill are within legislative competence.[50] In order to obtain this statement a copy of the draft Bill, together with a note of the government's view on its legislative competence, is sent to the Parliament's Director of Legal Services three weeks before the date set for its formal introduction. During this three-week period the Parliament's Directorate of Legal Services prepares advice to the Presiding Officer on the Bill's legislative competence. According to the Parliament's first Presiding Officer, if the Parliament's lawyers "find things they are worried about, they talk directly to the Executive lawyers – a very good and healthy dialogue goes on and the Bills are often amended".[51] This process has been criticised for failing to provide "the independent check on the legislative competence of bills intended by the Scotland Act".[52] The Calman Commission acknowledged that it was not a "particularly transparent process", but defended it on the ground that it "appears to be effective in identifying and resolving potential problems".[53]

G. THE PARLIAMENTARY STAGES

The Scotland Act provides that the parliamentary stages of the legislative process must include a minimum of three stages: a stage at which members can debate a Bill and vote on its general principles; a stage at which they can

---

49 On the Human Rights Committee, see D Feldman, "The impact of human rights on the UK legislative process" (2004) 25 *StatLRev* 91. The Calman Commission has now recommended that the explanatory notes published with a Bill should give a general account of the main considerations that informed the statement: *Serving Scotland Better: Scotland and the United Kingdom in the 21st Century* (2009) para 6.92.

50 Scotland Act 1998 s 31(2).

51 *Devolution: Inter-Institutional Relations in the United Kingdom* (n 2) question 776. "Although no Executive Bill has so far been given a 'negative' statement by the Presiding Officer, we understand that there have been a number of robust exchanges behind the scenes between Parliament and Scottish Government lawyers, which have led to changes to draft Bills prior to introduction": *Serving Scotland Better* (n 49) para 6.89.

52 I Jamieson, "Held in check" (2007) 52(6) *JLSS* 48-50.

53 *Serving Scotland Better* (n 49) para 6.89.

consider and vote on the details of a Bill; and a final stage at which a Bill can be passed or rejected.[54] There must also be an opportunity for the reconsideration of a Bill which is referred to the Supreme Court by the Law Officers or blocked by the Secretary of State after it has been passed (see below).

The parliamentary stages of the legislative process begin with the formal introduction of a Bill. A Bill must be accompanied on introduction by a number of documents which must be printed and published with the Bill. In the case of government Bills these comprise a government statement on legislative competence (see above), a statement by the Presiding Officer on legislative competence (see above), a financial memorandum, explanatory notes, and a policy memorandum, which sets out the Bill's policy objectives, what alternatives were considered, the consultation undertaken and an assessment of its effects on equal opportunities, human rights, island communities, local government, sustainable development and other matters considered relevant. Once a Bill has been published, together with its accompanying documents, it embarks upon its parliamentary stages.

The Stage 1 debate and vote on the general principles of the Bill take place in the Chamber. Once introduced, however, a Bill is referred to the relevant subject committee which considers and reports on the principles of the Bill to inform the debate and vote in plenary session; the Parliament's subject committees, which examine Bills before the Stage 1 debate and again at Stage 2, combine the roles of select and public Bill (formerly standing) committees at Westminster, the idea being to enable members "to develop an expertise in particular areas and to bring an informed view to the consideration of legislation and scrutiny of the Executive".[55] The Stage 1 inquiry is regarded as "crucial to the effectiveness of the Parliament's whole legislative process" in that, as well as taking place in public, it allows affected interests, including those who may not have been consulted, direct access to the legislature and with it an opportunity to "contribute to the formulation of a considered view both of the policy intention and of how it has been given detailed expression in legislation".[56] The Stage 2 consideration of the details of the Bill usually takes place in the relevant subject committee. The Bill is subjected to line-by-line scrutiny and amendments are considered and decided upon. At Stage 3 the Bill comes back to the Chamber. There is a further opportunity to amend the Bill, followed by a debate on whether to pass the Bill or reject it.

54 Scotland Act 1998 s 36(1).
55 *Shaping Scotland's Parliament* (n 8), section 2, para 13.
56 *Timescales and Stages of Bills* (n 39), para 112.

Amendments may be made at both Stage 2 and Stage 3. The assumption at the outset was that the relative lack of amending stages, compared with Westminster, would mean that Bills would be as near to the finished article as possible before their introduction:

> [the] paucity of amendable stages, compounded by the disinclination to pursue substantial amendment at Stage 2, is a strong factor which drives us to ensure that everything which is to be done in a Bill is included in it before introduction. The facility, which we enjoyed at Westminster, of adding substantial new material to Bills in Committee or at Report stages, including those stages in the second House, is noticeably diminished.[57]

Whatever inhibitions may have been felt at the outset about introducing significant amendments seem to have been shrugged off, however, leading to complaints that entirely new provisions are sometimes introduced late in the process, shortly before the legislation is passed, thereby bypassing detailed scrutiny in committee (see further below).

(1) Particular types of Bills

Government "programme" Bills are only one among several different types of Bills for which provision is made in the Parliament's standing orders.

(a) Members' Bills

A system in which the legislative initiative is confined to government could hardly be described as one in which the "power is shared". The Members' Bill procedure was used with some success in the first session to challenge government policy as well as to effect desirable but essentially minor changes in the law.[58] Faced with potentially competing demands for government and Members' Bills, the Parliament adopted new requirements for the introduction of Members' Bills early in the second session, which included raising the threshold (from eleven to eighteen), and the introduction of a requirement of cross-party support, the latter in line with the Procedures Committee's view that the main purpose of the Members' Bill procedure

---

57 McCluskie, "New approaches" (n 1) at 140-141. For the Hansard Commission, "the failure of all Governments 'to get bills right' – or more nearly right – before they are presented to Parliament has been, in our view, the basic defect in the legislative process and a grave indictment of those Governments' approach to law-making": *Making the Law* (1992) para 182.

58 The best example is Tommy Sheridan's Abolition of Poinding and Warrant Sales Act 2001, which led to the Debt Arrangement and Attachment Act (Scotland) Act 2002. The same pattern was repeated with his unsuccessful School Meals (Scotland) Bill, which provided the "inspiration" for the Education (School Meals) Scotland Act 2003.

is to provide a channel for legislative ideas with "broad general appeal".[59] Following their adoption, the number of successful Members' Bills fell sharply – from eight in the first session to three in the second session.[60] Once introduced, Members' Bills are subject to the same procedure as government Bills.

(b) Committee Bills

The Constitutional Convention's vision was of a Parliament that would operate through a system of powerful committees which would be able to initiate legislation as well as scrutinise and amend government proposals.[61] Committee Bills, however, have not featured prominently in the legislative output of the Parliament. Given the pressures on the committee system, and the substantial resources required to introduce legislation, Johnston suggests that the total of four Committee Bills enacted in the first two sessions is reasonable. He goes on to point out, however, that committees have not sought to exploit the gaps in their work programmes in the third session by bringing forward their own legislation. "Despite its minority status, the onus remains firmly on the government to bring forward its legislative programme."[62] Once introduced, Committee Bills are subject to the same procedure as government Bills, save that, at Stage 1, a Bill is not referred to a lead committee for a report on its general principles (the committee proposing the Bill having already reported on its general principles).

(c) Emergency Bills

The Scotland Act provided that the Parliament might expedite proceedings in relation to particular Bills.[63] An emergency Bill is a government Bill that Parliament agrees "needs to be enacted more rapidly than the normal timetable allows, for example to amend the law in response to a recent court judgment

---

59 *A New Procedure for Members' Bill* (6th Report, 2004). As well as a higher threshold and a requirement of cross-party support, the Committee recommended that there should be a minimum of twelve weeks' consultation on proposals for Bills, that there should be a limit on the number of proposals or Bills that members may promote at any time, and that the Scottish government should be able to pre-empt members' legislation where it or the UK government is planning similar legislation.

60 Two of the Members' Bills in the first session were to all intents and purposes government Bills: Leasehold Casualties, which the government would have introduced as part of the land tenure reform package (also including Abolition of Feudal Tenure, Title Conditions, and Tenements), and Mortgage Rights, the latter a classic "hand-out" Bill.

61 *Scotland's Parliament, Scotland's Right* (1995) 26.

62 Johnston, "The legislative process" (n 14) at 34.

63 Scotland Act 1998 s 36(2).

which has exposed a loophole or problem of interpretation in an existing enactment".[64] The first Bill passed by the Parliament was an emergency Bill: the Mental Health (Public Safety and Appeals) (Scotland) Act 1999. There have been a further five emergency Bills, the most recent being the Convention Rights Proceedings (Amendment) (Scotland) Act 2009, which imposed a one-year limit on the bringing of claims for breach of Convention rights against the Scottish Ministers. There is a risk that the procedure may be used to stifle or curtail debate on a Bill, as arguably happened with the Convention Rights Proceedings (Amendment) (Scotland) Act.[65]

(2) Effectiveness of scrutiny

For the Constitutional Convention it was important that as a single-chamber legislature the Parliament's procedures "provide for the rigorous scrutiny of proposed legislation".[66] Almost from the outset, however, concerns were expressed about the effectiveness of parliamentary scrutiny. The Parliament, it was said:

> does not yet have quite the same degree of legislative curiosity as at Westminster. … [It] tends to concentrate in its debates, even in Committee, on the policy and political dimensions of the Bills which it is scrutinising and tends to leave to one side questions about, for example, the particular application to particular cases of the provisions of its Bills.[67]

The implication was that the Parliament might yet develop that "curiosity". Other observers were less sanguine. For Lord Hope:

> The committee system, which was designed to provide an opportunity for careful, informed study of all the relevant detail, is not working as it should. Responsibility for both initial scrutiny of a Bill at Stage 1 and detailed scrutiny at Stage 2 rests with the same committee. At both stages this process tends to become the focus for political debate and point-scoring. Elected committee members lack the independence of mind and the opportunity for detachment and genuine self-criticism that is essential to effective scrutiny.[68]

Concern about the effectiveness of parliamentary scrutiny was reflected in calls towards the end of the first session for some form of second chamber or "revision" stage to compensate for the shortcomings of parliamentary

64 *Guidance on Public Bills* (n 39) para 3.45.
65 For discussion, see chapter 3 of this volume, by Aidan O'Neill; see also House of Lords Select Committee on the Constitution, *Fast-track Legislation: Constitutional Implications and Safeguards*, HL (2008-09) 116.
66 *Scotland's Parliament, Scotland's Right* (1995) 24.
67 McCluskie, "New approaches" (n 1) at 141.
68 Hope, "What a second chamber can do" (n 45) at 8.

scrutiny.[69] In the Parliament's defence the argument was that the parliamentary stages had been too rushed to allow for effective scrutiny. The Procedures Committee, in its examination of the application of the founding principles in the first session, found "clear evidence that the committee system in the Scottish Parliament is under severe pressure of work, and that the quality of output is threatened by the deadlines to which committees are working".[70] If the devolution settlement was to operate as the Parliament intended when it adopted the founding principles, it continued, the government had to ensure, "in seeking the time it needs to progress its electoral commitments, that committees are not so burdened that the quality of legislation, or other tasks that are central to committee work, is put at risk".[71] In its reply to the Procedures Committee, the government conceded that there had been pressures to complete Bill stages for Public Bills "more quickly than may have been ideal in some cases", before affirming its willingness "to discuss timetabling issues with the parliamentary authorities having regard to the concerns raised and the need to ensure the timely passage of legislation". Privately, it suggested that if the Parliament wanted to spend more time on legislation the answer might be for it to work harder; increased scrutiny, in other words, should not be at the expense of the government's legislative agenda.[72]

The Procedures Committee returned to the question of the speed of the process in the second session with a series of recommendations which

> should enable the quality and robustness of the Parliament's legislative output to be enhanced without threatening the legitimate expectation on the part of the Executive (and others) that they will be able to deliver legislative solutions within a reasonable timescale.[73]

The goal of improved scrutiny, however, is proving an elusive one. The Calman Commission reported continued concerns about the robustness of the Parliament's procedures for scrutinising legislation:

> In particular, we have heard concerns that, despite the focus early on in the process on consultation, and on an evidence-based approach, the later amending stages are often rushed giving outside interests insufficient opportunity to make representations. A related concern is that new provisions are sometimes introduced late in the process, shortly before the legislation is passed, thereby bypassing detailed scrutiny in committee.[74]

69 As to which, see Hope, "What a second chamber can do" (n 45) at 12-14.
70 *The Founding Principles of the Scottish Parliament* (n 8) para 1016.
71 *The Founding Principles of the Scottish Parliament* (n 8) para 1018.
72 Comments by the First Minister to this effect were reported in *The Scotsman*, 26 June 2003.
73 *Timescales and Stages of Bills* (n 34) para 170.
74 *Serving Scotland Better* (n 49) para 6.44

The Commission rejected the idea of introducing a second chamber or unelected element to provide detached and expert scrutiny of legislation, but raised the possibility that there might be scope for making the Parliament's procedures for scrutinising legislation more robust and effective, for example by separating the second main amending stage from the decision to pass a Bill, or by prohibiting amendments that raise new issues at a late stage.[75] It recommended that the legislative procedure should become a four-stage procedure, with the Stage 3 becoming limited to a second main amending stage, taken in the Chamber, while the final debate on whether to pass the Bill would become Stage 4.[76] Whether this recommendation will be pursued remains to be seen. Effective scrutiny, however, is not just a matter of procedures. As the Commission acknowledged, it also depends crucially on those doing the scrutiny and the spirit with which they are imbued.[77]

H. PRE-ASSENT SCRUTINY AND CHALLENGE

The "higher profile" of law in the constitution of the devolved Scotland is reflected in the procedures Bills go through after they have completed their parliamentary stages as well as before they are introduced. Once a Bill has been passed there is a four-week "holding" period before the Presiding Officer submits it for Royal Assent during which the three principal Law Officers – the Advocate General, the Lord Advocate and the Attorney General – and the Secretary of State may challenge it: the Law Officers by referring the question of whether it would be within the legislative competence of the Parliament to the Supreme Court, the Secretary of State by the making of an order prohibiting the Presiding Officer from submitting it for Royal Assent.[78]

While the Lord Advocate may refer a government Bill to the Supreme Court, it is the possibility of a reference by the two United Kingdom Law Officers that casts the longer shadow. Early dialogue and co-operation between the two governments have been seen as the key to eliminating the need for a reference in all but the most exceptional cases.[79] The Office of the Solicitor to the Advocate General (OSAG) examines Bills before they are first introduced, as well as formally when they have completed their

---

75 *The Future of Scottish Devolution within the Union: A First Report* (2008) para 8.15
76 *Serving Scotland Better* (n 49) para 6.44.
77 *Serving Scotland Better* (n 49) para 6.43.
78 Scotland Act 1998, s 33, 35; the Presiding Officer may submit a Bill for Royal Assent within the four-week holding period if the Law Officers and the Secretary of State notify him that they do not intend to exercise their right to challenge the Bill: ss 33(3), 35(4).
79 L Clark, "Three years on: the role of the Advocate General for Scotland" 2002 *SLT News* 139 at 142.

parliamentary stages, with a view to ensuring that the UK government has "early warning of issues of competence of bills of the Scottish Parliament or actings of the Scottish Executive, and can engage in constructive dialogue with the Scottish Executive to address them".[80] The threat of a reference was apparently sufficient to resolve such differences of opinion as arose during the first two sessions. Faced with the threat of a six-month delay to a Bill, and the consequent disruption to its legislative programme that a reference would have entailed, it would seem that the Scottish government preferred to remove offending sections or redraft the legislation rather than invite the UK government to test its arguments in court. This is not to say that a government of a different political complexion from the Westminster government would be equally amenable to the same threat. An administration which was keen to push the boundaries to devolved competence might well welcome the scope to "constitutionalise" a dispute a reference would afford. It might therefore invite the UK government to do its worst, in the knowledge that were it to succeed before the Supreme Court the UK government would then have no choice but to back off or to override the Supreme Court's decision, which might provoke a political crisis.

The grounds on which the Secretary of State may make an order prohibiting the Presiding Officer from submitting a Bill for Royal Assent are set out in the Scotland Act. The Secretary of State may intervene to prevent the Presiding Officer from submitting a Bill for Royal Assent where it contains provisions which he has "reasonable grounds to believe would be incompatible with any international obligations or the interests of defence or national security", or where it makes modifications to the law as it applies to reserved matters which he has "reasonable grounds to believe would have an adverse effect on the operation of the law as it applies to reserved matters".[81] The possibility of the Secretary of State's intervention is not confined to the initial four-week holding period; it may also take place within four weeks of a reference to the Supreme Court being decided.[82] These considerations therefore take precedence over the narrower question of *vires*. Like the power to refer Bills to the Supreme Court, this power is seen "very much as a matter of last resort".[83] Should disputes arise, the expectation is that these will be resolved

---

80 Hansard: 25 January 2002, col 1126 W. The Calman Commission's "understanding" was that UK government lawyers were sometimes involved in exchanges between Parliament and Scottish government lawyers before a Bill's introduction: *Serving Scotland Better* (n 49) para 6.89.
81 Scotland Act 1998 s 35(1).
82 Scotland Act 1998 s 35(3).
83 *Memorandum of Understanding and Supplementary Agreements between the United Kingdom Government, Scottish Ministers, the Cabinet of the National Assembly of Wales and the Northern*

bilaterally, or through the good offices of the Secretary of State, with the possibility of resort to the Joint Ministerial Committee in the event that these prove unsuccessful.[84]

(1) Reconsideration stage

The Scotland Act provides that there must be an opportunity for the reconsideration of a Bill which is referred to the Supreme Court or blocked by the Secretary of State after it has been passed.[85] Where a Bill is referred to the Supreme Court, the Parliament cannot reconsider it before the Supreme Court has reached a decision – if the Supreme Court decides that the Bill is within the competence of the Parliament, there is no need to reconsider the Bill unless, of course, the Secretary of State subsequently blocks it – or has referred a question arising from it to the European Court of Justice; in the latter case there is provision for the reference to be withdrawn to avoid the additional delay arising from the reference to the European Court.[86] The purpose of the reconsideration stage is to allow those provisions of a Bill subject to legal challenge to be amended so that the basis of the challenge is removed.[87] A Bill approved after reconsideration may be challenged by the Law Officers or the Secretary of State in exactly the same way as it was after it was first passed. There is no limit to the number of times a Bill may be approved or subsequently challenged.

I. ROYAL ASSENT

Once a Bill has been passed by the Parliament, or approved after reconsideration, and the four-week holding period has expired, the Presiding Officer submits it for Royal Assent; once it receives Royal Assent it becomes an Act of the Scottish Parliament.[88]

J. CONCLUDING REMARKS

Devolution has seen an explosion in purely Scottish law making – legislation that is made in Scotland by Scottish politicians – and with it what one politician has described as the "most far-reaching and rapid updating of Scots law

---

Ireland Executive Committee (Cmnd 5240: 2001) para 26.
84 *Memorandum of Understanding* (n 83) paras 23, 25.
85 Scotland Act 1998 s 36(4).
86 Scotland Act 1998 s 36(4).
87 *Guidance on Public Bills* (n 39) para 2.66.
88 Scotland Act 1998 s 28(2).

for three centuries".[89] As the legislature of the devolved Scotland, however, the Scottish Parliament is less different than some of the proponents of devolution had hoped. There are, of course, differences. The Parliament is a single-chamber legislature; the question of legislative competence has a significance that it lacks for Westminster, although its impact on the devolved legislative process is largely hidden from the public gaze; the Stage 1 process is more open and inclusive than the equivalent stage at Westminster, although one may question whether the rather mechanical approach committees have adopted to Stage 1 scrutiny represents the most effective use of limited scrutiny resources. Overall, however, the process emerges as no less executive dominated than the process at Westminster, notwithstanding a minority government since 2007. Nor, in the immediate short term, at least, does there appear to be any prospect of that changing.

89 W Alexander, in W Alexander (ed), *Donald Dewar: Scotland's First First Minister* (2005) 210.

Rights and Society

3 Human Rights and People and Society

Aidan O'Neill QC[*]

A. INTRODUCTION: A NEW KIND OF CONSTITUTION FOR SCOTLAND

In February 1998 the Judicial Committee of the Privy Council gave judgment in *Matadeen v Pointu*. This was an appeal to the Board sitting in London by the Mauritius Minister of Education and Science from a decision of the Supreme Court of Mauritius to the effect that, in introducing new school exam regulations without due notice, the government of Mauritius had acted unconstitutionally because, *inter alia*, it had acted in a manner contrary to art 3 of the Declaration of the Rights of Man and Citizen of 1793 (which provided that "all men are equal by nature and before the law"); as Lord Hoffmann notes, the 1793 Declaration had been "adopted by the *Assemblée Coloniale* of the *Île de France* on XIV *Thermidor* Year II (1 August 1794), no doubt unaware of the overthrow of the Robespierre government which had occurred five days earlier in Paris". In holding that, on its true construction,

* Ampersand Stable, Faculty of Advocates.

the Constitution of Mauritius entrenched the protection of the individual against discrimination only on a limited number of grounds, the Board noted that "a self-confident democracy ... may feel that it can give the last word, even in respect of the most fundamental rights, to the popularly elected organs of its constitution". The Board accepted, however, that the Diceyan theory of absolute parliamentary sovereignty was "an extreme case" and acknowledged that the experience of many other countries was that "certain fundamental rights need to be protected against being overridden by the majority ... by entrenching them in a written constitution enforced by independent judges". However, the Board concluded that there was no reason why a democratic constitution "should not express a compromise which imitates neither the unlimited sovereignty of the United Kingdom Parliament nor the broad powers of judicial review of the Supreme Court of the United States".[1]

We might bear this "compromise" in mind when comparing the constitutional conservatism of the Human Rights Act 1998 with the new constitutional model in the Scotland Act 1998. The enactment of the Human Rights Act – which received Royal Assent on 9 November 1998 – resulted in an amendment to the United Kingdom constitution to allow for a modified form of judicial review of primary statutes of the Westminster Parliament, albeit in a manner which was said to be consistent with continued adherence to the idea of the sovereignty of the UK Parliament. The Human Rights Act was consciously drafted on the basis of the precedent provided by the New Zealand Bill of Rights Act 1990. Like the New Zealand Act, its primary concern was to preserve the central constitutional concept of the sovereignty of the United Kingdom Parliament while allowing for an enhanced degree of legal protection under domestic law for the fundamental rights set out in the European Convention on Human Rights (hereafter "ECHR"). The model embodied in the Human Rights Act is one of delicate constitutional dialogue and a dance of deference between judiciary and legislature, but one where, ultimately, the UK Parliament has the last word.[2]

By contrast, the Scotland Act – which received Royal Assent on 19 November 1998 – was not drafted with a view to preserving any constitutional idea of the (devolved) legislature's sovereignty.[3] The constitutional structure which it embodied was modelled, instead, on the constitutions created by the Foreign and Commonwealth Office for the newly independent nations

---

1 *Matadeen v Pointu* [1999] AC 98 per Lord Hoffmann at 109-110.

2 See, further, Lord Irvine of Lairg, "The development of human rights in Britain under an incorporated Convention on Human Rights" [1998] *Public Law* 221 at 225.

3 See *Whaley v Lord Watson of Invergowrie and The Scottish Parliament* 2000 SC 340 (IH) per Lord Rodger at 348H, 350B-C:

emerging from the post-World War II transformation of the British Empire into the British Commonwealth.[4] The new constitution of post-apartheid South Africa was also taken, in part, as a model.[5] As a result, the Scotland Act contains quite different constitutional checks and balances from those which form the basis of the Human Rights Act. The protection of Convention rights under the constitutional settlement set out in the Scotland Act is embedded within the concept of limits on the powers or competence of the devolved authorities. Thus, the Convention-compatible interpretative obligation for UK legislation in the Human Rights Act s 3 is paralleled by an interpretative obligation for Scottish legislation in the Scotland Act s 101, relative to competence:[6] section 101(2) enjoins the courts, when faced with devolved Scottish primary and subordinate legislation which *could* be read in such a way as to be outside competence, to read the provision "as narrowly as possible as is required for it to be within competence, if such a reading is possible" and to give effect to it accordingly.[7] And the "implicit dialogue" provisions between court and legislature set out in the Human Rights Act s 4 in relation to Westminster legislation have their parallel in the Scotland Act s 102 as regards Scottish legislation: s 102(2)(a) permits the court to remove or limit the retrospective effect of any finding that legislation – whether passed by the Scottish Parliament or the Scottish Ministers – is beyond its legislative competence and hence *ultra vires*; and s 102(2)(b) of the Scotland Act allows

4 See A W Brian Simpson, *Human Rights and the End of Empire: Britain and the Genesis of the European Convention* (2004).

5 See, e.g., Scotland Act s 102 and art 172(1) of the Constitution of South Africa which both give power to the courts to suspend and/or modify the retrospective effect of their decisions as to the constitutional incompatibility of laws to give the legislature the opportunity of suitably amending the offending laws. *Minister of Home Affairs v Fourie* (2006) 20 BHRC 368 provides an example of the use of art 172(1) by the South African Constitutional Court.

6 See *DS v HM Advocate* 2007 SC (PC) 1 per Lord Hope at paras 21-24.

7 See *McCall v Scottish Ministers* 2006 SC 266. Section 101 of the Scotland Act also parallels and reflects the provision common in Commonwealth constitutions enjoining the courts to read statutes which appeared on their face to be incompatible with constitutional rights "with such modifications, adaptations, qualifications and exceptions as may be necessary to bring them into conformity with the constitution". See *Rojas v Berllaque (Attorney General for Gibraltar intervening)* [2004] 1 WLR 201, Lord Nicholls observing at 208-209, para 24:

Paragraph 2 of the transitional provisions [which states "the existing laws ... *shall* be construed with such modifications . ... as may be necessary to bring them into conformity with the Constitution'] imposes a far-reaching obligation on courts. As noted in *Director of Public Prosecutions of Jamaica v Mollison* [2003] 2 AC 411, 425-427, paras 16-17, this type of obligation goes beyond the limits of construction of statutes as usually understood. In the usual course the process of construction involves interpreting a provision in a manner which will give effect to the intention the court reasonably imputes to the legislature in respect of the language used. The exercise required by these transitional provisions is different. The court is enjoined, without any qualification, to construe the offending legislation with whatever modifications are necessary to bring it into conformity with the Constitution.

the court to suspend the effect of its decision on lack of legislative *vires* for such period and on such conditions as might allow the defect identified by it to be corrected by the legislature.

Significantly, however, there is no such power or discretion vested in the court to suspend its decisions in relation to administrative (non-legislative) acts of the Scottish devolved institutions, just as there is no discretion given to the courts to permit the Scottish Ministers to act in a manner which is incompatible with the Convention (see the Scotland Act s 57(2)). But the centrally important feature in the scheme of the Scotland Act – and the manner in which it differs fundamentally from the other devolution statutes – is that the Scottish Ministers are not given the Human Rights Act s 6(2) defence which is otherwise available to public authorities. No provision is made for the possibility of any "lawful" breach of Convention rights by the Scottish devolved authorities relying upon, or seeking to enforce, Convention-incompatible provisions of Westminster legislation.[8] Section 57(3) of the Scotland Act is the only provision of the Act which allows for the possibility of any member of the Scottish Executive – namely the Lord Advocate when acting in prosecuting any offence or in his capacity as head of the system of criminal prosecution and investigation of deaths in Scotland – acting in a manner which is incompatible with any of the Convention rights.[9] It is only by this member of the Scottish Executive, and only when exercising these functions "retained" by this office alone (see Scotland Act s 52(5)(b), that a Human Rights Act s 6(2) defence might be claimed. To date it has rarely been prayed in aid by the Scottish Law Officers,[10] and only once successfully.[11] It is clear from the parliamentary history that this failure to allow for *any* Convention-incompatible activity on the part of the Scottish Parliament or other member of the Scottish Executive was not a matter of inadvertence or oversight. The fact that no similar amendment was made in respect of the

---

8 As the First Division acknowledged in *Somerville v Scottish Ministers* 2007 SC 140 at 166 (italics added):

   [50] By s 6(2) of the Human Rights Act, subs (1) of that section (which renders unlawful incompatible acts of a public authority) is disapplied where, as a result of one or more provisions of primary legislation, the authority could not have acted differently; a similar disapplication applies to subordinate legislation where the authority is acting so as to give effect to or enforce primary legislation. *By contrast the existence of primary legislation having such results does not save acts amenable to the control of the Scotland Act.*

9 See Hansard: HL Deb 28 October 1998 at cols 2041-2042 per the then Lord Advocate, Lord Hardie.

10 See: *Starrs v Ruxton* 2000 JC 208 per LJ-C Cullen at 231B-C and Lord Reed at 256A; *Brown v Stott* 2000 JC 328 per the Lord Justice General, Lord Rodger of Earlsferry, at 334; and *Millar v Dickson* 2002 SC (PC) 30 per Lord Bingham at 43D-E, Lord Hope at 55A-D and Lord Clyde at 60H.

11 See *Dickson v HM Advocate* 2008 JC 181.

other Scottish Ministers – or for the Lord Advocate when acting other than as head of Scotland's criminal prosecution service – shows it was intended by Parliament that the Convention-based limits imposed on the powers of the Scottish devolved government would be subject to no exception.

The Scottish Ministers, then – unlike any other public body or devolved authority – are bound absolutely as a matter of *vires* by the requirements of the Convention. Thus, because the Scottish Ministers and Parliament have no Human Rights Act s 6(2) defence open to them, a declarator by a court (whether under the Human Rights Act s 4 or at common law) that a provision of Westminster legislation is incompatible with the requirements of the Convention will have the effect of rendering *ultra vires* any act or omission of the Scottish Ministers or Parliament which relies upon the Westminster provision in question. Since all those who hold office by virtue of their effective appointment by the Scottish Ministers within areas of devolved competence are governed by the *vires* controls of the Scotland Act s 57(2) – rather than by the lawfulness controls of the Human Rights Act s 6 – this means that a declaration of incompatibility made under the Human Rights Act s 4 has the effect of actually setting specific and particular limits on the power of those Scottish officials.[12] It is also to be noted in this regard that the Scotland Act s 57(2) refers to limitations on the powers of the Scottish Ministers under reference to both European Community law and Convention rights.[13] Because the Scottish Ministers have no Human Rights Act s 6(2) defence, Convention rights have the same effect against the Scottish Ministers as do directly effective provisions of Community law: both render their acts *ultra vires*. Thus, any Convention-incompatible provision of a Westminster statute effectively falls to be "disapplied" as regards the Scottish Ministers, just as any Community-law-incompatible provision of a Westminster statute is to be disapplied as regards acts of emanations of the UK State.[14] And the fact that the Scottish Parliament may pass a Sewel motion to allow for the UK Parliament to legislate in an area otherwise within devolved competence – for example in the case of sex offenders registration legislation – does

12 See *XY v Scottish Ministers* 2007 SC 631 for an argument that the declaration of incompatibility pronounced by the Registration Appeal Court in *Smith v Scott*, 2007 SC 345 in relation to the maintenance by the UK government of a blanket ban on convicted prisoners exercising the right to vote impacted upon the Scottish Ministers' powers to recall into custody a prisoner who had been released on licence.

13 See A O'Neill, "The constitutional supremacy of Community Law in the United Kingdom after the Human Rights Act", in de Sousa and Heusel (eds), *Enforcing Community law from Francovich to Köbler: Twelve Years of the State Liability Principle*, vol 37, Academy of European Law, Trier, Germany (2004) 87-116.

14 See *R v Secretary of State for Transport, ex p Factortame (No 2)* [1991] 1 AC 603.

not empower the Scottish Ministers to enforce (or make a commencement order in respect of) any resulting UK legislation in so far as it is Convention-incompatible.[15] In relation to the assessment of the lawfulness of acts of the Scottish Ministers, the Convention is placed on a par with Community law – with the result that Westminster statutes are placed in a position which is, from the viewpoint of the Scottish Ministers, normatively subordinate to the requirements of the Convention.

The Scotland Act, then, embodies the principle of judicial primacy in which the courts police and may strike down all and any "unconstitutional" acts of the devolved legislature and administration. As Lord Hope observed in his contribution to the House of Lords debate on the introduction of the Scotland Bill before the Second Chamber, the Scotland Act creates a "new kind of sovereignty" for Scotland. He distinguished the situation of the UK Parliament whose "power to legislate on whatever matter it chooses *cannot* be called into question before the courts" from that of the devolved Parliament for Scotland which "can only legislate within the powers which have been devolved to it". Scottish legislation, he said, was "vulnerable to attack on the ground that it is *ultra vires*" and "it is the judges, not the devolved parliament nor even the executive, who will have the last say as to whether or not it is within the powers of the parliament".[16]

Thus, within Scotland there now exist two wholly discrete constitutional models in relation to the protection of the fundamental rights of the individual against the organs of government. The Human Rights Act regime, which applies to all public authorities within the United Kingdom, is based on the principle of the ultimate supremacy of the (United Kingdom) legislature. The Scotland Act provisions for the protection of fundamental rights rest, instead, on the idea of the primacy of the judges within the Scottish legal system over the Scottish Parliament and the Scottish government. But it should not be assumed that the giving of greater powers to judges results in any stronger protection for fundamental rights in Scotland in comparison with the rest of the United Kingdom. If anything, the self-regarding complacency, the mulish resistance to change, the thrawn conservatism, which has for so long character-ised the ruling elites of Scottish society, not only its judiciary and its lawyers[17]

---

15 See *A v Scottish Ministers* 2008 SLT 412 (OH); [2007] CSOH 189.

16 Hansard: HL Deb 17 June 1998 per Lord Hope of Craighead at col 1637-9.

17 See W A Wilson, "The progress of the law 1888-1988" (1988) *JR* 207 at 231 (italics added):
> It cannot be said that the Scottish judiciary has been a major agency of change in the last hundred years. The House of Lords has made abrupt turns from time to time and perhaps that is the appropriate place for changes to be made. The Court of Session has been, on the whole, conservative; *it has refused to break new ground, not only because there was precedent*

but also its politicians, has meant that the promise of radicalism implicit in the new constitution for Scotland has not (yet) been fulfilled.

B. INTERNATIONAL (HUMAN RIGHTS) LAW AND THE SCOTTISH CONSTITUTION

The legal systems of both Scotland and England and Wales formally remain dualist, which is to say that, until formally incorporated by Parliament into domestic law, the domestic courts will not have regard to or seek in any way to enforce such treaty obligations as the United Kingdom may have assumed as a matter of public international law.[18] However, international law is not a thing writ on water. Section 126(10) of the Scotland Act defines "international obligations" for the purposes of the statute as meaning "*any* international obligation of the United Kingdom, *other than* obligations to observe and implement Community law or the Convention rights". Sections 35(1)(a) and 58 of the Scotland Act also create an enforcement mechanism whereby the UK Government can ensure that, when acting within their devolved responsibility, the Scottish Parliament and the Scottish Ministers will exercise their devolved functions and act in a manner which is compatible with the United Kingdom's international obligations. And the Scotland Act Sch 5 para 7 states that:

> (1) International relations, including relations with territories outside the United Kingdom, the European Communities (and their institutions) and other international organisations, regulation of international trade, and international development assistance and co-operation are reserved matters. (2) Sub-paragraph (1) does not reserve— (a) *observing and implementing international obligations*, obligations under the Human Rights Convention and obligations under Community law, (b) assisting Ministers of the Crown in relation to any matter to which that sub-paragraph applies.

The effect of these provisions is that observing and implementing international obligations which have been assumed by the United Kingdom (even if they have not – fully – been incorporated into national law) falls within the competence of the Scottish devolved institutions. And the United Kingdom is party to the following international human rights conventions, among others:

---

against it, but also because there was no precedent for it. ... The best that can be said for the judges is that they have kept the system going; that is, perhaps, their function.

18 The position is different as regards the norms of customary international law which are automatically incorporated into the domestic law of Scotland: *Lord Advocate's Reference (No 1 of 2000) re nuclear weapons*, 2001 JC 143 (HCJ). See too *In re McKerr* [2004] 1 WLR 807 (HL (NI)) per Lord Steyn at paras 49-50, 52.

- the UN International Covenant on Economic Social and Cultural Rights (1966);
- the UN International Covenant on Civil and Political Rights (1966);
- the UN Convention on the Elimination of All Forms of Racial Discrimination (1965);
- the UN Convention on the Elimination of All Forms of Discrimination against Women (1979);
- the UN Convention on the Rights of the Child (1989);
- the International Convention on the Protection of all Migrant Workers and Members of their Families (1990).

The intention of the UK Parliament, as revealed in the scheme of the Scotland Act, was that the Scottish government should *not* exercise the powers that were devolved to it in a manner which would put the United Kingdom in breach of its international treaty obligations.[19] As a matter of constitutional principle and good government, it is clear that if the United Kingdom's international obligations are to be breached, it will only be as a result of a deliberate and conscious decision on the part of Crown in right of the UK government. It is for this reason that the Scotland Act s 58 was enacted (to give the Secretary of State power to prevent action by the Scottish Ministers incompatible with international obligations). Further, in so far as the Scottish Ministers fail to act in a manner which might otherwise be required to be done in Scotland under and in terms of an international obligation binding upon the United Kingdom, they may be subject to enforcement action against them on the part of the Secretary of State by virtue of the Scotland Act s 58. There are no parallel provisions in the Human Rights Act which set out the continued significance of public authorities abiding by the United Kingdom's international obligations. Collectively these provisions of the Scotland Act might be said to bind the Scottish Ministers to exercise their powers in a manner which respects the whole range of international treaty obligations entered into by the United Kingdom – even where they have not been incorporated into the domestic law of the United Kingdom.[20]

The House of Lords in *Whaley v Lord Advocate* rejected an argument put forward by an unrepresented party litigant (and in the absence of any *amicus curiae* to make his case) that "the Scottish Parliament was obliged to observe and implement international obligations in just the same way as it was obliged

19 Compare *R (Hurst) v London Northern District Coroner* [2007] 2 AC 189 per Lord Brown of Eaton-under-Heywood at paras 55-59.
20 Compare, pre-devolution, *T, Petitioner* 1997 SLT 724 (IH) on the relevance of provisions of the ECHR prior to the incorporation of various of its provisions into domestic law by the Human Rights Act and the devolution statutes.

to implement and observe the Convention rights and Community law".[21] Nothing in their Lordships' decision or reasoning, however, forecloses the argument that a legitimate expectation enforceable by a private party[22] may exist to the effect that the actions of the Scottish devolved institutions will be compatible with the United Kingdom's "international obligations". Thus, while not making international obligations directly part of the domestic Scots law, the Scotland Act may itself be said to embody and create a legitimate expectation, enforceable by those with the necessary title and interest, that the actions of the Scottish devolved institutions will be compatible with the United Kingdom's "international obligations".

Further, as we have noted, the Scotland Act Sch 5 para 7(2)(a) provides that it is within devolved competence for the Scottish Ministers (and Lord Advocate) to observe and implement "international obligations, obligations under the Human Rights Convention and obligations under international law". Thus the Scottish Ministers have the power to take any action which might be said to implement the United Kingdom's international obligations, including all those under the international human rights treaties listed above. In granting the devolved institutions power to implement international obligations the Scotland Act Sch 5 para 7(2)(a) may in fact be used to expand the competences of the Scottish government even into areas (for example, anti-discrimination laws) which otherwise look to be reserved to the UK Parliament. There is Australian precedent in using the international law to affect the internal distribution of powers within a federal legal system. In *Commonwealth of Australia v State of Tasmania*[23] (the "Tasmanian Dam" case) the High Court of Australia upheld the claim of the Commonwealth of Australia that it could properly rely upon the external affairs powers granted it under the Australian constitution to give it the legal competence to pass the World Heritage Properties Conservation Act 1983. This federal Act was made in avowed implementation of a UNESCO declaration designating the Franklin River area a "world heritage site" and its purpose was to prevent the construction of the Franklin Dam by the Tasmanian government, a matter which would otherwise have fallen wholly within State competence. Again, we see the possibilities in the new Scottish constitutional model.

---

21 *Whaley v Lord Advocate* 2008 SC (HL) 107 per Lord Hope at 110-1 paras 8-9.
22 See *Salah Abdadou v Secretary of State for the Home Department* 1998 SC 504 (OH).
23 *Commonwealth of Australia v State of Tasmania* (1983) 158 CLR 1.

C. THE SCOTTISH PARLIAMENT AS A GUARDIAN OF HUMAN RIGHTS?

(1) No human rights committee of the Scottish Parliament

There is no committee or organ of the Scottish Parliament which plays any role equivalent or comparable to that played in Westminster by the UK Parliamentary Joint Committee on Human Rights ("JCHR"). All that the Scottish Parliament has had in the first ten years of its existence is an informal cross-party group on human rights and civil liberties which functions as a forum in which members of NGOs may meet some MSPs interested in human rights issues. But this cross-party group is not a committee of the Scottish Parliament and has none of the powers or prestige associated with that status. By contrast, Westminster's JCHR is made up of twelve members appointed from both the House of Commons and the House of Lords. The Joint Committee is charged with considering human rights issues in the UK and undertakes thematic inquiries on human rights issues, reporting its findings and recommendations to Parliament. It scrutinises all UK government Bills and picks out those with significant human rights implications for further examination. The JCHR also looks at UK government action to deal with judgments of the UK courts and the European Court of Human Rights where breaches of human rights have been found.

The failure by the Scottish Parliament to establish any analogous Scottish Human Rights Parliamentary Committee with the resources and expertise to be able and willing to test the Convention compatibility of the administrative and legislative action and inaction of the Scottish government casts grave doubt on the extent to which a human rights culture has indeed taken root at the heart of Scotland's institutions of government. What this means is that, by default, claims by the Scottish government as to the human rights compatibility of its actions and legislative programme go unchallenged before the Parliament. It is a cause of some disappointment that Scotland's democratic legislature should be so passive on the issue of human rights protection in Scotland and on holding the Scottish government to account on human rights grounds. The fact is that when criticisms are made of Scottish government policy by the Scottish Parliament, these criticisms would be immeasurably strengthened if they were also couched on human rights grounds: in so doing they would be drawing attention to absolute and enforceable legal limits on the powers which the Government was purporting to exercise, or failing to exercise.

(a) Slopping out

Certainly the fact that in the early days of the Scottish Parliament the Justice Committee was very proactive in calling the Scottish Ministers to account over their willingness to maintain a regime involving slopping out in Scottish prisons was crucial to the subsequent court finding in *Napier v Scottish Ministers*.[24] The court found that the regime in which remand prisoners were commonly being held in HM Prison Barlinnie, involving their being locked for up to twenty-three hours per day, two to a cell which had originally been intended for single occupancy and in which there was no provision for internal sanitation, requiring them to use a plastic potty for their sanitary needs, constituted – at least in Scotland by 2004[25] – "inhuman and degrading treatment" for the purposes of the ECHR art 3. But the fact that the court, in coming to its decision, took into account evidence, taken from the Scottish Parliamentary record, that the Scottish government had made a deliberate choice to move funds originally allocated for the elimination of slopping out to spend in favour of other projects was the subject of some public criticism on constitutional grounds. The former Solicitor General and Court of Session judge Lord McCluskey objected that

> the decision as to how limited public (i.e. taxpayers') funds are to be spent within the criminal system is a matter for elected politicians not for judges. How can it be for judges to decide that spending money on improving toilet facilities for convicted criminals is more important than spending that money on tackling domestic violence or on trying to fight the menace of dangerous drugs?

The Scottish Government failed to mark an appeal against the decision of the Lord Ordinary within the required time. Neither the Minister of Justice of the time nor the then Lord Advocate was willing to accept responsibility for this failure, each, apparently, being ready to blame the other. In the event, the Scottish government paid the pursuer's legal expenses and the sum of £2,100 damages which had been awarded to him at first instance, and it was given leave by the Inner House to appeal out of time, not on the merits of the actual case but only on the purely academic point as to whether the civil or criminal standard of proof was required to be met before a domestic court could hold in the context of a judicial review that conduct or inaction was in breach of the ECHR art 3. On this point the Inner House found in favour of the pursuer, and confirmed that the normal civil standard of proof on the balance of probabilities only applied on this question.[26]

24 *Napier v Scottish Ministers* 2005 SC 229 (OH).
25 See now a contrasting view expressed in *R (Wellington) v Secretary of State for the Home Department* [2009] 1 AC 335 per Lord Hoffmann at para 27.
26 *Napier v Scottish Ministers* 2005 SC 307 (IH).

(b) Tainted blood and the NHS

Another instance in which the court has felt able to support the views of the Scottish Parliament over those of the Scottish government is seen in the judicial review application *Kennedy v Lord Advocate*,[27] in which the decision of the Lord Advocate to refuse to hold a public inquiry into the deaths of individuals infected with hepatitis C virus from blood transfusions while in NHS care was overturned. The court held that a proper appreciation of the procedural duties implicit in the ECHR art 2 guarantee of the right to life required there to be a public inquiry into the issue raised by these deaths at which the families of those who had died could be properly represented. This decision by the court at first instance reflected and echoed repeated calls from the Scottish Parliament that such an inquiry should be set up and the incoming SNP administration expressly accepted the court's findings and decided not to appeal against the judgment and, in the light of the court's judgment, set up the Penrose inquiry to look into the issues raised by the judicial review.

(2) The Convention Rights Proceedings (Amendment) (Scotland) Act 2009

But by far the most egregious failure to date on the part of the Scottish Parliament to challenge or test the Scottish government's claim concerns the passing by the Scottish Parliament of the Convention Rights Proceedings (Amendment) (Scotland) Act 2009. This was a Scottish Executive Bill put before the Scottish Parliament to close the "loophole" said by the Ministers to have been exposed by the majority decision of the House of Lords in *Somerville v Scottish Ministers*.[28] This decision rejected the Scottish Ministers' argument that they could rely upon a time-bar provision contained in the Human Rights Act s 7(5) to defeat claims which had been brought against them under and in terms of the Scotland Act. Section 100 of the Scotland Act expressly contemplates the possibility of challenges being made under that Act on Convention rights grounds to Acts of the Scottish Parliament (ASPs) and to the action or inaction of the Scottish Ministers,[29] but the Scotland Act contains no provision for time limits for the making of such legal challenges. This had been expressly drawn to the attention of Parliament by Lord Hope

---

27 *Kennedy v Lord Advocate (No 1)* 2008 SLT 195 (OH); *Kennedy v Lord Advocate (No 2)* [2009] CSOH 1.

28 *Somerville v Scottish Ministers* 2008 SC (HL) 45 (Lord Hope of Craighead, Lord Rodger of Earlsferry and Lord Walker of Gestingthorpe forming the majority; Lord Scott of Foscote and Lord Mance dissenting).

29 See *R v HM Advocate* 2003 SC (PC) 21.

of Craighead – speaking in his then capacity as legislator – when the Scotland Bill was being debated in June 1998.[30] The majority decision of the Appellate Committee of the House of Lords in *Somerville v Scottish Ministers*, which was handed down in October 2007, simply confirmed the position but it was presented by the SNP administration as a revelation, if not a revolution. The difficulty for the Scottish government was that the *Somerville* decision turned upon the proper interpretation of the Scotland Act 1998. This is a reserved enactment which the Scottish Parliament has no power to amend. The Scottish government was therefore obliged to lobby the Westminster government for a change in the law.[31] In his statement to the Scottish Parliament on 11 March 2009, the Scottish Cabinet Secretary of Justice Kenny MacAskill MSP said this:

> The UK Government had suggested that we might address the *Somerville* issue by changing the law on time bar in Scotland more generally. However, that would reduce the rights of many *deserving* claimants, such as those who suffer from pleural plaques or been injured through the negligence of an employer.[32]

Three points can be made immediately in relation to these claims by the Justice Minister. First, the application to Convention rights ("just satisfaction") damages claim of the same (currently three-year)[33] period which applies to private law damages claims for personal injuries would *not* result in the reduction of any right of any existing claimants, since all that this would do would be to establish parity of treatment between these two categories of case. Secondly, an insinuation is being made by the Justice Minister to the effect that all who seek damages in respect of the violation of their Convention rights are *ipso facto* less deserving than those seeking damages for personal injuries. Finally, in any event, quite different rules, principles and procedures

30 See Lord Hope of Craighead in Hansard: HL Deb 17 June 1998 col 1638 (italics added):
    One has only to look at the devolution issues listed in paragraph 1 of Schedule 6 to see the scope which will exist for challenges to be made. No time limit is set for the making of those challenges. As has been pointed out by several noble Lords, there is to be no revising chamber. So in theory at least – I stress the word theory – subject to the exercise of the powers given to the court in Section 93 to vary retrospective decisions, *legislation by the Scottish parliament could be set aside as not being within that parliament's competence long after it had been put into effect.*
31 See, e.g., the Scottish Parliament, *Official Report*, Justice Committee, col 1181 (7 October 2008), per the Scottish Minister for Community Safety Fergus Ewing MSP:
    [T]he fundamental legal issue raised by the *Somerville* case … is that the Scottish ministers are the only public authority exposed to claims for damages arising from breaches of human rights without a one-year time bar. We asked the UK Government to assist us in tackling that. … Because we have not obtained a satisfactory response from Westminster, we are left facing these slopping out claims without the time bar that applies to every other authority. That seems to me to be a shocking neglect.
32 See Statement to the Scottish Parliament on 11 March 2009 by the Cabinet Secretary of Justice.
33 See Prescription and Limitation (Scotland) Act 1973 s 17.

already apply in relation to public law damages claims, since these are usually brought in the context of judicial review petitions. The introduction of changes in relation to the time limits applicable to such public law damages claims need not have any impact upon private law delictual damages brought by way of ordinary action. By April 2009 the Scottish government had managed to exert sufficient political pressure on the UK government – based mainly on repeated but quite unsubstantiated claims that a failure to change the law as it requested by the summer of 2009 would result in a further £50 million having to be paid out by the Scottish Ministers to convicted prisoners[34] – such that the Cabinet Secretary of Justice was able to advise the Scottish Parliament that the UK Government had agreed to vest the Scottish Parliament with power itself to amend the Scotland Act by introducing a time bar of one year or less in relation to proceedings brought by individuals against the Scottish Ministers on Convention rights grounds.[35] Less than a week after this power was granted, the Scottish Ministers introduced the Convention Rights Proceedings (Amendment) (Scotland) Bill before the Scottish Parliament. Two days after being published and introduced before the Parliament the Bill was passed, unamended, by a unanimous Scottish Parliament in one day on 18 June 2009. No proper reason was ever given by the Scottish government as to what emergency existed which required this legislation to be pushed through in one day without public consultation or debate almost two years after the House of Lords decision complained of. It is clear, however, that this change in the law allows for far more than setting a cap on the bringing of aged claims by prisoners for just satisfaction damages in respect of their slopping out, as was its professed rationale.[36] Instead, it provides for the imposition of a time bar of at most one year in relation to any Convention rights claim against the administrative action or inaction of the Scottish Ministers, regardless of whether just satisfaction damages were sought by the Convention rights victims in these actions, and regardless of whether these actions are brought by or on behalf of the apparently deserving

34 See statement to the Scottish Parliament on 11 March 2009 by the Cabinet Secretary of Justice (italics added):

> The situation created in Scotland by the judgment is untenable and unacceptable. Introducing a 1-year time bar would enable us to draw a line under our liability in relation to claims of the kind made in *Somerville, and so could release up to some £50m for spending on more worthwhile purposes.* It would also reduce our liability in relation to other human rights claims that might arise in the future. *£50m is a large amount of money. For instance, it could pay for 8 new primary schools or 500 new affordable housing units, or employ 1250 teachers or 1600 nurses for a year.* So this is a very real and important issue.

35 See the Scotland Act 1998 (Modification of Schedule 4) Order 2009, SI 2009/1380.
36 See Scottish Government Briefing Note (11 March 2009): "*Somerville*: time bar on human rights actions against Scottish Ministers" at para 19.

(for example, the pensioners whose situation was repeatedly mentioned in the Scottish Parliament) as contrasted with the allegedly undeserving (for example, convicted prisoners). This change in the law involves, under the guise of limiting prisoners' rights, a significant reduction in the level of judicial protection afforded to the (Convention) rights of every private individual in Scotland *vis à vis* the Scottish government. And all this was done without any public consultation,[37] in a helter-skelter rush to change the constitution to the Scottish government's advantage before anyone apparently noticed the implications of what was being done. It was an example of the Scottish government playing politics with the (Scottish) constitution and a supine, complaisant Scottish Parliament provided no protection, no scrutiny, against this.

D. THE SCOTTISH COURTS AND THE PROTECTION OF CONSTITUTIONAL RIGHTS

In another constitutional arrangement a second revising legislative or advisory chamber might have had a role to play in testing the factual and legal claims of the Scottish government in support of significant constitutional changes such as that contained in the Convention Rights Proceedings (Amendment) (Scotland) Act 2009. In the absence of such within the Scottish polity, might one then rely upon the courts in Scotland to carry out this constitutional function? The experience of the first ten years of litigation in a devolved Scotland makes this seem unlikely.

The purpose of litigation, as usually conceived of and judicially presented in the contemporary Scottish legal system, has been to obtain a resolution of a real dispute between individual parties about their respective rights and obligations *inter se*. The Scottish courts have, in the course of the twentieth century, insisted that there require to be both title and interest to sue as a prerequisite to an individual or body being permitted to raise any action in court. The passage constantly cited in support of this approach is some passing observations of Lord Dunedin in the 1915 case of *D & J Nicol v Dundee Harbour Trustees*, that for a person to have title to sue "he must be a party (using the words in its widest sense) to some legal relation which gives him some right which the person against whom he raises the action either infringes or denies".[38] This same test (which focuses on private rights)

---

37 See further the Scottish Government's Executive Note on the Scotland Act 1998 (Modification of Schedule 4) Order 2009 of 1 April 2009, repeated verbatim at para 22 of the Policy Memorandum to the Bill, which confirms that the only consultation was in the form of a statement to the Scottish Parliament.

38 *D & J Nicol v Dundee Harbour Trs* 1915 SC (HL) 12-13.

appears, then, to have been applied by default to public law challenges by way of judicial review,[39] notwithstanding that, as Sedley LJ has observed (italics added):

> Public law is not at base about rights, even though abuses of power may and often do invade private rights; it is about wrongs – that is to say misuses of public power; and the courts have always been alive to the fact that a person or organisation with no particular stake in the issue or the outcome may, *without in any sense being a mere meddler*, wish and be well placed to call the attention of the court to an apparent misuse of public power.[40]

In Scotland, by contrast, the interest which the party has to show he seeks to protect must also be considered by the court to be "a material or sufficient interest"[41] specific to him which will be prejudiced by the decision complained of.[42] The rationale for rules on standing was explained by Lord Ardwell in *Swanson v Manson* as follows:

> The grounds for this rule are (1) that the law courts of this country are not instituted for the purpose of deciding academic questions of law, but for settling disputes where any of the lieges has a real interest to have a question determined which involves his pecuniary rights or his status; and (2) that no person is entitled to subject another to the trouble and expense of a litigation unless he has some real interest to enforce and protect.[43]

Notwithstanding some judicial extra-curial criticisms[44] and observations in the Outer House authority to the effect that the Scottish rules on title and interest should not be applied in an artificial, technical or restrictive manner, particularly in a context such as judicial review,[45] it is clear that the rules on standing to take judicial reviews in Scotland have, to date, been applied far more restrictively than their equivalent rules in England and Wales.[46] In

---

39 See *Scottish Old People's Welfare Council v Secretary of State for Social Security* 1987 SLT 179 (OH) per Lord Clyde at 184; and *Adams v Advocate General* 2003 SC 171 (OH) for a discussion of the requirements of title and interest in public law cases.

40 *R v Somerset County Council, ex p Dixon* [1998] Env LR 111.

41 *Air 2000 v Secretary of State for Transport (No 2)* 1990 SLT 335. See also *Air 2000 v Secretary of State for Transport (No 1)* 1989 SLT 698.

42 See *Simpson v Edinburgh Corporation* 1960 SC 313 for a relatively narrow definition of what constitutes "prejudice" sufficient to ground an action for judicial review.

43 *Swanson v Manson* 1907 SC 426 per Lord Ardwell at 429. See, more recently, *Davidson v Scottish Ministers* 2002 SC 205 (IH) per Lord Hardie at 216.

44 Lord Hope of Craighead, "Mike Tyson comes to Glasgow" [2001] *Public Law* 294.

45 *MacColl v Crofters' Commission* [2007] Housing LR 46 per Lord Malcolm.

46 But see now *AXA Insurance v Lord Advocate* [2010] CSOH 2 per Lord Emslie at paras 57 and 59:

> [T]he domestic rules [on title and interest] may, like article 34 of the Convention, be seen as intended to exclude access to the courts where a pursuer's interest in, or connection with, the subject-matter of a proposed litigation is remote, tenuous, academic or theoretical. But ... where a party's personal, social, political, economic or proprietary interests are demonstrably

particular, the Scottish courts seem loath to admit the possibility of public interest challenges being taken before the courts to the lawfulness of executive or legislative action.[47] Scotland's restrictive rules on standing compared with the practice in England has meant that there is no real scope for public interest litigation by pressure groups or (quasi-) non-government organisations. Indeed, the Scottish Human Rights Commission – set up by the Scottish Parliament under the Scottish Commission for Human Rights Act 2006 – while permitted to intervene in legal proceedings "for the purpose of making a submission to the court on an issue arising in the proceedings", is expressly forbidden by its constituting statute to "provide assistance to or in respect of any person in connection with any claim or legal proceedings to which that person is or may become a party". And s 7 of the Equality Act 2006 also prohibits the Equality and Human Rights Commission from taking "human rights action" in Scotland, or even from considering the question whether a person's human rights have been contravened "if the Scottish Parliament has legislative competence to enable a person" to take such action or consider this question. The result has been a dearth in Scotland of what might be termed "public interest litigation". In so far as the public interest has been considered by the courts in Scotland, it appears at times to have become equated to the claims of the State - particularly as represented to the court on behalf of the government by the Scottish Law Officers.[48]

But the Lord Advocate exercises a far less prestigious and powerful role than prevailed in the pre-devolutionary settlement. The Lord Advocate is

---

affected by some real (as opposed to merely academic or theoretical) public law issue or grievance, then as a general rule he will be held to have title to raise proceedings for judicial review in that connection. ... [I]t seems to me, the broad and flexible principles enshrined in both domestic and Convention jurisprudence are intended to permit recourse to the court by those who can, in their own right, qualify a live, practical interest in the subject-matter of a public law complaint and who will themselves be materially affected by the outcome of proceedings.

47 See, e.g., *Glasgow Rape Crisis Centre v Secretary of State for the Home Department* 2000 SC 527 (in particular the latter at 534 per Lord Clarke). Compare, however, *Wilson v Independent Broadcasting Authority* 1979 SC 351.

48 See *Hester v McDonald* 1961 SC 370 per LP Clyde at 378-379 (italics added):

From time immemorial it has, therefore, been recognised, as Baron Hume puts it *Crimes*, vol. ii, p. 135 that "a constitutional trust is reposed in that high officer, selected by His Majesty from among the most eminent at the Bar; and *it will not be supposed of him, that he can be actuated by unworthy motives in commencing a prosecution, or fall into such irregularities or blunders in conducting his process, as ought properly to make him liable in amends*." As Alison says (vol. ii, p. 93) he is absolutely exempt from penalties and expenses. It is, therefore, an essential element in the very structure of our criminal administration in Scotland that the Lord Advocate is protected by an absolute privilege in respect of matters in connexion with proceedings brought before a Scottish Criminal Court by way of indictment.

See, too, *Crichton v McBain* 1961 JC 25 per LJ-General Clyde at 28-29.

no longer in charge, for example, of judicial appointments and preferment.[49] The office has become little more than a Scottish Director of Public Prosecutions. Under the influence of Convention rights jurisprudence, the courts have in more recent years begun to be willing to consider legal challenges to[50] – and at times to overturn[51] – decisions of the Lord Advocate exercising the role of the head of the system for investigation of deaths in Scotland.

More generally, the tradition of judicial deference to the "powers that be" may be seen to be changing under the devolved settlement. Thus, the peculiarly Scottish interpretation of the UK-wide provisions of s 21 of the Crown Proceedings Act 1947,[52] that it had the effect of prohibiting the courts from, in any circumstances, pronouncing any coercive or interim orders against the Crown, was eventually overturned, but only after a long and hard-fought campaign of litigation before the unwilling judges of the Court of Session,[53] and requiring three visits in the same case to the House of Lords.[54] The Scottish Ministers have also now been found to be guilty of contempt of court in their failure to ensure that an undertaking given to the court was duly respected by their civil servants.[55] And the judges of the First Division[56]

49 Judicial appointments are now in the hands of the Judicial Appointment Board for Scotland which, by virtue of s 14 of the Judiciary and Courts (Scotland) Act 2008, is required to have regard to the need to encourage "diversity" in the range of individuals available for selection for judicial appointments.

50 But see *Emms v Lord Advocate* 2008 SLT 2 (OH) and *Niven v Lord Advocate* 2009 SLT 876 (OH) on the duties of the Crown as regards an ECHR art 2 compliant investigation into a pre-Scotland Act death.

51 See, e.g., *Global Santa Fe Drilling Co (North Sea) Ltd v Lord Advocate* 2009 SLT 598 (IH), rejecting the Lord Advocate's submissions that it was not competent for a sheriff to make an award of expenses against the Crown in a fatal accident inquiry; and *Kennedy v Lord Advocate (No 2)* [2009] CSOH 1; *Kennedy v Lord Advocate* 2008 SLT 195 (OH) where the Lord Ordinary held that the refusal by the Lord Advocate to institute an inquiry into the deaths of individuals infected with hepatitis C virus from blood transfusions while in NHS care was incompatible with the requirements of ECHR art 6.

52 Set out by the Second Division in *McDonald v Secretary of State for Scotland* 1994 SC 234 (IH), refusing to follow the opposite interpretation by the House of Lords on the same statutory provision given in *M v Home Office* [1994] 1 AC 377 on the basis that this was an interpretation based on peculiarities of English law which were difficult for a Scots lawyer to understand or give effect to.

53 See, e.g., *Davidson v Scottish Ministers* [2002] 1 *Prison Law Reports* 58 (OH) per Lord Johnston and 2002 SC 205 (IH) per Lords Marnoch, Hardie and Weir; *Callison v Scottish Ministers* unreported, 25 June 2004, Lord Drummond Young (OH).; *Beggs v Scottish Ministers* 2004 SLT 755 (OH) (Lord Drummond Young); *McKenzie v Scottish Ministers* 2004 SLT 1236 (OH) (Lord Carloway); *Ralston v Scottish Ministers* 2004 SLT 1263 (OH) (Lady Smith).

54 See *Davidson v Scottish Ministers (No 3)* 2005 SC (HL) 1; *Davidson v Scottish Ministers (No 2)* 2005 SC (HL) 7; and *Davidson v Scottish Ministers* 2006 SC (HL) 42.

55 *Beggs v Scottish Ministers* 2006 SC 649 (IH).

56 *Napier v Scottish Ministers* 2005 SC 307 (IH) at para 7.

and the House of Lords in Scottish appeals[57] have been willing to give general declaratory judgment on legal issues which, by the time the cases were before them, had become academic as between the specific parties to the cause.

Yet the restrictive rules on standing remain stubbornly and capriciously[58] in place in Scotland, despite occasional judicial criticism and notwithstanding even the requirement – at least in areas of environmental law falling within the scope of the Aarhus Convention[59] – for wide public access to the courts to defend their (environmental) rights.[60] These restrictive rules on standing have significantly inhibited the development of public law in Scotland.

Notwithstanding the position of judicial primacy which the devolved settlement gives to the judges over the Scottish Parliament in the first full

57 See *Davidson v Scottish Ministers* 2006 SC (HL) 42 per Lord Rodger at para 58. See, too, *Beggs v Scottish Ministers* [2007] 1 WLR 455, 2007 SLT 235 (HL) per Lord Rodger at para 30.

58 See *Forbes v Aberdeenshire Council and Trump International Golf Links* [2010] CSOH 1 per Lady Smith.

59 Article 9(2) of the UNECE Convention on Access to Information, Public Participation in Decision-Making and Access to Justice in Environmental Matters (hereafter "the Aarhus Convention") provides as follows:

9(2) Each Party shall, within the framework of its national legislation, ensure that members of the public concerned

(a) Having a sufficient interest or, alternatively,

(b) Maintaining impairment of a right, where the administrative procedural law of a Party requires this as a precondition,

have access to a review procedure before a court of law and/or another independent and impartial body established by law, to challenge the substantive and procedural legality of any decision, act or omission subject to the provisions of article 6 and, where so provided for under national law and without prejudice to paragraph 3 below, of other relevant provisions of this Convention. What constitutes a sufficient interest and impairment of a right shall be determined in accordance with the requirements of national law and consistently with the objective of giving the public concerned wide access to justice within the scope of this Convention.

60 The Environmental Impact Assessment (Scotland) Regulations 1999 (which seek to implement in Scotland the Environmental Impact Assessment Directive 85/337/EEC) were amended with effect from 1 February 2007, apparently to increase NGOs' rights of access to the court by the following provisions:

46A *Access to review procedure before a court*

Any non-governmental organisation promoting environmental protection *and meeting any requirements under the law* shall be deemed to have an interest for the purposes of Article 10a(a) of the Directive and rights capable of being impaired for the purposes of Article 10a(b) of the Directive.

...

62A *Access to review procedure before a court*

Any non-governmental organisation promoting environmental protection and meeting any requirements under the law shall be deemed to have an interest for the purposes of Article 10a(a) of the Directive and rights capable of being impaired for the purposes of Article 10a(b) of the Directive.

This is apparently the only amendment which was considered necessary or desirable by the Scottish government to ensure that environmental rights accorded the individual under the Environmental Impact Assessment Directive and the Aarhus Convention were able to be protected before the court in Scotland.

ten years of its legislative programme, there have been only a handful of court challenges to the validity of provisions of primary legislation emanating from the Scottish Parliament. The Acts of the Scottish Parliament which have been subject to challenge in this period were: the Mental Health (Public Safety and Appeals) (Scotland) Act 1999, allowing for the continued detention in the state hospital of medically untreatable psychopaths on grounds of public safety;[61] the provisions of the Convention Rights (Compliance) (Scotland) Act 2001, which removed ministerial discretion on the matter of the date of release from prison of those serving a mandatory life sentence;[62] the Sexual Offences (Procedure and Evidence) (Scotland) Act 2002, which regulated the issue of disclosure of previous convictions in sexual offences cases;[63] the Protection of Wild Mammals (Scotland) Act 2002, which regulated fox hunting with hounds;[64] the Criminal Proceedings etc (Reform) (Scotland) Act 2007, which increased to twelve months the maximum sentence of imprisonment which could be imposed by the sheriff, sitting as a court of summary jurisdiction in respect of both common law and statutory offences;[65] and the Damages (Asbestos-related Conditions) (Scotland) Act 2009, which sought to ensure that delictual damages might continue to be claimed in respect of the development of asymptomatic pleural plaques and other specified asbestos-related conditions upon negligent exposure to asbestos fibres.[66] None of these challenges was said to have been taken in the general public interest. All were made by persons who claimed that they were "victims" in respect of a violation of their Convention rights. And none of these challenges has, to date, been successful in the sense of resulting in a finding by the court that either the Act of the Scottish Parliament or any of its provisions in question required to be disapplied or suspended or declared void on grounds that they had been made outwith the Scottish Parliament's legislative competence.

Perhaps the best one can hope for on the issue of the reform of public interest litigation in Scotland is not a series of individual court decisions (which ultimately would require to be taken to and upheld by the United Kingdom Supreme Court in order to have a chance of becoming properly established within the Scottish legal system) but by way of the systematic reform of the whole system promised by the Gill Review on civil justice reform. This promises the introduction of a new test of sufficient interest in

---

61 See *A v Scottish Ministers* 2002 SC (PC) 63.
62 *Flynn v HM Advocate* 2004 SC (PC) 1.
63 *DS v HM Advocate* 2007 SC (PC) 1
64 *Whaley v Lord Advocate* 2008 SC (HL) 107.
65 *Logan v Harrower* 2008 SLT 1049 (HCJ). See also *Martin v HM Advocate* [2010] UKSC 10.
66 *AXA General Insurance v Lord Advocate* [2010] CSOH 2.

judicial review, the imposition of a three-month time limit in which judicial review applications are to be brought, and new rules allowing specifically for class actions. Whether and when these reforms might be brought in is not clear. It seems unlikely that it would be a priority of the Scottish government to introduce reform in the court system which would make it easier for individuals and interest groups to take cases against them (at public expense) before the courts, though it is arguable that this is precisely what a properly constitutional democracy requires. What is clear, however, is that something has to be done. The Scottish judicial and legal system cannot continue to ignore the need for the very possibility of public interest litigation. The administration of justice is supposed to be blind (in terms of being impartial). It is not supposed to be deaf to the clamour for justice.

E. CONCLUSION: LONDON CALLING

In March 2001 Lord Bingham observed in his evidence on the constitution to the Joint Committee on Human Rights that "one of the anomalous, and to me surprising and unexpected, results of devolution is that for the first time one does have judges, Scots prominently among them but nonetheless judges, sitting in London ruling on questions relating to Scots criminal trials".[67] In almost 300 years of the Union with England, Scottish criminal law and procedure was developed in splendid isolation by the High Court of Justiciary, with little substantive input (or interference) from the (Westminster) legislature. But in the ten years of its existence the Privy Council's devolution jurisdiction was prayed in aid *only* in relation to appeals from Scotland, and these almost exclusively concerned issues of Scots criminal law and procedure, albeit dressed up in the language of Convention rights (primarily the fair trial rights set out in the ECHR art 6(1)). Although the criminal appeals from decisions of the High Court of Justiciary to the Privy Council were relatively few in number, they had a significant impact in opening up the traditionally insular (and almost wholly judge-made) world of Scottish criminal law and procedure to a degree of external scrutiny which does not now appear to be welcomed by the judges in Edinburgh.[68] This devolution jurisdiction of the Privy Council and the appellate jurisdiction of the House of Lords from Scotland were transferred to the UK Supreme Court by the Constitutional Reform Act 2005.

67 *http://www.publications.parliament.uk/pa/jt200001/jtselect/jtrights/66/1032607.htm.*
68 See, e.g., the collective submission of the judges of the Court of Session to the Calman Commission, 10 October 2008: *http://www.commissiononscottishdevolution.org.uk/uploads/2008-10-20-judiciary-in-the-court-of-session.pdf.*

The SNP is apparently committed to ending the possibility of any appeals, whether in civil or criminal matters from Edinburgh to London.[69] Paragraph 4(1) of Sch 4 to the Scotland Act, however, prevents the Scottish Parliament from modifying the Scotland Act itself. The Scottish Parliament has no *Kompetenz-Kompetenz*, which is to say no power to expand the range of its own powers. And Sch 6 to the Scotland Act makes provisions for appeals and preliminary reference on "devolution issues" to, ultimately, the UK Supreme Court. So it would seem to be outwith the legislative competence of the Scottish Parliament – and consequently not within the devolved competence of the Scottish Ministers – to alter, or indeed abolish, the current jurisdiction of the UK Supreme Court, at least as regards devolution issues. It may be competent, however, for the Scottish Parliament to legislate to alter, expand or indeed, abolish any appeals to that court from Scotland in non-devolution issues. But were the legality of any such measure to be challenged before the courts it would itself raise a "devolution issue". And under our current constitutional arrangements the ultimate resolution of such a challenge would lie with the UK Supreme Court itself, albeit acting pre-eminently in such a situation as *iudex in causa sua*. Certainly some Scottish-based judges,[70] academics[71] and politicians[72] have taken the opportunity of this inauguration of the UK Supreme Court to call into question the need for appeals outwith

---

69 See Scottish Executive, *Choosing Scotland's Future: A National Conversation* (2007), available at *http://www.scotland.gov.uk/Resource/Doc/194791/0052321.pdf*

70 See A Le Sueur, *A Report on Six Seminars about the UK Supreme Court* (2008) and, in particular, the remarks apparently to be attributed to Lord Gill on civil appeals from Scotland as noted at p 43.

71 See, e.g., J Chalmers, "Scottish appeals and the proposed Supreme Court" (2004) *Edinburgh Law Review* 4; and Professor H MacQueen, "Scotland and a Supreme Court for the UK?" (2003) *SLT (News)* 279 at 280:

    If difference of laws with an inevitable majority of non-Scottish members makes the House of Lords inherently unsuitable for Scottish criminal appeals, then the case is, if anything, stronger for private law appeals. One does not need to be a legal nationalist to see this.

72 Prompted by the imminent setting up of the UK Supreme Court, in December 2008, the Scottish Minister of Justice, Kenny MacAskill MSP, of the Scottish National Party, commissioned Professor Neil Walker of Edinburgh Law School to look into possible options for reform of the constitutional arrangements which currently allow for appeals to be taken to London from decisions of the courts in Scotland. The report Final Appellate Jurisdiction in the Scottish Legal System (available at *http://www.scotland.gov.uk/Publications/2010/01/19154813/14*) was published on 22 January 2010 and recommended that the appellate jurisdiction of the UK Supreme Court from Scotland be both extended and reduced. It should be extended so as to cover not only civil appeals from the Court of Session but criminal appeals from the High Court of Justiciary. It should be reduced so as no longer able to hear any appeal from Scotland unless the case raises "common UK issues". There would be no right of appeal from Edinburgh in any case which concern issues purely of Scots law. Professor Walker described this proposed re-arrangement of the appellate jurisdiction to London as transforming the UK Supreme Court, at least from the viewpoint of the Scottish legal system, into a "quasi-federal" Supreme Court.

Scotland to ensure that Scots law can develop in a manner uncontaminated by English law. But there is no intrinsic merit in having different legal systems, in all their integrity, existing for their own sake. What seems to be lost in such views is the fact that the legal system is of value only to the degree that it properly achieves and delivers justice to the people whose lives it governs.

Scotland is a small country and its legal system, lawyers and judges all benefit from appeals outside it.[73] It is important for all judges to think that they may be judged in another forum – the classic problem of *quis custodiet ipsos custodes*? – so that even if they are not appealed against, they know that they might be, and their reasoning analysed and held up to rigorous scrutiny. Arguably the possibility of appeals to the UK Supreme Court from Scotland does precisely that, and keeps the judges of the Court of Session and High Court of Justiciary and those who practise before them sharp, less likely to fall into unreasoned prejudice, more careful in how and what they decide. The European Court of Human Rights and the European Court of Justice perform a similar (but not as pervasive) function. The Scottish legal system will only flourish and serve the people of Scotland in so far as it and its practitioners remain open to the broader world. The mark of a mature legal system is the self-confidence to be open to outside influences. Scotland's people deserve nothing less.

---

73 As the then Lord Advocate Colin Boyd QC (now Lord Boyd of Duncansby) in a speech to the Conference of the Law Society of Scotland on the UK Supreme Court Proposals, 21 January 2004, observed at para 52:

As a legal system in a small country on the edge of Europe, we must be conscious of the risk of becoming self-centred and inward looking. It would be very easy for us to fall into the trap of defining our unique legal qualities and character in a negative sense, of simply not being the same as others.

4 Child and Family Law: Progress and Pusillanimity

Elaine E Sutherland[*]

A. INTRODUCTION

Any assessment of the Scottish Parliament's contribution to child and family law necessarily involves measuring its output against criteria. Happily, selecting the criteria is one of the privileges of the author. In this chapter, what the Parliament has achieved will be assessed in the light of the problems it was designed to solve; the promises held out for it by its creators; and the subject-specific goals of child and family law itself.

Scotland has long had an embarrassment of riches when it came to proposals for reform of child and family law, many emanating from the Scottish Law Commission. In common with other areas of Scots law, the pre-devolution problem lay in these proposals having to compete for precious parliamentary time at Westminster. Thus it was that no-fault divorce reached Scotland[1]

---

[*] Professor of Child and Family Law, School of Law, University of Stirling; and Professor of Law, Lewis and Clark Law School, Portland, Oregon.
1 Divorce (Scotland) Act 1976 s 1(1).

seven years after similar reform was implemented in England and Wales.[2] Other Commission proposals, like those on cohabitants, simply languished, unimplemented, in the bowels of the Scottish Office. There was also a perception of a degree of indifference at Westminster to Scottish matters: something demonstrated when Ian Lang, then Secretary of State for Scotland, rose to inform the House of Commons that he had published Lord Clyde's report on the highly controversial Orkney child protection case.[3] Such was the exodus from the House that the proceedings were interrupted by the noise of departing feet.[4] These concerns were acknowledged in *Scotland's Parliament*, the White Paper that preceded devolution, when it noted the need for a "more effective democratic framework"[5] for Scotland.

Since child and family law regulates our most intimate personal relationships, it touches upon our most profound beliefs about how we should be living our lives: beliefs that are a product of our personal morality, culture, religion (or absence thereof), history and politics. Its content and reform are of interest, not only to academics, practitioners and politicians, but to the wider public. Ideally, it ought to reflect the views of the people affected by it. While much pre-devolution legislation in the field was specific to Scotland and followed extensive consultation, both *Scotland's Parliament*[6] and the steering group that sought to implement it[7] promised an accountable and accessible legislative body and executive that would permit participation by the population. Of course, therein lies a challenge, since the people of Scotland are no more homogenous in their views on family structures and family life than is any other national group. If anything, this challenge has increased as Scottish society has become more racially and ethnically diverse.

Assessing whether the Scottish Parliament has measured up to the goals of child and family law requires that the discipline's subject-specific goals be identified – not a wholly uncontroversial process. The goals selected here are equality (and the associated values of inclusion and respect for diversity), empowerment (including freedom of choice) and protection, being goals that

---

2 Divorce Reform Act 1969.

3 *Report of the Inquiry into the Removal of Children from Orkney* in February 1991 (1992), following upon *Sloan v B* 1991 SLT 530.

4 Hansard: HC Deb 27 October 1992, col 865.

5 *Scotland's Parliament* (Cmnd 3658: 1997) para 2.1.

6 *Scotland's Parliament* (n 5) viii ("What [the reform] can do is connect and involve people with the decisions that matter to them").

7 *Report of the Consultative Steering Group on the Scottish Parliament* (1998) section 2, para 2 ("the Scottish Parliament should be accessible, open, responsive, and develop procedures which make possible a participative approach to the development, consideration and scrutiny of policy and legislation").

are widely accepted within the field itself.[8] Fortuitously, these coincide with express or implied goals set for the Scottish Parliament.[9]

Identifying precisely what the Scottish Parliament has done in respect of child and family law appears, at first glance, to be a straightforward task. One could simply analyse the legislation it has passed. But does it get the credit for matters it chose to hand off to Westminster through the legislative consent procedure, a device employed in respect of significant family law issues?[10] In the spirit of generosity, some credit will be given, but not without exploring why that particular approach might have been adopted. Nor does legislation tell the whole story. Parliaments and governments do more than make laws. They fund research, develop strategies and establish special projects and programmes. Again, credit will be given for relevant activities in the field.

B. CHILD LAW

(1) Children's rights

Since the creation of the Scottish Parliament, the administration in power at the time has sought to demonstrate its commitment to children's human rights, in general, and the United Nations Convention on the Rights of the Child ("UN Convention"), in particular. As the administration's final term drew to a close (albeit it did not realise that was happening), the (then) Scottish Executive published a progress report on its achievements on children's rights.[11] In the wake of the most recent findings of the United Nations Committee on the Rights of the Child in respect of the United Kingdom,[12] the Scottish government undertook a comprehensive audit of what more needed to be done, publishing its own draft response[13] and consulting further with professionals working with young people and young people themselves on priorities and

---

8 See, e.g., E M Clive, "Family law reform in Scotland: past, present and future" 1989 *JR* 133 (liberty, equality and protection); J Eekelaar, *Family Law and Personal Life* (2006) (power, friendship, truth, respect, responsibility and rights); L C McClain, *The Place of Families: Fostering Capacity, Equality and Responsibility* (2006) (capacity, equality and responsibility).

9 *Scotland's Parliament* (n 5) vii ("The Scottish parliament will reflect the needs and circumstances of all the people of Scotland regardless of race, gender or disability").

10 The legislative consent motion, formerly known as a "Sewel motion", its rationale and operation are discussed in ch 2.

11 Scottish Executive, *A Report on the Implementation of the UN Convention on the Rights of the Child in Scotland 1999-2007* (2007).

12 *Concluding Observations of the Committee on the Rights of the Child on the United Kingdom of Great Britain and Northern Ireland*, CCR/C/GBR/CO/4, 3 October 2008.

13 *Improving the Lives of Children in Scotland – Are We There Yet?* (2008), available at: *http://www. scotland.gov.uk/Publications/2008/12/18090842/0.*

future action.[14] So much for what politicians claim to care about, but what have they done?

An indication of serious commitment to children's rights was the creation of the office of Scotland's Commissioner for Children and Young People ("SCCYP"),[15] giving children and young people an independent voice in the political and legal system. A crucial part of the SCCYP's role is to consult with these very beneficiaries. Amid the so-called "bonfire of the quangos", it seemed as though the SCCYP might be under threat. In the event, overwhelming support for this crucial means of hearing Scotland's children won the day.[16]

However, breaches of children's rights remain, not least in respect of the children of unmarried parents, physical punishment of children, child protection and juvenile justice.[17] There are also systemic problems that impact upon children's rights. The first is a degree of adult ambivalence towards children and young people, something acknowledged by the UN Committee when it urged government to take "urgent measures to address the intolerance and inappropriate characterisation of children, especially adolescents, within the society, including the media".[18] That such negative images are found in the Scottish Parliament itself was illustrated during the debates on physical punishment of children, with one MSP referring to the beneficiaries of the much-needed protection as "ankle-biters".[19]

The second systemic problem relates to understanding the law and having access to legal advice and legal services. While this is a difficulty that young people share with many adults, whatever the obstacles faced by adults, they are all the greater for children. Since most children attend school, schools present a unique opportunity to address the problem of ignorance about the law and it is encouraging that providing public legal education in schools is in the exploratory stages in Scotland.

---

14 *Improving the Lives of Children in Scotland – Are We There Yet? Findings from National Seminars* (2009), available at: *http://www.scotland.gov.uk/Publications/2009/04/30132334/7*.

15 Commissioner for Children and Young People (Scotland) Act 2003.

16 Scottish Parliament, Review of SPCB Supported Bodies Committee, 1st Report, 2009, SP Paper 266, RSSB/S3/09/R1 paras 219-284 (21 May 2009).

17 Juvenile justice is largely outwith the scope of this chapter since there is an excellent chapter devoted to it later in this volume: see C McDiarmid, "Juvenile Offending: Welfare or Toughness".

18 *Concluding Observations of the Committee on the Rights of the Child on the United Kingdom of Great Britain and Northern Ireland* (n 12) para 25(a).

19 Scottish Parliament, *Official Report*, col 118 (24 February 2000) (Lyndsay McIntosh, Central Scotland, Conservative).

(2) Status of children

Much of the legal system's discriminatory classification of children, like the sexist notions of pupillarity and minority,[20] were distant memories by the time the Scottish Parliament came into being. Progress had already been made on minimising the impact of the invidious classification of children on the basis of their parents' marital status,[21] something rooted in the legal system's desire to express disapproval of extra-marital sex and child-bearing. This exercise in social control was failing abysmally and, by 2008, over half of the births in Scotland were outside marriage.[22] There was no doubt that discrimination against such children violated their rights under the UN Convention and the Human Rights Act 1998.[23] As long ago as 1992, the Scottish Law Commission recommended "completing the task" of ending the discrimination[24] and, following the method of further consultation that was to become the pattern for much of post-devolution child and family law reform,[25] it appeared that this goal would be achieved. The Family Law (Scotland) Act 2006 amended earlier legislation to provide:

> No person whose status is governed by Scots law shall be illegitimate; and accordingly the fact that a person's parents are not or have not been married to each another shall be left out of account in—
> (a) determining the person's legal status; or
> (b) establishing the legal relationship between the person and any other person.[26]

However, it would be a mistake to see this advance as delivering the "abolition of legal status of illegitimacy", as promised in the new section's heading. Two exceptions remain – the treatment of the non-marital father and its impact on the child, to which we will return presently,[27] and an anomaly that continues to affect a small number of members of the aristocracy for whom legitimacy remains as relevant as ever in the context of succession to titles

---

20 Age of Legal Capacity (Scotland) Act 1991. Previously, young women reached minority at the age of twelve while young men had to wait until they were fourteen.
21 Law Reform (Parent and Child) (Scotland) Act 1986 s 1(1) (original).
22 *Scotland's Population 2008: The Registrar General's Annual Review of Demographic Trends* (2009) 25. In 2008, 50.1% of births were to unmarried parents, a rise from 38.9% in 1998, and 25.4% in 1988. The trend continued in 2009: *Scotland's Population 2009: The Registrar General's Annual Review of Demographic Trends* (2010) 25.
23 *Marckx v Belgium* (1979) 2 EHRR 330. See, further, E E Sutherland, *Child and Family Law*, 2nd edn (2008) paras 6-050-6-065.
24 *Report on Family Law* (Scot Law Com No 135, 1992) 129.
25 *Parents and Children: A White Paper on Scottish Family Law* (2000) and *Family Matters: Improving Family Law in Scotland* (2004).
26 Law Reform (Parent and Child) (Scotland) Act 1986 s 1(1), as substituted by the Family Law (Scotland) Act 2006 s 21(2)(a).
27 See B. (3) below.

and honours.[28] There appears to be no public concern over the latter, perhaps because having an aristocracy in a modern democracy is, in itself, anachronistic. For many children born to unmarried parents, the goal of equality has been achieved, but it continues to elude others. Whether this can be justified in terms of protection (of the child or the mother), another of the goals of child and family law, is a matter to which we will return.

(3) Recognising and defining parents

Recognising a child's "parentage" has two distinct functions in Scots law. The first concerns recording genetic origins and the second involves parcelling out the automatic acquisition of parental responsibilities and parental rights, enabling the recipient to act as a child's social parent: that is, to engage in parenting.

Recording genetic origins is usually a factual matter and is effected through the process of birth registration, something that was modernised with the passing of the Local Electoral Administration and Registration Services (Scotland) Act 2006. However, that Act was concerned with the mechanics of the process and made no real difference to which parent controls registration. Either parent may register a child's birth where they are married to each other.[29] In the case of unmarried parents, the child's father may be registered as such only with the consent of both parents and, so, either can prevent his being registered, at least until court proceedings clarify the matter.[30]

Accurate recording of genetic parentage is crucial if the child's "right to know" about his or her ancestry is to be respected.[31] The long Scottish tradition of allowing adoptees access to their own birth records upon reaching the appropriate age (currently sixteen) was continued by the Children and Adoption (Scotland) Act 2007. There is no parallel provision for donor children to have access to identifying information about gamete donors. When Westminster dealt with this reserved matter, it felt the need to balance the child's rights with honouring promises of anonymity made to donors in the past and the new right of access to information will apply only to donations

28 Law Reform (Parent and Child) (Scotland) Act 1986 s 9. A person denied succession to a title on the basis of "illegitimacy" would have a persuasive case under the Human Rights Act 1998 and arts 8 (right to respect for private and family life) and 14 (prohibition of discrimination) of the Convention would be particularly helpful.
29 Registration of Births, Deaths and Marriage (Scotland) Act 1965 s 14.
30 1965 Act s 18.
31 That this right forms part of identity, implicating the right to private and family life, finds support in the European Convention on Human Rights art 8 (*Mikulic v Croatia*, Application No 53176/99, 7 February 2002; *Estate of K F Mortensen v Denmark* (Admissibility) (2006) 43 EHRR SE9; *Jäggi v Switzerland*, Application No 58757/00, 13 July 2006). See also the UN Convention arts 7 and 8.

made after the relevant regulations came into effect.[32] While a Public Petition presented to the Scottish Parliament sought a different approach, the Public Petitions Committee was aware that it could do nothing about the matter.[33]

The right to engage in parenting, through the automatic acquisition of parental responsibilities and parental rights, is governed by a number of presumptions, intended to reflect genetic reality, and legal fictions which, by definition, do not. The woman who gives birth to a child is presumed to be the child's mother,[34] an approach that was extended, by statute, to cover cases of assisted reproduction involving donated gametes.[35] Paternity is attributed on the basis of a number of long-standing rebuttable presumptions.[36] A legal fiction treats the adopters as the child's parents for most purposes[37] and, following the recommendations of the Adoption Policy Review Group,[38] the Scottish Parliament extended the categories of those eligible to apply to adopt a child to include civil partners and cohabiting couples.[39] A different set of legal fictions applies to cases involving assisted reproduction and the mother's husband or civil partner is treated as the child's second parent, whom failing the mother's male or female partner is so treated, provided that certain conditions are satisfied.[40] The current state of the law protects children, by providing them with social parents, and empowers adults, by respecting the range of choices they may make about the nature of their relationship and enabling them to become parents. By and large, the equality of children and adults, regardless of their family circumstances, is secured.

The blot on this inclusive landscape lies in the legal system's continued discrimination against non-marital fathers and their children. When the Scottish Parliament endowed non-marital fathers with automatic parental responsibilities and rights, in 2006, it limited its largesse to non-marital fathers who registered as such,[41] this being seen as a reflection of their commitment to their responsibilities. The amending legislation is of prospective effect, so only fathers who registered (or re-registered) after it came into

32 Human Fertilisation and Embryology Authority (Disclosure of Information) Regulations 2004, SI 2004/1511.
33 PE 1165, lodged 30 May 2008.
34 *Douglas v Duke of Hamilton* (1769) 2 Pat 143, a rare example of maternity being disputed.
35 Human Fertilisation and Embryology Act 2008 s 33. Egg donation is expressly stated not to be a means of being treated as the child's parent: 2008 Act s 47.
36 Law Reform (Parent and Child) (Scotland) Act 1986 s 5.
37 Adoption and Children (Scotland) Act 2007 s 28(2).
38 Adoption Policy Review Group, *Report of Phase II: Adoption: Better Choices for Our Children* (2005) para 3.42.
39 2007 Act s 29(3).
40 Human Fertilisation and Embryology Act 2008 ss 35, 36, 42 and 44.
41 Children (Scotland) Act 1995 s 3, as amended by the Family Law (Scotland) Act 2006 s 23.

force benefit,[42] something designed to protect mothers who had consented to registration when it gave the child's father no automatic rights. Only some 5% of fathers do not register,[43] so the new legislation will accommodate most children and fathers in the future.

The problem stems from the fact that either parent can impede the non-marital father's registration as the child's parent. If the mother chooses to prevent the father from doing so, he gains no automatic responsibilities or rights, prompting calls to amend the law in the attempt to "compel" registration, as has been done recently in England and Wales.[44] To date, such calls have been resisted, in part, because they appear unworkable and, in part, for fear of exposing the child's mother (and the child) to risk. At present, the father's only recourse, in the face of a resistant mother, is to seek to establish paternity in court.[45] Even then, the mother can block his path by refusing to permit a sample to be taken from the child for DNA analysis.[46] While the court may draw an inference from the mother's refusal to consent to testing,[47] it cannot substitute its own consent for hers. The mother's privileged position has been justified on the basis that it protects women and their children from unworthy or dangerous men,[48] but the law has other means to achieve that end. Then there is the mother's right to privacy but, as the European Court of Human Rights has noted, respecting her right comes at the price of the rights of the child and the father.[49] Empowering the court to compel the taking of samples for the purpose of DNA testing, something possible in the criminal context, would enable fathers to establish their paternity and, thus, secure registration. In addition, the issue would be in the court's arena, so any collateral consequences of establishing paternity, most notably the right to participate in parenting, could be regulated in the child's best interests. For the present, however, the goal of equality is proving elusive in this context.

Genetic parents, and persons treated as if they were, are the only people who gain automatic access to parenting, and two groups – step-parents and grandparents – have lobbied hard for greater recognition, using all the usual

---

42 Only registration under UK statutes counts and this may prove problematic under EU legislation.

43 Some 95% of non-marital fathers do register: *Scotland's Population 2009* (n 22) p 25.

44 Welfare Reform Act 2009 s 56 and Sch 6.

45 Law Reform (Parent and Child) (Scotland) Act 1986 s 7.

46 1986 Act s 6.

47 Law Reform (Miscellaneous Provisions) (Scotland) Act 1990 s 70. There is no guarantee that the court will draw a contrary inference, particularly if the child's mother is married: *Smith v Greenhill* 1993 SCLR 776.

48 The children resulting from rape or incest is the paradigm example cited here but such births make up a tiny fraction of the total.

49 *Söderbäck v Sweden* (1998) 29 EHRR 95; *Sahin v Germany* (2003) 36 EHRR 43.

methods including the public petitions procedure.[50] Neither group has been successful, and for good reasons.[51] Given the range of relationships encompassed, endowing blanket rights on either group would empower some adults at the expense of others and, more significantly, would involve failing to examine the nature of the specific relationship and what the particular adult had to offer the child. It does not serve equality to treat relationships as being the same when they are not. To permit a parent to hand over rights in respect of a child to his or her chosen partner risks the commodification of children – hardly consistent with protecting children or empowering them through permitting their participation in decision-making. Better, then, to leave resolution of intra-family disputes to the various methods of alternative dispute resolution available and to the courts.

(4) Resolving intra-family disputes

While the courts feature large in public perception of how disputes over parenting, whether between parents, between the child and the parent(s) or involving other family members, are resolved, informal negotiation has always played a large part. Successive Scottish governments have signalled support for mediation and other forms of alternative dispute resolution,[52] albeit funding has not always followed. In 2006, parents and others were armed with the tools to assist them in devising their own parenting agreements.[53] While all of this empowers parents to resolve their problems, the danger is that children and young people will be disempowered since there is no way to monitor whether parents comply with their obligation to give the child the opportunity to express views on the matter.[54] Nor is there any guarantee that everyone involved will understand their rights and obligations prior to embarking on negotiation.

Inevitably, some cases do reach the courts and they are resolved using the familiar tripartite test, giving paramountcy to the child's welfare, taking account of any views the child wishes to express and avoiding unnecessary orders.[55] In its original form, the statute offered no further guidance on assessing welfare and the absence of a statutory "welfare checklist" was quite

---

50 PE 124, lodged 8 March 2000; PE 1051, lodged 30 April 2007.
51 *The Charter for Grandchildren* (2006) was nothing other than a cosmetic sop to the grandparents lobby.
52 *Family Matters: Improving Family Law in Scotland* (n 25) pp 46-48.
53 *Parenting Agreements for Scotland – Guide*, available at: *http://www.scotland.gov.uk/Resource/Doc/112209/0027303.pdf.*
54 Children (Scotland) Act 1995 s 6.
55 1995 Act s 11(7).

deliberate since it was thought it might encourage a mechanistic approach.[56] Two issues emerged as particularly problematic: children being exposed to domestic abuse and unco-operative parents who obstruct contact with the child's other parent. There was intense, and very gendered, lobbying, including the use of the public petitions procedure,[57] and, without the usual consultation process taking place, the welfare test was amended. Welfare remains the paramount consideration, but the court must now "have regard in particular" to the need to protect the child from abuse and, when making an order that will require co-operation between two or more persons, to consider whether the order would be appropriate.[58]

While this might be held up as a shining example of the Scottish Parliament at its responsive best, what it really did was to split the difference and try to please the lobbying groups. The result is a statutory provision that is worse than it was before: a partial welfare checklist that not only renders the law untidy, but may divert attention from other, equally relevant, considerations.[59] Nor can it be claimed that judges were either unaware of these issues in the past or incapable of dealing with them.[60] In any event, the new provision does not tell them what they should do, having had regard, in particular, to either of them. It is only a matter of time until a petition, seeking to add another factor to the list, is lodged. It may be that the solution lies in a comprehensive statutory welfare checklist: the very thing the Scottish Law Commission counselled against.

(5) Child protection

The Scottish Parliament has made efforts to improve child protection in Scotland, building on existing legislation and introducing new initiatives, in what has long been a multi-faceted approach to protecting children from abuse and neglect. It has increased recognition of kinship care.[61] Following the recommendations of the Adoption Policy Review Group,[62] the legal remedies available have been improved with the introduction of the

---

56 *Report on Family Law* (n 24) paras 5.20-5.23.
57 PE 413, lodged 26 October 2001; PE 589, lodged 16 December 2002; PE 997, lodged 14 September 2006.
58 Children (Scotland) Act 1995 s 11(7A)-(7E), added by the Family Law (Scotland) Act 2006 s 24.
59 Parental substance abuse or mental illness may present equally pressing problems.
60 *M v S* 2009 Fam LR 149.
61 *Assessment and Support for Kinship Carers of Looked After Children* (Scottish Government, web only, 2008), available at *http://www.scotland.gov.uk/Publications/2008/09/11124435/0* and the Looked After Children (Scotland) Regulations 2009, SSI 2009/210.
62 *Better Choices for Our Children* (n 38) paras 5.12-5.36.

permanence order,[63] replacing the rather deficient parental responsibilities order.[64] Legislators at Holyrood have also sought to protect children from unsuitable carers and adult contact through vetting and barring procedures.[65] While some of the legislation aimed at actual and potential sex offenders is a product of Westminster,[66] the Scottish Parliament played its part with additional measures[67] and legislation targeting the "grooming" of potential child victims, particularly via the internet,[68] child pornography,[69] child prostitution,[70] human trafficking[71] and sex tourism.[72] In 2005, the Scottish Parliament took further steps to protect females from genital mutilation.[73]

New statutory age limits, designed to keep children away from harmful substances and activities, have been introduced.[74] Granted, these age limits disempower children, but such is the nature of protection. It is quite a different matter, however, to criminalise young people themselves in the name of protecting them, as the Scottish Parliament did when it passed legislation designed to discourage thirteen to fifteen year-olds from engaging with each other in what would be consensual sexual activity but for their age.[75]

It is when we turn to protecting children in their own families that the Scottish Parliament has failed the children of Scotland most severely. The fact that Scots law still permits parents to hit their children is an obvious example of wholly avoidable failure. Despite extensive lobbying for legislation that would outlaw all physical punishment of children, something supported wholeheartedly by the UN Committee on the Rights of the Child,[76] the

---

63 Adoption and Children (Scotland) Act 2007 Pt 2.
64 Children (Scotland) Act 1995 s 86. For a discussion of the deficiencies, see Sutherland, *Child and Family Law* (n 23) para 9-159.
65 Protection of Vulnerable Groups (Scotland) Act 2007, replacing earlier provision in the Protection of Children (Scotland) Act 2003.
66 Sexual Offences Act 2003 (sexual offences prevention orders and foreign travel orders).
67 Protection of Children and Prevention of Sexual Offences (Scotland) Act 2005 s 2 (risk of sexual harm orders).
68 2005 Act s 1.
69 2005 Act ss 9 and 10.
70 2005 Act s 11.
71 Criminal Justice (Scotland) Act 2003 s 22.
72 Sexual Offences (Scotland) Act 2009 s 55.
73 Prohibition of Female Genital Mutilation (Scotland) Act 2005.
74 Public Health, etc (Scotland) Act 2008 ss 95-96 (sunbeds) and Smoking, Health and Social Care (Scotland) Act 2005 (Variation of Age Limit for the Sale of Tobacco Purchase and Consequential Modifications) Order 2007, SSI 2007/437 (tobacco products).
75 Sexual Offences (Scotland) Act 2009 s 37, discussed later in this volume: see C. McDiarmid, "Juvenile Offending: Welfare or Toughness".
76 See, most recently, *Concluding Observations of the Committee on the Rights of the Child* (n 12), repeating the unequivocal criticisms expressed in previous reports. See, further, E E Sutherland, "Care of the child within the family", in A Cleland and E E Sutherland, *Children's Rights in Scotland*, 3rd edn (2009) paras 5-32-5-34.

Scottish Parliament refused to take that step. Instead, it sought to clarify the law on "justifiable assault" (the oxymoron that replaced "reasonable chastisement")[77] and thereby sent a message to parents that it is acceptable for them to hit their children, provided they stick to the rules. By permitting some violence against children, it undermined the whole climate for child protection. Arguably, legislators at Holyrood were responding to public opinion or, at least, opinions expressed in the tabloid press, but that hardly absolves them of their failure to protect children and their rights from harm perpetrated by enfranchised and, thus, more powerful adults.

On a more general level, there are the repeated failures of the child protection system, exemplified by numerous children who were left to face further abuse or to die at the hands of family members when the local social work department was well aware of cause for concern. In this, legislation is only part of the problem since social work practice plays such a pivotal role. However, the ultimate responsibility for both lies with the Scottish Parliament. Attempts to reform law and practice began in the early days of devolution with an audit, designed to identify shortcomings,[78] and extensive consultation.[79] New standards and practices were promulgated. Legislation was drafted,[80] but it was so flawed that the new Scottish government was correct in listening to informed opinion and rethinking it. The result was the Children's Hearings (Scotland) Bill – again, a product of extensive consultation.[81] Child protection is a complex matter and the hope is that consultation is more likely to produce effective responses, but it takes time – and time was something the children who died did not have.

C. ADULT RELATIONSHIPS

(1) The recognised relationships and their formation

Traditional marriage – of the one male, one female variety – has long held a central place in the Scottish legal system. The law worked reasonably well and the legislation passed by the Scottish Parliament has been aimed largely

77 An assault will never be "justifiable" if it involves a blow to the head, shaking or the use of an implement: Criminal Justice (Scotland) Act 2003 s 51(3). In other cases, the court is directed to a checklist of factors in assessing justifiability: 2003 Act s 51(1).
78 *"It's everyone's job to make sure I'm alright": Report of the Child Protection Audit and Review* (2002), available at *http://www.scotland.gov.uk/Publications/2002/11/15820/14032.*
79 *Getting it Right for Every Child* (GIRFEC), available at *http://www.scotland.gov.uk/Topics/People/Young-People/childrensservices/girfec.*
80 Draft Children's Service (Scotland) Bill (2006), available at *http://www.eastrenfrewshire.gov.uk/draft_children_s_services_bill_consultation.pdf.*
81 SP Bill 41 (2010). On the Bill and the extensive consultation, see *http://www.scotland.gov.uk/Topics/People/Young-People/c-h-bill/Bill.*

at either relaxation of unnecessary restrictions or clarification of the rules. One exception is the substantial and prospective abolition of marriage by cohabitation with habit and repute, Scotland's last remaining form of irregular marriage.[82] Much loved by law examiners, this relic of a bygone era was thought, with some justification, to pose a threat to subsequent formal marriages, rendering them void.[83] Existing irregular marriages were not affected by the legislation but, for the future, they will be possible only to cure defective foreign marriages where one of the parties died domiciled in Scotland and the survivor is so domiciled. Thus, the reform here is designed to protect two, quite distinct, groups of people who have attempted to marry, but are in danger of finding that they have not done so.

Prompted by favourable responses to a consultation paper,[84] this time from the Registrar General for Scotland, and driven on by a Private Member's Bill,[85] the Scottish government of the day took up the issue of where civil marriage ceremonies could take place.[86] The Marriage (Scotland) Act 2002 made it possible for couples who want a civil marriage ceremony to hold it somewhere other than in a registration office and has opened the way to lucrative business at places, or on vessels in Scottish waters, approved under regulations for that purpose. More significantly for our analysis, it empowers intending spouses to exercise freedom of choice on the matter. Similarly, freedom of choice was extended to the tiny number of former children-in-law and parents-in-law wishing to marry, since the previous restrictions on such marriages were removed.[87]

Among the many recommendations from the Scottish Law Commission that had lain unimplemented for years were those aimed at clarifying and, in one case, amending the old common law rules on defective consent to marriage.[88] Following the now-familiar consultation process,[89] the Family Law (Scotland) Act 2006[90] implemented most of these recommendations and the law dealing with incapacity, duress and error is clearer as a result and effects greater protection of the vulnerable and those who may have been pressured or misled. In the attempt to deal with sham marriages, tacit withholding of

82 Family Law (Scotland) Act 2006 s 3, effective 4 May 2006.
83 *Sheikh v Sheikh* 2005 Fam LR 7 at [23].
84 Registrar General for Scotland, *Consultation Paper on Civil Marriages outwith Registration Offices* (1998).
85 The proposal for a Civil Marriages Bill was lodged by Euan Robson, MSP, on 24 March 2000.
86 *Civil Marriages outwith Registration Offices* (2001).
87 Family Law (Scotland) Act 2006 s 1, amending the Marriage (Scotland) Act 1977 s 2.
88 *Report on Family Law* (1992) (n 24) paras 8.16-8.20.
89 *Parents and Children* (n 25); *Family Matters: Improving Family Law in Scotland* (n 25).
90 2006 Act s 2, inserting a new s 20A in the Marriage (Scotland) Act 1977.

consent to marriage, by itself, no longer results in a marriage being void.[91]

In its purest form, a sham marriage is the willing misuse of legal formalities by the parties. Forced marriage is a different matter entirely since it occurs where one (or both) of the parties is coerced into participating in the ceremony. Scots law already offers a number of civil[92] and criminal[93] mechanisms designed to protect against such abuse. However, since forced marriages continue to occur, it is clear that existing sanctions are not wholly effective. The Scottish government has explored what more needs to be done but, to date, has failed to bring forward legislation. The reasons for this failure are complex and, to be fair, relate more to racial and cultural sensitivity and the desire to find an *effective* response, rather than a lack of government will. Since forced marriage usually arises in the context of minority ethnic groups in the community, there is a need to avoid perpetuating racial stereotypes[94] or alienating people who may already feel marginalised from seeking protection. Thus, the option of creating a specific offence of forcing (or attempting to force) a person to enter a marriage was explored and rejected, not least because many victims would be reluctant to report offenders (usually their relatives) if prosecution would result.[95] Another option would be to create a new civil order of protection that would enable the victim, or a person acting on his or her behalf, to seek a civil order from a court, requiring a third party to stop certain conduct, such as threatening to abduct the victim, or take positive action, such as surrendering a passport.[96] Consultation on introducing such an order produced mixed results, with many respondents taking the view that existing civil remedies were sufficient but emphasising the need to improve support, legal advice and financial assistance in accessing the courts, so that victims utilise these remedies.[97]

Arguably, the most challenging family law debate of the late twentieth and

91 Lord Clarke had attempted this reform by judicial decision, but was overturned on appeal: *Hakeem v Hussain* 2003 SLT 515 (OH); *H v H* 2005 SLT 1025 (Ex Div). Further steps to counteract sham marriages were effected through UK immigration law.

92 The marriage will be void: Marriage (Scotland) Act 1977 s 20A(2). For examples of marriages declared void due to family pressure amounting to duress, see *Mahmood v Mahmood* 1993 SLT 589; *Mahmud v Mahmud* 1994 SLT 599; and *Sohrab v Khan* 2002 SLT 1255.

93 Depending on the circumstances, offences might include abduction, assault, child cruelty, rape or other sexual offences and a variety of statutory offences relating to harassment or protective orders.

94 This is exemplified in the occasional confusion between arranged, but consensual, marriage and forced marriage.

95 Home Office, *Forced Marriage: A Wrong Not A Right* (2005); *Forced Marriage: A Civil Remedy?* (2008) 2.

96 Such an order is available in England and Wales: Family Law Act 1996 s 63, as amended by the Forced Marriage (Civil Protection) Act 2007.

97 *Consultation on Forced Marriage: A Civil Remedy? Analysis of Responses* (2009) 7-31.

early twenty-first centuries was over what, if any, legal recognition should be accorded to same-sex relationships. The last decade saw the European Court of Human Rights[98] and the House of Lords[99] extending increasing recognition to same-sex relationships, as did European Union law.[100] While the Scottish Parliament was already including both same-sex and different-sex couples in legislation on specific issues,[101] it showed no great inclination to address the matter squarely. Eventually, and after some prompting from the Department of Trade and Industry[102] and a Scottish Private Member's Bill,[103] the (then) Scottish Executive consulted on the compromise solution of creating a new formal relationship – civil partnership – a marriage-equivalent for same-sex couples in Scotland, using the legislative consent procedure so that the necessary legislation could be passed at Westminster.[104] Responses to the consultation were substantially positive,[105] albeit there remained (and remain) pockets of vehement opposition to legal recognition of same-sex relationships.

At the beginning of this chapter, it was promised that the Scottish Parliament would be given some credit for legislation it authorised Westminster to pass on its behalf, subject to exploring why it did so. Its own justification – that reserved matters were implicated and, thus, there were efficiency gains in passing UK-wide legislation – is not wholly without merit.[106] However, when one remembers the context in which the decision was made, it becomes clear that political expediency played its part. Politicians in the Scottish Parliament were still smarting from the bruising battle there had been over the repeal of homophobic legislation in the context of education.[107] They were not anxious

---

98   *Da Silva Mouta v Portugal* (2001) 31 EHRR 47; *Karner v Austria* (2004) 38 EHRR 21; *Schalk and Kopf v Austria*, Application No 30141/04 judgment on 24 June 2010.

99   See, e.g., *Fitzpatrick v Sterling Housing Association* [2001] 1 AC 27 and *Ghaidan v Godin-Mendoza* [2004] 2 AC 557.

100   Employment Directive 2000/78, expressly prohibiting discrimination on the basis of sexual orientation in employment and training. Thus, denying same-sex partners access to pensions and other benefits resulting from employment would be a breach of the Directive. See also, Charter of Fundamental Rights of the European Union, 2000/C 364/01.

101   See, e.g., the Adults with Incapacity (Scotland) Act 2000, the Protection from Abuse (Scotland) Act 2001, the Housing (Scotland) Act 2001, the Mortgage Rights (Scotland) Act 2001, the Agricultural Holdings (Scotland) Act 2003 and the Mental Health (Care and Treatment) (Scotland) Act 2003.

102   *Civil Partnership: A Framework for the Legal Recognition of Same-Sex Couples* (2003).

103   The proposal for a Civil Registered Partnerships (Scotland) Bill was lodged by Patrick Harvie, MSP, on 12 May 2003. It fell on 12 November 2004.

104   *Civil Partnership Registration: A Legal Status for Committed Same-Sex Couples in Scotland* (2003).

105   See, V Strachan et al, *The Consultation on Civil Partnership Registration: Analysis of the Responses* (2004).

106   *Civil Partnership Registration* (n 104) ch 4.

107   The repeal of the Local Government Act 1986 s 2A by the Ethical Standards in Public Life etc (Scotland) Act 2000 s 34.

to have another confrontation with the homophobes on their own doorstep.

Thus, civil partnerships were created, for Scotland, by the Civil Partnership Act 2004. That this was a Westminster statute may explain why the need to amend some existing Scottish legislation was missed in the process, occasioning a slew of later statutory instruments and other amendments.[108] To a large extent, the legal formalities for registering a civil partnership parallel those for marriage.[109] However, often in the attempt to appease opponents of recognition, legislators imposed distinctions. Some appear accidental and are probably of no moment.[110] Others, like the need to create a statutory bigamy equivalent, are the inevitable result of civil partnership being a new creature of statute.[111] Yet others are designed to signal that civil partnership "is not marriage" and to placate the religious opponents. So, for example, a civil partnership may be created only through the civil registration procedure and, unlike marriage, there is no possibility of a religious ceremony.[112] Finally, there are those flowing from the legislature's consistent resistance to acknowledging any sexual dimension to same-sex relationships. Thus, while a civil partnership may be void for much the same reasons as a marriage may be void,[113] there is no provision in the 2004 Act for a voidable Scottish civil partnership, although the concept is relevant to civil partnerships from other jurisdictions.[114]

For some, civil partnership was *the* compromise solution: for others, it is a temporary stage on the road to same-sex marriage. Like many compromise solutions, it failed to satisfy anyone entirely. Opponents of recognising same-sex relationships remain as vocal as ever. While the consequences of civil partnership are almost identical to those of marriage, empowering many couples to gain legal recognition of their relationship, it remains the case that same-sex couples are denied the opportunity to marry and, thus, to have

108 See, e.g., the Civil Partnership Act 2004 (Consequential Amendments) (Scotland) Order 2005, SSI 2005/623.

109 As a result, the requirements in terms of capacity and consent mirror those for marriage, allowing for necessary adaptations: Civil Partnership Act 2004 s 128. There is no provision in respect of tacit withholding of consent in the civil partnership context.

110 The witnesses to a civil partnership must "have attained the age of sixteen", not simply "profess" that this is the case, as with marriage: 2004 Act s 85(1)(b).

111 Since bigamy is a common law offence, the civil partnership equivalent is a statutory creation, it being an offence to register a civil partnership while married or in a civil partnership: 2004 Act s 100.

112 2004 Act s 85. Similarly, specific registrars are designated "authorised registrars" for the purpose of registering a civil partnership: 2004 Act s 87.

113 2004 Act ss 86 and 123.

114 2004 Act s 204. It will be remembered that the only ground on which a marriage is voidable (as opposed to void), in Scotland, is incurable impotency at the time of the marriage.

wholly equal recognition of their relationships. The real frustration here is that the Scottish Parliament had the opportunity to embrace equality and pass legislation permitting same-sex marriage. Fear of offending vocal, largely religious, groups prevented it from doing so. Such craven conduct should not be mistaken for respecting freedom of religion. To permit religious minorities to dictate the content of law is to ignore the rights of those who do not subscribe to that (or any) religion and to join in the oppression of those whose conduct some religious groups find objectionable. Nor should it be seen as respecting the right of the public to participate, since allowing one group to oppress another is inconsistent with true democracy. Certainly, this was not the Scottish Parliament's finest hour.

The extent to which non-marital (non-civil partnership) cohabitation should be accorded legal recognition was, again, controversial. While some opponents were adherents of the view that different-sex marriage is the only valid form of intimate relationship, the real difficulty here stems from the reasons why couples cohabit, rather than opting for one of the more formal relationships, and the resulting conflict between the goals of family law. Some couples cohabit with the express intention of avoiding the legal consequences of the formal options, and respect for their freedom of choice militates against imposing these very consequences on them. For other couples, cohabitation is the product of simple inertia. Even where it results from conscious choice, substantial sections of the population have little or no accurate understanding of the legal consequences of the decision. In addition, many cohabitants make sacrifices, incur economic and other disadvantages and develop levels of economic dependence that parallel those of their counterparts in the more formal relationships. If the law has a role in protecting adults from ignorance and inequality, then there is a case for attaching at least some consequences to cohabitation.

The legal system attached limited consequences to different-sex cohabitation long before the creation of the Scottish Parliament, most notably in offering limited protection against domestic abuse.[115] In 1992, the Scottish Law Commission had recommended modest expansion of the legal consequences of cohabitation, while keeping it quite distinct from marriage.[116] Post-devolution, these recommendations found favour with the (then) Scottish Executive[117] and whole sections of the public, not least because many

---

115   Matrimonial Homes (Family Protection) (Scotland) Act 1981 s 18.
116   *Report on Family Law* (n 24) ch 16.
117   *Parents and Children* (n 25) 29; and *Family Matters: Improving Family Law in Scotland* (n 25) 21-22.

people thought that at least some of the consequences already flowed from cohabitation.[118] Again, the solution was a compromise but, this time, it was one designed to accommodate principle, and the Scottish Parliament took ownership of the solution by passing the legislation itself. The legal consequences of cohabitation are discussed below[119] and, for now, suffice to note that empowerment through freedom of choice is enhanced by couples being able to contract out of them.

Since cohabitation is not preceded by the neat legal step of registration, it was necessary to define precisely which couples qualified. The Family Law (Scotland) Act 2006 provides that they are couples who "are (or were) living together as if they were" husband and wife or civil partners,[120] and offers further statutory guidance in the form of a non-exclusive list of relevant factors.[121] While the legislation has been in effect for a comparatively short time, it appears to be serving the courts well.[122]

(2) Consequences of recognition

Given the antiquity of marriage, the legal system had long since worked out what its legal consequences should be. On a personal level, there is the obvious bar to entering another formal relationship while already married and marriage had long been the ticket to recognition as a child's parent, whether through presumptions or fictions. During the currency of a marriage, the system of separate property is encroached on only a little by the obligation to aliment a spouse,[123] certain rebuttable presumptions that household goods and housekeeping allowances are shared equally,[124] and the special treatment of the family home, designed to protect against domestic abuse.[125] Far more significant property consequences may attach, of course, on divorce or death.

Civil partnership simply slotted into the system operating for spouses, with most of the same consequences applying to civil partners. It was not until the Scottish Parliament passed the Adoption and Children (Scotland) Act 2007 and Westminster addressed the reserved matter of assisted reproduction, in

---

118 L Nicholson, *Improving Family Law in Scotland: Analysis of Written Consultation Responses* (2004).
119 See p 76 below.
120 Family Law (Scotland) Act 2006 s 25(1).
121 2006 Act s 25(2). The factors are the length of time the parties lived together, the nature of the relationship, and the nature and extent of any financial arrangements subsisting. Notably absent from the list is a minimum length of time that will raise a presumption of cohabitation.
122 *Chebotareva v King's Executrix* 2008 Fam LR 66; *Fairley v Fairley* 2008 Fam LR 112.
123 Family Law (Scotland) Act 1985 s 1(1).
124 1985 Act ss 25 and 26.
125 Matrimonial Homes (Family Protection) (Scotland) Act 1981.

the Human Fertilisation and Embryology Act 2008, that civil partners gained access to the benefits of legal fictions surrounding parentage.

The 2007 Act aside, the Scottish Parliament legislated only a little on the consequences of marriage and civil partnership, much of it relating to curing, or seeking to cure, existing defects in the law. Measures were directed at further protecting spouses and civil partners in respect of occupation of the family home, dealings with third parties in respect of it, special destinations,[126] and protection of a partner's occupation of the home in the event of bankruptcy.[127] If the Scottish Parliament did little in this area, it was because little needed to be done.

Cohabitants face no legal consequences should they form a new relationship while cohabiting and, for some, this freedom is one of the attractions of cohabitation. Thus it was that, in extending the opportunity to apply to adopt a child to cohabiting couples, the Scottish Parliament chose to formulate the qualification in terms of them being "in an enduring family relationship",[128] a provision designed to protect the children concerned from instability. Of course, stable cohabitation is no more of a guarantee of permanence than is marriage or civil partnership. Again, it fell to Westminster to regulate how partners gained recognition as the second parents of donor children, but it is worth noting that the status derives from agreement, and cohabitation is not a prerequisite.[129]

When the Scottish Parliament decided to extend legal recognition to qualifying cohabitants, it was never seeking to replicate the system that applied to spouses and civil partners where, it will be remembered, the property consequences are not all that extensive in any event. Rather, it was seeking to offer certain minimal protection. So it was that the Family Law (Scotland) Act 2006 extended the limited rebuttable presumptions that household goods and housekeeping allowances are shared equally to qualifying cohabitants.[130] The 2006 Act also sought to place same-sex cohabitants on an equal footing with their different-sex counterparts, extending to them the protection in the family home[131] and the right to claim damages in respect of a cohabitant's death.[132]

---

126 Family Law (Scotland) Act 2006 ss 5-9 and 19, amending the Matrimonial Homes (Family Protection) (Scotland) Act 1981.
127 Bankruptcy and Diligence (Scotland) Act 2007.
128 Adoption and Children (Scotland) Act 2007 s 29(3).
129 Human Fertilisation and Embryology Act 2008 ss 36 and 43.
130 Family Law (Scotland) Act ss 26 and 27. "Qualifying cohabitant" is as defined in s 25, discussed at p 75, above.
131 2006 Act s 34, amending the 1981 Act s 18.
132 2006 Act ss 30 and 35, amending the Administration of Justice Act 1982 and the Damages (Scotland) Act 1976.

The most significant omission – the fact that cohabitants still do not owe each other any obligation of aliment – is consistent with the Scottish Law Commission's original proposals.[133] This creates a certain inconsistency, since the rules for some state benefits assume financial support from a cohabitant. As we shall see, certain support and property consequences may apply when cohabitation terminates, whether by choice or by death.

(3) Protection from domestic abuse

Scots law had long sought to tackle the scourge of domestic abuse through common law civil remedies, criminal sanctions and legislation, most notably the Matrimonial Homes (Family Protection) (Scotland) Act 1981. Almost from its inception, the new government of Scotland sought to address domestic abuse comprehensively: developing a national strategy; establishing a national domestic abuse helpline; funding an advertising campaign designed to highlight the issues; funding projects aimed at tackling abuse; and commissioning research on various aspects of the problem. Scotland's first specialist domestic abuse court began operating, in Glasgow, in October 2004, and proved highly successful.[134] It would be all the more regrettable, then, if taking this effective model to other parts of the country were to be delayed for financial reasons.[135]

The narrow ambit of the 1981 Act was addressed by the Protection from Abuse (Scotland) Act 2001, the first Committee Bill to pass.[136] While the 1981 Act was limited to protecting spouses and cohabitants, the 2001 Act makes interdict available to anyone seeking protection from abuse, a term defined widely in the Act as "violence, harassment, threatened conduct, and any other conduct giving rise, or likely to give rise, to physical or mental injury, fear, alarm or distress".[137] Not only can it be used to protect former spouses, civil partners and cohabitants in the post-relationship context, but its provisions are available to their future partners or to other family members, should the aggressor turn his or her attentions to them. A later statutory amendment implemented another old Scottish Law Commission recommendation,[138] and was designed to strengthen the protection offered by the 1981 Act by

133 *Report on Family Law* (n 24) paras 16.5-16.6.
134 Reid Howie Associates, *Evaluation of The Pilot Domestic Abuse Court* (2007), web only, available at *http://www.scotland.gov.uk/Publications/2007/03/28153424/15*.
135 D Leask, "Abuse court roll-out in jeopardy", *Scotland on Sunday*, 20 December 2009.
136 It had its origins in a report from the then Justice and Home Affairs Committee: *Proposals for Protection from Abuse (Scotland) Act* (9th Report 2000, SP Paper 221, 23 November 2000).
137 2001 Act s 7.
138 *Report on Family Law* (n 24) paras 10.29-10.52.

extending the places that could be covered by a matrimonial interdict.[139] Yet another clarified the rules on attaching powers of arrest to interdicts.[140]

Domestic abuse remains a problem and reported incidents increase year on year.[141] Some of this increase may be explained by the fact that victims are now more willing to report abuse. Legislation and government policy can go only some way in tackling reprehensible human behaviour, but that is no reason to give up on the effort. It is encouraging, then, to see that a Private Member's Bill, designed to make legal aid available to enable all domestic abuse victims to pursue remedies and to strengthen sanctions for breach of protective orders, was introduced in the Scottish Parliament in 2010.[142]

(4) Divorce and civil partnership dissolution

Despite the fiction that the Divorce (Scotland) Act 1976 made divorce available on the sole ground of irretrievable breakdown, the reality was that a mixed system, encompassing fault (adultery, desertion and behaviour) and no-fault (non-cohabitation) grounds, operated. Following the usual consultation process,[143] the Family Law (Scotland) Act 2006 implemented the Scottish Law Commission's modest recommendations on reform of divorce law, dating, this time, from 1989.[144] The periods of non-cohabitation required for the no-fault grounds were shortened from two and five years to one and two respectively; desertion was abolished as a ground for divorce; certain, rather obsolete, defences were removed;[145] and the court acquired a new, discretionary power to postpone granting decree of divorce in order to accommodate parties who required further formalities to be complied with before they could enter a subsequent marriage under religious law.[146]

When civil partnership was created, a system for dissolution was put in place that paralleled divorce, with one notable difference: the absence of any equivalent of the adultery ground for divorce.[147] While this can be explained

---

139 Family Law (Scotland) Act 2006 s 10, amending the 1981 Act s 14.
140 2006 Act s 32, amending the Protection from Abuse (Scotland) Act 2001 s 1.
141 *Statistical Bulletin Crime and Justice Series: Domestic Abuse Recorded by the Police in Scotland 2008-09* (2009), web only, available at: *http://www.scotland.gov.uk/Publications/2009/11/23112407/0.*
142 Domestic Abuse (Scotland) Bill, SP Bill 45 (2010). The Bill began its life as the proposal for the Civil Protection Orders and Access to Justice (Scotland) Bill, lodged by Rhoda Grant, MSP, on 30 November 2009.
143 *Parents and Children* (n 25) 15-18; and *Family Matters: Improving Family Law in Scotland* (n 25) pp 16-17.
144 *Report on Reform of the Grounds of Divorce* (Scot Law Com No 116, 1989).
145 Family Law (Scotland) Act 2006 ss 11-14, amending the Divorce (Scotland) Act 1976 ss 1 and 9.
146 2006 Act s 15, adding s 3A to the 1976 Act.
147 Civil Partnership Act 2004 s 117.

on the basis of the hetero-normative definition of "adultery" in Scots law,[148] it does not explain the absence of a ground of divorce that would cover a civil partner engaging in sexual intercourse with someone of the opposite sex. In truth, the omission is simply another example of the legislature's desire to avoid all recognition of the sexual dimension of same-sex relationships. Happily, it is of little practical significance since sexual infidelity by a civil partner would qualify under the behaviour ground for dissolution.

The passing of the Gender Recognition Act 2004 posed a new challenge to the established order since Scots law does not recognise same-sex marriage, nor different-sex civil partnership. The solution was to delay full recognition of gender change until the applicant had terminated an existing marriage or civil partnership. Thus, obtaining an interim gender recognition certificate became a new and separate ground for divorce or civil partnership dissolution.[149]

In short, both marriage and civil partnership can be terminated fairly easily, at least in legal terms. Undoubtedly, this empowers the party who wishes to leave the relationship. Inevitably, a partner who would like the marriage or civil partnership to continue may feel disempowered, but there is nothing to be gained by a legal system that traps unwilling partners in empty legal relationships.

(5) Consequences of dissolution

Financial provision on divorce had long been regulated by the Family Law (Scotland) Act 1985. With the advent of civil partnership, again, it was slotted into the existing system. The 1985 Act had been amended, not least to take account of the need to accommodate pension sharing and pension splitting, but the legislation was widely regarded as providing an equitable, principled and predictable method for addressing the economic fallout of divorce and civil partnership dissolution. While the highly respected Law Lord, Lord Hope, was critical of aspects of the legislation, academic opinion was at variance with him on the issue,[150] practitioners were generally happy with it and the Scottish system has been eyed with admiration from south of the border.[151] Thus, all that was required was for the Scottish Parliament to

---

148 Adultery is voluntary sexual intercourse with a person of the opposite sex who is not one's spouse and requires "the introduction of the male organ into the female": *MacLennan v MacLennan* 1958 SC 105 per Lord Wheatley at 112.

149 1976 Act s 1(1)(b) and 2004 Act s 117(2)(b).

150 For discussion of that particular disagreement, see Sutherland, *Child and Family Law* (n 23) paras 16-181-16-182.

151 See, e.g., *Charman v Charman* [2007] 1 FLR 1246 at [107], where Sir Mark Potter noted the "clarity and certainty" of the Scottish system.

amend the 1985 Act in respect of a number of practical issues that had proved problematic, including the date of valuation of heritable property and variation of agreements on aliment.[152]

Hitherto, there was no parallel system available to separating cohabitants. Occasionally, property disputes were resolved using more general concepts, such as unjustified enrichment,[153] but these were of limited application. Yet again, a solution had been proposed in 1992[154] and, following further consultation,[155] it was implemented by the Family Law (Scotland) Act 2006. Consistent with distinguishing cohabitation from marriage and civil partnership, what the court can do for separating cohabitants is more limited than its comprehensive powers applicable in the context of the formal relationships.[156] A qualifying cohabitant must raise the action seeking financial provision "not later than one year after the day on which the cohabitants ceased to cohabit"[157] and the court has no discretion to extend this period of time. Thereafter, the court may order the payment (on a specified date or by instalments) of a capital sum,[158] in order to balance economic advantages and disadvantages sustained by one party in the interests of the other or a "relevant child";[159] order payment (not limited to a capital sum) in respect of any economic burden of caring for the couple's child after the cohabitation has ended;[160] and it may make "such interim award as it thinks fit".[161] Cohabitants may opt out of claims for financial provision under section 28, subject to the ordinary rules on the validity of contracts.[162] The legislative framework is now being applied and elucidated through individual court decisions.[163]

---

152   Family Law (Scotland) Act 2006 ss 16-20, amending the Family Law (Scotland) Act 1985.
153   *Shilliday v Smith* 1998 SC 725.
154   *Report on Family Law* (n 24) paras 16.14-16.23.
155   *Parents and Children* (n 25) 29; and *Family Matters: Improving Family Law in Scotland* (n 25) 21-30. See also *Improving Family Law in Scotland: Analysis of Written Consultation Responses* (2004) para 5.1 and Table 3.
156   The court has no power to transfer property from one former cohabitant to the other, nor to make any of the orders relating to pensions that are available to spouses and civil partners.
157   2006 Act s 28(8). *Lawley v Sutton* 2010 GWD 14-257.
158   2006 Act s 28(2)(a) and (7).
159   2006 Act s 28(3)-(6). A "relevant child" includes both a child of whom the cohabitants are parents and a child, under the age of sixteen, "accepted" as a member of the family: 2006 Act s 28(10).
160   2006 Act s 28(2)(b). Only a child under the age of sixteen "of whom the cohabitants are parents" is covered this time and not an "accepted" child.
161   2006 Act s 28(2)(c).
162   However, such contracts are not open to the sort of challenge available to spouses and civil partners under the Family Law (Scotland) Act 1985 ss 8 or 16.
163   *Fairley v Fairley* 2008 Fam LR 112; *M v S* 2008 SLT 871; *Jamieson v Rodhouse* 2009 Fam LR 34; *F v D* 2009 Fam LR 111; *Gow v Grant* 2010 Fam LR 21; *Cameron v Leal* 2010 Fam LR 82.

D. CONCLUSIONS

What, then, is the verdict, overall, on the contribution of the Scottish Parliament to child and family law? There can be no doubt that it has been active and productive, passing a myriad of statutes devoted to the field and numerous others impacting significantly on aspects of it. That many of the statutory provisions had their roots in pre-devolution recommendations of the Scottish Law Commission is no criticism of Holyrood, since one of the problems it was designed to overcome was the lack of time available at Westminster to implement them. Nor is it a criticism of the Scottish Parliament that it sometimes passed legislation that mirrored or developed provisions already in place in England and Wales.[164] There are many parallels in law reform initiatives around the world and learning from other jurisdictions is part of a long Scottish tradition of comparativism. The trick is to adopt and adapt the best and reject the rest.

Arguably, there has been overuse of the legislative consent procedure. That gender recognition and same-sex relationships were dealt with thus prompts the suspicion that it can sometimes be convenient for politicians at Holyrood to distance themselves from issues that are particularly politically sensitive in Scotland by handing them over to Westminster. Other relevant matters were put beyond the reach of the Scottish Parliament by the Scotland Act itself. That this was done in respect of assisted reproductive technology and abortion is difficult to justify, since they are so obviously tied to family formation and intimate relationships and, arguably, ought to reflect local preferences. Nonetheless, when one looks at the combined effects of delegating legislative competence and reserved matters, there is no escaping the shadow of Scotland's puritanical past and a sense of "No sex please, we're Scottish". These shortcomings aside, it can be concluded that the creation of the Scottish Parliament has addressed the problem of the lack of legislative time available to address Scottish child and family law.

What of our second criterion: the promise held out of a legislature and executive that would be accessible and responsive, permitting public participation in the legislative process? While one's answer to that question may be influenced by whether one's own preferences prevailed, there is no denying that there was extensive consultation on almost all aspects of proposed legislation. Where that was not done, as was the case in reform of the welfare test, the law is the worse for it. One hopes that Holyrood will learn from its mistakes. While the newly created public petitions procedure was used by

164   For example, extending adoption to civil partners and cohabiting couples.

various interest groups to put forward their proposals, the proposals were often partisan and flawed and went no further. That is no criticism of the procedure itself. Rather, it is simply recognition that special interest groups often make lousy legislators. Their role highlights another challenge posed by responsiveness. Creating an equal and inclusive society involves more than simply counting heads in favour and against or deferring to those groups with the resources and determination to shout loudest and longest. Thus, while it can be concluded that the Scottish Parliament has been accessible, responsive and participatory, the real test of what it has done requires assessing the content of child and family law reforms in the light of the goals of the discipline itself, these being: equality (and the associated values of inclusion and respect for diversity), empowerment (including freedom of choice) and protection.

Despite assertions of commitment to children's rights from various administrations, the Scottish Parliament has a rather mixed record in terms of what it has done for children and young people. In terms of equality, while it took steps to abolish the status of illegitimacy, the process has been left incomplete and remains marred by obstacles faced by non-marital fathers in establishing and retaining links with their children – something that can deny a child two active parents. In terms of empowerment, a positive step was the creation of Scotland's Commissioner for Children and Young People but, that aside, the thrust of legislative efforts has been directed at protecting children or criminalising thirteen- to fifteen year-olds for engaging in sexual activity that the adult world would, probably wisely, prefer them to postpone. It is no criticism of Holyrood that it has sought to protect children and young people, albeit that offering protection is an inherently disempowering process. The regret is that legislators concentrated on sunbeds and cigarettes while failing to address adequately the more challenging issue of physical chastisement of children: it is so much easier to limit the freedom of young people than to restrict that of adults.

Couples, whether different-sex or same-sex, have undoubtedly been empowered by the availability of a range of legally significant relationships. Where the Scottish Parliament has fallen down is over the principle of equality through its willingness to participate in the wholly unnecessary creation of a new form of relationship: the civil partnership. It could have followed the path, chosen by many other jurisdictions, of creating same-sex marriage, respecting the legitimate choice of same-sex couples to enter that secular, legal institution and extending to them the same dignity and respect as are currently afforded to different-sex couples. Given the range of options available across Europe and the European Court's recent decision on the matter,[165] the Scottish Parliament's failure is safe from a human rights challenge for the time being. However, it is only a matter of time before a consistent picture on same-sex marriage emerges across the continent and the European Court finds that art 12 (the right to marry and to found a family) of the European Convention requires the availability of same-sex marriage. The regret is that Scotland will be a follower in this process, rather than a leader.

That cohabitation has different consequences to the formal relationships of marriage and civil partnership is no offence to the principle of equality, since it does not require that different things be treated as though they were the same. Indeed, retaining the distinction increases choice and, thus, respect for diversity. By attaching limited, protective legal consequences to cohabitation, legislators at Holyrood furthered that particular goal.

It is in the context of protection that the Scottish Parliament has made so little progress. Countless children have been failed by the child protection system and adult domestic abuse remains all too commonplace. Undoubtedly, that is due, in part, to the fact that no amount of laws and policies can eradicate reprehensible human behaviour. It is, however, the task of legislators to find new and better ways to offer protection and it has made a start through domestic abuse courts and the associated support they offer. Thus, it is encouraging that further legislation, designed to tackle both child[166] and adult[167] domestic abuse, is in the pipeline.

Any assessment of the early years of the Scottish Parliament requires acknowledgement of an obvious truth. It was never going to be possible to do all that needs to be done in ten or so years. Nonetheless, progress has been made in the child and family law context, and the Scottish Parliament shows no signs of flagging. The challenge now is to complete some of the tasks it has started and to focus on the pursuit of equality, empowerment and protection.

---

165 *Schalk and Kopf v Austria*, Application No 30141/04, judgment of 24 June 2010.
166 Children's Hearings (Scotland) Bill, SP Bill 41 (2010).
167 Domestic Abuse (Scotland) Bill, SP Bill 45 (2010).

5 Culture

Dr Robert Dunbar°

A. LANGUAGE
B. A CULTURE BILL AND CREATIVE SCOTLAND

The Scottish Parliament generally has the competence to deal with most issues which would be considered to relate to culture,[1] with the important exception of broadcasting.[2] The creation of the Parliament has arguably resulted in greater discussion of a range of Scottish cultural issues than had been possible at Westminster, prior to devolution. There has, for example, been a committee with responsibility for culture since the creation of the Scottish Parliament,[3] and it has produced a number of significant reports. These include a report in 2000 on an inquiry into the national arts companies;[4] reports in 2001 on the Gaelic Broadcasting Committee[5] and on Scottish Ballet;[6] a report in 2003 on the role of education and cultural policy in supporting Gaelic, Scots and minority languages in Scotland;[7] a 2004 report on broadband in Scotland;[8]

° Reader in Law and Celtic, the University of Aberdeen. The author is a board member of Bòrd na Gàidhlig and MG Allan, but the views expressed herein are solely his own.

1 Head K, in Sch 5 to the Scotland Act 1998 (c 46) (which sets out the reserved matters which remain, by virtue of s 29 of the Act, in the sole legislative competence of Westminster), refers to "Media and Culture", but aside from broadcasting, matters referred to are quite limited in scope.

2 Broadcasting is a reserved matter and therefore outside the legislative competence of the Scottish Parliament: s 29(2)(b), s 30(1), and Schedule 5, section K1, "Broadcasting": Scotland Act 1998 (c 46).

3 In the first Session (1999-2003), the Education, Culture and Sport Committee; in the second Session (2003-2007), the Enterprise and Culture Committee, and in the third Session (2007-2011), the Education, Lifelong Learning and Culture Committee.

4 Education, Culture and Sport Committee, 1st Report 2000, *Report on Inquiry into the National Arts Companies*, SP Paper 65, Session 1 (2000).

5 Education, Culture and Sport Committee, 14th Report 2001, *Report on the Gaelic Broadcasting Committee*, SP Paper 473, Session 1 (2001), 18 December 2001.

6 Education, Culture and Sport Committee, 12th Report 2001, *Report on Report on Inquiry into Scottish Ballet*, SP Paper 457, Session 1 (2000), 29 November 2001.

7 Education, Culture and Sport Committee, 2nd Report 2003, *Report on Report on Inquiry into the Role of Education and Cultural Policy in Supporting and Developing Gaelic, Scots and Minority Languages in Scotland*, SP Paper 778, Session 1 (2003), 20 February 2003; the report was produced in Arabic, Bengali, Chinese, Gaelic, Punjabi, Scots and Urdu, as well as English.

8 Enterprise and Culture Committee, 4th Report 2004 (Session 2), *Report on Broadband in Scotland*, SP Paper 158, Session 2 (2004), 20 May 2004.

reports in 2005 on arts in the community[9] and on the implications of BBC Scotland's internal reviews;[10] and a 2008 report on the Creative Scotland Bill;[11] as well as reports on the Gaelic Language (Scotland) Bills and on the Public Services Reform (Scotland) Bill, referred to below. The Scottish Government has a Minister for Culture[12] and a division which deals with Arts and Culture;[13] its annual budget for culture is currently approximately £201.9 million.[14]

The fruits of all this interest and activity, in the form of new legislation (which is the focus of this contribution) have, however, been relatively sparse. There has been significant legislative activity with respect to the Gaelic language. Provisions on Gaelic education were included in the Standards in Scotland's Schools etc Act 2000, and two Bills on the language have come before the Scottish Parliament. One, the Gaelic Language (Scotland) Bill, introduced as a Private Bill in November 2002 by Michael Russell, then a member of the SNP opposition, received assent at the Preliminary Stage, but ultimately died when the first Scottish Parliament was dissolved in March 2003. The second Gaelic Language (Scotland) Bill, introduced into the Scottish Parliament by the Labour-Liberal Democrat Scottish Executive in September 2004, was ultimately passed, in amended form, unopposed in the Scottish Parliament in April 2005, and became the Gaelic Language (Scotland) Act 2005. There has been much less activity – and no legislation – with respect to Scotland's other languages, most notably Scots. It should be noted that the Scottish Parliament is precluded from dealing with at least some aspects of broader minority policy because some important policy areas – most notably equal opportunities issues – are reserved matters which can only be dealt with by the Westminster Parliament.[15]

Also significant have been the legislative developments relating to a proposed new agency, Creative Scotland. A Consultation Draft of a Culture

9   Enterprise and Culture Committee, 1st Report 2005 (Session 2), *Report on Arts in the Community*, SP Paper 302, Session 2 (2005), 3 March 2005.
10 Enterprise and Culture Committee, 6th Report 2005 (Session 2), *Report into the Implications of BBC Scotland's Internal Reviews*, SP Paper 365, Session 2 (2005), 31 May 2005.
11 Education, Lifelong Learning and Culture Committee, 3rd Report 2008 (Session 3), *Report on the Creative Scotland Bill*, SP Paper 105, Session 3 (2008), 2 June 2008.
12 At the time of writing, the present minister is Fiona Hyslop.
13 See *http://www.scotland.gov.uk/Topics/ArtsCultureSport/arts*.
14 This is the draft budget for 2009-10 for Culture and Gaelic; within that budget, £55.1 million is allocated to Creative Scotland, £97.4 million to cultural collections (such as the National Galleries), £24.9 million to national performing companies (such as Scottish Opera), and £19.7 million to Gaelic: see Scottish Budget, Draft Budget 2009-2010, available at *http://www.scotland.gov.uk/Publications/2008/09/12140641/3*.
15 Head L, Sch 5 to the Scotland Act 1998, s L2: "Equal opportunities, including the subject-matter of – (a) the Equal Pay Act 1970, (b) the Sex Discrimination Act 1975, (c) the Race Relations Act 1976, and (d) the Disability Discrimination Act 1995."

(Scotland) Bill was launched by the Labour-Liberal Democrat Scottish Executive in December 2006, but no Bill was introduced before the second Session of the Scottish Parliament ended in April 2007. One of the core aspects of the Consultation Draft was the creation of Creative Scotland, to assume the functions of certain other public bodies active in the area of culture. This aspect of the Consultation Draft has been carried forward into a Creative Scotland Bill, introduced by the SNP government in March 2008. This was defeated in the Scottish Parliament in June 2008, only for the idea to be revived in the Public Services Reform (Scotland) Bill, introduced by the SNP government in 2009 and presently working its way through the Parliament.

There have been three other Acts of the Scottish Parliament to which brief reference should be made, as each could be said to relate broadly to cultural matters. First, there is the National Galleries of Scotland Act 2003, which resulted from a Private Bill introduced in October 2002 and promoted by the Board of Trustees of the National Galleries of Scotland. In spite of its title, it was an extremely narrow Act which simply amended existing legislation that limited development in Princes Street Gardens, Edinburgh, in order to allow for the construction of an underground link between the National Gallery of Scotland and the Royal Scottish Academy.[16]

Given the iconic status of tartan in Scottish culture, the Scottish Register of Tartans Act 2008 deserves brief mention. The result of a Private Bill first introduced by the MSP Jamie McGrigor, the legislation introduced a Scottish Register of Tartans which is to be "a repository for the preservation of tartans" and "a source of information about tartans" (s 1), to be maintained by the Keeper of the Records of Scotland (ss 3, 4; when exercising his functions in respect of the Register, the Keeper of the Records of Scotland is to be referred to as the "Keeper of the Scottish Register of Tartans"). Interestingly, the Act has defined "tartan" in the following terms: "For the purposes of this Act, a tartan is a design which is capable of being woven consisting of two or more alternating coloured stripes which combine vertically and horizontally to form a repeated chequered pattern" (s 2).

The third piece of legislation which could be said to have a cultural aspect, and one which is notable in relation to the cultural practices of certain cultural minorities in Scotland, is the Prohibition of Female Genital Mutilation (Scotland) Act 2005. This Act criminalises the excision, infibulation or other mutilation of the female genitalia (s 1(1) and (2)). The Act specifies, however, that a surgical operation conducted by a registered medical

---

16 A Rehfisch and F McCallum, "National Galleries of Scotland Bill", The Scottish Parliament, the Information Centre. SPICe Briefing 03/02 (2003).

practitioner which is necessary for the patient's physical or mental health, or one conducted by a registered medical practitioner, a midwife or a person training to be such a practitioner or midwife performed on a women who is in labour or has just given birth, for purposes connected with the labour or birth, is not an offence (subss 1(3), (4) and (5)). Significantly, in determining whether an operation is necessary for the mental health of the patient, it is immaterial whether the patient or any other person believes that the operation is required as a matter of custom or ritual (subs 1(6)). It appears that multiculturalism has some limits when it comes to cultural practices such as these. It is important to recall, however, that female genital mutilation was criminalised in the UK by an Act of the Westminster Parliament in 1985: the Prohibition of Female Circumcision Act 1985. This Act was repealed in England, Wales and Northern Ireland by the Female Genital Mutilation Act 2003, which simply re-enacted the provisions of the 1985 legislation, gave them extra-territorial effect, and increased the penalties available. The Scottish parliamentary legislation is for much the same purpose and has much the same effect.

Given this relatively limited legislative record, it is perhaps not surprising that culture has received scant attention in recent texts on Scottish politics;[17] developments relating to Gaelic have, however, received some academic analysis.[18] Nevertheless, it is difficult, on the whole, to avoid the conclusion that the legislative achievements have generally been modest.

A. LANGUAGE

Assessment of the impact of devolution on legislation and policy for Gaelic requires some consideration of the activity of the Westminster Parliament in respect of the language. Until relatively recently, that record could be described as one of malign neglect. Most demographers of the Gaelic language will, for example, point to crucial legislation such as the Education

17 See, e.g., C Jeffery and J Mitchell (eds), *The Scottish Parliament 1999-2009: The First Decade*; J Curtice and B Seyd (eds), *Has Devolution Worked? The Verdict from Policy Makers and the Public* (2009); N McGarvey and P Cairney, *Scottish Politics: An Introduction* (2008); C Bromley, J Curtice, D McCrone and A Park (eds), *Has Devolution Delivered?* (2006); M Keating, *The Government of Scotland: Public Policy Making after Devolution* (2005).

18 See, e.g., R Dunbar, "The Gaelic Language (Scotland) Act 2005" 9 *Edinburgh Law Review* (2005) 466; W McLeod, "Securing the status of Gaelic? The Gaelic Language (Scotland) Act 2005", 57 *Scottish Affairs* (2006) 19; R Dunbar, "Gaelic in Scotland: the legal and institutional framework", in W McLeod (ed), *Revitalising Gaelic in Scotland: Policy, Planning and Public Discourse* (2006); R Dunbar, "Scotland: language legislation for Gaelic", 38 *Cambrian Law Review* (2007) 39; J Walsh and W McLeod, "An overcoat wrapped around an invisible man? Language legislation and language revitalisation in Ireland and Scotland", 7 *Language Policy* (2008) 21.

(Scotland) Act 1872, which introduced universal state-supported education, but made no provision either for the teaching of Gaelic as a subject
or teaching through the medium of the language. Gaelic had, until that
time, been used as a medium of instruction in many of the Highland schools
run by various religious bodies, and the effective exclusion of Gaelic from
the classroom by the 1872 legislation is thought to have had a profoundly
negative impact on the health of the language.[19] The omission of Gaelic in
the 1872 legislation was partially addressed by the inclusion in the Education
(Scotland) Act 1918 of an obligation on education authorities to provide for
the teaching of Gaelic in Gaelic-speaking areas, a provision that has been
carried forward in subsequent Scottish Education Acts of the Westminster
Parliament, including the Education (Scotland) Act 1980 s 1(5)(a)(iii)). The
difficulty is that the implications of this provision have never been adequately
spelled out and, until 1985, such Gaelic education provision which did exist
took the form of classes in the language at secondary level, primarily in the
Highlands and Islands, and usually taught through the medium of English.
In 1985, teaching at primary level through the medium of Gaelic began at
two Scottish schools, one in Glasgow and one in Inverness, and by 2009-2010
this had expanded to sixty schools, with two, again one in Glasgow and one
in Inverness, being all-Gaelic schools. This development has, however, not
resulted from any changes in primary legislation, but from local education
authority policy, although since 1986, development has been supported by a
funding mechanism, the so-called "Gaelic specific grant" that was introduced
by way of Westminster secondary legislation.[20]

A small amount of other Westminster legislation has either made reference to Gaelic or had provisions of relevance for Gaelic, although the impact
of such provisions is relatively narrow. While Gaelic found no place in education legislation of the 1870s, it did obtain recognition in ground-breaking
crofting legislation of the 1880s. The Crofters Holdings (Scotland) Act 1886
required that at least one member of the Crofters Commission should be a
Gaelic-speaker, a provision which has been carried forward into the current
legislation, the Crofters (Scotland) Act 1993 s 3(3). The Scottish Land Court
Act 1993 also requires a Gaelic-speaking member for the Land Court, which
deals with non-crofting land disputes (s 1(5)). The British Nationality Act
1981 requires a sufficient knowledge of English, Welsh or Scottish Gaelic for

19 K MacKinnon, *Gaelic: A Past and Future Prospect* (1991) 74-97.
20 Grants for Gaelic Language Education (Scotland) Regulations 1986, 1986 No 410, made under s
    73 of the Education (Scotland) Act 1980.

naturalisation.[21] The Local Government (Gaelic Names) (Scotland) Act 1997 permits local authorities to adopt a Gaelic name.[22]

Of more importance has been the Westminster Parliament's legislative activity in respect of Gaelic broadcasting. The Broadcasting Act 1990 created the Comataidh Telebhisein Gàidhlig (the "CTG", the "Gaelic Television Committee", renamed Comataidh Craolaidh Gàidhlig ("CCG", the "Gaelic Broadcasting Committee") under the Broadcasting Act 1996, when its remit was expanded to include the funding of Gaelic-medium radio programming) to administer a fund to finance the making of Gaelic-medium television programming (s 183(3) and (4)). Originally worth £8.5 million, this fund was expected to finance about 200 hours of new programming a year. This Act also placed obligations on Channel 3 licence-holders in Scotland (Grampian Television and Scottish Television) to ensure that a "suitable proportion" of Gaelic programmes was broadcast, and that a "suitable proportion" of such programmes funded by the CCG would be broadcast at peak viewing times (s 184(1)(a) and (b)). These statutory obligations, together with pump-priming through the CCG, facilitated a significant expansion in Gaelic television broadcasting on both the BBC and the Channel 3 services – it is important to remember that the CCG was not itself a broadcaster, but was reliant on other broadcasters such as these to transmit Gaelic programming. In the Communications Act 2003, the CCG was reconstituted as Seirbhis nam Meadhanan Gàidhlig (the "Gaelic Media Service" – since rebranded as "MG ALBA") and given an expanded remit which included not only financing but also *engaging in* the making of programmes in Gaelic (s 208), thereby apparently allowing the organisation to develop into a Gaelic-medium broadcaster itself. While MG ALBA kept open this possibility, it also entered into discussions with BBC Scotland on possible co-operation between the two organisations with a view to jointly launching a service. One of the main obstacles was financial; however, considerable extra funding committed by the Scottish Executive (now the Scottish Government), from within the BBC, and some additional money from the Westminster Department of Culture, Media and Sport[23] paved the way, and in 2007 a co-operation agreement between MG ALBA and the BBC was concluded. In September 2008 BBC ALBA,[24] the Gaelic

21 Sch 1 subpara 1(1)(c).
22 One has done so: the Western Isles Council, which is now Comhairle nan Eilean Siar.
23 The Scottish Government contributed over £3 million, the BBC committed approximately £2.5 million, and DCMS £250,000 of additional money to facilitate the creation of the new service. Some funding was also received from Scottish Television in compensation for the reduction of its obligations with respect to broadcasting Gaelic programmes.
24 See *http://www.bbc.co.uk/alba/*.

digital television service, was launched, and it presently broadcasts approximately six and a half hours of programming a day.

Controversially, in authorising the creation of the service, the BBC Trust delayed making any decision on whether the new service would be available on Freeview until 2010, as part of a wider review of BBC ALBA – at present, the service is only available to viewers via satellite, to which only about 40% of Scottish viewers have access. The BBC Trust launched the consultation on its review of BBC ALBA in October 2009,[25] and it closed in January 2010. Although the results of the consultation have not yet been released, it is understood that there was widespread support for making BBC ALBA available on Freeview; significantly, that support included the Scottish Government[26] and all parties in the Scottish Parliament.[27] However, the BBC Trust released the news in March 2010 that it would further delay its decision on Freeview until later in the year, when it intends to publish its final view on what the future strategy for the BBC as a whole should be.[28] Given the support of the Scottish Government and Scottish Parliament for early access to Freeview for BBC ALBA, this BBC Trust decision may prove to be even more controversial than its original one.

The foregoing events and decisions highlight one of the anomalies of the devolution settlement: although, as noted, Westminster continues to have sole authority for broadcasting, since the creation of the Scottish Parliament, the funding of the CCG and now MG ALBA has come through the Scottish Executive (now the Scottish Government). Indeed, with the election of an SNP government in May 2007, the question of broadcasting has taken on added prominence in the Scottish Parliament. There is widespread recognition that television broadcasting is not only of considerable importance to the so-called "creative economy", but is also of broader cultural and, indeed, political importance. There is also widespread concern in Scotland that Scotland's share of network production is well below its percentage of the population of Britain.[29] In its manifesto for the 2007 campaign, the SNP argued that "Scotland needs a dedicated news service and more quality programming made in Scotland", said it would "push for the devolution of broadcasting

25 http://www.bbc.co.uk/bbctrust/assets/files/pdf/consult/alba/bbc_alba_consultation.pdf.
26 See http://openscotland.net/Topics/ArtsCultureSport/arts/Broadcasting/Broadcasting.
27 Minutes of Proceedings vol 3, no 54 Session 3, 11 February 2010, available at: http://www.
    scottish.parliament.uk/business/chamber/mop-10/mop10-02-11.htm.
28 See   https://consultations.external.bbc.co.uk/departments/bbc/bbc-alba-review/consultation/
    consult_view.
29 P Schlesinger, "The SNP, cultural policy and the idea of the 'creative economy'", in G Hassan (ed),
    The Modern SNP: From Protest to Power (2009) 137.

powers to the Scottish Parliament", and highlighted its claim that Scotland currently "generates 8.8% of BBC revenues in licence fees and only receives 5.7% of the revenues raised".[30] In August 2007, the First Minister, Alex Salmond, announced the establishment of a Scottish Broadcasting Commission ("SBC") to investigate the current state of television production and broadcasting in Scotland and to identify ways of advancing the industry. One of the key recommendations of the SBC was the creation of a new Scottish network comprising a digital public service television channel and an extensive and innovative online platform.[31] Another key recommendation was that both the BBC and Channel 4 should secure a share of network television production from Scotland that is in line with the Scottish share of the UK population.[32] In a motion which gained all-party support, the Scottish Parliament welcomed the SBC final report, accepted that the Parliament should "take an active role in considering the broadcasting industry and services as they relate to Scotland", and welcomed "the key recommendation for the creation of a new public service Scottish digital network, which represents a major opportunity to develop Scotland's broadcasting industry".[33] In this context, and given its support for making BBC ALBA available on Freeview, it will be interesting to see how the Scottish Parliament – and, indeed, the Scottish Government – will respond to the most recent delay by the BBC Trust in resolving this issue.

Returning to the role that Westminster has played in relation to Gaelic, two other matters deserve comment. First, the Scotland Act 1998 reserves to Westminster all matters relating to international relations,[34] and the Westminster government has used its powers to enter into treaties to ratify two Council of Europe treaties which create considerable obligations for both the Westminster Parliament and the Scottish Parliament in relation to Gaelic and, indeed, Scots. These are the Framework Convention for the Protection of National Minorities,[35] ratified by the UK on 15 January 1998, and the European Charter for Regional or Minority Languages,[36] ratified by

30 Scottish National Party, *Manifesto 2007* (2007) 56.
31 Scottish Broadcasting Commission, *Platform for Success: Final Report of the Scottish Broadcasting Commission* (2008) 5.
32 Scottish Broadcasting Commission, *Platform for Success* (n 32) 8-9.
33 Minutes of Proceedings vol 2, no 25 Session 3, 8 October 2008, available at: *http://www.scottish.parliament.uk/business/chamber/mop-08/mop08-10-08.htm.*
34 Paragraph 7, Sch 5 to the Scotland Act 1998.
35 Council of Europe, ETS no 157, Strasbourg, 1.II.1995, available at: *http://conventions.coe.int/Treaty/en/Treaties/Html/157.htm.*
36 Council of Europe, ETS no 148, Strasbourg, 5.XI.1992, available at: *http://conventions.coe.int/Treaty/EN/Treaties/HTML/148.htm.*

the UK on 27 March 2001. The latter is particularly important, as it creates a range of quite specific obligations in respect of Gaelic, and requires both the Westminster Parliament and the Scottish Parliament to base their legislation, policy and practices with regard to both Gaelic and Scots on a number of principles, including the recognition of both languages as an expression of cultural wealth, the need for resolute action to promote them in order to safeguard them, and the facilitation and/or encouragement of their use, in speech and writing, in public and private life (art 7 subparas 1(a), (c) and (d)).

The final matter which deserves to be mentioned in respect of Westminster's legislative record for Gaelic is that, in spite of the various measures of legislative support that have just been considered, the Westminster Parliament did not manage to create legislation of a broader nature in relation to the official status of Gaelic, similar to the Welsh Language Act 1967 or the Welsh Language Act 1993. In 1980, the SNP Member of Parliament for the Western Isles, Donald Stewart, introduced a Private Member's Bill, the Gaelic (Miscellaneous Provisions) Bill, which would have, among other things, authorised the use of Gaelic in legal proceedings and the provision of official forms in the language. However, the Bill died on 13 February 1981, when it got caught up in delaying tactics that were being employed to ensure that an unrelated measure did not come to a vote.[37]

Inspired in part by the passage of the Welsh Language Act 1993, Comunn na Gàidhlig (CNAG), the main Gaelic development organisation at the time, began a campaign for more all-encompassing language legislation for Gaelic. Its proposals for a Gaelic Language Act, encompassed in a package entitled "Inbhe Theàrainte dhan Ghàidhlig/Secure Status for Gaelic" (Comunn na Gàidhlig, 1997), included the creation of right to education through the medium of Gaelic ("Gaelic-medium education" or "GME") at all levels wherever there was "reasonable demand" therefor,[38] and the obligation on education authorities to create Gaelic-medium schools where there was "sufficient demand" (undefined) therefor. CNAG also proposed a requirement that a range of public bodies be required to prepare Gaelic policies within three years of the coming into force of the legislation, and which would require commitments in relation to communication with the public through the medium of Gaelic, the use of Gaelic on signage, and the use of Gaelic in the provision of social services. The level of commitment required depended on the size of the Gaelic-speaking population served by a particular public body, but where the Gaelic-speaking population constituted at least

---

37 K MacKinnon, *Gaelic: A Past and Future Prospect* (1991) 111.
38 Defined as demand on behalf of five or more pupils.

30% of the population being served, the commitments in these areas should be to full bilingualism and full equality of treatment between Gaelic and English. CNAG proposed the creation of a Gaelic Language Advisory Board to assist in the preparation of the policies, but specified that the policies would ultimately be approved by government. CNAG also recommended the creation of a general statutory right for all persons appearing before all courts of general jurisdiction (both criminal and civil), administrative tribunals and all other judicial or quasi-judicial bodies to present cases and give evidence through the medium of Gaelic. Finally, CNAG recommended the creation of an Office of the Gaelic Language Commissioner to regulate and monitor implementation of the proposed legislation, and the creation of a special remedy in the legislation which would give access to the courts in respect of any failure to implement rights, obligations or policy commitments.

The proposals were delivered to Brian Wilson, the minister in the Westminster Labour government at the time with responsibility for Gaelic; however, although he and his successor, Calum MacDonald, directed their officials to discuss the proposals with CNAG, no further action was taken, and, with the creation of the Scottish Parliament in 1999, it was thought that it would be more appropriate for that parliament, which would have legislative responsibility for most of the areas implicated in the CNAG proposals, to consider them. With that in mind, CNAG repackaged the proposals (with further recommendations with regard to the use of Gaelic in the Scottish Parliament itself), and presented them in July 1999 to Alasdair Morrison, the minister in the Labour-Liberal Democrat Scottish Executive with responsibility for Gaelic.[39]

Initially, there was little response. In early 2000, when the Scottish Executive launched a wide-ranging Education Bill, the Standards in Scotland's Schools etc Bill, CNAG saw the opportunity of at least having those aspects of its Secure Status proposals relating to education included in the Bill as it made its way through the parliamentary process. The Executive was unwilling to consider a right to GME of the sort being proposed by CNAG, instead offering what CNAG ultimately perceived to be an insufficiently limited provision. The SNP MSP Michael Russell together with John Farquhar Munro of the Liberal Democrats introduced an amendment to the Bill based on the right proposed by CNAG, but this amendment failed to gain sufficient support. The Executive did, however, ultimately advance amendments in an attempt to meet some of the concerns that had been raised by CNAG. The

39 Comunn na Gàidhlig, *Dreach iùl airson Achd Gàidhlig/Draft brief for a Gaelic Language Act* (1999).

result was that under the Standards in Scotland's Schools etc Act 2000, local education authorities are required to provide an annual account of the ways or circumstances in which they will provide GME and, where they already provide GME, an account of how they will seek to develop their provision (s 5(2)(c)). The Act also created a system of "national priorities" in education under which local education authorities must prepare annually a statement of education improvement objectives in respect of each of the national priorities defined by the Scottish Executive (s 5(1), (2) and (4)). One of the national priorities is to promote equality and help every pupil benefit from education, with particular regard to Gaelic and other lesser-used languages.

The Executive's response during the first session of the Scottish Parliament to other aspects of the CNAG proposals was essentially to study the matter. In December 1999, it established a task force with the relatively limited remit of examining the arrangement and structures for the support of Gaelic organisations in Scotland. When it reported in September 2000, the task force recommended, among other things, the creation of "a small Gaelic-speaking Department of the Gaidhealtachd" within the Executive to advise ministers on policy, to establish a transitional advisory group, and to establish a Gaelic development agency to produce an overarching strategy and formulate plans with clear targets for the language, and to "[f]acilitat[e] the process of Secure Status for the language";[40] the use of the term which CNAG had used to describe its legislative proposals led some to interpret this as a nod to the need for legislation broadly in line with CNAG's proposals. In December 2000, the Executive then duly appointed the advisory group which had been recommended by the task force. Among the recommendations in the first part of its report, delivered in December 2001, were the creation of a Gaelic development agency, Bòrd na Gàidhlig, established as a non-departmental public body. Although legislation was not specifically recommended, the report insisted that the new agency "must have powers to plan for Gaelic nationally, and to require other public sector bodies to work with it in that process",[41] a recommendation which bore some similarity to the language policies which CNAG had proposed.

In June 2002, the Scottish Executive announced that it would act on one of the recommendations, by the establishment of a Gaelic development agency, Bòrd Gàidhlig na h-Alba, as a non-departmental public body; in

---

40 *Taskforce on Public Funding of Gaelic, Revitalising Gaelic: A National Asset/Ag Ath-Bheothachadh Gaidhlig: Neamhnuid Naiseanta* (2000) 4.
41 Ministerial Advisory Group on Gaelic, *A Fresh Start for Gaelic/Cothrom Ùr Don Ghàidhlig* (2002) 6-7.

October 2002 its chairperson was appointed and in March 2003 its member-ship was announced. In the absence, however, of any other significant action on the two reports, Michael Russell of the Opposition SNP energised matters by introducing in November a Gaelic Language (Scotland) Bill, as a Private Bill. The Bill was a rather short one of seven sections and one schedule; significantly, it did not include any of the rights that CNAG had recommended, such as a right to GME or a right to use Gaelic in the courts. It did, however, adopt the use of Gaelic language plans as a means of increasing the use of Gaelic by public bodies. Most public bodies operating in an area essentially comprising the Highland, Western Isles and Argyll and Bute council areas would have to prepare a Gaelic language plan setting out the measures the public body proposed to take as to the use of Gaelic in connection with its internal processes and in its provision of services to the public (s 1(1) and (2), s 6(2)). The purpose of the measures to be taken was to give effect, "so far as is both appropriate in the circumstances and reason-ably practicable", to the principle that in the public body's internal processes and in its provision of services to the public, Gaelic and English "should be treated on the basis of equality" (s 1(3)). CNAG, other Gaelic organisations and activists welcomed the proposals, and were particularly pleased with the inclusion of the concept of treatment of Gaelic and English on the basis of equality, a formulation similar to that used in the Welsh Language Act 1993. It was also pleased with the Schedule, which set out the minimum content that had to be in every Gaelic language plan, and which included matters such as response to external and media communication, documents and other materials, translation services, details of any Gaelic-only services, details of training in the Gaelic language for staff, and of posts for which Gaelic language skills would be an essential job requirement. It was less pleased with the fact that the Bill effectively drew a Highland Line on the map, below which public services would be untouched; in the 2001 census, it was noted that almost half of Scotland's roughly 58,000 speakers lived outside of the traditional "heartlands" and on the wrong side of the line, and both the CNAG proposals and the Executive-appointed task force and advisory group had taken the view that Gaelic policy needed to be national in scope.

As noted at the start of this chapter, the Bill received assent at the prelimi-nary stage, but died at the end of the first session, in March 2003. It helped to change the dynamic with regard to Gaelic language legislation, however, as the Scottish Labour Party and the Scottish Liberal Democrats, as well as the SNP, pledged to introduce legislation for Gaelic in their manifestos for the

2003 Scottish parliamentary elections. "A Partnership for a Better Scotland",[42] the partnership agreement between Scottish Labour and the Scottish Liberal Democrats to form the Scottish Executive, contained a commitment to "legislate to provide secure status for Gaelic through a Gaelic Language Bill". A consultation draft of the Bill, also entitled the Gaelic Language (Scotland) Bill, was released in October 2003, the Bill itself was introduced into the Scottish Parliament in September 2004, and it was passed unopposed in the parliament in April 2005.

The Gaelic Language (Scotland) Act 2005 is undoubtedly the single most important piece of legislation that has ever been passed in support of the language and, given the relatively limited legislative developments in other areas relating to culture, is arguably the most notable piece of legislation on cultural matters that has yet been passed.[43] There are four main aspects to the legislation. The first is the creation of a statutory language planning body, Bòrd na Gàidhlig, which effectively replaced Bòrd Gàidhlig na h-Alba (s 1(1)). The Bòrd is given four main functions, including that of promoting the use and understanding of the Gaelic language and of Gaelic education and Gaelic culture, and of advising the Scottish Executive and public authorities on matters relating to the Gaelic language, Gaelic education and Gaelic culture (s 1(2)). The Bòrd must exercise all its functions "with a view to securing the status of the Gaelic language as an official language of Scotland commanding equal respect to the English language" in three ways: first, through increasing the number of persons who are able to use and understand Gaelic; second, through encouraging the use and understanding of Gaelic; and third, through facilitating access to the Gaelic language and Gaelic culture (s 1(3)).

The second main aspect of the Act is a requirement on the Bòrd to submit to the Scottish Executive (now the Scottish Government) a national Gaelic language plan within a year of the legislation coming into force and every five years thereafter (s 2(1)). The plan must include proposals for how the Bòrd will exercise its functions, and a strategy for promoting the use and understanding of the Gaelic language, as well as of Gaelic education and Gaelic culture (s 2(2)). The Bòrd's first national Gaelic language plan was approved by the Scottish Executive in 2007.[44]

---

42 *http://www.scotland.gov.uk/Resource/Doc/47095/0025772.pdf*; see p 43.
43 For a more detailed account of the Act and its context, as well as a critical assessment, see R Dunbar "The Gaelic Language (Scotland) Act 2005", 9 *Edinburgh Law Review* (2005) 466 and W McLeod, "Securing the status of Gaelic? The Gaelic Language (Scotland) Act 2005", 57 *Scottish Affairs* (2006) 19.
44 Bòrd na Gàidhlig, *The National Plan for Gaelic 2007-2012/Plana Nàiseanta na Gàidhlig* (2007).

The third main aspect of the Act is perhaps its most important one: the creation of a mechanism for the development of Gaelic language plans by public bodies in Scotland. Both the creation of the Bòrd and of this mechanism were inspired to a significant degree by the model of the Welsh Language Act 1993. Similar to that legislation, the Bòrd has the power to require any Scottish public authority to prepare a Gaelic language plan (s 3(1)), although the public authorities can appeal both the requirement to prepare such a plan and the timetable required by the Bòrd for doing so to the Scottish Government (s 3(1) and (2), s 4(1) and (8)). The Act provides that, in its Gaelic language plan, the Scottish public authority must set out the measures it will take in relation to the use of Gaelic in its internal processes as well as in the provision by it of any services to the public, and the date by which such measures will be taken (s 3(4)). In preparing its plan, the public authority must have regard to the following: the national Gaelic language plan; the extent to which the public it serves comprises Gaelic speakers; the potential for developing the use of Gaelic in its internal processes and in the provision by it of services to the public; any representations in respect of the plan that have been made by the public; and any guidance provided by the Scottish Government or by the Bòrd (s 3(5)). The Bòrd prepared such guidance in 2007.[45] Finally, all Gaelic language plans must be approved by the Bòrd (s 5(1)), although if disagreement emerges between the public authority and the Bòrd, the matter will be referred to the Scottish Government (s 5(5)(c)). To date, the Bòrd has authorised six Gaelic language plans, including that of the Scottish Parliament Corporate Body. It is still too early to tell how effective this mechanism has been, but it certainly has the potential to allow for a significant expansion in the use of Gaelic in dealing with the public sector in Scotland.

The final main aspect of the Act relates to Gaelic education, defined in the Act to include not only GME but also the teaching of Gaelic as a subject (s 10(1)). In particular, the Bòrd can prepare guidance for local authorities on Gaelic education, and in providing its annual account under the Standards in Scotland's Schools etc Act 2000 as to what it is doing in respect of Gaelic education, local authorities would be required to have regard to such guidance. To date, the Bòrd has not yet prepared any such guidance. The Bòrd could, of course, require an education authority (or the local authority of which it is a part) to prepare a Gaelic language plan in which there could be articulated objectives with respect to education provision.

45 Bòrd na Gàidhlig, *Guidance on the Development of Gaelic Language Plans/Stiùireadh air Deasachadh Phlanaichean Gàidhlig* (2007).

By way of conclusion, the following points should be made with respect to the impact of the Scottish Parliament on legislation for Gaelic. First, an Act of the Scottish Parliament, the Gaelic Language (Scotland) Act 2005 is the single most important legislative development in the modern history of the Gaelic language. While such legislation could have been introduced at Westminster, the existence of a Scottish Parliament seems to have created conditions which facilitated such legislation by, for example, providing a forum in which issues of particular relevance to Scotland such as Gaelic and which would have been very marginal issues at Westminster could be more fully debated. It has been noted that one effect of devolution has been a general increase in separate Scottish Bills.[46]

Second, some commentators have noted that the process for Members' Bills at Holyrood is simpler than that at Westminster, giving "many MSPs a reasonable chance of legislative progress or, at the least, a strong agenda-setting tool".[47] In this regard, it is worth noting that Michael Russell's 2002 Member's Bill may have acted as a catalyst for subsequent legislative action, in sharp contrast to the effects of Donald Stewart's Westminster Bill of the early 1980s.

Third, the general spirit of cross-party goodwill towards the language at Holyrood is evident in much of the foregoing discussion. The Gaelic Language (Scotland) Act 2005, the other legislative initiatives, and various other Gaelic matters including Gaelic broadcasting have been dealt with seriously and with care in both committees and the full Scottish Parliament. It is also worth noting that some Committee evidence and some parliamentary debate has occurred in Gaelic, something specifically permitted by the Parliament's Standing Orders (and something that would not have occurred at Westminster). The quality of debate stands in sharp contrast with that heard during the consideration of Donald Stewart's Bill at Westminster in 1981, which "was marred by an extraordinary series of hostile attacks and offensive, patronising remarks" based on hoary stereotypes about Gaelic and Gaelic-speakers.[48]

Finally, there is the much greater presence of Gaelic in the work of the Scottish Parliament itself. Partly as a result of the Scottish Parliament

---

46 M Keating and P Cairney, "The New Scottish Statute Book: The Scottish Parliament's legislative record since 1999", in Jeffery and Mitchell, *The Scottish Parliament 1999-2009*, 37.

47 Keating and Cairney, "The New Scottish Statute Book" (n 47) 39.

48 W McLeod, "Official Status for Gaelic: Prospects and Problems" 21 *Scottish Affairs* (1997) 21, 95-118. McLeod provides this example: "First, there were declarations of raw prejudice against Gaelic and Gaelic speakers, like that of Martin J O'Neill, Labour member for Clackmannan and East Stirlingshire, who mused about the possible difficulties from 'a drunken Highlander appearing in court on a Monday morning claiming the right to give evidence in Gaelic'".

Corporate Body's statutory Gaelic language plan,[49] and partly as a result of its earlier and ongoing commitment to Gaelic, the Parliament has a bilingual corporate identity, there is expanded bilingual public signage at Holyrood, and front-line staff receive Gaelic awareness training; also, members of the public can correspond to or call the Parliament using Gaelic, a wide range of information and educational resources are available in print and on-line in Gaelic, Gaelic public tours are available, and Gaelic or bilingual sessions are available for school, college and university groups as part of the Parliament's education programme. And, as noted, it is possible to use Gaelic in parliamentary debates and committee meetings.[50] Quite simply, none of this would be conceivable at Westminster.

In contrast to Gaelic, Scots has been relatively neglected at Holyrood. There has, for example, been no attempt to legislate for Scots, and the formalised use of Scots within the Parliament's operations has not been developed. Indeed, it could be argued that the most important legal step that has been taken in respect of Scots was the ratification by the UK government of the European Charter for Regional or Minority Languages, which, as noted earlier, applies to and provides protection for Scots. As noted at the beginning of this chapter, however, there was a report by the Education, Culture and Sport Committee near the end of the first Session of the Parliament in 2003 on the role of education and cultural policy in supporting Gaelic, Scots and minority languages in Scotland, and a version of the report was produced in Scots (as well as other languages; see note 8, above). In the third Session of the parliament, under an SNP administration, there has been some non-legislative activity, such as a 2009 Scottish Government *Audit of Current Scots Language Provision in Scotland*[51] and a Scottish Government-commissioned 2010 study *Public Attitudes towards the Scots Language*.[52]

B. A CULTURE BILL AND CREATIVE SCOTLAND

The Scottish Labour-Scottish Liberal Democrat coalition which formed the Scottish Executive during the second Session of the Parliament showed an interest in taking a broad look at all aspects of cultural policy; in an April 2004 Cultural Policy Statement,[53] the Executive noted the need for "a new

49 *http://www.parlamaid-alba.org/gaelicplan.*
50 See Scottish Parliament/Pàrlamaid na h-Alba (2009). *Gàidhlig ann am Pàrlamaid na h-Alba/ Gaelic in the Scottish Parliament* (2009).
51 *http://www.scotland.gov.uk/Publications/2009/01/23133726/0.*
52 *http://www.scotland.gov.uk/Resource/Doc/298037/0092859.pdf.*
53 Scottish Executive, *Cultural Policy Statement* (2004).

cultural vision for our country and a radically different way of delivering and sustaining our cultural services", reasserted its commitment to a general review of the cultural sector, and established a Cultural Commission to carry out this review, which the Executive specifically asked to

- explore the notion of cultural rights for the Scottish citizen, and those of its creative community and define how these might be translated into a scheme of entitlements;
- redefine the institutional infrastructure and governance of the Scottish cultural sector to enable it to deliver the entitlements that spring from rights.[54]

The Cultural Commission's final report, submitted to the Scottish Executive in June 2005, was an extremely lengthy and wide-ranging document containing 124 separate recommendations.[55] In response to this report, in January 2006 the Scottish Executive announced its new cultural policy, *Scotland's Culture*.[56] Recognising that legislation was needed in order to achieve some of its proposals in *Scotland's Culture*, the Executive decided in December 2006 to publish a Draft Culture (Scotland) Bill Consultation Document,[57] as well as draft guidance, in a Draft Culture (Scotland) Bill Guidance Document [58] in respect of the implementation of aspects of the draft Bill.

The draft bill had four main aspects. The first, set out in Pt I and in the draft guidance document, contained proposals on the provision by local authorities of "cultural services". A key part of the proposals was the draft guidance to which local authorities would have to have regard, which, drawing on the work of the Cultural Commission, contained the notion of "cultural entitlements", specific activities and opportunities to take part in and enjoy culture; local authorities would have been required to develop entitlements that included local access to the arts, heritage resources, museums, libraries and archives.[59] While the proposals were complex, they did represent an innovative attempt to give content to a rather vague concept of "cultural rights" which can be found in international instruments such as the 1948 United Nations Universal Declaration of Human Rights (art 27(1)) and the 1966 United Nations International Covenant on Economic, Social and Cultural Rights (art 15(1)). The second aspect of the draft Bill, set out in Pt II, was the creation of a new public body, Creative Scotland, to act as Scotland's national cultural development body. As the new body would take over the

---

54 Scottish Executive, *Cultural Policy Statement* (n 54) 10.
55 *http://www.scotland.gov.uk/Resource/Doc/54357/0013577.pdf*.
56 Scottish Executive, *Scotland's Culture/Cultar na h-Alba* (2006).
57 Scottish Executive, *Draft Culture (Scotland) Bill, Consultation Document* (2006).
58 Scottish Executive, *Draft Culture (Scotland) Bill, Guidance Document* (2006).
59 Scottish Executive, *Draft Culture (Scotland) Bill, Guidance Document* (n 59) 12, para 1.33.

functions then being carried out by the Scottish Arts Council, the Scottish Executive was given the power to disband the arts council. The third aspect of the draft Bill, set out in Pt III, contained a range of changes to legislation governing various national cultural bodies, including the National Library of Scotland, the National Galleries of Scotland and the National Museums of Scotland, with a view to updating their functions and facilitating co-operation between them. It also proposed the dissolution of the Royal Commission on the Ancient and Historical Monuments of Scotland and its effective replacement by a new body, the National Record of Scotland. The final aspect of the draft Bill were proposed changes in the law in respect of dealing in tainted cultural objects, being objects of historical, architectural or archaeological interest which had been unlawfully removed from a building or structure, or from a monument, of historical, architectural or archaeological interest.

As noted earlier in this chapter, no Bill based on the Consultation Draft of a Culture (Scotland) Bill was introduced before the end of the second Session of the Scottish Parliament in April 2007. One aspect of the draft has survived in the third Session of the parliament: the creation of a new body to be called Creative Scotland (and with it, the dissolution of the Scottish Arts Council and the transfer of its staff and property to the new body). As also noted, the Scottish Government of the SNP introduced into the Scottish Parliament a Creative Scotland Bill which was defeated in June 2008.[60] However, the substance of that Bill has reappeared in the 2009 Public Services Reform (Scotland) Bill, SP Bill 26, Session 3 (2009) which is now before the Scottish Parliament.

The core aspects of the creation of Creative Scotland have not changed very much. The Scottish Arts Council will be dissolved and its staff and property will be transferred to Creative Scotland (ss 31 and 32). It is also intended that Creative Scotland will subsume Scottish Screen, a company limited by guarantee which was set up in 1997 as a non-departmental public body to operate as the national development body for the screen industries.[61] Under the most recent Bill, Creative Scotland will have a range of general functions, including identifying, supporting and developing quality and excellence in the arts and culture; promoting understanding, appreciation and enjoyment of the arts and culture; encouraging as many people as possible to access and participate in the arts and culture; encouraging and supporting artistic and other creative endeavours which contribute to an understanding

---

60 For a good account of the Creative Scotland saga, at least up to this point in the story, and a critical assessment of it, see Schlesinger, "The SNP, cultural policy" (n 30).

61 Schlesinger, "The SNP, cultural policy" (n 30) 136.

of Scotland's national culture; and promoting and supporting industries and other commercial activity, the primary focus of which is the application of creative skills (s 27(1)).

It remains to be seen what impact the establishment of Creative Scotland will have. However, aside from the significant legislative developments relating to Gaelic, it will stand as the single most important legislative product of eleven years of deliberation at Holyrood. It is important to remember that the devolved institutions impact on the cultural life of Scotland in a large number of ways, and that it would be inappropriate to judge the impact of devolution by reference to legislative output alone.[62]

Nonetheless, if one were to consider the legislative record of over ten years of devolved government alone, there might be some cause for disappointment. This is likely, however, to be more of a reflection on the priorities and preoccupations of Scotland's political class than on the Scottish Parliament *per se*, for where there has been engagement, as has been the case with Gaelic, the legislative accomplishments, clearly facilitated by devolved law-making powers, have been considerable.

---

62 N McGarvey and P Cairney. *Scottish Politics: An Introduction* (2008) 199-218, esp. 210-213.

6 Charity Law:
An Issue of Choice

Stuart Cross[*]

A. INTRODUCTION

The passing of the Charities and Trustee Investment (Scotland) Act 2005[1]
was a landmark occurrence in the development of charity law in Scotland.
It introduced a dedicated charities regulator, created a new definition of
"charity" for Scottish charities and introduced a new regulatory regime to

---

* Senior Lecturer in Law, University of Dundee.
1 Hereafter "the 2005 Act".

allow for the effective monitoring of and potential intervention in the affairs of Scottish charities, built on the information contained in the new Scottish register of charities. Although the public perception may have been that these changes to the landscape of charity law in Scotland only took place as a result of the need to develop a regime which could cope with issues such as those which had arisen from a number of high-profile scandals involving Scottish charities, that would be to ignore the detailed consideration of the potential shape of charity law and regulation which had been ongoing across the United Kingdom in the fifteen years preceding the 2005 Act. The 2005 Act is a product of the Scottish Parliament and it incorporates a range of provisions and mechanisms which reflect choices made during the passage of the legislation. Some of those choices were overtly political in nature yet result in distinct legal consequences. This chapter considers the fundamental changes to charity law in Scotland that resulted from the passing of the 2005 Act and discusses how particular choices and approaches to the key provisions in the Act have resulted in a legislative outcome which is both distinctively Scottish in approach but pragmatically cognisant of a broader United Kingdom social and legal context.

B. REGULATION OF CHARITIES IN SCOTLAND PRE-2005

Scotland has a long established common law of "charitable and public trusts"[2] which, as the late Lord President Cooper commented, had nothing to do with "the statute of Elizabeth and the artificial structure which has been erected upon it"[3] – namely, the concept of charity developed by the English courts which has its foundations in the preamble to the Charitable Uses Act 1601.[4] Charitable trusts in Scotland are part of a specific class[5] of the broader species of Scottish public trusts.[6] Although it has been argued that the development of the Scots common law charitable and public trusts regime could have provided Scotland with a strong, indigenously rooted regime for the regulation of charities,[7] that approach was not followed when the first statutory

---

2 *Wink's Executors v Tallent* 1947 SC 470.

3 *Wink's Executors* (n 2) at 476 per LP Cooper.

4 More commonly referred to as "the Statute of Elizabeth" or "the 1601 Act".

5 Being a class which is concerned principally with the provision of benefit to that section of the public which can be categorised as "the poor": see *Special Commissioners for the Purposes of Income Tax v Pemsel* [1891] AC 531 at 561 per Lord Watson.

6 Scottish public trusts are trusts where "the beneficial interest is intended for the benefit of a section of the public": *The Laws of Scotland: Stair Memorial Encyclopaedia*, vol 24 xxiv, para 6.

7 See, in particular, P J Ford, "Supervising charities: a Scottish-Civilian alternative (2006) 10(3) *Edin LR* 352, and P J Ford, "The Charities and Trustee Investment (Scotland) Bill: falling between two stools? (2005) 16 *KCLJ* 1 at 4.

regime for the regulation of Scottish charities was introduced by means of the Law Reform (Miscellaneous Provisions) (Scotland) Act 1990 ("the 1990 Act"). The main influence and drive for regulatory change in Scotland in respect of charities in the late 1980s came not from Scotland but from England. In Sir Philip Woodfield's report, *Efficiency Scrutiny of the Supervision of Charities*,[8] it was commented that it would be "imprudent" to leave matters as they were in Scotland.[9] What followed, in the form of the 1990 Act, was a regime which was built around recognition of the fact that many Scottish organisations which were not-for-profit in nature were entitled to seek and obtain relief from United Kingdom taxes on the basis that these bodies' purposes were "charitable" in the technical sense of the concept as developed from the 1601 Act.[10] The 1990 Act was constructed around this linkage, and once a not-for-profit body had been able to satisfy the (then) Inland Revenue that it was entitled to relief from taxation on the basis of its purposes, having satisfied the 1601 Act derived threshold, then those bodies would be entitled to refer to themselves as "Scottish charities" and would be subject to regulation as such under the 1990 Act.[11] The outcome of this approach was effectively to subrogate the role of legal form in respect of the regulation of charities. A "Scottish charity" might well have been a species of public trust for the purposes of classification of form in Scots law but for regulatory purposes as a charity the critical element was the purpose or purposes pursued by the body. This approach was not greatly surprising because the use of the *Pemsel* test for fiscal purposes was well established in Scotland[12] and the extended application of the use of the fiscal definition of "charity" for regulatory purposes in effect created a common notion of "charity" in England and Scotland. One of the key effects of the 1990 Act was, therefore, to create a statutory species of Scottish charities which was defined and circumscribed by the same English derived rules as were applied by the Charity Commission in England and Wales.

8 *Efficiency Scrutiny of the Supervision of Charities* (1987) (hereafter "Woodfield Report").
9 Woodfield Report para 144.
10 See *Income Tax Commissioners* v *Pemsel* (n 5) at 570 and 587 per Lord Macnaghten. The main relief from taxation sought by charities was in respect of income tax, which relief is set out in the Income and Corporation Taxes Act 1988 s 505.
11 1990 Act s 1(7).
12 See, e.g., *IRC* v *Falkirk Temperance Cafe Trust* 1927 SC 261 and *IRC* v *City of Glasgow Police Athletic Association* [1953] AC 380.

C. THE REFORM OF CHARITY LAW IN SCOTLAND

(1) Structural deficiencies and sectoral scandals

The 1990 Act was the subject of criticism and calls for its reform were made almost from the time it came into force. The regulatory structure introduced by the 1990 Act was broadly based on the regime for small charities in England and Wales in terms of the Charities Act 1960, and it introduced formal accounting requirements[13] for Scottish charities and provided powers of official inquiry and intervention[14] which were structurally similar to but far less comprehensive than those conferred on charity commissioners in England and Wales. Notable absences from the 1990 regime were any form of dedicated charity regulator such as existed in England and Wales in the form of the Charity Commission[15] or a properly constituted public register of charities.[16] A series of reviews were undertaken into these and other perceived inadequacies in the 1990 regime, with the three main reports being the Kemp Report,[17] the report by Dundee Law School's Charity Law Research Unit,[18] and the McFadden Report.[19] Of these, the McFadden Report was the most significant and most directly influential on the reform agenda that ensued. The most striking recommendation from the McFadden Report was for the creation of a new regulator for Scottish charities. Other key recommendations which echoed proposals made in the Kemp Report and the Dundee University Report were for the creation of a new and publicly available register of charities, a revised definition of "charity" which would incorporate a stronger emphasis on public benefit as a central requirement and the introduction of a new and dedicated legal form for charities. More than two years passed before the (then) Scottish Executive made a clear commitment

---

13 See 1990 Act ss 3 and 4.

14 1990 Act ss 6-8. The powers of investigation into mismanagement and misconduct were conferred on the Lord Advocate, who also had very limited powers of intervention. The Court of Session was given fuller powers of intervention

15 For further information about the Charity Commission, see: *http://www.charity-commission. gov.uk/About_us/About_the_Commission/Our_status_index.aspx*, where it describes itself as "a non-Ministerial Government Department, part of the Civil Service. The Commission is completely independent of Ministerial influence and from the sector it regulates. It has a number of quasi-judicial functions where it uses powers similar to those of the High Court".

16 The Inland Revenue maintained an informal register of charities in Scotland which had received confirmation from the Revenue that their purposes were charitable in terms of the Income and Corporation Taxes Act 1988 s 505.

17 The Report of the Commission on the Future of the Voluntary Sector in Scotland, *Head and Heart* (1997).

18 *Scottish Charity Legislation: An Evaluation* (2000).

19 The Report of the Scottish Charity Law Review Commission, *Charity Scotland* (2001). The Commission was chaired by Ms Jean McFadden.

to the introduction of legislation for the reform of charity law in Scotland and it seems clear that the direct impetus for the commitment to reform was the level of public concern raised over the effectiveness of the existing supervisory and monitoring regimes triggered by the high-profile failures of two large Scottish charities, Moonbeams and Breast Cancer Research (Scotland).[20] In 2003 both charities were the subject of petitions to the Court of Session at the instance of the Scottish Charities Office under the intervention procedures contained in the 1990 Act.[21]

(2) Cabinet Office Strategy Unit review of the third sector and English developments

Reform discussions in respect of charity law did not take place in isolation in Scotland and the debate as to possible reform in England and Wales in respect of a variety of matters relating to charity law[22] was intended to refine the existing system for English and Welsh charities by amendment of the 1993 Act.[23] This process of debate generated a series of reports, the most significant of which were the Deakin Report,[24] the report of the Charity Law Reform Advisory Group,[25] and *Public Action: Private Benefit*.[26] With some modifications,[27] the recommendations in *Public Action: Private Benefit* were directly reflected in the Bill which subsequently became the Charities Act 2006 and developed the English and Welsh charity law regime by amending the 1993 Act. Although *Public Action: Private Benefit* carefully avoided offering any recommendations in respect of charity law in Scotland,[28] the coincidence in the timing of the passage of the separate pieces of legislation in Scotland and England and Wales gave rise to an opportunity for convenient and almost parallel scrutiny of the development and refinement of legislative treatment of similar concepts and issues by the Scottish and Westminster Parliaments.

---

20 See the statement from the Minister for Communities, Scottish Parliament, *Official Report*, cols 133-136 (28 May 2003). See also further statement, Scottish Parliament, *Official Report*, cols 1955-1958 (24 September 2003).
21 The Scottish Charities Office exercised the Lord Advocate's powers under the 1990 Act.
22 In relation to the debate on the definition of "charity" in English law see, e.g., C Mitchell, "Redefining charity in English law" (1999) 13 *Trust Law International* 21.
23 In England and Wales the Charities Act 1960 (c 58) was replaced by the Charities Act 1993 (c 10), which also consolidated the changes to the 1960 Act contained in the Charities Act 1992 (c 41).
24 Report of the Commission on the Future of the Voluntary Sector, *Meeting the Challenge of Change-Voluntary Action in the 21st Century* (1996).
25 *For the Public Benefit? A Consultation Document on Charity Law Reform* (2001).
26 Report of the Strategy Unit of the Cabinet Office, *Public Action, Private Benefit: A Review of Charities and the Wider Not-for Profit Sector* (2002).
27 See the Home Office report, *Charities and Not-for-profits: A Modern Legal Framework* (2003).
28 See *Public Action: Private Benefit* (n 26) para 1.7.

D. THE PASSAGE OF THE 2005 ACT

(1) Restraints on the Scottish Parliament

The Scottish Parliament has competence to legislate in respect of the "creation, operation, regulation and dissolution of charities"[29] and in respect of the fiscal treatment of charities by virtue of local taxation[30] but has no competence to legislate in respect of United Kingdom taxes, as that is a reserved matter. This restraint on the legislative competence of the Scottish Parliament was of particular significance in respect of charities as the existing regulatory regime for Scottish charities, as established by the 1990 Act, relied on the English definition of "charity" which was also the definition relied upon by the Inland Revenue in assessing the provision of tax relief to charities. This was an effective constraint on choice for the Scottish Parliament in respect of its approach to reforming legislation. It could, if it wished, retain, modify or replace the 1990 approach to the definition of "charitable" and "Scottish charity" for the purposes of creation, operation, regulation and dissolution of charities but it could not change the definition of "charity" which would be applied in deciding whether a Scottish charity was entitled to receive relief from United Kingdom taxes. This restraint aside, it is clear that, *prima facie*, the legislative competence and freedom of choice afforded to Scottish Ministers in relation to the promulgation of legislation in respect of the regulation of Scottish charities was, and is, broadly unfettered.

(2) Interaction between the Scottish and English reforming legislation

The timing of the early stages of the respective parliamentary processes for the Scottish and English legislation was remarkably close. The original Charities Bill for England and Wales was issued as a consultation draft in May 2004 and then introduced into the House of Lords in December 2004. The Scottish Bill (which ultimately led to the 2005 Act) was introduced as a consultation paper in June 2004 and introduced into the Scottish Parliament in November 2004. This closeness in terms of process was lost when the English Bill was temporarily dropped at the time of the general election in May 2005.[31] By that stage, however, it was clear that the Scottish Executive had at the very least been mindful of the way issues were being addressed in the draft legislation for England and Wales. In evidence given to the

29 Scotland Act 1998 s 30, Sch 5, Pt II Head C1.
30 1998 Act s 30, Sch 5 Pt II Head A1.
31 But ultimately re-introduced and passed as the Charities Act 2006 (hereafter "the 2006 Act").

Communities Committee at Stage 1, the then head of the Scottish Bill team commented that "the bill sets out a Scottish definition of a charity that is based on the principle of public benefit and is compatible with the definition that the United Kingdom Government is proposing" and that "The charitable purposes have been changed to bring them more into line with those proposed by the Home Office for the rest of the UK".[32] Those remarks were neither questioned nor debated at the Committee Stage of the Scottish legislation and the general acceptance of an approach which either explicitly drew upon or sought to accommodate provisions in the parallel English legislation is an interesting example of an apparently pragmatic approach to the development of Scottish legislation in an area where there were no constitutional requirements for Scottish Ministers to adopt such a compatible position.[33]

E. THE CURRENT LAW

(1) Policy

The Policy Memorandum[34] which accompanied the publication of the Charities and Trustee Investment (Scotland) Bill[35] clearly set out a number of key policy objectives for the legislation.[36] The central objective was to deliver a "robust, proportionate and transparent regulatory framework that satisfies public interest in the effective regulation of charities in Scotland and meets the needs of the Scottish charity sector".[37] The approach to be taken to achieve this end would involve repealing "existing provision for the recognition, supervision and reorganisation of Charities" and creating "one single, modern framework for charity regulation in Scotland".[38] Ministerial interpretation of and comment upon these policy objectives made it even clearer that the new legislation was squarely aimed at protecting the charity brand and that the new Act should protect against "the corrupt use and abuse of the word 'charity' and against the abuse of people who give their time and resources to support good works".[39] Given that the proposed Scottish

---

32 Scottish Parliament, *Official Report*, Communities Committee, col 1474 (8 December 2004).

33 See para D. (1) above.

34 The policy memorandum can be located electronically at *http://www.scottish.parliament.uk/business/bills/32-charitiesTrustee/b32s2-introd-pm.pdf* (hereafter "the Policy Memorandum").

35 As introduced to the Scottish Parliament on 15 November 2004.

36 It should be noted that the Policy Memorandum sets out the objectives determined by the Scottish Executive and not the Scottish Parliament.

37 Policy Memorandum (n 34) para 1.

38 Policy Memorandum (n 34) para 5.

39 Remarks of Ms Johann Lamont, Deputy Minister for Communities, Scottish Parliament, *Official Report*, col 17821 (9 June 2005).

egislation would have no direct impact on the principal benefit associated with charitable status – relief from income tax – it was inevitable that the real focus in the new Act would be on the extent to which the new regulatory structure could achieve these policy objectives and not on how control of the benefits of a concessionary tax regime might influence the use of the charity brand.

(2) Structure of the Act

The 2005 Act is split into four parts. Part 1 introduces the new regime for the regulation and supervision of Scottish charities, doing so in a way which implements a substantial proportion of what was recommended in the McFadden Report, and addresses the principal objectives for the legislation as set out in the Policy Memorandum.[40] The model adopted for the new Scottish regime is much closer to the pre-existing regime in England and Wales, with appropriate modifications to reflect the recommendations set out in McFadden and other specifically Scottish requirements. The key elements of the new regime addressed in Pt I are the creation of a new Scottish charities regulator named OSCR;[41] the creation of a new register of charities in Scotland;[42] controls on charity names;[43] restrictions on references to charitable status;[44] powers of inquiry and intervention for OSCR;[45] powers of intervention for the Court of Session;[46] new arrangements in relation to the reorganisation of charities;[47] a new accounting regime which is broadly similar but not identical to the relevant English regime;[48] a new legal form for charities, to be known as the "Scottish Charitable Incorporated Organisation";[49] detailed provisions in respect of the duties, remuneration and disqualification of trustees;[50] and the creation of a new Charity Appeals Panel[51] to hear appeals from decisions by OSCR[52] before

---

40 Policy Memorandum (n 34) para 1.
41 "Office of the Scottish Charity Regulator": 2005 Act s 1. OSCR replaced the Scottish Ministers' executive agency which had the same name and exercised the powers of the Scottish Ministers under the 1990 Act.
42 2005 Act s 3.
43 2005 Act ss 10-12.
44 2005 Act ss 13-15.
45 2005 Act ss 28-33.
46 2005 Act s 34.
47 2005 Act ss 39-43.
48 2005 Act ss 44-48.
49 2005 Act ss 49-64.
50 2005 Act ss 66-70.
51 Known as SCAP ("the Scottish Charity Appeals Panel"): 2005 Act s 75.
52 2005 Act ss 75-78

any final hearing before the Court of Session.[53] Parts 2, 3 and 4 of the 2005 Act deal respectively with fundraising for benevolent bodies, investment powers for trustees and a range of general and supplementary matters. Part 1 of the 2005 Act undoubtedly deals with the key structural issues and components of the new regulatory regime for Scottish charities established by the 2005 Act but it is arguable that the matters addressed in Pts 2-4 of the Act would have had to be addressed at some stage and that while the Act could arguably have delivered on the key objectives set out in the Policy Memorandum had it only included those issues addressed by Pt I of the Act, the inclusion of Pts 2-4 results in a more rounded and complete approach to the overhaul of Scottish charity law.

(3) OSCR

(a) Substance and form

The first recommendation contained in the McFadden Report was that "a new body should be established in Scotland with powers to determine eligibility for status as a Scottish Charity".[54] This recommendation was followed and OSCR[55] was established as the Scottish Charity Regulator. The creation of OSCR is a direct reference to the Charity Commission in England and Wales and OSCR is modelled on that body, albeit with lesser powers.[56] There was no discussion in the McFadden Report as to the legal form the new body should adopt. The approach taken in the 2005 Act is to establish the office, which is named as OSCR,[57] and then establish a body corporate known as the Scottish Charity Regulator which will be the holder of the office.[58] OSCR operates as a non-ministerial officeholder of the Scottish government, making it a non-ministerial department. This model is relatively uncommon in Scotland and such departments[59] are usually headed by individuals who are senior civil servants. OSCR was the first non-departmental body in Scotland to be established as a body corporate and, as such, it has a relatively conventional

53 The abolition of SCAP has already been announced by Scottish Ministers as part of a broader move by the Scottish Government to merge or abolish a number of bodies scrutinising public services. See the Scottish Government news release (dated 6 November 2008) at *http://www. scotland.gov.uk/News/Releases/2008/11/06103757*. This step will see part of the 2005 Act cease to have effect before the entire Act has come into force (the provisions in respect of the Scottish Charitable Incorporated Organisation are not yet in full force and effect).

54 McFadden Report (n 19), recommendation 1 and paras 1.25 and 1.26.

55 See n 41.

56 See para E. (3)(b) below.

57 2005 Act s 1(1).

58 2005 Act s 1(2).

59 Which include bodies such as the General Register Office for Scotland and the Registers of Scotland.

corporate structure, with a non-executive board, a chairman,[60] a deputy chairman[61] and not less than four members.[62] The nature of the legal form to be adopted by OSCR generated little discussion during the progress of the Scottish Bill but there was considerable discussion as to the level of independence the new body would enjoy, particularly in dealings with the Scottish Ministers, and the structure adopted is an attempt to provide an appropriate degree of distance and separation between OSCR and the Scottish government. During the parliamentary progress of the Scottish Bill the Charity Law Association expressed concerns about the status of OSCR and was of the view that it should be "further from the Scottish Executive". Admittedly, those concerns were focused on the then proposed mechanism which would have obliged OSCR to comply with ministerial directions on the form and content of OSCR's annual report and accounts and the Charity Law Association's own suggestion that OSCR should be under a duty to advise[63] Scottish Ministers.[64] There was clearly recognition within OSCR that the sector within which it would be operating in Scotland would be sensitive as to the degree of separation between the regulator and Scottish Ministers and the chief executive of OSCR, in giving evidence to the Communities Committee, commented that "it was critical to get the balance right between our having sufficient authority and our having sufficient operational independence. I am content that the model which has been developed secures that".[65]

(b) Functions and powers

In terms of functional competence, the similarities between OSCR and the Charity Commission are notable. OSCR determines whether bodies are charitable[66] and, in so doing, applies the new statutory charity test;[67] OSCR maintains a public register of charities[68] which is in many respects similar to the English register;[69] OSCR regulates those names which may and may

---

60 2005 Act s 1(10) Sch 1, para 3(1)(a).
61 2005 Act s 1(10) Sch 1, para 3(1)(b).
62 2005 Act s 1(10) Sch 1, para 1(1).
63 Written evidence from the Charity Law Association (Scottish Parliament, Communities Committee, Stage 1 Report on the Charities and Trustee Investment (Scotland) Bill, 1st Report, 2005 (Session 2) Vol 2 (31st Meeting, Session 2 (2004)) (15 December 2004).
64 Neither of which issues is dealt with in the 2005 Act in the manner originally suggested.
65 Scottish Parliament, *Official Report*, Communities Committee, cols 1680-1681 (26 January 2004).
66 2005 Act s 1(5)(a).
67 2005 Act s 7.
68 2005 Act ss 1(5)(b) and 3.
69 With one significant difference between the two being that any body holding itself out as a charity in Scotland must be registered in Scotland unless the activities undertaken in Scotland are limited in nature: 2005 Act ss 13 and 14.

not be used by charities:[70] OSCR operates a regime for the submission of annual accounts and returns;[71] OSCR has a wide range of new powers in relation to the reorganisation of charities,[72] an inquiry and intervention role;[73] and it has a function very similar to that of the Registrar of Companies to be exercised in respect of the proposed new Scottish Charitable Incorporated Organisation.[74] Each of these functions as allocated to OSCR has a direct parallel in functions exercised in England and Wales by the Charity Commission. In one area, however, there is a notable difference in the nature and extent of the powers attributed to OSCR. The powers of inquiry and intervention given to OSCR in the 2005 Act are more extensive than those which were available under the 1990 Act and they represent a significant extension of the powers which may be exercised by the regulator without having to make reference to the Court of Session. In that respect the regime is closer to the regime operated by the Charity Commission in England and Wales than the previous regime under the 1990 Act. The powers of intervention which are given to OSCR[75] are, however, significantly less extensive than those enjoyed by the Charity Commission. The most obvious example is the short-term duration of OSCR's powers of intervention[76] when compared with the Charity Commission's power to intervene in a potentially permanent manner.[77] OSCR's jurisdiction over bodies which may be subject to inquiry and supervision is, however, wider than the Charity Commission's jurisdiction. OSCR's powers[78] cover not only charities entered in the Scottish Charity Register but also bodies which are not charities but hold themselves out as though they were,[79] whereas the Charity Commission has only a supervisory jurisdiction over those bodies which are charities under English law. The rather different approach adopted in Scotland in respect of supervisory powers and jurisdiction is one of the clearer examples in the 2005 Act where an approach taken in the English regime has not been slavishly copied but modified to reflect a clear Scottish policy objective. In this instance the mix of powers and jurisdictional competence given to OSCR is clearly directed towards allowing OSCR to focus on the prevention of any misleading use of

70 2005 Act ss 10-12.
71 2005 Act ss 45-48.
72 2005 Act ss 39-43.
73 2005 Act ss 28-33.
74 2005 Act ss 49-64.
75 In particular, those under s 31 of the 2005 Act.
76 Under s 31 of the 2005 Act.
77 Charities Act 1993 s 18; and Charities Act 2006 ss 19-21.
78 Under ss 28 and 21 of the 2005 Act.
79 See, e.g., s 28(1)(c) of the 2005 Act.

the charity brand or label and allowing those who are entitled to enjoy the goodwill and benefits of charitable status to do so in an untarnished manner.

(4) The Scottish Charity Register

Before the 2005 Act there was no statutory requirement for any body associated with the regulation of charities in Scotland to maintain any form of central register containing information about charities which could be publicly accessed. The 1990 Act[80] gave the Commissioners of Inland Revenue power to release basic contact details to the public in respect of bodies with charitable status in Scotland[81] but the resulting index of Scottish charities maintained by HMRC was the subject of criticism[82] and the McFadden Report recommended that a Scottish charity register should be established.[83]

In policy terms, the creation of the Scottish Charity Register is a central element of the aim behind the 2005 Act to ensure that the charity label or brand is protected and that there is as much protection as possible against the abuse of the word "charity". Entry to the register is given only to bodies whose purposes satisfy the charity test.[84] Bodies appearing on the register are subject to the protective measures in the 2005 Act dealing with names[85] and bodies appearing in the register are subject to OSCR's compliance regime in respect of the use of the word "charity".[86]

There are considerable similarities between the Scottish Charity Register and the Register of Charities in England and Wales maintained by the Charity Commissioners, but there are also notable differences. Registration under the 2005 Act is not compulsory and it is, therefore, a matter of choice as to whether a body should register as a charity in Scotland. This opens up the possibility that, for example, a body may obtain relief from income and other taxes by being recognised by HMRC as having charitable purposes[87] but choose not to be a Scottish charity by virtue of non-registration in terms of the 2005 Act. In practice there are two strong reasons why many bodies

---

80 Via s 1(1) and (7).
81 The provisions specifically related to "recognised bodies", being bodies recognised by the Inland Revenue Commissioners as entitled to tax relief under s 505 of the Income and Corporation Taxes Act 1988 because of their charitable purposes and also being bodies located in Scotland or established under Scots law.
82 See the Kemp Report para 7.9.3, where particular criticism was made as to the adequacy of the index.
83 McFadden Report (n 19) para 3.18.
84 2005 Act ss 3(1) and 4-9
85 2005 Act ss 10-17.
86 2005 Act ss 3 and 13-15.
87 In terms of ICTA 1988 s 505.

will choose to opt for registration. First, only a body which is registered as a Scottish charity will be allowed to represent itself as a charity in Scotland[88] and, secondly, mandatory rates relief[89] will be available only to a body appearing in the Scottish Charities Register. By contrast, registration is *prima facie* compulsory in England and Wales for all English and Welsh charities.[90]

Another difference between the two registers relates to what might be referred to as "non-domiciled" charities. Under the English regime there is no requirement for a body established outwith England and Wales to register in the Charity Commission's register. The Scottish regime requires any body[91] to register in the Scottish charity register if it intends in any circumstances to refer to itself as a charity in Scotland,[92] which has the direct result that such bodies will be subject to the compliance regime contained in the 2005 Act.

The final difference relates to the fiscal consequences associated with entries in the respective registers. An entry in the Scottish charity register will only be conclusive as to a body's entitlement to mandatory rates relief[93] and a Scottish charity will also have to satisfy HMRC as to whether the body qualifies for tax relief at a UK level in terms of the definitions of "charity" and "charitable purposes" in English law as applied by HMRC.[94] Conversely, an entry in the Charity Commission's register will be conclusive as to a body's entitlement to UK level tax relief as the definitions applied by the Charity Commission and HMRC are one and the same. Central to this difference in approach is, therefore, the application of differing charity tests.

(5) The charity test and public benefit

(a) The nature of the charity test

In assessing the range of possible definitions of "charity" which could be used to determine charitable status for Scottish charities (i.e. the charity test) the Policy Memorandum discussed whether a viable option would have been to rely on a definition set by Westminster.[95] Such an approach would have been

---

88 2005 Act ss 13 and 14.

89 Under s 4(2) of the Local Government (Financial Provisions etc) (Scotland) Act 1962.

90 Subject to limited exceptions in respect of groups such as small charities: see 1993 Act s 3.

91 Irrespective of the location of establishment.

92 With a limited exception for those bodies which are established as "charities" outwith Scotland and have no direct territorial connection with Scotland. See 2005 Act s 14.

93 See n 89.

94 HMRC and OSCR have entered into a Memorandum of Understanding which sets out the basis for co-operation between the two bodies. For details of the Memorandum of Understanding, visit OSCR's website at *http://www.oscr.org.uk/publicationitem.aspx?id=bb71672b-c53b-4ea7-96aa-a56b883d9736*.

95 Policy Memorandum (n 34) para 53.

a straightforward continuation of the approach taken in the 1990 Act and it was noted that "This might be considered particularly helpful in some circles as charity status is currently based on Inland Revenue decisions, based on a UK definition".[96] This approach had not been favoured in the McFadden Report[97] and it was not the approach taken in the Bill and ultimately in the 2005 Act. The Policy Memorandum makes it clear that this was an essentially political decision and remarks that "the regulation of charities is specifically devolved to the Scottish Parliament under the Scotland Act and many people would consider it wholly inappropriate for the Parliament to abdicate this responsibility".[98] This inherently political approach was tempered by a pragmatic compromise which suggested that the proposed new Scottish definition would "for good reasons" (which were not clearly elucidated in the Policy Memorandum) be "very similar and compatible with that currently being proposed for England and Wales".[99] Given this approach, what is the nature of the definition of "charity" used in the 2005 Act to establish charitable status?

There are three central elements to the charity test as it appears in the 2005 Act. A body will meet the test only if, first, "its purposes consist only of one or more of the charitable purposes"[100] set out in the 2005 Act.[101] Secondly, a body must "provide … public benefit in Scotland or elsewhere".[102] Finally, in determining whether the charity test has been met there is no presumption that any particular purpose is to be for the public benefit.[103] Each element of the charity test has substantial similarities to the English definition of "charity" but there are noteworthy differences which merit consideration.

(b) Charitable purposes

The list of charitable purposes set out in the 2005 Act has the same origins as the list which appears in the 2006 Act.[104] The lists are substantially similar but have differences in approach and construction which give rise to notable differences between the two. The Scottish list contains sixteen headings

---

96   Policy Memorandum (n 34) para 53.
97   Which did not favour reliance on "precedents based on English law": McFadden Report (n 19) para 1.30.
98   Policy Memorandum (n 34) para 53.
99   Policy Memorandum (n 34) para 53.
100 2005 Act s 7(1)(a).
101 See s 7(2) of the 2005 Act.
102 2005 Act s 7(2)(b).
103 2005 Act s 8(1).
104 Being the classification set out by Lord Macnaghten in *Pemsel* as drawn from the statement of uses set out in the preamble to the Charitable Uses Act of 1601. See n 5 above.

instead of the thirteen set out in the 2006 Act but this does not mean that the Scots test contains a broader or wider list of charitable purposes. In fact, it is arguable that the Scots test is narrower. The thirteenth head in the 2006 Act[105] and the sixteenth head in the 2005 Act[106] have a broadly similar purpose. That is to allow the extension of each list to permit the inclusion of other purposes which are analogous to existing purposes. There are, however, differences in outcome which arise from the treatment in both Acts of pre-legislative purposes. The approach taken in England and Wales in the 2006 Act is to permit as a charitable purpose not only those purposes listed in the 2006 Act but also those purposes recognised as charitable prior to the 2006 Act list but which are not set out in the 2006 Act list.[107] This mechanism is not mirrored in Scotland which means that the list of purposes set out in the 2005 Act is, with the exception of the analogous purposes extension, definitive. The English approach to charitable purposes is, therefore, wider in two respects. First, it maintains pre-2006 list purposes, which the 2005 Act does not. Secondly, the analogising approaches taken in the respective heads of purpose in the 2006 and 2005 Acts also differ. The English approach allows analogies to be drawn not only with the listed purposes but also the "safety net" protected prior purposes. The English approach is also wider in another respect. In the 2005 Act other purposes may be recognised only if they are "analogous to any of the preceding purposes".[108] The English approach allows analogies to be drawn with purposes which are "within the spirit"[109] of other permitted purposes.

(c) Public benefit

This element of the charity test contains perhaps the clearest manifestation of the political choice to develop a distinct Scottish approach to the definition of "charity" which does not rely on English case law for the purposes of construction and interpretation. The significance of the public benefit element of the test was evidenced by the ministerial comment that it was "the bill's central keystone".[110] The Scottish approach to the public benefit element of the test focuses on the activities undertaken[111] by a body and places the responsibility

---

105 2006 Act s 2(2)(m).
106 2005 Act s 7(2)(p).
107 2006 Act s 2(4)(a).
108 2005 Act s 7(2)(p).
109 2006 Act ss 2(2)(m) and 4(b).
110 Comment from the Minister for Communities at Stage 3 of the Bill. See Scottish Parliament, *Official Report*, Plenary Session, col 17881 (9 June 2005).
111 In the case of a body which has not yet been formed and which has not carried on any activities,

on OSCR to assess whether the activities being pursued by a body in connection with its charitable purposes actually provide public benefit.[112] This may be contrasted with the English approach which continues to focus on a body's purposes. If those purposes, as opposed to activities, provide public benefit as defined by existing case law[113] then the body will satisfy the English public benefit test. The continuing reliance in England and Wales on pre-existing rules and the provision of statutory principles of law in respect of the determination of public benefit may also be contrasted with the approach in the 2005 Act. The Scottish approach to defining "public benefit" is to provide statutory guidance as to those matters in respect of which OSCR must have regard "[i]n determining whether a body provides or intends to provide public benefit".[114] The statutory statement is a distillation of the English criteria, and, although OSCR may draw on the pre-statutory public benefit case law, there is no intention or requirement that OSCR, the Scottish Charities Appeal Panel or the Court of Session should be bound by it.[115] The existence of and application of the differing definition and test were clearly understood from the outset to give rise to the possibility of differing and increasingly divergent interpretations of "charity" in Scotland and England, at least for regulatory purposes.[116] Scottish Ministers accepted that there were "no means of ensuring that these definitions ... will eventually end up similar following ... interpretation by different charity regulators and courts".[117] What the Scottish approach to public benefit attempts to do is to encapsulate in a single section what is dealt with in English law by means of a complex body of law. In so doing, it has to attempt to deal with a wide range of complex and disparate issues. These include what is meant by "a section of the public", the status of bodies campaigning for law reform, the status of self-help organisations,[118] and even more controversial elements such as fee-charging, particularly in relation to schools. While the restraints on related issues such as profit distribution,[119]

OSCR will assess the public benefit criterion on the basis of the body's intended activities. See para 8.1 of OSCR's *Guidance on Meeting the Charity Test* (hereafter "OSCR Guidance").

112   2005 Act s 7(1)(b).
113   See 2006 Act s 3(3).
114   2005 Act s 8(2).
115   See the comments of the Deputy Minister for Communities in evidence to the Communities Committee, Scottish Parliament, *Official Report*, Communities Committee, col 1742 (2 February 2005).
116   Noting that, in respect of relief from income and other taxes, a unitary approach and single definition continue to apply across the United Kingdom.
117   Policy Memorandum (n 34) para 53.
118   See, e.g., *Dingle v Turner* [1972] AC 601.
119   2005 Act s 7(4)(a).

ministerial or Crown control[120] and political campaigning[121] are welcome in the provision of some statutory guidance on restraints on charitable status, the interpretation of the public benefit test is left to OSCR. It is this approach and mechanism which are at the heart of the difference in approach to the treatment of public benefit in the 2005 Act. OSCR is charged with determining whether a body meets the public benefit test set out in the 2005 Act and, in so doing, is subject only to the constraints set out in s 8 of the 2005 Act. These require OSCR to have regard as to how any benefit gained by members of the body or any other person[122] or any disbenefit incurred or likely to be incurred by the public[123] as a result of a body exercising its functions compares with any benefit gained by the public and, where benefit is provided only to a section of the public, whether any condition as to obtaining that benefit[124] is unduly restrictive.[125] These criteria are expressed in the very broadest of terms, with no definitions given in respect of such issues as disbenefit, and OSCR is only bound to have "regard"[126] to these issues. This highlights the fundamental difference in approach between the 2005 Act and the 2006 Act which flows directly from a political decision. In the 2005 Act the public benefit formulation is general in its terms and is an attempt to provide some form of synthesised interpretation of the key principles in the relevant English common law. The English approach is to continue to rely on that body of common law. Leaving aside the political merits or otherwise of adopting this approach, the necessary outcome is fundamentally different. OSCR is placed in a position of having to devise and develop principles in respect of what is meant by "public benefit" as a key requirement of the charity test, whereas the Charity Commission in England and Wales is responsible for making accessible those principles in respect of public benefit which are to be found in English case law. This places responsibility firmly with OSCR in deciding how to interpret and apply the public benefit test. In so doing, OSCR is obliged to issue guidance on how it determines whether a body meets the charity test.[127] OSCR has produced such guidance.[128] Although the guidance produced by OSCR is useful and informative, it is merely guidance. It remains

---

120 2005 Act s 7(4)(b).
121 2005 Act s 7(4)(c).
122 2005 Act s 8(2)(a)(i).
123 2005 Act s 8(2)(a)(ii).
124 Which includes any charge or fee: see 2005 Act s 8(2)(b).
125 2005 Act s 8(2)(b).
126 2005 Act s 8(2).
127 2005 Act s 9.
128 Which is to be found at OSCR's website at *http://www.oscr.org.uk/PublicationItem.aspx?ID =aec25378-896e-448a-bb07-906b8b715a96*.

open for a decision by OSCR as to the application of the charity test to be reviewed[129] and thereafter appealed to the Scottish Charity Appeals Panel[130] and potentially thereafter to the Court of Session.[131] Until decisions by OSCR in respect of the broader charity test or the narrower public benefit element of the test have been subjected to appeal to the Court of Session, the basis upon which such decisions will have been made will continue to be regulatory based guidance.

Given the approach which has been taken to the structure of the charity test and the key public benefit element of the test, there remains the very real prospect that Scots law in this area could develop in a direction which differs fundamentally from that which remains applicable in England and Wales. From a political perspective, such an outcome was accepted as a potential outcome[132] but the consequence attached to the divergent approaches in Scotland and England and Wales is the potential for legal uncertainty at two levels. First, and while there is no evidence at present to suggest that this is the case, OSCR could interpret the provisions in the 2005 Act in a manner which differs fundamentally from the approach deployed in England and Wales in respect of the definition of "charitable purposes" and the associated public benefit requirement. Secondly, even if OSCR construes charitable purposes and public benefit in a manner which is broadly consistent with the approach adopted in England and Wales, until such time as those decisions have been the subject of full review and appeal, there can be no absolute certainty as to the fundamental validity of the interpretations made in respect of purposes and public benefit. The outcome of political choice in the structure of the 2005 Act in this particular area is, therefore, legal uncertainty.

(6) Cross-border charities

The 2005 Act has a strong central policy theme which is protection against "the corrupt use and abuse of the word 'charity'".[133] In attempting to deliver against this policy theme, the 2005 Act recognises that it is important that the Scottish public should be able to donate to and engage with non-Scottish charities operating in Scotland with a level of confidence and security comparable to those bodies which are Scottish charities for the purposes of the 2005 Act. The clearest origins of this approach to protection of the charity brand are

129   2005 Act s 71(a).
130   2005 Act s 76.
131   2005 Act s 78.
132   See n 117 above.
133   See n 39 above.

to be found in the McFadden Report which recommended that "any organisation that wants to get any benefits of being a Scottish Charity – including collecting money from the Scottish public by way of public charitable collections – should be registered with [the Scottish charity regulator]".[134] The substantive manifestation of this policy approach is to be found in ss 13 and 14 of the 2005 Act, the combined effect of which is to require that any body which wishes to represent itself as a Scottish charity must register with OSCR and be subject to the regulatory regime contained in the 2005 Act. There is a limited exception to this requirement which applies when a non-Scottish charity has no significant operations in Scotland. Section 14 of the 2005 Act specifies that a non-Scottish charity may refer to itself as a Scottish charity provided (i) that it does not "occupy any land or premises in Scotland, or (ii) carry out activities in any office, shop or similar premises in Scotland".[135]

The dual registration requirement for non-Scottish charities with a significant Scottish presence is in marked contrast with the approach taken in England and Wales where registration by non-English charities is not mandatory. The requirement to register in Scotland brings with it the full force and effect of the Scottish regulatory regime and means, for example, that an English charity with significant operations in Scotland will be subject to dual regulation by OSCR and the Charity Commission in England and Wales. While both regulators have agreed to "minimise the burden of dual regulation on cross border charities",[136] it does not alter the fact that dual regulation is a direct consequence of the approach taken to non-Scottish charities in the 2005 Act and an undoubted additional burden for such charities. A substantial number of cross-border charities have registered with OSCR.[137] However, the existence of a regulatory compact between the OSCR and the Charity Commission and the implementation by OSCR of a relatively "light touch" monitoring regime for cross-border charities[138] are all potential indicators that the dual registration and regulation mechanisms have not, in the short term, served to act as a disincentive to cross-border charitable activity. It is, however, another example of how the actual effect of certain provisions in the 2005 Act differs from what was originally anticipated[139] and the recent

134 McFadden Report (n 19) paras 3.22-3.28.
135 2005 Act s 14(b)(i) and (ii).
136 Memorandum of Understanding between OSCR and the Charity Commission (2007) para 1.1.
137 More than 450 as of 2009. See OSCR's *Cross Border Monitoring Consultation Evaluation Report* at *http://www.oscr.org.uk/publicationitem.aspx?id=347c4355-3b21-48bc-b1bf-226519983444*.
138 See OSCR's guidance on *Cross border charity regulation in Scotland* at *http://www.oscr.org.uk/publicationitem.aspx?id=f7f4d972-2197-4a0b-9654-b0f1ca664a9e*.
139 For a clear view of what was anticipated by Scottish legislators, see Scottish Parliament, *Official Report*, Communities Committee, Stage 1 Report, vol 1, paras 21, 77 and 78 (2005).

Commission on Scottish Devolution recommended that there should be no such requirement for separate registration.[140]

F. CONCLUSION

The very issue of whether or not to seek charitable status is an issue of choice which faces those charged with the responsibility of governing a body whose purposes and activities may be, or could be intended to be, charitable. In assessing whether to exercise that choice, trustees, committee members or directors of a body will have regard to a range of factors to consider and upon which they will ultimately exercise their choice. These will include the perceived benefits or otherwise of obtaining relief from local and national taxation, the benefits attributable to being associated with the charitable brand and the accessibility which charitable status may provide to income sources and opportunities for engagement which are available only to charities. Balanced against the positive attributes which may be associated with charitable status are the initial and ongoing registration and monitoring requirements, specific accounting obligations and the general responsibilities and duties imposed on charities and their trustees which flow from the regulatory regime now enshrined in the 2005 Act. The 2005 Act incorporates a range of mechanisms which will be broadly familiar to ongoing and putative charities in the form of criteria for the grant of charitable status, potential intervention in the affairs of a charity and standards such as the need to prepare accounts. What marks out the current regime as different from that which prevailed under the 1990 Act is the extent to which it establishes, as a matter of political choice, a regime which has an inherently Scottish approach to certain issues but which seeks to accommodate charitable activity across and within jurisdictions within the United Kingdom by taking account of other legal and regulatory structures and mechanisms, particularly those in England and Wales. The most striking example of this approach is to be found in the Scots approach to the charity test and public benefit. New approaches to the definitions of "charity" and "public benefit" have been deployed in Scotland which have their origins in, but diverge from and may or may not ultimately become significantly different from, those used in England and Wales. At the same time, however, one of the core benefits of charitable

140 See recommendation 5.3 of the Report of the Commission on Scottish Devolution, *Serving Scotland Better: Scotland and the United Kingdom in the 21st Century* (2005) at *http://www.commissiononscottishdevolution.org.uk/uploads/2009-06-12-csd-final-report-2009fbook marked.pdf* (hereafter "the Calman Commission" after its chair, Sir Kenneth Calman).

status – relief from national taxes – continues to be dealt with by HMRC on a national level, based on nationally applicable criteria derived from English common law, and although it has been argued that this approach should be changed,[141] it seems unlikely that any such change will be forthcoming in the foreseeable future. The net result is that bodies which are currently charities or seek to become charities in Scotland will have to exercise their choice to retain or acquire that status on the basis of a legal regime which has an increasingly distinctive Scottish dimension but which is nonetheless strongly influenced by English concepts and principles and a fiscal regime which is unreservedly national. The exercise of choice in respect of charitable status is not, however, solely restricted to those who seek to enjoy that status. OSCR has been afforded a unique role by the Scottish Parliament in the ongoing development of key issues such as the concept of public benefit, and, in so doing, OSCR will be exercising choice, within the framework of the 2005 Act, as to how such pivotal issues develop. Choice is, therefore, at the heart of charity law in Scotland. What will be fascinating to record over the next fifteen years is whether the exercise of choice by all involved in the use and shaping of charity law in Scotland sees a continuing interaction and dialogue between jurisdictions at fiscal, legal, regulatory and user levels or the development of increasingly distinctive Scottish mechanisms, approaches and outcomes.

141   The Calman Commission (n 140) recommendation 5.2.

Public Administration and Services

7 Local Government

Francis McManus°

A. INTRODUCTION

Local government has been described as "big business".[1] With the exception of Northern Ireland, local authorities in the United Kingdom are responsible for education, housing, personal services, transport, planning, fire and rescue services, policing, libraries and museums, leisure and recreation, waste services, consumer protection and environmental health.[2] This chapter examines the role which has been played by the Scottish Parliament in the development of local government.

Local government falls within the legislative competence of the Scottish Parliament.[3] Further, local authorities are creatures of statute, with legislation defining their geographical areas, the way in which their members are elected, how their business must be conducted, the services they can or must

---

° Professor of Law, Edinburgh Napier University. The author would like to thank Bonnie Holligan, Jean McFadden and Jill Stavert for commenting on an earlier draft of this chapter. Thanks are also due to Professor Gavin Little for his very valuable input. However, all errors and other shortcomings remain the sole responsibility of the author.

1 A McConnell, *Scottish Local Government* (2004) 1.
2 C Jeffery, "Devolution and local government" (2006) 36 *Publius: The Journal of Federalism* 57 at 58.
3 Scotland Act 1998 ss 29, 30 and Sch 5.

provide, the powers they may exercise, many of the duties they must fulfil and how they may be controlled by central government and the courts.[4] The key features of local authorities are summarised by Hart who states that they are legally independent entities, which are popularly elected, have independent powers of taxation and are to a certain degree autonomous. He then underscores the significance of local government by stating that local authorities are neither legally nor politically mere agents of central government.[5] It is, therefore, interesting to consider how the Scottish Parliament, which itself is a creature of the Scotland Act 1998, has used its legislative powers in relation to local authorities.

B. HISTORICAL CONTEXT

In the 1980s, there was an uneasy, highly political tension between Labour-controlled local authorities in Scotland and the UK Conservative government which, particularly after the 1987 general election, had very little parliamentary representation north of the Border. Indeed, McFadden argues that Labour councillors in Scotland regarded themselves as the "front-line troops" in a war against Thatcherism.[6] The conflict between central government and local government was at times fought out in the courts. For example, Stirling District Council, Dundee District Council and Lothian Regional Council were "rate capped" by the Secretary of State and subsequently were the subject of action by the Commission of Local Authority Accounts in Scotland.[7] However, the system of two-tier regional and district-level Scottish local government which was established by the Local Government (Scotland) Act 1973 and the Local Government and Planning (Scotland) Act 1982 remained structurally unscathed throughout the 1980s.[8]

In 1991, the Conservative Secretary of State for Scotland announced that the UK government intended to abolish the two-tier structure and replace it with a single-tier system. Its first consultation paper, *The Structure of Local Government in Scotland: The Case for Change. Principles of the New System,* was published in 1991. The government expressed the view that the two-tier system was not readily understood. There was confusion in the mind of the

---

4 A Henney, *Inside Local Government* (1984) 33.

5 W O Hart and J F Garner, *Hart's Local Government and Administration,* 9th edn, (1973) 6.

6 J McFadden, *Local Government Law in Scotland* (2nd edn), (2008) 12. See also Jeffery, "Devolution and local government" 59.

7 *Commission for Local Authority Accounts in Scotland v Stirling District Council* 1984 SLT 442.

8 J McFadden, "The reorganisation of Scottish local government: a councillor's perspective" (1993) 19 *Local Government Policy Making* 4 at 23.

public about which tier was responsible for what.[9] Old allegiances, particularly to the pre-1973 counties and county towns, lived on. Perhaps the most
damning indictment of the two-tier structure was the view that the regional
authorities were too large and that the system resulted in duplication of
services and time-wasting.[10]

Although the 1991 paper was criticised by some for a lack of evidence
and analysis,[11] a further consultation paper, *The Structure of Local Government in Scotland*, was published by the government in 1992. It reiterated the
government's view that the two-tier system of local government should be
reformed.[12] A White Paper, *Shaping the Future*,[13] was then published in 1993.
Notwithstanding the fact that there was doubt in many quarters in Scotland
about the desirability of local government reform, the government introduced the Local Government Bill at the end of the year. It had a protracted
passage through Parliament but received Royal Assent in November 1994.
Crucially, the two-tier system of local government was replaced by a single-
tier system which comprised twenty-nine unitary authorities. The structure
of the three islands councils remained unchanged by the reforms, leaving
thirty-two unitary local authorities in Scotland. This basic structure, which
has its origin in the often bitter political disputes between Scottish local
government and UK central government of the 1980s and early 1990s, has
remained in place to this day.

On the election of the Labour government in 1997, a White Paper[14] setting
out the general principles which would underpin the relationship between
the new Scottish Parliament and Scottish public bodies, including local
authorities, was published. It was the government's view that the Scottish
Parliament should set the national framework within which other Scottish
public bodies operate.[15] Furthermore, the government viewed the establishment of the Scottish Parliament as an opportunity to re-examine the roles
and responsibilities of some of these bodies. It went on to emphasise the
importance of the relationship between the Scottish Parliament, the Scottish
Executive and local authorities in terms of the good governance of Scotland
and the provision of services to the people of Scotland: there was a clear
intention to move on from the conflict which had prevailed during the

9 *The Structure of Local Government in Scotland: The Case for Change* 7.
10 *The Structure of Local Government in Scotland: The Case for Change* 7.
11 McFadden, *Local Government Law in Scotland* (n 6) at 24.
12 At iii.
13 Cm 2267: 1993.
14 *Scotland's Parliament* (Cm 3658: 1997).
15 *Scotland's Parliament* (n 14) at 19.

preceding Conservative administrations. The government agreed to establish an independent committee to advise on how to build relations between the Scottish Parliament, the Scottish Executive and a "strong and effective local government". It had already demonstrated its commitment to the principle of local government by signing the Council of Europe Charter of Self-Government[16] only one month after coming into office. Such commitment and action appears to have been well timed. McFadden argues that some local authority members and officers saw (and, indeed, continue to see[17]) the establishment of a Scottish Parliament as a threat to local government and feared that the Parliament might want to take control of some of its services.[18] It was beyond doubt that the Parliament would carry greater legal and political status than local authorities. Indeed, Bailey and Elliott argue that the devolved institutions are more obviously imbued with constitutional status than their local counterparts: they enjoy a particular status in popular consciousness which derives from the fact that they are bound up with and constitute a focal point for a sense of nationhood.[19] They also enjoy an obvious democratic legitimacy which local authorities do not, in that they were endorsed by the 1997 referendum.[20]

As promised in the 1997 White Paper, a Commission on Local Government was established by Donald Dewar (who was then Secretary for State for Scotland) in 1998, under the chairmanship of Neil McIntosh. The formal remit of the Commission was:

> to examine how to build the most effective relations between local government and the Scottish Parliament and the Scottish Executive so that collectively they can best serve the people of Scotland; and how councils can best make themselves responsive and democratically accountable to the communities which they serve.

The more specific remit of the Commission included consideration of the approaches used by councils to involve communities, alternatives to political management structures, electoral arrangements and the role and remuneration of councillors. The Report of the Commission (which, perhaps surprisingly, devoted simply a mere eight pages to the subject of the relationship between the Scottish Parliament and local government) recognised that the arrival of the Parliament represented a fundamental change in the political

---

16 Strasbourg 15 x 1985.
17 J McFadden and M Lazarowicz, *The Scottish Parliament*, 4th edn (2010) 147.
18 McFadden *Local Government in Scotland* (n 6) at 151.
19 S Bailey and M Elliott, "Taking local government seriously: democracy, autonomy and the constitution" [2009] *CLJ* 436 at 455.
20 Bailey and Elliott, "Taking local government seriously" at 456.

landscape within which Scottish local authorities operate.[21] Indeed, the new Parliament would have the ultimate power of determining what should become of local government. The Commission recognised that relations between the Parliament and local government ought to be conducted on the basis of mutual respect and also parity of esteem, if not formal power and status.

The final main recommendations of the Commission, as far as the relation-ship between local government and the Scottish Executive was concerned, were as follows. First, it recommended the voluntary adoption by all local authorities and the Scottish Parliament of a joint agreement or covenant which set out an agreed statement of the principles defining the working relationship of the respective institutions. A draft covenant was appended to the report, containing the general principles, including: respect for each other's roles, partnership on strategic issues, genuine consultation prior to any major restructuring of local government, full pre-legislative discussion on local government issues, commitment to the principle of subsidiarity, and commitment to openness and accountability.[22] The covenant was to be enforced simply by the political necessity of keeping to it, in contradistinction to it being enforced under black-letter law: there was no suggestion that formal legislation would underpin the relationship.[23] Second, the Report recom-mended the establishment of a separate standing joint conference with equal membership, which would be drawn from local government and the Scottish Parliament. The conference would oversee the covenant and also monitor the working relationship between local government and the Parliament and also that between local government and Scottish Ministers. The rationale for the setting-up of a conference, as opposed to a formal committee, was to give the conference independence from the Scottish Parliament.[24] Third, it was recommended that there should be a joint agreement which would set out the terms of the working relationship between local government and the Scottish Ministers. Interestingly, no covenant or conference has been established. As far as the last-mentioned proposal is concerned, a concordat was reached between the Convention of Scottish Local Authorities (COSLA) and the Scottish Ministers. The concordat is not binding on individual local authorities. The concordat sets out the relationship between the Scottish Government and local government based on mutual respect and partnership.

21 McIntosh Report, *Moving Forward Local Government and the Scottish Parliament* (1999) at 11.
22 McIntosh Report (n 21) at 46.
23 McIntosh Report (n 21) at 15.
24 McFadden, *Local Government Law in Scotland* (n 6) at 154.

C. LEGISLATION OF THE SCOTTISH PARLIAMENT

The Scotland Act 1998 made no express provision which affected the future status, structure or functioning of local government in Scotland. Local government (with the exception of the local government franchise)[25] was not, however, designated a "reserved matter" under the Act. Therefore, responsibility for all aspects of local government automatically came within the legislative competence of the Scottish Parliament. The control which the Parliament can wield over local government is therefore considerable. Indeed, Himsworth observes that it would clearly be within the legislative competence of the Parliament fundamentally to reorganise the structure of local government and, furthermore, because nearly all the functions of local authorities are also within its competence, the Parliament can modify these functions by adding new ones and taking others away.[26] Only a small number of local authority functions are outwith the Parliament's competence (for example, consumer protection and weights and measures).[27] Therefore, it has wide scope to exercise its legislative imagination. It is, however, perhaps inevitable that the Parliament's law making would be influenced by a number of contextual factors, not least the long tradition of local government in Scotland and also the recent history of central-local government relations which had not always been amicable.

(1) Conduct of councillors

One of the first Acts passed by the fledgling Scottish Parliament was the Ethical Standards in Public Life etc (Scotland) Act 2000 (hereafter "the 2000 Act"). The 2000 Act introduced a new ethical framework for those in public life, such as local authority elected members. The concept of a code of conduct was not a new idea in the local government context. Indeed, a non-statutory code, which governed the conduct of elected members in local government throughout the United Kingdom, had been issued by the government in 1975. However, this had simply provided informal guidance. McFadden observes that its existence was not widely known among either elected members or the general public. Furthermore, few councils regularly brought the provisions of the code to their members' attention. Councillors were, therefore, not as conscious of its provisions as they might have been.[28]

---

25 Scotland Act 1998 Sch 5.
26 C Himsworth, "Local government in Scotland", in A McHarg and T Mullen, *Public Law in Scotland* (2006) 154 at 168.
27 Himsworth, "Local government in Scotland" (n 26) at 168.
28 McFadden, *Local Government Law in Scotland* (n 6) at 134.

Prompted by the recommendations of the Widdicombe Committee on the Conduct of Local Authority Business,[29] the National Code of Local Government Conduct was placed on a statutory footing under the Local Government and Housing Act 1989.[30] However, notwithstanding the fact that the National Code was given more gravitas, no formal machinery for enforcing it was put in place.

The main significance of the 2000 Act is, therefore, that it effectively gave "teeth" to the old councillors' code. The Act places a duty on the Scottish Ministers to issue a code of conduct for councillors,[31] and the code was duly published in 2002. [32] A general duty is placed on every council to promote the observance of high standards of conduct by its members and also to assist them in observing the code. The principles which are contained within the code require to be achieved in accordance with any guidance which is issued by the Standards Commission for Scotland.[33] The office of Chief Investigation Officer (CIO) was established.[34] The main function of the CIO is to investigate, and also to report to the Commission on, cases where it is alleged that a councillor[35] has breached the code. The CIO has the same powers as the Court of Session when dealing with civil proceedings to enforce the attendance and examination of witnesses and the production of documents.[36] If a councillor has breached a relevant code, the Standards Commission is required to impose one of three sanctions, namely: censure, suspension or disqualification.[37] An appeal against any sanction which is imposed lies to the sheriff principal.[38] The fundamental change which the Act brings about is that sanction in the face of misconduct does not, as was the case previously, lie with the electorate but, rather, with an unelected regulatory body.[39]

A further important provision of the 2000 Act is the duty which is placed on local authorities to both establish and maintain a register of councillors' interests and to make the register available for public inspection.[40] The inter-

29 Cm 9797: 1986 at para 6.23.
30 Section 31 (repealed).
31 2000 Act s 1.
32 The key principles of the code are set out at *Councillors' Code of Conduct* (2002) para 2.1.
33 2000 Act s 5.
34 2000 Act s 9.
35 Or member of a public body: C Himsworth and C O'Neill observe that the majority of complaints have concerned councillors: *Scotland's Constitution: Law and Practice*, 2nd edn (2009) 216.
36 2000 Act s 13.
37 2000 Act s 19.
38 2000 Act s 22.
39 McFadden and Lazarowicz, *The Scottish Parliament* (n 17) at 157.
40 2000 Act s 7. See also the Ethical Standards in Public Life etc (Scotland) Act 2000 (Register of Interests) Regulations 2003, SSI 2003/135, as amended by SSI 2003/203.

ests that require to be registered may be financial or non-financial.[41] The code also places a responsibility on councillors to make a declaration of their interests.[42] The effect of such a declaration is to preclude the councillor from participating in discussion and voting. If the declaration relates to a financial interest, the councillor is also required to leave the meeting room until discussion of the item of business is concluded.[43]

The 2000 Act also abolishes[44] the controversial surcharge on both elected members and officials, replacing such a penalty with sanctions similar to those which obtain in relation to a breach of the councillors' code.

(2) The Scottish Public Services Ombudsman

Members of the public in Scotland who had sustained injustice as a result of acts of maladministration by local authorities had been able to complain to the Local Government Ombudsman for Scotland since 1975. The Scottish Public Services Ombudsman Act 2002 (hereafter "the 2002 Act") replaced this scheme[45] and, in effect, introduced a "one-stop shop" by means of which complaints against all Scottish public authorities could be made.[46] On the face of it, the 2002 Act makes little difference to the substantive powers of the ombudsman to regulate the conduct of local authorities. Thus, after completing an investigation the ombudsman is required to send a report to Scottish Ministers and also lay a report before the Scottish Parliament:[47] even in the face of a local authority failing to implement a recommendation of the ombudsman, the sole action which the ombudsman can take is to lay a special report before the Parliament.[48] But the 2002 Act does bring local authorities into a special relationship with the Parliament. No formal machinery of enforcement is introduced by the Act, and neither the Scottish Government nor the Parliament can impose sanctions under statute in the face of maladministration on the part of a local authority – the ultimate sanction lies in the hands of the local electorate. However, the very fact that the ombudsman now has the power to lay such a report before the Scottish Parliament sends the message to local authorities that they are responsible not only to the local electorate but also to the Parliament and, therefore, the Scottish people.

41 See *Councillors' Code of Conduct* (n 32) s 4.
42 *Councillors' Code of Conduct* (n 32) s 5
43 *Councillors' Code of Conduct* (n 32) para 5.16.
44 The Act amends the Local Government (Scotland) Act 1973 by adding a new s 103.
45 Scottish Public Services Ombudsman Act 2002 Sch 6.
46 See, generally, B Thompson, "The Scottish Public Services Ombudsman: revolution or evolution", in McHarg and Mullen, *Public Law in Scotland* (n 26) 281 at 290-304.
47 Scottish Public Services Ombudsman Act 2002 s 15(1).
48 Scottish Public Services Ombudsman Act 2002 s 16(3).

Notwithstanding this provision, it may be argued that the Scottish Public Services Ombudsman remains as "toothless" as his predecessor, at least in relation to the measures which he can take if a local authority declines to implement his recommendations. Indeed, some commentators[49] have argued that the 2002 Act renders the ombudsman weaker than before, in that the Local Government Ombudsman could require a local authority which had failed to remedy an injustice to publish a statement in a local newspaper which gave details of the ombudsman's recommendations and explain why such recommendations had not been followed.[50] Furthermore, prior to 2002, where a councillor had been engaged in maladministration by reason of which he breached the National Code of Local Government Conduct, the ombudsman had the power to name the councillor concerned.[51] No similar provisions are made in the 2002 Act.

(3) Local government elections

The Scottish Local Government (Elections) Act 2002 introduced a four-year cycle for local government elections, in contrast to the previous three-year cycle. This Act also made provision for the synchronisation of polling at local government and Scottish Parliament elections.[52] However, the system which was put in place by the Act caused confusion among some of the electorate as a result of which, during the 2007 Scottish Parliament and local government elections, many ballot papers were rejected as invalid, much to the annoyance of the candidates and political parties. An independent review of the Scottish parliamentary and local government elections[53] recommended the de-coupling of Scottish Parliament and local government elections. The main reasons which the review body gave for such a change was that de-coupling would not only reduce confusion among voters, but also prevent national issues from dominating local issues at election time.[54] These recommendations were given effect by the Scottish Local Government (Elections) Act 2009 which severed the link between the two types of election. Local government elections and Scottish Parliament elections are no longer to be

---

49 McFadden *Local Government Law in Scotland* (n 6) at 130.
50 Local Government (Scotland) Act 1975 s 29 (as amended).
51 Local Government (Scotland) Act 1975 s 32.
52 The Act also made provision, *inter alia,* for new electoral procedures and allowed the Scottish Executive to run pilot schemes of innovative electoral procedures at particular local government elections.
53 Which was chaired by Ron Gould and reported in October 2007.
54 *Independent Review of the Scottish Parliamentary and Local Government Elections* (3 May 2007) at 115.

held in the same year. In future, local government elections are to take place at the mid-point of the Scottish Parliament elections.

Arguably the most important legislative reform of Scottish local government which has been made by the Scottish Parliament is the replacement of the so-called "first past the post" or relative majority voting system in local government elections. The McIntosh Report advocated that the existing system of electing councillors should be replaced by a system of proportional representation.[55] In turn, the Kerley Working Group advocated that the form proportional representation should take should be that of the single transferable vote (STV).[56] Many members of the Labour Party were of the view that proportional representation would lead to instability in terms of administrative control in local government and, perhaps more to the point, would lose Labour seats.[57] Notwithstanding this, the STV system of election featured in the partnership agreement between the Scottish Labour Party and the Scottish Liberal Democrats in 2003, which was the basis of their coalition for office as the Scottish Executive.

Despite Labour Party concerns, the Local Governance (Scotland) Act 2004[58] (hereafter "the 2004 Act") introduced the STV system to Scottish local government. Under the STV system of voting, each ward is multi-member. The number of councillors to be returned for each ward is three or four as determined by delegated legislation.[59] The system is controversial in as much as it breaks the member-ward link which was valued by most councillors.[60] The STV system in local government elections came into effect in 2007. The Scottish Labour Party's fears as to the consequences of an STV system coming into existence were realised in the local government elections of that year which saw that party losing 161 seats while the SNP gained 182. This may suggest that the Labour Party's historically strong performance in local elections and consequent strong grip over Scottish local government may have been attributable in no small measure to the "first past the post" electoral system, rather than majority support from the electorate. The advantages of the STV system for smaller parties were also evident in the performance of the Green Party (which had not contested the local elections in 2003) securing eight seats.[61] Indeed, McFadden observes that the STV system

55 McIntosh Report (n 21) 25.
56 Kerly Report, *The Report of the Renewing Local Democracy Working Group* (2000) 63.
57 McFadden, *Local Government Law in Scotland* (n 6) at 32.
58 Local Governance (Scotland) Act 2004 (hereafter "the 2004 Act") ss 1-3.
59 2004 Act s 1(2).
60 McFadden, *Local Government Law in Scotland* (n 6) at 32.
61 For more details of the 2007 local government election, see McFadden, *Local Government Law*

has changed the face of local government in Scotland. While she concedes that the STV system is more representative than the "first past the post" system, with the former system bringing about proportionality in the political composition of local authorities, it has also led to the decline of single-party administration and an increase in the likelihood of coalitions.[62] Although it is obviously disliked by the Labour Party, others would perhaps consider it more advantageous. It is certainly a significant and profound reform of the system of local government in Scotland.

The other changes which were made by the 2004 Act include the removal of the disqualification of local government officers standing for election to their employing authority.[63] The Act also reduces the age at which one can stand for election to a local authority from twenty-one to eighteen,[64] and removes the automatic disqualification of officials from participating in a range of political activities by virtue of the level of their salary.[65]

(4) Local government service provision

(a) Best value

With regard to the role of local authorities in Scotland as "providers" of public services, the most significant statute which has been passed by the Scottish Parliament to date is the Local Government in Scotland Act 2003 (hereafter "the 2003 Act"). Arguably, the most important provision of the 2003 Act relates to the principle of "best value" in local government service provision. Such a concept is not new. Indeed, the need for local authorities to make efforts to secure more efficient services lies in the concept of compulsory competitive tendering which was introduced by the Conservative government in the 1980s, in order to reduce the amount of work which was carried out in-house by councils' own workforces and to increase the amount of work which was carried out by the private sector.[66] The expression "best value" is a term of art and is defined as the "continuous improvement of the performance of the authority's functions".[67] In securing "best value" a

---

in Scotland (n 6) at 167.

62 McFadden, *Local Government Law in Scotland* (n 6) at 168. McFadden observes that of the twenty-seven local authorities in Scotland, no party is in overall control. In a very few local authorities a single party attempts to run the council as a minority administration but in most cases there are coalitions formed from alliances of various parties and independents.

63 2004 Act s 7.

64 2004 Act s 8.

65 2004 Act s 9.

66 McFadden, *Local Government Law in Scotland* (n 6) at 57.

67 2003 Act s 1(2).

local authority is required to maintain an appropriate balance between the quality of its performance of its functions, the cost to the authority of that performance and also the cost to individuals who are charged for the service which is provided.[68] In maintaining such a balance, the authority is required to have regard to efficiency, effectiveness, economy and also the need to meet equal opportunities requirements.[69] Furthermore, the authority has an obligation to discharge its duties in a way which contributes to the achievement of sustainable development.[70] In securing "best value" the authority is required to have regard to any guidance which is provided by the (then) Scottish Executive.[71] While the Act is rather brief on the subject of "best value", the guidance by the Scottish Executive which was published in 2004 is wide ranging in its setting of performance outcomes by means of which an authority can demonstrate that it has secured "best value".[72] The Act also extends the roles of both Audit Scotland and also the Accounts Commission for Scotland to include consideration of best value.[73]

(b) Community planning

The amorphous concept of "best value" in the 2003 Act is complemented by that of "community planning". The Act[74] places a duty on, *inter alia*, a local authority to maintain and facilitate a process by means of which the public services which are provided in the local authority area and planning activity takes place after consultation among all the public bodies which are responsible for providing those services and also with relevant community bodies. The authority is also placed under a duty to publish from time to time reports on how it has implemented the community planning process in its area.[75]

Another significant provision which is made by the Act is the power of a local authority to advance the well-being of the community, which implements one of the recommendations of the McIntosh Report.[76] The 2003 Act[77] gives a local authority power to do anything which it considers is likely to promote or

---

68 2003 Act s 1(3).
69 2003 Act s 1(4).
70 2003 Act s 1(5).
71 2003 Act s 2.
72 The guidance also covers sustainable development and equal opportunities.
73 2003 Act ss 3-5.
74 2003 Act s 15.
75 2003 Act s 16.
76 The concept of general competence for local authorities has its origins in art 4(2) of the European Charter of Self-Government which was drawn up by the Council of Europe in 1985. See C Himsworth, "New devolution: New dangers for local government" (1998) 24 *Scottish Affairs* 6 at 15.
77 2003 Act ss 20-22.

improve the well-being of its area and the persons within that area, bringing Scotland into line with the rest of the EU.[78] The power is, however, circumscribed. For example, a local authority may not do anything which it is prohibited from doing by statute,[79] and the authority may not use its general power to promote or improve the well-being of the community if the exercise of such power would unreasonably duplicate anything which someone else has the duty or power to carry out.[80] Nor may the authority impose a tax or charge in order to advance the well-being of the community.[81] Power is given to the Scottish Government to take enforcement action against local authorities which exceed the power of general competence which has been conferred on them by the Act.[82] Interestingly therefore, control over local authorities which abuse their legal powers is removed, at least in the first instance, from judicial control in the form of judicial review to political control in the form of the Scottish Executive.[83]

D. CONCLUSION

In relation to the organisation and structure of Scottish local government, and in sharp contrast to the position south of the Border (where the Local Government Act 2000 required most councils in England and Wales to choose between an elected mayor and executive, an appointed leader and executive, or an elected mayor and council manager) the Scottish Parliament has been largely non-interventionist, preferring to allow local authorities to review and also reform their own organisational and decision-making structures on an informal basis.[84] In the aftermath of the strongly politicised statutory re-structurings of the 1980s and early 1990s, the Parliament has, perhaps wisely, not sought to reform the structure of Scottish local government to any significant extent.[85]

78 McFadden and Lazarowicz, *The Scottish Parliament* (n 17) 152.
79 2003 Act s 22(2).
80 2003 Act s 22(4).
81 2003 Act s 22(7).
82 2003 Act s 26.
83 See McFadden, *Local Government in Scotland* (n 6) at 57.
84 See the report of the Leadership Advisory Panel which was established by the Scottish Executive (and reported in 2001), the remit of which was to advise councils on the review of their decision-making and policy development processes and the working practices which support those processes: Scottish Local Government's Self-Review of its Political Management Structures (2001) (the McNish Report).
85 Although the Planning (Scotland) Act 2006 gives Scottish Ministers increased powers in relation to the development of land, substantially limiting the powers of local planning authorities in relation to a development which is designated as a national development. Furthermore, the

While the fears which were entertained by some that the new Scottish Parliament would constitute a powerful rival to local government have, thus far, proved to be unfounded, some of the legislation which has been passed in the Parliament's first decade has, however, been significant and controversial. In particular, the Parliament has implemented fundamental reform of the electoral system for Scottish local government, which has given rise to a profound change in its political composition. Other legislation dealing with matters such as standards of conduct for councillors and service provision is less contentious, and in the case of provision for the review of local government maladministration perhaps less than effective, but it is nonetheless positive and worthwhile in its objectives.

Looking to the future, however, it remains possible that the Parliament could legislate to re-allocate local authority functions that have traditionally been considered core areas. For example, it is certainly possible that the Scottish Parliament could establish a national police force. In the final analysis, therefore, while the future existence of Scottish local government is secure, it may be that its powers will be eroded by the Parliament: the first ten years of relatively non-interventionist law-making may not necessarily continue. Indeed, McFadden argues that there is a feeling in some local government circles that both the Scottish Parliament and the Scottish Government are of the opinion that if services require to be improved, they require to be in central government control:[86] in future, there may be doubt about the value of the "localness" of Scottish local government.[87]

Transport (Scotland) Act 2005 institutes a National Transport Agency which has responsibility for delivering concessionary fare schemes and also for co-ordinating public transport in Scotland, a matter which was formerly a local authority function.

86 McFadden, *Local Government Law in Scotland* (n 6) at 170.

87 Parenthetical reference should be made to the present freezing of the council tax by the Scottish Executive with a financial penalty for local authorities who do not freeze it. This has reduced the percentage which councils can raise from 20% to about 15%, thereby eroding the "government" element of local government.

8 Housing

Peter Robson[*]

A. INTRODUCTION
B. BACKGROUND
C. THE SCOTTISH PARLIAMENT AND HOUSING
(1) Homelessness
(2) Regulation of landlords
(3) Repairs
D. CONCLUSION

A. INTRODUCTION

Housing has been a major feature of the first ten years of the Scottish Parliament. Legislation in relation to housing has been a major part of the work of the Holyrood legislature. There have been no fewer than three major pieces of legislation focusing solely on housing, as well as housing featuring significantly in three other Acts. Indeed, one of the first pieces of legislation to reach the statute books from the new Scottish Parliament was the Housing (Scotland) Act 2001 and, at the time of writing, a Housing (Scotland) Act is likely to be passed in 2010. Looking, then, at the overall picture of the law, policy and economics of housing in this era, it is possible to make some kind of initial judgment on the first decade of housing under devolution. In crude terms, the lot of those in Scotland who are homeless, in poor-quality housing or suffering from absentee landlords is probably better than their equivalents in England and Wales over the first decade of the twenty-first century. However, the effectiveness of the changes continues to lie in the level of resources devoted to them and, just as in William Kelso's Paisley,[1] what happens on the ground in the lives of badly housed or homeless citizens depends not on what powers are enshrined in statute but on whether financial resources make these provisions meaningful.

---

* Professor of Social Welfare Law, University of Strathclyde.
1 W Kelso, *Sanitation in Paisley: A Record of Progress 1488-1920* (1922).

B. BACKGROUND

The regulation of housing has been confronted by common elements as well as differences in the past. These have been legal as well as cultural. There are some areas of property law where there are major differences between Scots and English law and where separate legislation has a long tradition. These differences would be expected whether or not there were any form of devolution. This chapter is not concerned with these issues such as registration of title, land conditions and the nature of land tenure.[2] Nor is the principal focus on the contrasting fortunes of owner-occupiers over this period. The differences in their experiences are largely outwith the control of the devolved government and tell us little about a possibly distinctive Scottish approach to housing.

In terms of rental property, the core concepts in Scots land law and also landlord and tenant law are quite distinct from the English system and dictate that this aspect of social policy be devolved in the first place. These include in particular the long established concepts of tacit relocation and the automatic obligation to provide habitable and tenantable residential accommodation. These have no direct equivalent in English law. Most of the areas in the modern regulation of housing, however, have a purely statutory basis which has overlaid common law and which often involves no specific Scots law element. In pre-Holyrood statutory housing interventions, three distinct approaches to housing legislation were encountered. There was an initial tendency for the solutions to housing issues to be addressed in common legislation. Hence we find the Rent Acts which took the issues of rent fixing and security of tenure out of traditional market mechanisms being covered by common British legislation. This occurred, with one minor exception,[3] from 1915 through to the Rent Act 1965.[4] From the mid-1960s there was a trend over the next twenty years for there to be separate but parallel legislation.[5]

---

2 I am keenly aware that the impact of the changes in relation to feuing conditions and how common conditions in tenement dwellings are enforced has an impact on the daily lives of many of us living in Scotland. The twenty-first-century changes, however, are not reliant on the existence of the Scottish Parliament for their implementation and involve technical changes rather than issues of policy. For further information, see L Xu, "Problems in the law of the tenement" [2008] *JR* 131.

3 The regulation of furnished accommodation was initially excluded from the Rent Acts. Control was, however, introduced in Scotland in 1943 with the Rent of *Furnished Houses* (Scotland) *Act 1943.* An English equivalent, the *Furnished Houses* (Rent Control) *Act,* was introduced in 1946.

4 Increase of Rent and Mortgage Interest (War Restrictions) Act 1915; Rent Act 1920; Rent Act 1923; Rent Act 1945; Rent Act 1957; Rent Act 1965.

5 **England and Wales**   **Scotland**
  Rent Act 1968   Rent (Scotland) Act 1971
  Rent Act 1977   Rent (Scotland) Act 1984
  Housing Act 1980   Tenants' Rights etc (Scotland) Act 1980

Finally, in the period from 1986, distinct local solutions have been sought in the housing field and quite significant differences have developed in the rules on either side of the border in relation to homelessness.[6]

Any examination of the development of housing in Scotland needs to acknowledge the very specific historical circumstances and make-up of the housing stock in Scotland as it developed in the twentieth century. The most important interventions into the market, which I would describe as constituting modern housing law, started to take place in the early twentieth century. At that time, in Scotland 53.2% of the housing stock consisted of one- or two-room houses, compared with only 7.1% in England. Overcrowding occurred in 45.1% of Scottish dwellings compared with 9.1% of their English equivalents.[7]

Starting with a base of 90% private rental housing in 1914, the investment in public-sector housing was much greater than that in England and Wales, peaking in 1981 at 55% of stock compared with a figure of 29.1% south of the Border.[8] The dynamism to create municipal housing for the benefit of local people was very much dependent on local initiatives.[9] In addition, the Scottish Special Housing Association was set up in 1937, expanding the role of the Scottish National Housing Company and with the express purpose of providing accommodation to promote new economic activity.[10] It promoted new construction systems and built up a stock of some 100,000 houses by the mid-1970s.[11] By contrast, housing association activity was very sporadic.[12] Although traditionally often described as the "third arm of housing",[13] this

---

Housing Act 1985   Housing (Scotland) Act 1987
Housing Act 1988   Housing (Scotland) Act 1988
Note, however, that the common approach in the case of the Housing (Homeless Persons) Act 1977 was displaced by separate legislation in the form of the Housing Act 1985 and Housing (Scotland) Act 1987. The special circumstances of this legislation and its application, at the last minute, to Scotland is well documented: P Robson and M Poustie, *Homeless People and the Law* (1996) 42-46, and P Gibson, "How Scotland got the Housing (Homeless Persons) Act", in N Drucker and H Drucker (eds), *Scottish Local Government Yearbook* (1979).

6 Robson and Poustie, *Homeless People* (n 5) *passim*.
7 Figures from the 1911 Census, cited in A Murie, "Scottish housing: the context", in D Sim (ed), *Housing and Public Policy in Post-Devolution Scotland* (2004) at 24.
8 D Maclennan, "Owner occupation", in C Jones and P Robson (eds), *Owner Occupation: New Patterns, Policies and Parliament* (2001) at 152.
9 Barrhead Community Council, *Housing the Heroes: The Struggles of a Small Town, 1919-1939* (undated, c 1985).
10 T Begg, *50 Special Years: A Study in Scottish Housing* (1987) at 58. Chapters 2 and 3 in particular provide an account of inter-war social housing developments in Scotland.
11 D Robertson, "Scottish Homes: a legacy", in C Jones and P Robson (eds), *Health of Scottish Housing* (2001) at 112.
12 R Young, "Housing associations: the new kid on the block", in Jones and Robson, *Health of Scottish Housing* (n 11) at 90.
13 J Short, *Housing in Britain: the Post-War Experience* (1982) 189.

sector remained very minor in terms of its contribution to housing stock until the mid-1970s. Thereafter, numbers of completions rose from 1,859 houses in 1979/1980 to 2,840 in 1989/1990[14] and stock increased from 1.7% of housing in Scotland in 1981 to 4.5% in 1996.[15]

Similarly, the shift in the Housing (Scotland) Act 1988 to provide a local frame of regulation in the form of Scottish Homes provided a level and form of policy-making outwith the day-to-day control of politicians. Decisions on such crucial issues as development were thus taken for a decade by a body described as "a Tory quango whose prime objective was the privatisation of public sector housing in Scotland".[16] Merely looking at the bland text of the Housing (Scotland) Act 1988 does not disclose the full significance of this development and its consequences for Scottish housing. What the next decade witnessed was the shift in the role of Scottish Homes. While SSHA had a strategic role in the expansion of publicly owned housing in Scotland in locations where they were required for reasons of economic expansion, Scottish Homes' role was to enable rather than to retain a strategic role as a landlord. Hence its stock was transferred principally to newly formed housing associations.[17] It could be described as a "national housing agency" but was initially focused on ceasing to be a landlord.

Housing regulation is resources dependent. The extent to which the words of the Code of Guidance on homelessness provide useful pointers to likely outcomes or merely improbable aspirations depends on structural factors. The statement, for instance, that under the Homeless Persons (Unsuitable Accommodation) (Scotland) Order 2004 local authorities "cannot put households with children and pregnant women into 'unsuitable' temporary accommodation unless exceptional circumstances apply"[18] cannot be seen as a straightforward guarantee that accommodation will be suitable. It takes its meaning from the nature and extent of the pool of accommodation which those allocating housing have at their disposal. Reports and case law from the past suggest that this has not always been impressive.[19]

Hence in all the significant areas where the Scottish Parliament has been active – homelessness, expansion of tenants' rights to decent accommoda-

14 Scottish Homes, *Statistical Supplement 1989/90* (1990), cited in Young, "Housing associations" (n 12) at 98.
15 Young, "Housing associations" (n 12) at 105.
16 Robertson "Scottish Homes: a legacy" (n 11) at 110.
17 Robertson "Scottish Homes: a legacy" (n 11) at 120. Not all the transferees adhered to the standard housing association model but encompassed not-for-profit structures like Waverley Homes and WESLO, with tenant directors as well as employee and independent board members.
18 Code of Guidance (2005) para 9.9.
19 *R v Wycombe DC ex p Holmes* (1988) 22 HLR 150; *R v Brent LBS ex p Omar* (1991) 23 HLR 446.

tion and regulation of landlords – we need to take into account not only the regulations incorporated in the legislation but also the likelihood of these rules and directives being rendered effective.

C. THE SCOTTISH PARLIAMENT AND HOUSING

As indicated above, there have been four major pieces of legislation impacting upon the governance of housing in Scotland. Space here dictates that an overview is provided rather than a section-by-section analysis of this welter of legislative material. The principal broad themes that strike me as of major impact are the changes in relation to homelessness, regulation and repairs. They provide a distinct approach to housing in Scotland and mean that a Scots-trained housing practitioner returning from a ten-year sojourn in England or Wales would find the legal framework of Scottish housing transformed. Focusing on these broad categories rather than on trying to cover every single statutory change means that some fascinating developments outwith the broad themes cannot receive extensive analysis. The first extension of tenancy succession rights in Britain to same-sex couples and the single social tenancy are examples.[20] These, however, broadly support the thesis that Scots housing law has adopted an agenda of expanding tenants' rights more readily than has occurred in England.

(1) Homelessness

The Scottish Executive, shortly after commencing its life, set up a Housing Task Force. Part of the remit was to examine the legislation in relation to homelessness in Scotland. There had long been a sense among homelessness practitioners in Scotland that the problems of London and specific "magnet" authorities in England had had a disproportionate impact on policy-making in relation to homelessness. In practice the tests were operated in a random and irrational way and diverted attention away from the issue of provision of affordable homes onto an agenda of legal pecksniffery and moral evaluation as exemplified by "intentionality".[21] The most dramatic result of the shift of homelessness legislation to the Scottish Parliament was to restore the original principles underlying Stephen Ross's 1977 Housing (Homeless Persons) Private Member's Bill. This had originally envisaged an uncomplicated right to housing for homeless applicants. The limiting factors – the hurdles in the

---

20 Housing (Scotland) Act 2001, Pt 2; s 22 and Sch 3 para 2(1)(a) (succession).
21 S Halliday, *Judicial Review and Compliance with Administrative Law* (2004).

"homeless persons' obstacle race"[22] – of priority need, local connection and intentionality were introduced during the passage of the legislation. Given the fact that the government of the day supported the Bill but itself operated as a minority administration, these limiting factors had to be accepted or the principle would have been lost.

The shift came in two stages. In the first place, *ad hoc*-ery was banished. Local authorities no longer simply had enforceable duties to priority non-intentional homeless applicants. They were required to have a strategy. This was built on in the 2003 legislation in a gradualist way, allowing councils to develop their response to homelessness. In terms of crude numbers, the nature of applications has changed and the level has steadily increased over the years[23] and the numbers on Scottish waiting lists have reached 200,000. It is clear that while the existence of planned strategies is an advance on early practice, it can only provide a more coherent plan for priority for those still waiting.

In the short term, the categories of those in priority need was extended to include a whole range of people who might have qualified as "vulnerable" through special reason[24] but where litigation was often required to establish their status. As from 2012, the restrictions on who had to be provided with accommodation or assisted into accommodation will disappear. As far as intentionality is concerned, there will no longer be a duty to investigate whether a person is deemed to have brought the misfortune on their own heads. The astonishing amount of litigation and the technical gymnastics evolved in the first thirty-five years of this concept may become a thing of the past. Authorities will have the option of looking at this issue and, where there is a finding of intentionality, have the possibility of granting short-term tenancies through the mechanism of the short Scottish secure tenancy[25] and the related housing support appropriate to such a tenancy.

It is, of course, impossible, writing in 2010, to assess how the abolition of the priority need and intentionality restrictions changes will work out in

22 A metaphor used by P Robson and P Watchman in "The homeless persons' obstacle race" (1981) *Journal of Social and Welfare Law* 1-15; 67-82 to describe the process of obtaining rights under the Housing (Homeless Persons) Act 1977 and borrowed from Germaine Greer's account of women artists and their struggle for recognition in *The Obstacle Race: The Fortunes of Women Painters and Their Work* (1979).
23 1988/1989: 24,741; 1998/1999: 45,700; 2002/2003: 51,999; 2003/2004: 56,523; 2004/2005: 57,454; 2005/2006: 59,970; 2006/2007: 59,096; *Statistical Bulletin Operation of the Homeless Persons Legislation in Scotland: National and Local Authority Analyses 2006–07* (2007); *Operation of the Homeless Persons Legislation in Scotland: 2008–09* (2009).
24 Homelessness etc (Scotland) Act 2003: "vulnerable" includes those with a personality disorder; learning disability; physical disability; chronic ill health; women who have suffered a miscarriage or had an abortion; people discharged from hospital, prison or the armed forces.
25 Housing (Scotland) Act 2001 ss 34-37.

practice. The impact of the expansion of the categories of who is regarded as automatically coming within the coverage of priority need does not seem to have resulted in major problems. The 2012 changes enacted do have the merit of returning the law to the vision of the originators of the homeless persons legislation in the 1970s and tuning in with twenty-first-century commitments to human rights. In England and Wales the legislation, with its restrictions on those covered by its terms, remains unaltered and it is not unreasonable to adjudge that, although this legislation only alters who receives housing rather than adding to the housing stock, advances have been made through the work of the Scottish Parliament. Housing is more likely to be allocated on the grounds of need than on highly legalistic and often perverse local inter-pretations of moral worth involved in interpreting "vulnerable" and "inten-tionality" and operating the "local connection" rules.

(2) Regulation of landlords

Both private and social rented landlords are now covered by detailed regula-tion. The reluctance to interfere directly with the operation of private-sector landlords has always been based on the belief that most landlords and tenants get along fine most of the time and was borne out by research in the more fractious 1970s.[26] There is, however, acceptance that there are a few "rogue" landlords in a position to abuse their power in a market with more demand than supply. The Minister for Communities stressed the benefits for strategic planning which registration should achieve:

> Registration will allow local authorities to get to grips with the private rented sector in their areas and to understand what the sector provides and the contribu-tion it makes to meeting housing need. It will help them to plan strategically for housing need, to work in partnership with the sector and, if necessary, to intervene to raise the quality of the sector and to drive out the few exploitative landlords about whom members have talked.[27]

In the private sector the approach has been to recognise that this is an area for education rather than for rigid application of the rules.[28] Exceptions have been made for areas where the consumer has limited bargaining power, such as at the lower end of the market in shared accommodation or houses in multiple occupancy (HMOs). The requirement to have a licence for an HMO property was introduced by statutory instrument in 2000.[29] The number of

26 B Paley, *Attitudes to Letting* (1978).
27 Scottish Parliament, *Official Report*, col 9312 (17 June 2004).
28 Scottish Government, *Review of the Private Rented Sector (vol 1) Key Finding 2* (2009).
29 Civic Government (Scotland) Act 1982 (Licensing of Houses in Multiple Occupation) Order 2000, SI 2000/177.

HMOs registered in the past decade indicates a significant area of housing provision. The problem with regulation where small business is concerned is the withdrawal of suppliers from the market and disinvestment from this area of provision. There were some anecdotal claims from Edinburgh that the costs and "hassle" had led to some withdrawal of supply. Whether or not this is a long-term shift is not yet clear, although signs are that returns outweigh the administrative inconvenience. Since 2001, the number has steadily risen to the most recent figure of 11,400, with 24% of this number being new applications.[30]

In the modern era, the idea of having minimum standards as to who could be private landlords was briefly hinted at by John Patten prior to the 1987 general election.[31] The notion of "approved independent landlords" never saw the light of day thereafter, with reliance instead on market mechanisms through the relaxation of any kind of rent controls and removal of security of tenure in the Housing Act 1988 and the Housing (Scotland) Act 1988. It was only when the issue of HMO landlords was under discussion that the point was raised. It was agreed that the principle of approval of fit and proper persons to run HMOs could well be applied to the whole sector. As a result, we have a policy for which there had been no planning. The introduction of the "fit and proper" test was bedevilled by delays in implementation. Even when finally introduced, the Scottish Executive changed its mind as to who should decide what fee should be paid for this service. Initially local authorities were given the task but just a couple of weeks before the process of registration of private landlords commenced, new regulations were brought in and this became a centrally determined charge. The contrast with the care and detail behind the other policies introduced by the Homelessness etc (Scotland) Act 2003 and (as we will see below) the Housing (Scotland) Act 2006 was marked.

Since 30 April 2006 anyone seeking to rent out property to non-relatives must pay a fee and apply to be registered with the relevant local authority. They can only be registered if the local authority where they have their property is satisfied that they are a "fit and proper" person. In determining this, the local authority must have regard to a number of issues relevant to the kinds of problems their tenants might face. So, the local authority must look to whether or an applicant has committed any offence involving fraud or other dishonesty, violence or drugs. In addition it must look to whether or not the would-be landlord has practised unlawful discrimination on the grounds

---

30 Scottish Government, *HMO Statistics for Scotland – Houses in Multiple Occupation* (2009).
31 *Weekend World*, "Private renting – ripe for development", 22 March 1987.

of sex, colour, race, ethnic or national origins or disability in business. Finally, it must look at whether the applicant has contravened any provision of the law relating to housing or landlord and tenant law.[32] If a landlord has a history of illegal eviction, refusing to return tenants' deposits when due or having discriminatory letting policies, then the implication is that any tenant is likely to suffer similar kinds of abuse from such a person. If a landlord is unregistered, then it is a criminal offence for which there is provision for a fine.[33]

After a slow and confused start, the level of applications by landlords to register has reached a reasonably high level. The Scottish Government estimated that in Scotland in 2009 there were 173,000 private rented properties. There were 101,778 registrations by June 2008 and by February 2009 these had reached 138,000.[34] The vast majority of landlords registering are individuals – 94.7% – with an average holding of 1.3 properties – 74.9% of private rented properties. The rest of the market is composed of companies (22.6%)[35] and charities (2.6%).[36] Most landlords operate on a part-time basis and two-thirds of rented properties are dwellings owned by landlords who started renting in the last decade.[37]

The expectation of the government is that this regulation is to be "light touch", with an ethos of education rather than strenuous intervention. It is aimed at achieving minimum standards rather than benchmark standards and has been criticised for "not applying the fit and proper person test in a meaningful way".[38] The aim is to tackle the spectre of Rachmanism which still looms over the private rented sector. The simplicity of the issues contrasts with the complexity of the Scottish Housing Quality Standard discussed below and exemplifies the limited nature of private-sector tenancy regulation. At the time of introduction, the Scottish Executive stressed its position as limited:

> Scottish Ministers have powers to regulate on various aspects of how landlord registration and antisocial behaviour notices will operate in practice, and to issue guidance to local authorities. Ministers are clear that, while landlord registration provides a very powerful tool to deal with bad landlords, the system should be as light-touch as possible to minimise the impact on the majority, who provide a good service for their tenants.[39]

32 Antisocial Behaviour etc (Scotland) Act 2004 s 85.
33 Level 5: £5,000 at the time of writing.
34 Scottish Government, *Review of the Private Rented Sector (vol 1)* (2009) para 2.5.
35 Scottish Government (n 34), average holdings 7.3.
36 Scottish Government (n 34), at para 2.5, average holding 12.4.
37 Scottish Government (n 34), above, at para 2.11.
38 Shelter, *Landlord registration in Scotland: three years on* (Shelter, April 2009).
39 Regulation of Private Landlords under the Antisocial Behaviour etc. (Scotland) Act 2004: Consultation on the Implementation of Parts 7 and 8, 8 July 2005.

Deputy Communities Minister Johann Lamont explained in July 2005 that "applicants are regarded as fit and proper unless there are grounds to suggest otherwise".[40]

The difference between the private-sector landlord registration and that in the social rented sector is marked. The question of financial information is different because of the nature of the risk of public grant. Here, with the Housing Corporation Housing Association model in operation, registered social landlords must submit detailed information about their individual policies and practices on a very wide range of issues from rent arrears levels, equality policies and repair turn-round times.

At the time of writing, the regulatory framework in operation encompassing social landlords – housing associations and local authorities – is found principally in the Housing (Scotland) Act 2001. This made provision for a new concept: the registered social landlord. This covered housing associations and other bodies providing social housing. The message of the Housing (Scotland) Act 2001 appeared to be simplification – a single social tenancy, a single regulatory framework and a single regulatory body.

Part 3 of the 2001 Act transferred the regulatory function from Scottish Homes to a new body: Communities Scotland. Scottish Homes had been a quango at arm's length from government but with its membership and terms of reference determined by the then Scottish Office. Communities Scotland was an executive agency. This meant that it reported direct to Scottish Ministers and was accountable, through them, to the Scottish Parliament. A number of specific statutory functions were made its responsibility, covering "performance standards to ensure the delivery of good quality housing and related services".

The most recent incarnation of regulation in the Scottish social rented sector is to be found in the creation of the Scottish Housing Regulator whose work now also encompasses Scottish local authority landlords. The framework and guidance is hugely complex and involves extensive detailed information on a wide range of issues. It is centred around meeting peer group performance standards. Where landlords have underperformed, there are powers to put members on the boards of associations. During 2008/2009, appointments were made to the boards of five organisations,[41] and in two of these instances support was given to transfer to other housing associa-

40 News release, 12 July 2005, on launch of Consultation document.
41 Scottish Government, *Review of the Private Rented Sector* (2009) 24: St John (Glasgow) Housing Association; Moray Housing Partnership; Four Walls Housing Co-operative; Forth Valley Housing Association; and Cumbernauld Housing Partnership.

tions.[42] All this information is available in public reports available online.[43] The regulation of private landlords, welcome though it is, is far less visible.

The extent to which this level of scrutiny of social landlords is likely to be maintained in the future is not entirely clear at the time of writing. The current body charged with the task of regulating social rented landlords, the Scottish Housing Regulator, has indicated that it intends to target its work in the future to focus on risks rather than a mechanistic and predictable form of bureaucratic inspection. This process, already in train, is likely to be extended by the Housing (Scotland) Bill which further extends the range of issues under scrutiny.

As indicated, these changes indicate two crucial aspects. First, we can see that the levels of regulation in the private sector and the social rented sector are very different. The social rented regulation is much more extensive, structured and ongoing. It relies on the establishing of peer-led targets and best practice, and involves regulatory penalties rather than the possibility of court proceedings. What they do share, however, is a dependence on the input of the regulators. At the time of writing, one would expect the level of staffing involved in social renting regulation to be rising as the burden becomes more and more complex. That, however, is not scheduled to take place. Recent moves to replace automatic re-inspection with targeted inspection mean that, in the social rented sector, regulation is likely to become diluted and focused on easily measurable outcomes. The extent to which this provides adequate protection for tenants from underperforming landlords remains to be seen. Private-sector tenants are faced with the illusion of protection and the reality of an opaque and inaccessible system with few resources devoted to it. It is, nonetheless, an advance on the situation south of the Border where, at the time of writing, anyone can set up in the business of providing private-sector tenancies with no need to satisfy even the most rudimentary of checks.

(3) Repairs

Two strangely contradictory developments have taken place in relation to the right to sanitary and tenantable housing. One the one hand, the complex and confusing sets of remedies available to tenants of rental housing have been significantly clarified into statutory form. On the other hand, what were once rules common to both public- and private-sector tenancies have been

42 Four Walls Housing Co-operative to Tenants First Housing Association, and St John (Glasgow) Housing Association to Loretto Housing Association Ltd.
43 http://www.scottishhousingregulator.gov.uk/stellent/groups/public/documents/webpages/shr_homepage.hcsp.

separated into distinct and slightly different codes. Prior to 2001, as far as
repairs and habitability were concerned, tenants had rights under their lease
agreements. There were, however, minimum common law and statutory
standards where the lease agreement was silent on repair obligations, as was
often the case. In addition, any attempt to shift the burden of repairs onto
tenants through the terms of the lease could not override statutory rights.
The rights to habitable property were expressed in slightly different forms
in both the common law cases and institutional writings and in a number of
different statutes.[44] Tenants might seek to pursue remedies under either the
common law, para 1 of Sch 10 to the Housing (Scotland) Act 1987 (fit for
human habitation) or para 3 of Sch 10 to the 1987 Act (implied obligation to
keep property and fixtures and fittings in repair). This position has now been
substantially simplified in the first decade of the twenty-first century. Tenants
of social landlords – local authorities and housing associations – now look to
the six short paragraphs of Sch 4 to the Housing (Scotland) Act 2001 to find
their repair rights. Tenants in the private sector, on the other hand, have
their repair rights enshrined in eighteen sections of the Housing (Scotland)
Act 2006 which set out the nature of the required "repairing standard" which
landlords must satisfy in relation to their rented property. There are differences in the extent of the detail as between the social rented sector Sch 4
obligations and the much more extensive private rented sector s 14.

More significantly, however, the remedies for enforcing the repair rights are
completely distinct. Just like their predecessors in the 1980s and 1990s, dissatisfied tenants renting from local authorities and housing associations will have
to take their cases to the sheriff court.[45] Their fellow tenants whose landlords
are in the private sector have the opportunity to approach a newly constituted
tribunal. Based on the structure of the rent assessment committees, which
have a role in the fixing of rents for private tenancies, the private rented
housing committee offers a free informal mechanism for the adjudication
of complaints where houses do not meet the statutory "repairing standard".

Prior to embarking on the changes to the private rental system, the Scottish Executive remitted the whole question to a Housing Improvement Task

---

44 For a discussion of these parallel rights, see P Robson and S Halliday, *Residential Tenancies*
   (1998).
45 There is provision in the social renting sector for tenants to carry out small "qualifying repairs"
   under a ceiling of £350. The major issue, though, in the extensive litigation over the past three
   decades has been much more fundamental problems of dampness through an ineffective combination of heating, ventilation and insulation: see Robson and Halliday, *Residential Tenancies* (n 44)
   ch 3. Although there is no equivalent in the private sector, the speed and nature of the Private
   Rented Housing Panel set up under the Housing (Scotland) Act 2006 process renders such a right
   limited.

Force. This concluded that the market itself did not provide a strong enough incentive to ensure that landlords in the private sector kept their property in good condition.[46] The result, as indicated above, was an obligation on landlords to ensure that their properties met the "repairing standard" – an amalgam of the common law, fitness for human habitation standard and the statutory implied repair obligations found in the Housing (Scotland) Act 1987. These are now incorporated into the Housing (Scotland) Act 2006. The accessible mechanism for enforcement is the innovation.

In the social renting sector, individual complainants have no such recourse. They must make their way through the sheriff court procedure. The most recent cases which are reported suggest that this is a long, drawn-out process. For instance, in typical cases in the past decade we are talking between four and six years from the issue being notified to the social rented sector landlord to determination in the sheriff court.[47] In practice, for the majority of tenants, the principal impetus to alter the conditions in which tenants live is less likely to come from any kind of individual actions but rather from the central statutory obligation laid on social landlords to meet the non-statutory Scottish Housing Quality Standard. This is a highly technical set of requirements much resembling the Building Regulations. Not only are houses required to meet standards in terms of being tenantable and habitable but there must be such things as a specified numbers of wall sockets in kitchens.

This obligation is enforced indirectly, through pressure by the Scottish Housing Regulator in the social rented sector, like the obligation on local authorities to secure that housing in their areas meets the "tolerable standard".[48] Although the obligation specifically relates to a start date of 2015, it is an ongoing obligation. How effective it will be will depend on the sanctions which it is reasonable to visit on those who fail to meet its exacting standards. Given the levels of investment available from the Scottish Government into housing, this is an assessment which is difficult to make. While those involved in the provision of social rented housing remain committed to bringing the benefits of the Scottish Housing Quality Standard to their tenants, the costs are significant.

The first two years of the operation of the private-sector Private Rented Housing Panel and its committees suggest that the problem of disrepair in the private sector is also extensive. What is particularly interesting is that

46 Housing Improvement Task Force, *Issues in Improving Quality in Private Housing* (2002), Conclusion 45.
47 *Deans v Glasgow Housing Association* 2009 Hous LR 92 (2003 to July 2009); *Campbell v Aberdeen City Council* 2007 Hous LR 26 (March 2003 to February 2007).
48 Housing (Scotland) Act 1987 Pt IV ss 85–87.

problems appear to be spread throughout most of Scotland. Hence we find that while the largest numbers of complaints come from the major cities – some 55% of cases involved cities and large towns[49] – the rest were from rural and small-town Scotland.[50] The nature of the complaints ranges from apparently minor issues such as a shoogly stair tread to more serious ones such as a defective roof.[51]

D. CONCLUSION

There is, then, a major set of changes which have been effected during this period. It feels to someone involved in providing training to practising lawyers that there is an almost continuous process of explaining new regulations. The question, though, is whether or not most of these changes would have occurred anyway. To assess this we have noted whether or not there have been equivalent changes in the same period in England and Wales. The changes have been major and, one must infer, would have been less likely to have taken place without devolution. As far as regulation is concerned, there is, at the time of writing, a consultation document in England canvassing views on whether or not there should be a "fit and proper" test, with private-sector landlords being licensed. Repair complaint mechanisms have not been introduced in England. Looking, then, at homelessness, the changes which have occurred in Scotland have not been mirrored by developments in England.

What has happened south of the Border during the past ten years is a crude but worthwhile yardstick to measure the achievements of the Scottish Parliament. In the fields of regulation of private landlords Scottish legislation has belatedly shown the way forward. As far as homelessness in concerned, the situation continues to reflect the distinct local nature of the phenomenon in a way which its predecessor Acts did not.

For any individual holding property on both sides of the Border which they seek to rent out, the challenges facing them are now significantly different. In Scotland, a good degree of activism is required. It is no longer enough to find some willing tenants, give them possession and sit back. Active engagement with the condition of the property, rapid responses to tenants' complaints and active intervention in relation to tenants' bad behaviour are now legal

---

49 Cities and large towns: 94 complaints [55%]. Analysis, by author, of Private Renting Housing Panel data: *http://www.prhpscotland.gov.uk/prhp/127.html*, last accessed 6 May 2010.
50 Small towns and rural locations: 78 complaints, analysis as above, note 49.
51 *http://www.prhpscotland.gov.uk/prhp/127.html*.

requirements rather than merely advisory. The unengaged absentee landlord in England has a rather easier time.

For the homeless applicant in Scotland the reality is that the applications have risen and the waiting lists too.[52] This is, to a degree, a legacy from the continued loss of community-owned housing to the right to buy[53] and its bizarre extension under Labour in Scotland to housing associations.[54]

The prospects for the future are, as ever, hard to gauge. The ideas and imagination are available in abundance, from minimum standards for tenants to an all-encompassing policy towards homeless people. What is vital, though, in all these and other plans is a level of commitment that makes these forms of regulation meaningful. Forming a judgment on the first ten years of the Scottish Parliament's work cannot be done by simply examining what has happened in terms of legislative provisions. It is the material context in which we operate that is crucial. William Kelso and his colleagues in Paisley at the end of the nineteenth century were faced with enormous problems in securing sanitary and healthy housing in Paisley.[55] Their problem was not the law. The legislation they were operating[56] managed to survive for a century and is remarkably similar to the powers enjoyed by modern-day environmental health departments. What was lacking then was financial commitment. This comes in the form of the provision of housing just as much, if not more so, than elaborate schemes concerning the allocation or maintenance of existing property. With social rented housing stock from which housing allocated by need can be drawn plunging from 612,000 to 420,000, the prospects for the 200,000 people on the housing waiting list give cause for concern.

At the time of the passage of the Housing (Homeless Persons) Bill in 1977, Baroness Young pointed out that for all the elaborate provisions and notion of rights the Bill was limited:

> while deeply sympathising with the terrible problem of the homeless, whether they be young people or families, may I ask how ... this Bill will help, since it will provide for no more houses to be built and no more houses to be let?[57]

That chilling reminder of the impotence of rights in the face of economic restrictions remains as true after a decade of cutting-edge Scottish housing legislation as it did when all decisions were taken in London and the hopes of

---

52 Scottish Government, *Operation of the Homeless Persons Legislation in Scotland 2008-9* (2009).
53 150,000 houses were sold to sitting tenants between 30 September 1997 and 30 September 2009: Scottish Government, *Local Authority Housing – Income and Expenditure 2008-9 and 2009-10*.
54 Housing (Scotland) Act 2001 s 43.
55 Kelso, *Sanitation in Paisley* (n 1).
56 Public Health (Scotland) Acts 1887 and 1897.
57 *HL Deb 20 April 1977 vol 382 cols 129-132*.

Scots for decent affordable housing were an afterthought. The most recent proposals for affordable housing in Scotland focus on the process[58] and, while admirable, are dependent for their success on the levels of finance available. The record of the Scottish Parliament on levels of investment in housing since devolution has to be a cause for a degree of scepticism. As Gavin Corbett points out, the recent budget plans represent a major fall in investment levels of almost 30%.[59] Ten years on, the law looks tidier and more coherent to the professional lawyer but the concrete gains for the homeless and ill-housed remain limited.

58 Scottish Government, *Firm Foundations: A Discussion Paper for Scotland* (2007); Scottish Government, *Investing in Affordable Housing: A Consultation* (December 2008); Scottish Government, *The Way Forward* (June 2009).
59 Shelter, *Submission to Scottish Government* (2009): The budget for affordable housing investment has been the single biggest loser in the draft 2010-2011 budget, falling by 30% between 2009-2010 and 2010-2011. The published figures show that, from 2009-2010 to 2010-2011, the housing budget fell by £169 million or 29%. Back in 2007, the last Comprehensive Spending Review anticipated the affordable Housing Programme rising from £566 million in 2009-2010 to £591 million in 2010-2011: a rise of £25 million. A projected rise in the original CSR of £25 million turns into a fall of £204 million. This fall of £204 million represents a decline of 30% from 2009-2010 to 2010-2011: *http://scotland.shelter.org.uk/__data/assets/pdf_file/0014/210650/Building_solutions.pdf.*

9 Education:
Could Do Better

Janys M Scott QC[°]

A. CHILDREN'S RIGHTS
B. STANDARDS IN EDUCATION
C. SOCIAL EDUCATION AND WELFARE
D. PARENTAL INVOLVEMENT IN SCHOOLS
E. SCHOOL CLOSURES
F. INDEPENDENT SCHOOLS
G. PRE-SCHOOL EDUCATION
H. CURRICULUM
I. PROVISION FOR ADDITIONAL SUPPORT NEEDS
J. FURTHER AND HIGHER EDUCATION
K. RESERVED AND DEVOLVED ISSUES
L. CONCLUSIONS

The Scottish Parliament passed no less than fourteen education statutes between the beginning of 2000 and the end of 2009. This is hardly surprising given the importance of education to the future of Scottish society and the proud independent tradition of education in Scotland. The Parliament has been keen to make a mark on the international stage in recognition of children's rights. Aspirations for the quality of Scottish education are clear. Under previous Westminster administrations, parents were considered the best guardians of education for their children. This administration has not agreed. Parents are to be interested and involved, but education authorities are to exercise power, under the guidance of the Scottish Ministers. Maintaining the quality of education takes money. The education budget forms a significant part of the expenditure of Scottish local authorities. This was recognised in 2007 in a concordat between the Scottish Government and the Convention of Scottish Local Authorities (COSLA)[1] in which the government gave certain commitments to authorities in relation to funding and

---

[°] Murray Stable, Faculty of Advocates.
[1] Available at *http://www.scotland.gov.uk/Publications/2007/11/13092240/concordat.*

authorities undertook to do what was required to deliver various key policies and programmes, including certain commitments in the field of education. The recognition that funding is key to implementation of policy has been apparent in the field of further and higher education as well as school education.

This analysis is focused on change to the law. Legislation provides the framework within which education is offered, but it does not describe what happens in schools, colleges and universities. In any discussion of education law it has to be recognised that education is principally driven by the quality and commitment of the teachers and others involved in its provision.

A. CHILDREN'S RIGHTS

In the Scottish Parliament's first education measure its attention was focused on the United Nations Convention on the Rights of the Child.[2] Article 28 of that Convention requires states to recognise the right of the child to education. Article 29 records agreement that the education of the child should be directed towards the development of the child's personality, talents and mental and physical abilities to their fullest potential. Article 12 demands a commitment to assuring to the child who is capable of forming his or her own views the right to express those views freely in all matters affecting that child and to giving those views due weight in accordance with the child's age and maturity. These articles are given statutory recognition in ss 1 and 2 of the Standards in Scotland's Schools etc Act 2000. Statutory recognition of the rights of the child looks good, but unless it makes a difference to children it is mere grandstanding.

Taking the first section of the Standards in Scotland's Schools etc Act 2000, this contains the statement of the child's right to be provided with education by, or by virtue of arrangements made or entered into by, an education authority. The section was unnecessary to attain any practical end in the domestic context. The structure of Scottish education law was already effective to recognise the right of the child to education. Education authorities are required to secure adequate and efficient provision of school education for their area.[3] It was, and remains, the duty of the parent of every child of school age to provide efficient education for the child, suitable to his or her age, ability and aptitude, either by causing the child to attend a public school

2 20 November 1989 (TS 44 (1992); Cm 1976), ratified by the United Kingdom on 16 December 1991.
3 Education (Scotland) Act 1980 (hereafter "E(S)A 1980") s 1(1).

regularly or by other means.[4] The Human Rights Act 1998 gives effect in domestic law to art 2 of the First Protocol of the European Convention on Human Rights and Fundamental Freedoms. This article provides that "No person shall be denied the right to education". Despite the negative formulation, this is a right to such education as the state provides.[5] All children in Scotland have access to state education, subject to alternative education being provided at the choice of their parents.[6]

Section 2(1) of the 2000 Act is similar. Of course, school education should be directed towards the development of the child's personality, talents and mental and physical abilities to their fullest potential, but education authorities are constrained by their resources. They have a duty to provide adequate and efficient school education for their area.[7] A child who is a budding tennis genius will have physical education alongside other pupils, but it is doubtful whether he or she could insist that the education authority provide top-flight tennis coaching. It is interesting that when the principle of school education directed towards the development of the child's personality, talents and mental and physical abilities to their fullest potential is restated in the Education (Additional Support for Learning) (Scotland) Act 2004,[8] the Parliament goes on to qualify the obligations of an education authority which is not required to do anything that would result in unreasonable public expenditure being incurred.[9] There is no reported instance of successful challenge to education authority provision on the basis of s 2(1).

As regards the views of the child in s 2(2), children are not going to be able to express views unless opportunity is given for them to do so. The 2000 Act itself did provide for consultation of pupils when education authorities and schools were preparing statements of objectives and schools were preparing development plans[10] (of which more later), but there was otherwise very limited scope for the expression of views. The principle that children should have the right to express views has not otherwise been carried forward in relation to many of the issues that arise in the course of school education. For example, if a parent appeals against a child's exclusion but the child does not appeal, there is no requirement for appeal committees or the sheriff court

---

4 E(S)A 1980 s 30(1).

5 *Belgian Linguistics Case (No 2)* (1968) 1 EHRR 252.

6 Parental choice is preserved by E(S)A 1980 s 30(2).

7 E(S)A 1980 s 1(1).

8 Education (Additional Support for Learning) (Scotland) Act 2004 (hereafter "E(ASL)A 2004") s 1(2).

9 E(ASL)A 2004 s 4(2)(b).

10 Standards in Scotland's Schools etc Act 2000 (hereafter "SSSA 2000") ss 5(1) and 6(1).

dealing with the case to seek out the views of the child and to have regard to those views. There is a similar *lacuna* when a parent appeals in relation to the school in which a child may be placed. Some thought has been given to the matter in relation to appeals to the Additional Support Needs Tribunal. Rule 33 of the Additional Support Needs Tribunals for Scotland (Practice and Procedure) Rules 2006[11] provides that the tribunal may permit a child under the age of twelve to give evidence only where it considers (a) that the evidence of the child is necessary to enable a fair and just hearing of the reference; and (b) that the welfare and interests of the child will not be prejudiced by so doing. If the child is allowed to give evidence, the convenor may appoint a person with appropriate skills or experience to facilitate the giving of evidence by the child. The tribunal rules do not wholly embrace the principle in s 2(2) of the 2000 Act. The Scottish Parliament finally took a step towards providing a structure for children's views to be taken in relation to school closures and other proposals affecting schools in the Schools (Consultation) (Scotland) Act 2010.[12] The 2010 Act requires pupils at an affected school to be consulted, in so far as the education authority considers them to be of a suitable age and maturity.[13]

The Standards in Scotland's Schools etc Act 2000 did make an advance for the individual pupil who was allowed to appeal in relation to his or her own exclusion from school,[14] but the provision itself has significant flaws. Only a pupil with legal capacity may appeal. Legal capacity is defined by reference to the Age of Legal Capacity (Scotland) Act 1991 s 2(4A) and (4B). The test of legal capacity in these subsections of the 1991 Act is whether the child concerned has a general understanding of what it means to instruct a solicitor. The first stage of any appeal against exclusion is to an appeal committee. No legal aid is available for an appeal to an appeal committee. A test based on an understanding of what it means to instruct a solicitor is unlikely to be applied. There are no reported instances of a child appealing. Further, if a child does appeal against exclusion, the legislation does not specify how such an appeal would relate to an appeal brought by a parent in respect of the same exclusion. Both may have an interest in appealing but their positions may differ.

---

11 SSI 2006/88.
12 Passed on 19 November 2009 and received Royal Assent on 5 January 2010.
13 Schools (Consultation) (Scotland) Act 2010 (hereafter "S(C)(S)A 2010") s 2 and Sch 2 paras 1(d), 2(d), 3(d), 4(d), 5(d), 6(d), 7(d), 8(d), 9(d) and 10(d).
14 SSSA 2000 s 41.

B. STANDARDS IN EDUCATION

The Standards in Scotland's Schools etc Act 2000 attempts to set a framework for aspiration in the standards of education in Scotland. A duty to "endeavour to secure improvement in the quality of school education" is imposed both on the Scottish Ministers and on education authorities.[15] The Scottish Minsters are required to define national priorities in education, and to publish measures of performance.[16] National priorities were defined by statutory instrument in 2000.[17] The priorities include raising standards of educational attainment for all in schools, especially in the core skills of literacy and numeracy, supporting and developing the skills of teachers, promoting equality, working with parents to teach pupils respect for self and one another, and equipping pupils with the foundation skills, attitudes and expectations necessary to prosper in a changing society. The list of priorities does look like an articulation of what education should be about. It is by no means novel.

Education authorities are to prepare annual statements of improvement objectives. They are to carry out a consultation exercise each year, involving bodies representative of teachers, parents, employees other than teachers, pupils and other persons who have an interest. Schools are required to publish an annual development plan. The development plan should include an account of the ways in which, and the extent to which, the head teacher of a school will consult the pupils in attendance and seek to involve them when decisions require to be made concerning the everyday running of the school.[18] Education authorities should define and publish measures and standards of performance for the schools they manage and review the quality of education provided by individual schools, having regard to those measures and standards.[19]

Scotland retained a system of inspection of schools by Her Majesty's Inspectors. The 2000 Act reinforces that system by providing for inspection of education authorities to review how they are carrying out their functions in relation to the provision of school education.[20] Scottish Ministers may issue codes of practice in relation to inspection of authorities[21] and educational establishments generally.[22] Further enforcement measures

15 SSSA 2000 s 3(1) and (2).
16 SSSA 2000 s 4.
17 Education (National Priorities) (Scotland) Order 2000, SSI 2000/443.
18 SSSA 2000 s 6.
19 SSSA 2000 s 7.
20 SSSA 2000 s 9.
21 SSSA 2000 s 10.
22 SSSA 2000 s 12, inserting E(S)A 1980 s 66A.

were added by the School Education (Ministerial Powers and Independent Schools) (Scotland) Act 2004. Where Her Majesty's Inspectors carry out an inspection and identify steps that should be taken to secure improvement, they should give an opportunity to make the necessary improvement. If the opportunity is not taken and the seriousness of the failure is such that an enforcement direction is justified, they are required to make a reference to the Scottish Ministers. The legislation provides for a preliminary notice requiring a written response from the managers of the school or the education authority. The final step is an enforcement direction, which should be complied with by the recipient.[23]

It is one thing to legislate for a framework that focuses on improvement. It is another to secure the improvement itself. On one view, the imposition of such a framework adds significantly to the burden of teachers, head teachers and education authorities and takes them away from the primary task of providing education. Without financial and human resources, the aspiration for improvement may be impossible to attain. The Scottish Executive clearly decided that more was required and decided to limit the numbers of pupils in classes. Circular 1/2007 set out formal guidance to education authorities to the effect that classes in the first year of primary education should be no more than twenty-five and the number of pupils in maths and English classes in the first two years of secondary education should be no more than twenty. This was seen as a first step towards having only eighteen pupils in all lower primary classes and better pupil/staff ratios generally. This policy has, to date, been impossible to implement. In part the problem was one of resources, but in part it was due to a failure to understand the law.

The Scottish Parliament inherited a system in which class sizes in the first three years of primary education were restricted by regulation to thirty pupils, subject to certain exceptions.[24] The guidance on Primary One class sizes in Circular 1/2007 allowed the same exceptions to the maximum numbers in a class as the regulations. One such exception applies where the child is placed as a result of a decision by the sheriff or appeal committee and the decision to place is taken after 30 April immediately preceding the start of the school year.[25] This drove a coach and four through the policy on reduction of class sizes. If a school was popular, there would tend to be placing requests. These could not be resisted on the ground that the authority would need to employ

23 School Education (Ministerial Powers and Independent Schools) (Scotland) Act 2004 (hereafter "SE(MPIS)(S)A 2004") ss 1 and 2, adding E(S)A 1980 ss 66B, 66C and 66D and SSSA 2000 ss 10A, 10B and 10C.
24 Education (Lower Primary Class Sizes) (Scotland) Regulations 1999, SI 1999/1080.
25 SI 1999/1080 regs 3(3), 4(1), (2), Sch para 4, read with reg 2(2).

an additional teacher. Classes in popular schools could not be held at twenty-five in terms of the guidance.[26] They could not even be held at thirty in terms of the regulations. The debacle tends to indicate that the Executive had a poor understanding of the different roles of guidance and legislation and a poor grasp of the tensions in education between national aspiration and the aspiration of individual parents for their own children.

C. SOCIAL EDUCATION AND WELFARE

The Schools (Health Promotion and Nutrition) (Scotland) Act 2007 also imposed a requirement that the Scottish Ministers and education authorities endeavour to ensure that schools and hostels managed by them are "health-promoting". This involves providing activities and an environment and facilities which promote the physical, social, mental and emotional health and well-being of pupils in attendance at the school or residing in the hostel.[27] This provision simply adds to a long line of similar policy objectives, embedded in the legislation, and stranded there over time. For example, the Schools General (Scotland) Regulations 1975 provide that education authorities in the day-to-day conduct of every school under their management are to:

> ensure that care is taken to develop, in pupils in attendance at that school, reasonable and responsible social attitudes and relationships, to cultivate in such pupils consideration for others, and to encourage in such pupils the practice of good manners, good attitudes to work, initiative and self-reliance and habits of personal hygiene and cleanliness.[28]

Children may be subject to medical and dental examinations at school[29] and may in particular be examined in the "interests of cleanliness" to ensure that neither they nor their clothes are "infested with vermin or in a foul condition".[30] There is nothing particularly new about the promotion of health and social welfare in schools. What is new is the level of financial support involved in social welfare provision in schools and the detail of aspects of control.

Free school meals have long been available to children whose parents are in receipt of benefits.[31] The Education (School Meals) (Scotland) Act 2003

---

26 *East Lothian Council, Petrs* 2008 SLT 921.
27 Schools (Health Promotion and Nutrition) (Scotland) Act 2007 (hereafter "S(HPN)(S)A 2007") s 1, adding SSSA 2000 s 2A.
28 SI 1975/1135 reg 11.
29 E(S)A 1980 s 57.
30 E(S)A 1980 s 58.
31 E(S)A 1980 s 53.

extended the power to provide free school meals to children whose parents were in receipt of tax credits and other benefits prescribed by the Scottish Ministers.[32] In the Schools (Health Promotion and Nutrition) (Scotland) Act 2007 the Scottish Parliament went further and imposed a duty on education authorities to take reasonable steps to ensure that every pupil entitled to a free lunch actually received that lunch.[33] To spare such pupils embarrassment, which may deter them from receiving lunch, education authorities are statutorily required to take reasonable steps to protect their identity.[34] Between October 2007 and June 2008 the government ran a pilot project providing free lunches to all Primary One to Three children in five local authority areas.[35] On the basis of that project, regulations have been passed to allow all education authorities to provide free lunches to all pupils in the first three years of primary education, with the intention that free school meals will be provided with effect from August 2010.[36] Further extension to all pupils in education authority primary schools has been recommended.[37] The policy of free school meals was part of the concordat between the Scottish Ministers and education authorities that saw additional funding for councils in return for services that formed part of government policy, but plans to widen provision of free school meals to later stages of primary education have been opposed by councils struggling with recession. The provision of free school meals for pupils in Scotland has been seen as part of a costly programme of social policy funded via the Barnett formula, and as such is a source of resentment south of the Border.

Provision of free school lunches is linked to new nutritional requirements for food provided in schools managed by the education authority.[38] These requirements are set out in regulations.[39] The regulations may include specification of food and drink which satisfies, or fails to satisfy, nutritional

32 This power was exercised in the Education (School Meals) (Scotland) Regulations 2003, SSI 2003/350, in respect of pupils whose parent was awarded child tax credit but not working tax credit, and extended in the Education (School Lunches) (Scotland) Regulations 2009, SSI 2009/178 (replacing SSI 2003/350) to pupils whose parent was in receipt of working tax credit in addition to child tax credit, based on an income not exceeding a certain threshold.
33 S(HPN)(S)A 2007 s 7, adding E(S)A 1980 s 53A(2).
34 S(HPN)(S)A 2007 s 8, adding E(S)A 1980 s 53B.
35 Provision of School Lunches (Disapplication of the Requirement to Charge) (Scotland) Order 2007, SSI 2007/451. The pilot ran in East Ayrshire Council, Fife Council, Glasgow City Council, Scottish Borders Council and West Dunbartonshire Council.
36 Provision of School Lunches (Disapplication of the Requirement to Charge) (Scotland) Order 2008, SSI 2008/400. See also Executive Note to this Order.
37 "National food and drink policy – walking the talk – getting government right" (April 2009).
38 S(HPN)(S)A 2007 s 3, adding E(S)A 1980 s 56A.
39 Nutritional Requirements for Food and Drink in Schools (Scotland) Regulations 2008, SSI 2008/265.

requirements; specification of the circumstances where food or drink may be provided to a pupil even if it does not satisfy nutritional requirements; and requirement that drinking water is made available.[40] The regulations contain detailed provisions for school meals, including a requirement for not less than two types of vegetables per day and a ban on confectionery (including chocolate).[41] There are strict limitations on food and drink which may be provided in schools, which exclude, for example, sugary carbonated drinks.[42] These provisions do not apply to food or drink brought onto school premises by pupils, for example in a lunch box, nor to food and drink that is provided as part of a social, cultural or recreational activity.[43]

D. PARENTAL INVOLVEMENT IN SCHOOLS

There is an uneasy tension in education law between the provision offered by education authorities and the role of the parent. The basic structure of Scottish education law is that education authorities offer school education, but in the exercise and performance of their duties are bound to have regard to the general principle that, so far as is compatible with the provision of suitable instruction and training and avoidance of unreasonable public expenditure, pupils are to be educated in accordance with the wishes of their parents.[44] This does not mean that parents' wishes should prevail: simply that regard should be had to them.[45] The balance shifted in favour of parents with the Education (Scotland) Act 1981, which gave parents the right to make "placing requests" for children to attend a school of the parents' choice.[46] This provision has resulted in a challenge to the policy aspirations of the Scottish Executive in respect of numbers in Primary One classes, as seen above. The Standards in Scotland's Schools etc Act 2000 introduced two new grounds for refusing parental placing requests.[47] In this and other respects the Scottish Parliament has shifted the balance of power in education away from parents.

The School Boards (Scotland) Act 1988 gave parents the power to elect a board which would have a role in the management of schools. Once a school

40 S(HPN)(S)A 2007 s 83, adding E(S)A 1980 s 56B.
41 SSI 2008/265 reg 3, Sch 1, paras 1, 6.
42 SSI 2008/265 regs 3 and 4, Schs 2 and 4.
43 E(S)A 1980 s 56A(2)(b)(ii) and (3).
44 E(S)A 1980 s 28(1).
45 *Harvey v Strathclyde Regional Council* 1989 SLT 612.
46 E(S)A 1980 s 28A, inserted by E(S)A 1981 s 1(1).
47 SSSA 2000 s 44, adding E(S)A 1980 s 28A(3)(a)(vi) and (vii) allowing refusal on the ground that the education authority would require to create an additional class or employ an extra teacher in the future or that the capacity of the school would be exceeded in terms of pupil numbers.

had a board, the board could hold a ballot of parents and "opt out" of education authority control, under the Self-Governing Schools etc (Scotland) Act 1989. There was no particular rush to self-governing status. A handful of schools initiated the procedure. Two became self-governing. One of the two, Dornoch Academy, returned to education authority management in 1999. The other, St Mary's Episcopal Primary School, secured self-governing status and wished to remain self-governing. The Scottish Parliament repealed the provisions for self-governing status and provided for return of self-governing schools to education authority management.[48] An attempt by St Mary's to remain self-governing was rejected in both the Outer House and the Inner House of the Court of Session.[49]

The Scottish Parliament went on to repeal the School Boards (Scotland) Act 1988 and to replace it with the Scottish Schools (Parental Involvement) Act 2006. The ostensible purpose of the 2006 Act was to promote parental involvement in schools managed by education authorities. It followed a "National Debate on Education" undertaken by the Scottish Executive. This was a large-scale consultation exercise involving pupils, parents, teachers, employers and others with an interest in the future of school education. One finding was that parents were deterred from contributing to school boards by the formality of the statutory requirements associated with boards. This was confirmed by independent research commissioned by the Scottish Executive in 2004. Further consultation on a draft Bill in 2005 produced a wide range of views, the majority being in favour of some changes requiring primary legislation. Most individual responses were from people who already had significant levels of involvement in schools. The Scottish Ministers commissioned a telephone survey of 1,000 randomly selected parents and held a series of focus group discussions. This resulted in changes to the draft Bill. Considerable effort was made to produce a piece of legislation that would improve parental involvement in schools.[50]

The Scottish Schools (Parental Involvement) Act 2006 imposes general duties on the Scottish Ministers and on education authorities to promote the involvement of parents in the education provided to pupils in public schools.[51] Education authorities are to prepare strategies to further parental involvement[52] and schools

48 SSSA 2000 ss 17-23, s 60(2) and Sch 3.
49 *Dove, Petrs* 2002 SC 257, 2002 SLT 640 affd 2002 SLT 1296.
50 See Stage 1 Report on the Scottish Schools (Parental Involvement) Bill by the Education Committee of the Scottish Parliament, available at *http://www.parlamaid-alba.org/business/committees/education/reports-06/edr06-02.htm*.
51 Scottish Schools (Parental Involvement) Act 2006 (hereafter "SS(PI)A 2006") s 1.
52 SS(PI)A 2006 s 2.

must include a strategy for parental involvement in their development plans.[53] One of the measures of the quality of education provided by a school is the extent to which a pupil's parents are involved in the education provided to a pupil.[54] All parents of pupils attending a particular school are automatically members of the "parent forum". The forum may establish a "parent council" to represent the forum.[55] Unlike the old school boards, there is no set model for a parent council. Parents can choose a scheme for the parent council for their particular school. The most significant difference between a parent council and an old school board is that the parent council has no management powers. It exists to support the school management, to make representations to the head teacher and education authority, and to promote contact between the persons and bodies involved with the school.[56]

It is interesting that in an Act designed to foster parental involvement, the term "involvement" is not defined. It is not clear whether the involvement to be fostered relates to involvement of the individual parent in relation to the education offered to his or her own child, or involvement in the education offered by the school or facilities at the school. It might be designed to cover involvement of groups of parents. Involvement could mean anything from passive receipt of information to active participation in the classroom. It is not clear why it was necessary to take away parents' role in management in order to promote their involvement. The result is that the initiative has been securely returned to education authorities.

E. SCHOOL CLOSURES

Education authorities are required to consult before making certain changes to school education and in some cases they require the consent of the Scottish Ministers. Falling school rolls and pressure on local authority budgets have led to proposals to close rural schools. In January 2008, a Private Member's Bill was proposed to introduce a presumption against closure of rural schools. The government then introduced its own Bill, which in due course became the Schools (Consultation) (Scotland) Act 2010. While motivated by the issue of rural schools, the Act repeals and replaces convoluted measures[57] relating to consultation and change. It represents a change in emphasis in a number

53 SS(PI)A 2006 s 3.
54 SS(PI)A 2006 s 4.
55 SS(PI)A 2006 s 5.
56 SS(PI)A 2006 s 8.
57 E(S)A 1980 ss 22A and 22B and Education (Publication and Consultation Etc) (Scotland) Regulations 1981, SI 1981/1558, as amended.

of respects, including a change in the circumstances when consent of the Scottish Ministers has been required to close schools or to change catchment areas. In the past, consent has been required to close schools or to change catchment areas where schools are relatively full.[58]

Under the 2010 Act an education authority must prepare and publish an "educational benefits statement" explaining among other things the likely educational effects on pupils and other users of the schools facilities of the change proposed and giving a description of the educational benefits which the authority believes will result from implementation of the proposal.[59] Her Majesty's Inspectors of Education must receive a copy of the proposal paper and are required to prepare a report on the educational aspects of the proposal.[60] There are additional requirements when an authority proposes to close a rural school, including an assessment of the likely effect on the local community if the proposal is implemented. Provided that they comply with the requirements of the Act, education authorities will be given a free hand to make changes in the provision of education. The Scottish Ministers may call in decisions relating to closure of schools, including discontinuance of a school or a particular stage of education and discontinuance of English-medium or Gaelic-medium education in nursery classes or a stage of educa-tion[61] if it appears that the education authority may have failed to comply with the requirements of the Act or failed to take proper account of a material consideration relevant to the decision to implement the proposal.[62]

Having taken the opportunity to modernise the general provisions for consultation and change, the Scottish Parliament has left unaltered the existing provisions relating to changes to denominational schools.[63] These provisions suffer from significant lack of clarity and have been criticised in the Outer House of the Court of Session, the Inner House and the House of Lords.[64] Denominational schools are, however, a difficult issue and one that the Scottish Parliament has avoided thus far.

58 SI 1981/1558, reg 9, Sch 2; *King v East Ayrshire Council* 1998 SLT 1287.
59 S(C)(S)A 2010 ss 1(3)(a) and 3.
60 S(C)(S)A 2010 ss 1(3)(e) and 8.
61 S(C)(S)A 2010 ss 2(1)(b), Sch 1 para 1.
62 S(C)(S)A 2010 s 17(2).
63 E(S)A 1980 ss 22C and 22D.
64 *Scottish Hierarchy of the Roman Catholic Church v Highland Regional Council* 1988 SC (HL) 1.

F. INDEPENDENT SCHOOLS

Consistent with the centralisation of education, there has been a tightening of control on independent schools. The School Education (Ministerial Powers and Independent Schools) (Scotland) Act 2004 extended the definition of an "independent school". Previously, a school with fewer than five pupils was not regulated under the legislation relating to education. Now all schools are regulated, regardless of the number of pupils. There are new provisions for registration.[65] It is no longer possible for an independent school to receive provisional registration pending inspection. Operating an unregistered school is a criminal offence. The 2004 Act provides for disqualification of premises, proprietors and teachers at independent schools, imposition of conditions and removal from the register.[66]

Indirect steps have also been taken to impose conditions on independent schools. The nutritional requirements imposed on schools managed by education authorities pursuant to the Schools (Health Promotion and Nutrition) (Scotland) Act 2007 do not apply in terms to independent schools, but an education authority cannot award a bursary for a pupil to attend a fee-paying school, nor can it make special arrangements for attendance at a particular independent school without regard to whether food and drink provided at the school would comply with those nutritional requirements.[67]

Deliberate steps have been taken to restrict education authorities' responsibilities for children whose parents choose an independent education. If children attending independent schools may have additional support needs, education authorities have no obligation to assess or provide for such needs. They have a discretion to assess, if asked to do so by a parent, the young person, or the managers of the school. They can establish whether the pupil has additional support needs and whether, were the education authority responsible for the pupil's school education, a co-ordinated support plan would be required, but they cannot prepare a plan.[68] Parents send children to independent schools at their peril. If the child comes to require additional support, they may not have access to education authority resources.

Meantime, independent schools are faced with the implications of the Charities and Trustee Investment (Scotland) Act 2005. This Act provides for

65 E(S)A 1980 s 98A, added by SE(MPIS)(S)A s 4.
66 See E(S)A 1980, as amended by SE(MPIS)A ss 4, 5 and 6.
67 E(S)A 1980 ss 49(2ZA), 50(1ZA) and 50A, added by S(HPN)(S)A 2007 s 5.
68 E(ASL)A 2004 s 7.

a new Scottish Charity Regulator[69] and a new Scottish Charity Register.[70] To be included on the Register, independent schools must show not only that their purposes consist only of one or more charitable purposes, in this case the advancement of education, but that they provide public benefit in Scotland or elsewhere.[71] In practice, schools that provide assistance by way of means-tested bursaries have retained charitable status, and the associated benefits.

G. PRE-SCHOOL EDUCATION

One of the developments of the late twentieth and early twenty-first centuries has been the increasing emphasis on pre-school education. Before the intervention of the Scottish Parliament, education authorities had the power to provide education for children under school age, but no duty to do so. The Education (Scotland) Act 1996 instituted a voucher system, where parents were issued with vouchers to "purchase" pre-school education from providers who themselves were given grants. The system was fiercely criticised by education authorities. It was repealed by the Standards in Scotland's Schools etc Act 2000.[72] In its place the 2000 Act imposed a new duty on education authorities to provide adequate and efficient school education for certain children under school age.[73] Broadly speaking, education authorities are obliged to provide a certain number of hours of nursery education for those children between the ages of three and five whose parents seek such education,[74] and have power to provide education for other children under school age. Education authorities did not and do not have sufficient nursery schools or classes and have been empowered to enter into arrangements with private providers.[75] This represents a concession to private education, but a necessary one, if the ambition of nursery education for all whose parents wished this was to be achieved.

Having provided for nursery education, the Scottish Parliament proceeded to try to resolve the long-standing controversy as to whether a parent could make a placing request requiring an education authority to provide a primary

---

69 Charities and Trustee Investment (Scotland) Act (hereafter "CTI(S)A 2005") s 1.
70 CTI(S)A 2005 s 3.
71 CTI(S)A 2005 s 7.
72 SSSA 2000 s 39.
73 SSSA 2000 s 32(3), amending E(S)A 1980 s 1 by inserting subss (1A), (1B) and (1C).
74 Provision for School Education for Children under School Age (Prescribed Children) (Scotland) Order 2002, SSI 2002/90.
75 SSSA 2000 s 35.

school place in respect of a child who was too young to be eligible to commence primary education. There were sheriff court decisions that proceeded on the basis that such an "early age placing request" was competent,[76] and decisions to the effect that such a request was not competent.[77] Different education authorities responded in different ways to such requests. The Standards in Scotland's Schools etc Act 2000 made it clear that despite an entitlement to pre-school education, a parent could not insist on a place at any particular nursery.[78] The parent of a child under school age may ask for a school place, and the education authority for the area in which the parent is ordinarily resident should admit the child to school if the school education usually provided in the class is suited to the ability and aptitude of the child.[79] This is, however, a matter for the judgment of the authority. The parent cannot make a placing request. Placing requests for children under school age were effectively proscribed.

Unfortunately, the Act went further than necessary to achieve the objective of preventing placing requests for children too young to attend school. It restricted placing requests to children of school age.[80] This had the effect of preventing a parent from making a placing request for a child due to start primary school. It also prevented a request from being made for a child who had actually started school, if the child was not of school age. Corrective legislation had to be passed in 2002 to allow parents to request places at their school of choice for children starting their primary education.[81] The policy of preventing placing requests for children under school age was then further undermined by the Education (Additional Support for Learning) (Scotland) Act 2004. Gifted children may have additional support needs.[82] Placing requests can be made for pre-school age children with additional support needs.[83] Given that most early age placing requests were based on an assertion that the child was unusually advanced, then the obvious route for a parent seeking a place at school for a child under school age is to proceed under the 2004 Act.

---

76 See, e.g., *Boyne v Grampian Regional Council*, 15 April 1983, unreported, Sh Pr Bell, Aberdeen; *Laverty v Strathclyde Regional Council* 1988 GWD 2-69; *Coates v Lothian Regional Council* 1999 Fam LR 8.

77 See, e.g., *Shiels v City of Edinburgh Council* 1999 Fam LR 86.

78 SSSA 2000 s 43, amending E(S)A 1980 s 28A(1).

79 SSSA 2000 s 38.

80 E(S)A 1980 s 28A(1) (as added (see n 46 above) and amended by SSSA 2000 s 44(2)).

81 E(S)A 1980 s 28A(6), added by the School Education (Amendment) (Scotland) Act 2002 s 1(1) (c).

82 See, e.g., *B v Highland Council* [2007] CSOH 126, 2007 SLT 844.

83 E(ASL)(S)A 2004 s 22, Sch 2 para 2.

H. CURRICULUM

The Scottish Parliament has adhered to Scottish tradition by refraining from legislation in relation to the curriculum, with one notable exception. Until 2000 there was a restriction preventing local authorities from intentionally promoting homosexuality in any public school, nursery school or special school.[84] There were strong views for and against repeal of the restriction when this was debated early in the life of the Parliament. The provision was repealed[85] but a positive duty was imposed on education authorities in the exercise of their functions to have regard to the value of stable family life in a child's development. This was combined with a duty to have regard to the need to ensure that the content of instruction relating to persons of school age is appropriate, having regard to each child's age, understanding and stage of development.[86]

The curriculum in secondary education is effectively controlled by the examination system. The Scottish Parliament inherited an examination system instituted by the Education (Scotland) Act 1996 which combined the Scottish Examination Board and the Scottish Vocational Education Council. The new examination body was the Scottish Qualifications Authority (SQA) and the first year of operation was in 1999/2000, just as the Scottish Parliament started work. The first year of examinations was a disaster: 2.7% of the results and 16,748 candidates were affected by missing or incomplete data. A review of the results revealed a wide range of managerial and organisational weakness.[87] The Parliament responded with the Scottish Qualifications Authority Act 2002. This is a relatively short piece of legislation – just six sections. It reduces the size of the SQA board from between sixteen and twenty-five members to just eight to ten members. It removes the four-year maximum term for membership of the board, and it allows the SQA to pay remuneration to all members of the board, including the chair.[88] The Scottish Ministers assumed the power to make regulations about the procedure of the SQA and its committees,[89] and the power to establish an advisory council.[90] The authority now appears to be operating smoothly.

---

84 Local Government Act 1986 s 2A (added by the Local Government Act 1988 s 28).
85 Ethical Standards in Public Life etc (Scotland) Act 2000 (hereafter "ESPL(S)A 2000") s 34.
86 ESPL(S)A 2000 s 36(a) and (b).
87 *A Review into Examination Results Concerning the Scottish Qualifications Authority*, available at *http://www.scotland.gov.uk/library3/education/sqar-04.asp*.
88 Scottish Qualifications Authority Act (hereafter "SQAA 2002") s 1, amending Education (Scotland) Act 1996.
89 SQAA 2002 s 2.
90 SQAA 2002 s 3; see Advisory Council (Establishment) (Scotland) Regulations 2002, SSI 2002/293.

I. PROVISION FOR ADDITIONAL SUPPORT NEEDS

The Education (Scotland) Act 1980 was amended in 1981[91] to provide for children with "special educational needs". The Scottish Parliament completely revamped provision for such children in the Education (Additional Support for Learning) (Scotland) Act 2004. There is now legislative provision for children and young people who have "additional support needs". Additional support is provision which is additional to, or otherwise different from, the educational provision made generally in state schools for pupils of the same age.[92] A child has additional support needs where, for whatever reason, he or she is, or is likely to be, unable, without the provision of additional support, to benefit from school education provided or to be provided.[93] The statutory intention was to widen the group of children whose needs required to be recognised. Disability and illness may give rise to additional support needs, but so too may difficult family circumstances, or bereavement, or even giftedness. Every education authority is required to make adequate and efficient provision for such additional support as is required by a child or young person for whose school education the authority is responsible. Further, the authority must make appropriate arrangements for keeping under consideration the additional support needs and the adequacy of the support provided for each such child and young person.[94]

This is not unmitigated good news for children, young people and their parents. The duties of education authorities are qualified. Authorities cannot be required to do anything that would result in unreasonable public expenditure being incurred.[95] More seriously, the identification of what provision is required is left in the hands of education authorities, save in a particular category of cases. Challenge would be difficult. Matters are different in the category of cases where a child or young person requires a "co-ordinated support plan". The requirement for such a plan is not solely linked to the severity of the need. It relates to the requirement for co-ordination of support between different agencies. Co-ordinated support plans are available only to pupils for whose education an education authority is responsible. The child or young person must have additional support needs arising from one or more complex factors or from multiple factors. Those needs must be likely to continue for more than a year, and they must require significant additional

---

91 E(S)A 1981.
92 E(ASL)(S)A 2004 s 1(3)(a).
93 E(ASL)(S)A 2004 s 1(1).
94 E(ASL)(S)A 2004 s 4(1).
95 E(ASL)(S)A 2004 s 4(2)(b).

support to be provided by the education authority in the exercise of any of its other functions as well as in the exercise of its functions relating to education or by one or more other agencies as well as by the education authority itself.[96] When a co-ordinated support plan is prepared, then an education authority must ensure that additional support is provided by it for the child or young person in accordance with the plan.[97] In other words, the education authority can be held accountable by reference to the plan, at least in so far as it is in its power to make the provision specified in the plan. If the plan identifies another person to provide the support, the education authority should seek to ensure that the additional support is provided by that person in accordance with the plan. The authority should, so far as possible, co-ordinate the provision of additional support for the child or young person.[98]

New battle lines have been drawn up between parents anxious to have their child's needs identified and met, and who see a co-ordinated support plan as a means to this end, and education authorities who find the procedure for assessment, preparation of a plan, and the obligation to make specified provision onerous, time-consuming and expensive.[99] This appears to have come as something of a surprise to the Members of the Scottish Parliament, who seem to have anticipated that the 2004 Act would function in a consensual manner. There is a strong emphasis in the Act on resolving differences of view. There is express provision for education authorities to provide mediation services[100] and, in addition, for dispute resolution by an independent adjudicator.[101] A new tribunal service, the Additional Support Needs Tribunals for Scotland,[102] was established, with jurisdiction in relation to matters related to co-ordinated support plans and placing requests for pupils with such plans. No legal aid is available for the tribunal. The tribunal rules require cases to be dealt with in a way that is proportionate to the complexity of the issue and the resources of the parties, with an objective of seeking informality and flexibility and ensuring that parties are on an equal footing procedurally and able to participate fully in the proceedings.[103]

---

96 E(ASL)(S)A 2004 s 2(1); see *JT v Stirling Council* 2007 SC 783.
97 E(ASL)(S)A 2004 s 11(5)(b).
98 E(ASL)(S)A 2004 s 11(5)(c) and (d).
99 See *B v Highland Regional Council* 2007 SLT 844; *JT v Stirling Council* 2007 SC 783; *WA's Legal Representative v Highland Council* [2008] CSIH 5, 2008 Fam LR 130.
100 E(ASL)(S)A 2004 s 15.
101 E(ASL)A 2004 s 16; see Additional Support for Learning Dispute Resolution (Scotland) Regulations 2005, SSI 2005/501.
102 E(ASL)A 2004 s 17.
103 Additional Support Needs Tribunals for Scotland (Practice and Procedure) Rules 2006, SSI 2006/88; see in particular r 3.

The 2004 Act provided for an appeal to the Court of Session on a point of law.[104] This was the first time that appeal to the Court of Session had been possible in relation to the education of children with additional support needs. There was a series of appeals.[105] These were greeted with some dismay, as they exposed deficiencies in the drafting of the Act and an unexpectedly "adversarial" context. A new amending Bill was framed. The debates on the Bill are instructive of the approach of the Parliament. The minister responsible for education, in a comment to the Education, Lifelong Learning and Culture Committee, was critical of the involvement by education authorities of lawyers in the Additional Support Needs Tribunal, a criticism echoed by the committee. There was little appreciation of the role of lawyers in elucidating legislation and assisting parties to apply the law in circumstances involving children with complex needs, where there may be a tension between parental concern and a shortage of resources.

The Education (Additional Support for Learning) (Scotland) Act 2009 does not impress as easily comprehensible at first sight, but with scissors and paste and a good deal of patience it is possible to discern that the draftsman is seeking to reverse a number of the decisions of the Court of Session in relation to the interpretation of the 2004 Act. In particular, parents of children with additional support needs will be able to make placing requests at schools in the area of education authorities other than the area in which they live.[106] A restrictive interpretation of "additional support needs" as limited to educational support offered in a teaching environment will be expanded to cover provision other than educational provision.[107] The jurisdiction of the Additional Support Needs Tribunal will extend to placing requests for pupils for whom education authorities propose to establish a co-ordinated support plan.[108] The 2009 Act also tidies up certain deficiencies in the 2004 Act, including the rather awkward relationship between placing request cases that may oscillate between the Additional Support Needs Tribunal and the ordinary process of appeal committees and the sheriff court, depending on

104   E(ASL)A 2004 s 21.
105   *Gordon, Appellant* 2007 FamLR 76; *SM, Appellant* 2007 FamLR 2; *B v Highland Council* [2007] CSOH 126, 2007 SLT 844; *JT v Stirling Council* [2007] CSIH 52, 2007 SC 783; *G v Argyll and Bute Council* [2008] CSOH 61, 2008 SLT 541; *C v City of Edinburgh Council* [2008] CSOH 60, 2008 SLT 522; *WA's Legal Representative v Highland Council* [2008] CSIH 5, 2008 Fam LR 130; *WD v Glasgow City Council* [2007] CSOH 139, 2007 SLT 881, affd [2007] CSIH 72, 2008 SC 117; *Edinburgh City Council v K* [2009] CSIH 46, 2009 SC 625.
106   Education (Additional Support for Learning) Act 2009 (hereafter "E(ASL)A 2009") s 1, reversing *WD v Glasgow City Council* [2007] CSIH 72, 2008 SC 117.
107   E(ASL)A 2009 s 6, reversing *C v City of Edinburgh Council* [2008] CSOH 60, 2008 SLT 522.
108   E(ASL)A 2009 s 1(7)(d), reversing *Gordon, Appellant* 2007 FamLR 76.

whether or not a co-ordinated support plan is required.[109] It also tackles issues of enforcement in so far as a parent will be able to complain to the Additional Support Needs Tribunal if an education authority fails to provide additional support identified in a co-ordinated support plan[110] and gives the president of the tribunal the power to monitor implementation of the tribunal's decisions and refer failures to the Scottish Ministers.[111] Sadly, the increased powers of enforcement will serve to increase the gap between pupils with a co-ordinated support plan and those without.

J. FURTHER AND HIGHER EDUCATION

Further and higher education have traditionally each adopted a different focus. Further education has generally been directed towards vocational qualifications, while degree studies have been the province of higher education. Since devolution there has been a movement in policy towards lifelong learning and an erosion of the distinction between further and higher education. Further education colleges have become known as "Scotland's colleges" in recognition of higher education level work carried out there. Some colleges have been recognised as higher education institutions or universities with power to grant their own degrees. For example, UHI Millennium Institute is a partnership of a number of colleges and research institutions in the Highlands and Islands. It was awarded higher education status by the Scottish Parliament in 2001[112] and the right to grant degrees in 2008.[113]

The Further and Higher Education (Scotland) Act 2005 reduced the distinction between the two branches of tertiary education by abolishing separate funding councils and establishing a single Scottish Funding Council for Further and Higher Education. The Scottish Ministers provide support to the Council[114] and the Council has a general duty to exercise its functions for the purpose of securing coherent provision by the bodies it funds of a high quality of further education and higher education and the undertaking of research.[115] The Council must promote the use of a credit and qualifications framework for further and higher education as a whole, through which

---

109   See E(ASL)A 2009 s 1(8)(b), amending E(ASL)A 2004 s 19(5).
110   E(ASL)A 2009 s 18(1)(a), adding E(ASL)A 2004 s 18(3)(d)(ia).
111   E(ASL)A 2009 s 21, adding E(ASL)A 2004 s 11A.
112   Designation of UHI Millennium Institute (Scotland) Order 2001, SSI 2001/39.
113   Academic Awards and Distinctions (UHI Millennium Institute) (Scotland) Order of Council 2008, SSI 2008/212.
114   Further and Higher Education (Scotland) Act 2005 (hereafter "FEH(S)A 2005") s 4.
115   FHE(S)A 2005 s 3.

programmes of learning and courses of education may be compared and understood in relation to one another.[116] There are also general duties for the Council in relation to Scotland. It is required to have regard to skills needs in Scotland and to have a skills committee for the purpose of advising on matters relating to skills.[117] It must have regard to issues affecting the economy of Scotland and social and cultural issues in Scotland.[118] It should have regard to the desirability of achieving sustainable development, and encourage the further and higher education bodies eligible for funding to contribute to this aim.[119] While the opportunity has been taken in this Act to focus on the needs of Scotland in particular, the Council must, in exercising its functions, have regard to the United Kingdom context and the international context.[120]

The Parliament also addressed the support needs of individual students to access lifelong learning. Young people over the school leaving age but under the age of twenty are eligible for payment of an education maintenance allowance to encourage them to stay in full-time education, whether at school or in further education.[121] The Education and Training (Scotland) Act 2000 provides a framework for payment of grants to meet the cost of certain courses. The Act gave the power to pass regulations allowing grants to be paid to or in respect of individuals.[122] This power was exercised to provide for individual learning accounts[123] available for courses of further education. Individual learning accounts are not available for school education, full-time higher education, training statutorily required for a particular employment or driving lessons.[124] Individual learning accounts may be used to provide for tuition fees and costs such as registration and examination fees associated with a particular course. They may also be used for part-time higher education or professional qualifications. They are available, for example, to assist students undertaking part-time Open University courses.

Shortly before devolution, the Westminster Parliament had passed the Teaching and Higher Education Act 1998 which provided for university students to pay a means-tested contribution towards tuition fees, while living costs were to be supported by loans, repayable on the basis of income after graduation. The new Scottish Parliament set up an independent committee

116 FHE(S)A 2005 s 14.
117 FHE(S)A 2005 s 20(1)(a), Sch 1 para 11.
118 FHE(S)A 2005 s 20(1)(b), (c) and (6).
119 FHE(S)A 2005 s 20(2)(a), (b).
120 FHE(S)A 2005 s 20(3)(a), (b).
121 Education Maintenance Allowances (Scotland) Regulations 2007, SSI 2007/156.
122 Education and Training (Scotland) Act 2000.
123 Individual Learning Account (Scotland) Regulations 2004, SSI 2004/83.
124 SSI 2004/83 reg 10(3).

of inquiry into Student Finances, chaired by Andrew Cubie. The recommendations of that committee resulted in the Education (Graduate Endowment and Student Support) (Scotland) Act 2001. Scottish students, unlike their English counterparts, were not to be required to make an immediate contribution towards tuition fees, but instead a Scottish graduate endowment scheme was introduced. Students were expected, on graduation, to make a payment to cover the cost of tuition, subject to certain exemptions.[125] Bursaries were available for young people from low-income families and for mature students. In 2008, the graduate endowment was abolished by the Graduate Endowment Abolition (Scotland) Act 2008. Students who complete their course on or after 1 April 2007 are not required to pay the endowment. There is now a major difference between student support for Scottish students studying at Scottish universities and higher education institutions and their English counterparts. The English and those Scottish students who choose to study in England pay tuition fees. English students studying in Scotland are required to pay tuition fees, albeit these are lower than the fees at English universities. Scottish students studying in Scotland do not pay any tuition fees. Scottish students remain eligible for loans to cover living costs and are required to repay those loans after graduation.[126]

One difference between England and Scotland introduced in the Further and Higher Education (Scotland) Act 2005[127] is the extension of the role of the Scottish Public Services Ombudsman. Whereas England and Wales have established the Office of the Independent Adjudicator for Higher Education to deal with student complaints, in Scotland complaints of injustice or hardship as a result of maladministration on the part of institutions of further or higher education may be referred to the existing office of the Ombudsman. The service is free and regularly investigates allegations by students, as can be seen from its website.[128] Referral to the Ombudsman is an attractive alternative to the more cumbersome and expensive alternatives of an action for judicial review or for breach of contract. Extension of the Ombudsman's jurisdiction has been a creative use of a Scottish institution to fulfil a particular need in relation to Scottish further and higher education.

---

125   Education (Graduate Endowment and Student Support) (Scotland) Act 2001, ss 1 and 4.
126   Education (Student Loans) (Scotland) Regulations 2007, SSI 2007/154.
127   FHE(S)A 2005 s 27, adding to Scottish Public Services Ombudsman Act 2002 Sch 2 Pt 3 para 90.
128   Available at *www.spso.org.uk*.

K. RESERVED AND DEVOLVED ISSUES

While education law is devolved under the Scotland Act 1998, there are matters reserved to the Westminster Parliament that bear upon education. On occasion these have called for legislation. For example, the Data Protection Act 1998 allows pupils access to records processed by an authority for the purposes of its function in securing school education which relate to the discharge of that function in respect of that pupil.[129] Parents are not the subject of such data and there were concerns that they could not access pupil records. The Scottish Parliament dealt with this in the Education (Disability Strategies and Pupils' Educational Records) (Scotland) Act 2002 by providing for new regulations in relation to the keeping, transferring and disclosure of educational records.[130] The regulations govern disclosure to parents.[131]

The same Act deals with an issue related to the disability discrimination legislation. Equal opportunities are a reserved matter under the Scotland Act 1998, but encouragement of equal opportunities and the observance of equal opportunities requirements is devolved, and is the responsibility of the Scottish Parliament. Bodies responsible for schools are obliged to prepare an accessibility strategy to increase the extent to which pupils with a disability can participate in the school's curriculum. The strategy should deal with improving the physical environment of the school and improving communication with pupils with a disability.[132] Education authorities have duties to promote disability equality, gender equality and race equality. The Scottish Ministers have exercised powers to impose by order duties to ensure better performance of equality duties of education authorities.[133]

L. CONCLUSIONS

In the debate on the Education (Additional Support for Learning) Scotland Bill in 2009 Members of the Scottish Parliament expressed dismay about the complexity of the law. They were referring to the law in relation to just one area of education, but the comment could be applied to the whole of Scottish

---

129 Data Protection Act 1998 ss 1(1)(d), 68(1)(b), Sch 11 para 5.
130 Education (Disability Strategies and Pupils' Educational Records) (Scotland) Act 2002 (hereafter "E(DSPER)(S)A 2002") s 4.
131 Pupils' Educational Records (Scotland) Regulations 2003, SSI 2003/581.
132 E(DSPER)(S)A 2002 s 1.
133 Disability Discrimination (Public Authorities) (Statutory Duties) (Scotland) Regulations 2005, SSI 2005/565; Sex Discrimination (Public Authorities) (Statutory Duties) (Scotland) Order 2007, SSI 2007/32; Race Relations Act 1976 (Statutory Duties) (Scotland) Order 2002, SSI 2002/62.

education law. Before devolution this was a patchwork of measures in need of rationalisation. Ten years later, the problem has been exacerbated by grafting yet more measures onto the Education (Scotland) Act 1980 and by legislation designed to operate alongside the 1980 Act. Some measures were necessary to keep in step with modern developments across the United Kingdom in areas such as data protection and the requirements of the equality legislation. Others have been driven by considerations of Scottish policy. While there is now an urgent requirement for codification, such a project would require a greater understanding of education law than that displayed by the draftsmen to date. It is disappointing that two out of fourteen statutes have been required principally to correct deficiencies in earlier statutes out of the fourteen.

The Scottish Parliament clearly has significant aspirations for education. The trend towards centralising power and marginalising parents emphasises the responsibilities of education authorities and the Scottish Ministers. It is interesting that statutes focusing on structural reform of the Scottish Qualifications Authority and the organisation of funding of further and higher education appear to meet their policy objectives. Developments that depend on the continued availability of resources may have an uncertain future. Free school meals and reduced primary class sizes are already under pressure. Support for lifelong learning and, in particular, free tuition for Scottish students at Scottish universities look precarious.

Looking at the Parliament's record on education law over the first ten years, it is not clear that legislation has consistently been seen as a framework for delivery of education. There has, on occasion, been a lack of realism about the need for practical measures to put policy into practice and a tendency to rely on guidance where legislation was required. There has been a failure to recognise the tensions inherent in the provision of education and the constitutional role of the courts and of legal practitioners in understanding and applying the law. The difficulties of legislating for education should not be underestimated, but reflection on the statutes of the past ten years does indicate there is scope for improvement in the next decade.

Justice and Legal System

10 The Reform of the Scottish Judiciary

Gavin F M Little[°]

A. INTRODUCTION

Scottish judges[1] possess considerable power over their fellow citizens and under the constitution. The Scottish Parliament has, in its first decade of law-making, introduced important statutory reforms of the judiciary with the objective of modernising its position in the constitution and strengthening its internal structures and processes. Indeed, for the higher judiciary in the Court of Session in particular, the passing by the Parliament of the Judiciary and Courts (Scotland) Act 2008[2] (hereafter "the 2008 Act") is one of the most significant legislative landmarks since the Act of Union 1707.

This chapter is set out as follows. First, brief consideration is given to the importance of a strong, independent judiciary for the maintenance of the rule of law. Second, the constitutional and legal provision for Scottish judges prior to the 2008 Act is evaluated. Third, the main reforms introduced by the 2008 Act are analysed. The chapter then concludes with a short assessment of the Parliament's contribution to the area.

° Professor of Law, School of Law, University of Stirling. I would like to thank my colleague, Dr Kay Goodall, for her insightful comments.

1 That is, judges of the Court of Session, temporary judges, the chairman of the Scottish Land Court, sheriffs principal, sheriffs, part-time sheriffs and justices of the peace. Court of Session judges are, of course, also judges in the High Court of Justiciary.

2 2008 asp 6.

B. THE JUDICIARY AND THE RULE OF LAW

The independence, impartiality and competence of the judiciary are fundamental to maintaining the authority of the courts. Judicial independence is sustained by the legal and constitutional protections which seek to ensure that judges are collectively and individually safeguarded from external influences when adjudicating.[3] Impartiality requires that individual judges are unbiased decision-takers.[4] Scottish judges have tended to take a pragmatic approach to the distinction between independence and impartiality, recognising that they may be inter-linked. For example, while an independent judge may be biased, it is also the case that insufficient provision for judicial independence may give rise to bias or the impression that it exists. It is axiomatic that there must be public confidence in the professional competence of judges, given their central role in the courts.[5] While the levels of competence will vary from one judicial office to another, the degree of responsibility and complexity involved in judging even relatively minor cases is often substantial.

Legal and constitutional provision must therefore ensure that appropriately qualified judges can take decisions impartially on the basis of the law and the arguments presented to them, and that, in so doing, they are protected from external influence or pressure.[6] Moreover, the effectiveness of this provision should be ostensive – that is, it should be clearly demonstrative in order to maintain public confidence in the judicial decision-taking process.

It should also be appreciated that the concept of judicial independence in particular has profound constitutional significance. In Scotland, as throughout the UK, it is a long established constitutional convention that judges should be independent in the sense that they should not be subject to political influence, pressure, interference or threats. As Lord Cullen has stated, "An independent judiciary is a feature of every democracy which is worth the name".[7] Indeed, the traditional conceptualisation of judges as independent legal shamans detached from political influences constitutes an iconic idealisation of the judicial function within the constitution, which has deep historical roots.[8]

3 Lord Hope, "Judicial independence" (2002) *SLT* 105. See also S C Styles, "The Scottish judiciary", in A McHarg and T Mullen (eds), *Public Law in Scotland* (2006) 174 at 177-178.

4 Styles, "The Scottish judiciary" (n 3).

5 *Starrs v Ruxton* 2000 JC 208, per Lord Prosser at 232; and *Clancy v Caird* 2000 SC 441 per Lord Sutherland at 455 and per Lord Coulsfield at 459-460. See also Lord Hope, "Judicial independence" (n 3) 106 and Styles, "The Scottish judiciary" (n3) at 177-178.

6 Second Principle, UN Basic Principles on the Independence of the Judiciary endorsed by General Assembly Resolution 40/32 (1985).

7 Lord Cullen, "The judge and the public" (1998) *SLT (News)* 261.

8 For example, the attempt by King James VII to weaken judicial independence by changing judicial tenure was countered by the Claim of Right 1689. Thereafter, tenure *ad vitam aut culpam* was a feature of holding office as a Court of Session judge: see Erskine, I, 2, 32.

Society expects a higher standard of decision-taking from judges than from others, such as government ministers, and independence is central to the ideal of what judges are meant to be. Thus, as articulated in the *Latimer House Guidelines*,[9] which provide an influential Commonwealth-wide statement of good practice to govern the inter-relationships between the judiciary, the executive and the legislature, there should be effective rules and procedures for, *inter alia*, judicial appointments, salaries, training, conduct and removal from office, in order to maintain judicial independence and public confidence.[10]

Crucially, however, what makes judicial independence of fundamental constitutional importance is that it is essential for the maintenance of the rule of law. Although rule of law theory has long stimulated lively debate in the UK, the significance attached to the independence of the judiciary in maintaining the rule of law is a unifying theme.[11] Without an independent judiciary which is able to decide cases on the facts and according to the law without fear or favour, the consequences are not simply widespread injustice and abuse of power but also a more fundamental lack of social and constitutional certainty and cohesion, as individuals attempt to plan their futures without effective recourse to the law.[12] Judicial independence is a vital constitutional indicator of the importance ascribed to the rule of law in Scotland, as elsewhere, and is essential to its perpetuation.

C. PROVISION FOR SCOTTISH JUDGES PRIOR TO THE 2008 ACT

Although schooled in the pragmatic context of legal practice rather than rule of law theory, Scottish judges have long felt themselves to be independent of political and other influences. In the absence of a formal constitution, however, the separation of powers between the executive and the judiciary has been haphazard in Scotland. The successful challenge in 2000 to the appointment by the Scottish Executive of temporary sheriffs for renewable one-year fixed terms on the grounds that it breached the right to trial before an independent and impartial tribunal under the European Convention on Human Rights provided a salutary reminder of just how ad hoc arrangements can be.[13]

9 The *Latimer House Guidelines* were first drafted in 1998. They were annexed to the *Commonwealth Principles on the Three Branches of Government*, and re-issued in 2009.

10 *Latimer House Guidelines*. See also Lord Hope, "Judicial independence" (n 3).

11 A V Dicey, *Introduction to the Study of the Law of the Constitution*, 9th edn (1941) 202-203, 409-410; J Raz, "The rule of law and its virtue" (1977) 93 *LQR* 195 at 200-201; and T R S Allan, *Law, Liberty and Justice* (1993) 49-50.

12 Raz, "The rule of law and its virtue" (n 11) 205.

13 *Starrs* v *Ruxton* 2000 JC 208.

In this context, it is perhaps surprising that the independence of the judiciary has not been called into question more often in Scotland.[14] That this has not happened is likely to be because, notwithstanding the issue of temporary sheriffs, Scottish judges have for the most part enjoyed strong *de facto* security of tenure, which is a key prerequisite of independence. In addition, the setting and payment of judges' salaries, which could have an obvious influence on judicial independence, has not been a matter of concern in Scotland[15] and judges effectively have immunity from legal suit.[16] Indeed, despite the occasional tussle with government, such as over the issue of criminal sentencing, it is clear from their decisions and extra-judicial statements that Scottish judges do not feel themselves to be subject to direct political pressure,[17] and no Court of Session judge has been removed from office since before 1707.[18] Moreover, the issue of judicial impartiality has not been a significant concern in Scotland. Although the common law rule against bias (which provides for judicial impartiality by requiring that a person may not be a judge in his or her own cause) is not without complexity, the impartiality of Scottish judges is seldom called into question.[19] Similarly, public confidence in the collective professional competence of the judiciary is generally high, although some individual judgments may, inevitably, be controversial.

The absence of a clear separation of powers has, however, influenced how judges throughout the UK have defined their independence from the political process. Traditionally, they had tended, by focusing on individual rights and limiting their own discretion, to avoid involvement in areas that could lead to the boundaries of judicial activity being expanded into the public policy arena, thereby voluntarily pre-empting conflict with the government and Parliament.[20] By exercising their inherent common law power to

---

14 There has, however, been some academic commentary arguing that the homogenous social conditioning of judges may influence their decision-taking. This approach was developed in the Scottish context in I D Willock, "Scottish judges scrutinised" 1969 *JR* 193; and S C Styles, "The Scottish judiciary 1919-1986" 1988 *JR* 41.

15 A A Paterson et al, *The Legal System of Scotland: Cases and Materials* (1999) at 237; and Lord Hope, "Judicial independence" (n 3) at 107.

16 See C M G Himsworth and C M O'Neill, *Scotland's Constitution: Law and Practice* (2009) at 309-310.

17 Although there are no grounds for complacency about the relationship between the judiciary and the executive: see Lord Hope, "Judicial independence" (n 3) at 106-111.

18 A number have, however, resigned. Only two sheriffs have been removed from office since the Sheriff Courts (Scotland) Act 1971: see Paterson et al, *The Legal System of Scotland* (n 15) at 232-237.

19 Himsworth and O'Neill, *Scotland's Constitution* (n 16) at 312-318. *Starrs v Ruxton* (n 13) was, *inter alia*, a challenge to judicial impartiality: for a further rare example, see *Hoekstra v HM Advocate (No 2)* 2000 SLT 602.

20 Lord McCluskey, *Law, Justice and Democracy: the Reith Lectures 1986* (1987) 24; and Lord Devlin, *The Judge* (1979) at 5-17.

make law under the self-imposed restraints of statutory interpretation and *stare decisis*, judges defined as if by osmosis their relationship with political authority[21] and, arguably, Scottish judges have tended to be more reluctant to extend their law-making powers in public policy areas than their English equivalents.[22]

The Scotland Act 1998 and the Human Rights Act 1998, however, require Scottish judges to exercise a very much more direct and powerful role within the political constitution than was previously the case – a role which Aidan O'Neill examines critically in chapter 3 of this book. The allocation to judges of major constitutional review functions under these Acts was not without controversy. In particular, although judges in England do not have the Scotland Act to contend with, the extension of their power to review government and public authority decision-taking under the Human Rights Act created considerable tension with the UK government. Matters came to a head in 2003, when, against the background of aggressive criticisms of the judiciary's handling of human rights cases by the then Home Secretary, the UK government announced major proposals for judicial reform south of the Border.[23] Although the announcement was rushed and inept,[24] the UK government's main proposals were, after compromise with the judiciary, enacted in the Constitutional Reform Act 2005 ("the Constitutional Reform Act"), which made significant provision for England and Wales. It reformed the post of Lord Chancellor and the system of judicial appointments,[25] established the Lord Chief Justice as the head of the judiciary,[26] provided statutory protection for judicial independence,[27] and created new systems and processes for judicial conduct and discipline.[28] Similar changes were introduced for Northern Ireland.[29] In a UK-wide context, the Act has, of course, replaced the historic system of law lords operating as a committee of the House of Lords with the UK Supreme Court.[30]

21 For analysis, see Lord Steyn, "Deference: a tangled story" 2005 *PL* 346.
22 For example, until *T, Petr* 1997 SLT 724 per LP Hope at 733, the Scottish courts had held that the European Convention on Human Rights was, as an international treaty, not even an aid to interpreting domestic law: see *Kaur v Lord Advocate* 1980 SC 319. The courts in England had taken a less restrictive view: see *R v Secretary of State for the Home Department, ex parte Brind* [1991] AC 696.
23 S Prince, "The law and politics: upsetting the judicial apple-cart" 57/2 (2004) *Parliamentary Affairs* 288.
24 Prince, "The law and politics" (n 23) 289-290.
25 Constitutional Reform Act ss 2, 61-98.
26 Constitutional Reform Act s 7.
27 Constitutional Reform Act s 3.
28 Constitutional Reform Act ss 62, 99-114.
29 Constitutional Reform Act ss 4, 10-11 and Pt 5.
30 Constitutional Reform Act ss 23-60.

Importantly, the reform of the Scottish judiciary was not included in the Constitutional Reform Act, as this was a matter for the Scottish Parliament. The Act had, however, left Scottish provision for the judiciary looking anachronistic and unstructured. That this was so is unsurprising. While there was piecemeal statutory provision for the appointment, tenure and removal of sheriffs and justices of the peace,[31] the rules and procedures applying to Court of Session judges in the immediate post-devolution period were ad hoc and archaic. Although the appointment process for Court of Session judges had been reformed under the Scotland Act,[32] the legal qualifications required for appointment were provided for by the Union with England Act 1707, as amended.[33] Tenure of office for Court of Session judges had been determined by custom and, under the Claim of Right 1689, had long been *ad vitam aut culpam*, or during good behaviour,[34] with a compulsory retirement age fixed under statute.[35] Remarkably, there had been no formal system for the removal of a Court of Session judge from office until one was introduced by the Scotland Act,[36] which also added a further ground to the old test of *culpa*.[37] As was the case south of the Border before the Constitutional Reform Act, there was no statutory provision to protect judicial independence.

Although a non-statutory Judicial Appointments Board for Scotland ("JAB") was established by the Scottish Executive in 2002 to make recommendations for appointment to the Bench,[38] there had been concern for some time that the judicial appointments process lacked transparency and was open to abuse.[39] Since candidates for the most senior judicial posts emerged from the small "pool" of the Scottish Bar, it had been "open to attack on grounds of

---

31 Sheriffs were appointed under the Scotland Act 1998 s 94 and the Sheriff Courts (Scotland) Act 1971 s 5. Provision for removal from office was made under the Sheriff Courts (Scotland) Act 1971 s 12. Justices of the peace were appointed under the District Courts (Scotland) Act 1975 ss 9, 11 and 14, and could be removed from office under s 15.
32 Scotland Act 1998 s 95.
33 Union with England Act 1707 s 19; and Law Reform (Miscellaneous Provisions) (Scotland) Act 1990 s 35 and Sch 4. Under the 1707 and 1990 Acts, appointees were to be advocates, sheriffs principal or solicitors of at least five years' standing who had rights of audience in the Court of Session and the High Court of Justiciary.
34 Art 13.
35 Judicial Pensions and Retirement Act 1993: retirement is compulsory at age seventy, extendable to seventy-five.
36 Scotland Act 1998 s 95. See C Himsworth, "Securing the tenure of Scottish judges" (1999) *PL* 14.
37 That is, inability.
38 This had been suggested in Scottish Executive, *Judicial Appointments: An Inclusive Approach* (2000).
39 C M Campbell, "Judicial selection (and judicial impartiality)" 1973 *JR*, 254.

patronage, social class bias and narrowness of experience".[40] There was also pressure to increase the small number of woman judges, particularly on the Court of Session Bench.[41]

Prior to the establishment of the JAB, while there was no suggestion of impropriety or of interference with judicial independence, there was, disturbingly, no clear separation of powers in the judicial appointment process which, on the face of it, was controlled by the government. In the period immediately following devolution, and notwithstanding the reforms introduced by the Scotland Act, appointment to the Court of Session Bench by the Queen was based on the recommendation of either the Prime Minister following nomination by the First Minister (for the posts of Lord President and Lord Justice-Clerk) or the First Minister alone (in relation to other Court of Session judges).[42] It is not, of course, necessarily problematic for politicians to have a role in the appointment of judges: indeed, some political involvement may be appropriate to confer the imprimatur of democratic authority to the judiciary. Crucially, however, the Lord Advocate – a member of the government – had a key role in deciding who should be recommended, and the deliberations were secret.[43] The system of appointment to the Scottish Bench was therefore potentially open to abuse and political manipulation, notwithstanding the integrity of those involved.

Even more disturbingly, until the creation of the JAB, Lords Advocate could also succeed to the posts of Lord President or Lord Justice-Clerk, or the Court of Session Bench, if a vacancy occurred during their term of office. Under a long-standing system of patronage, Lords Advocate could (and would), notwithstanding their position as members of the government, and apparently on their own nomination, be appointed to the most senior posts in the Scottish judiciary when they fell vacant. Despite some academic criticism,[44] this anachronistic practice had gone largely unnoticed and, within

---

40 Campbell, "Judicial selection" (n 39) at 278-279; and Paterson et al, *The Legal System of Scotland* (n 15) at 228.

41 Paterson et al, *The Legal System of Scotland* (n 15) at 230.

42 The Prime Minister must only recommend those who have been nominated by the First Minister: Scotland Act 1998 s 95.

43 Before devolution, the Lord Advocate was the chief UK government Scottish law officer, head of the Scottish prosecution service and a member of the government. After devolution, the Lord Advocate performs similar legal functions for, and as a member of, the Scottish Executive (or Government, as it is now called): see the Scotland Act 1998 s 44. For discussion of the "pivotal" role of the Lord Advocate in judicial appointments at this time, see HL Deb 2 November 1998, cols18-27, per Lord Hope at col 20.

44 See Willock, "Scottish judges scrutinised" (n 14); C M Campbell, "Judicial selection" (n 39); R Black, "The Scottish Parliament and the Scottish judiciary" 1998 *SLT (News)* 321; and C O'Neill, "The constitutional position of the Lord Advocate", *The Journal*, 1 March 2000.

the confines of the Scottish legal establishment, caused little comment.[45] Once matters had become subject to the more local scrutiny of the Scottish Parliament, however, the appointment of Lord Hardie, who was Lord Advocate in the first Scottish Executive, to the Court of Session Bench in 2000 caused a bare-knuckled political brawl.[46]

Moreover, until the 2008 Act, there was no formal mechanism governing the conduct or disciplining of Scottish judges, short of removal from office.[47] Broadly, the Lord President was responsible for overseeing the conduct of Court of Session judges, with sheriffs principal supervising the sheriffs in their sheriffdoms. Notwithstanding this, it was unclear how complaints against judges could be raised, how they would be investigated, and even how many were being made.[48] The power of the Lord President and sheriffs principal was essentially informal. This absence of structured rules and procedures and general lack of transparency was criticised by the Scottish Government, which stated in the policy memorandum on the Judiciary and Courts (Scotland) Bill that the lack of a formal process for investigating judicial conduct was "inconsistent with modern day standards".[49]

Reservations had also been expressed about the level of training for Scottish judges by comparison with their counterparts in England and Wales. While training should not compromise judicial independence and should accordingly be provided by judges themselves, it is an obvious means of improving competence, facilitating professional development and maintaining public confidence.[50] It is potentially a cause for concern that provision for judicial training in Scotland, which is provided by the Judicial Studies Committee, has historically lagged behind that which is available for judges south of the Border.[51]

45 Although the move of Lord Rodger (who was Lord Advocate in John Major's Conservative government) to the post of Lord President in 1997 gave rise to some criticism of the appointments system: see Paterson et al, *The Legal System of Scotland* (n 15) at 226.

46 Scottish Parliament, *Official Report*, cols 1221-1224 and 1230-1259 (17 February 2000). Note that it was stated that Lord Hardie had not been involved in the appointment process: the main cause of controversy was the effect that his resignation as Lord Advocate to take up a judicial post would have on the Lockerbie bomber trial.

47 J Harrison, "Judging the judges: the new scheme of judicial conduct and discipline in Scotland" (2009) *ELR* 427 at 431.

48 J Harrison, "Judging the judges (n 47).

49 Policy Memorandum on the Judiciary and Courts (Scotland) Bill, SP Bill 6-PM, Session 3 (2008) para 82.

50 Note that the creation of a culture of training is an important aspect of the *Latimer House Guidelines*: see *Commonwealth Principles* (n 12) at 18.

51 Paterson et al, *The Legal System of Scotland* (n 15) at 230-231. See also the comments of Sheriff Crowe, formerly Director of the Judicial Studies Committee, in "Sheriff calls for increased judicial training", *The Journal*, 15 September 2008.

Prior to the 2008 Act, therefore, the overall provision for the Scottish judiciary was a piecemeal "patchwork quilt" of constitutional doctrine, statute, custom and administrative arrangements, dating from the seventeenth century to the present. Some parts of the system were transparent and others were not and, like Topsy, it had "just growed". Importantly, there was no doubt that Scottish judges were strongly independent. Nonetheless, in the context of the judges' new responsibilities for constitutional review under the Scotland Act and the Human Rights Act, the controversies over the judicial appointments process, and the comprehensive re-structuring of the judiciary elsewhere in the UK under the Constitutional Reform Act, the anachronistic and somewhat Heath Robinson nature of the arrangements for the Scottish judiciary was increasingly apparent.

D. THE JUDICIARY AND COURTS (SCOTLAND) ACT 2008

Against this backdrop, the Scottish Executive published its consultation document *Strengthening Judicial Independence in a Modern Scotland* in 2006.[52] Its objective was to prepare the ground for legislation which would give the judiciary "greater opportunities to secure the speedier and more efficient and effective disposal of the business of the courts".[53] Significantly, the consultation was based on the premise that the judiciary was best placed to carry out this responsibility, but that the way in which it was organised worked against the development and implementation of consistent policies throughout the court system.[54] The core theme was that the Scottish Executive wished to strengthen judicial independence by removing itself from the administration of the courts, after having modernised "the organisation and leadership" of the judiciary.[55]

The consultation and subsequent passage of the Judiciary and Courts (Scotland) Bill through the Scottish Parliament in 2008 generated relatively little controversy, at least by comparison with the furore which had surrounded the Constitutional Reform Act at Westminster. Although the Lord President and other judges criticised particular proposals, the Bill was, after amendment, passed unanimously.

---

52 Scottish Executive, *Strengthening Judicial Independence in a Modern Scotland* (2006) 1. See also Scottish Executive, *Proposals for a Judiciary (Scotland) Bill* (2007).
53 Scottish Executive, *Strengthening Judicial Independence* (n 52).
54 Scottish Executive, *Strengthening Judicial Independence* (n 52).
55 Scottish Executive, *Strengthening Judicial Independence* (n 52) 2.

Now that the Act has come into force,[56] and notwithstanding that it was influenced initially by the Constitutional Reform Act, it will constitute a significant reform of the Scottish judiciary. The rest of this chapter focuses on the following key areas: the statutory guarantee of continued judicial independence;[57] the establishment of the Lord President as the head of the Scottish judiciary;[58] the designation of the JAB as a statutory body;[59] the new provision for judicial conduct, discipline and removal from office;[60] and the role of the Lord President in the Scottish Court Service.[61]

(1) Guarantee of continued judicial independence

The 2008 Act echoes the Constitutional Reform Act by commencing with a specific statutory duty for the First Minister, the Lord Advocate, Scottish Ministers, Members of the Scottish Parliament and all other persons with responsibility for matters relating to the judiciary or the administration of justice to uphold the continued independence of the judiciary.[62] Importantly, this duty does not displace the existing common law offence of attempting to interfere with the course of justice. The Act also makes specific provision that, "[i]n particular", the First Minister, the Lord Advocate and Scottish Ministers must not "seek to influence particular judicial decisions through any special access to the judiciary" and that they must "have regard" to the need to provide the judiciary with the necessary support in order that they can perform their functions.[63] Although not defined in the Act, "special access" is intended to mean any access which the relevant individuals may have by virtue of their positions which an ordinary member of the public may not have.[64] Interestingly, the use of the phrase "[i]n particular" does not exclude other forms of influence from the ambit of the Act, thereby recognising that there is a multitude of ways in

---

56 The 2008 Act received the Royal Assent on 29 October 2008, and its provisions have been brought into force in phases (subject to specific transitional provisions and savings) by the Judiciary and Courts (Scotland) Act 2008 (Commencement No 1) Order SSI 2009/83; the Judiciary and Courts (Scotland) Act 2008 (Commencement No 2) Order SSI 2009/192; the Judiciary and Courts (Scotland) Act 2008 (Commencement No 3) Order SSI 2009/318; and the Judiciary and Courts (Scotland) Act 2008 (Commencement No 4, Transitional Provisions and Savings) Order SSI 2010/39.
57 2008 Act s 1.
58 2008 Act s 2.
59 2008 Act ss 9-18.
60 2008 Act ss 35-41.
61 2008 Act s 60.
62 2008 Act s 1.
63 2008 Act s 1(2).
64 Explanatory Notes, Judiciary and Courts (Scotland) Act 2008 2.

which ministers might potentially seek to pressurise judges.[65]

Although Lord McCluskey[66] was dismissive in his evidence to the Parliament about the guarantee of judicial independence on the grounds that it sought to "follow slavishly and plagiarise the English legislation"[67] and could be repealed by the Scottish Parliament, the Lord President, Lord Hamilton, took a more conciliatory view. He indicated that it was "a signal, if nothing more" which recognised the importance of judicial independence and sent out the "right message".[68] Lord Hamilton went on to comment that "We live in pleasant times. Times may not always be pleasant, and conflicts could arise between the judiciary and the executive".[69]

Thus, the principal significance of the statutory guarantee is that it articulates the importance of judicial independence within the constitution. It makes explicit what was previously only implicit, which is surely to be welcomed, and establishes the legislative policy context for the rest of the Act. Although the guarantee could, of course, be amended or repealed in subsequent legislation, this must be considered unlikely, given the political implications of doing so. Viewed in this context, the creation of a statutory guarantee of continued judicial independence is essentially of symbolic value. It expresses the Scottish Parliament's recognition of the importance of judicial independence and, more broadly, the rule of law, which, it may also be hoped, could "influence the culture and practice of executive government and even the wider community".[70]

(2) The Lord President as head of the Scottish judiciary

In a significant provision,[71] the Act establishes the Lord President as the head of the Scottish judiciary before going on to stipulate a number of weighty *ex officio* duties. Following pressure from Lord Hamilton and senior judges,[72] the Lord President's role is more extensive than of the Lord Chief Justice (who became head of the judiciary in England and Wales under the Constitutional

---

65 For discussion, see Scottish Parliament, Justice Committee Stage 1 Report on the Judiciary and Courts (Scotland) Bill, SP Paper 91, 11th Report, Session 3 (2008) para 33.
66 A former Lord Advocate and a retired Court of Session judge.
67 Scottish Parliament, *Official Report*, Justice Committee, cols 629 and 639 (18 March 2008).
68 Scottish Parliament, *Official Report*, Justice Committee, col 568 (11 March 2008).
69 Scottish Parliament, *Official Report*, Justice Committee, col 568 (11 March 2008).
70 Professor Alan Paterson, quoted at Scottish Parliament, Stage 1 Report on the Judiciary and Courts (Scotland) Bill (n 65) para 34.
71 2008 Act s 12.
72 See statement by the Cabinet Secretary for Justice, Scottish Parliament, *Official Report*, col 8553 (14 May 2008); Written Submission of the Lord President, Document JC 8, 2-3; and Response by the Judges' Council on behalf of the Judges of the Court of Session para 4.

Reform Act[73]), as it includes responsibility for the court service. The Lord President's statutory duties can be summarised as: ensuring the efficient disposal of business in the courts; representing the views of the judiciary to the Scottish Parliament and Scottish Ministers; making written representations to the Scottish Parliament on matters that he thinks are of importance in relation to the judiciary or the administration of justice; the management of appropriate arrangements for judicial welfare, training and guidance; and the investigation and determination[74] of matters arising in respect of judicial conduct.[75]

The Lord President also has a new statutory power to issue directions, which must be complied with, to sheriffs principal.[76] Sheriffs principal have been allocated similar powers, subject to the Lord President's overall authority, to direct sheriffs, justices of the peace, magistrates and Scottish Court Service staff.[77] Importantly, these powers of direction are administrative only, and are to secure efficiency in the disposal of the business of the court. Neither the Lord President nor sheriffs principal are empowered to give directions in respect of judicial decisions: the independence of individual judges is therefore maintained.

In this context, it should also be noted that the Lord President has been made subject to a specific duty to require judges to attend such training as he thinks appropriate.[78] By the time of the Bill's passage through the Parliament, the issue of training had been referred to the Judicial Council, a non-statutory body composed of judges which was established to provide information and advice to the Lord President on the administration of justice.[79] The question of whether or not judges should receive mandatory training generated some controversy in the Parliament.[80] Indeed, the Justice Committee recommended that training should be mandatory, a view which was rejected by the Cabinet Secretary for Justice on the basis that the Lord President should, in accordance with the principle of judicial independence, "be free from legislative constraints".[81] This position was accepted subsequently by

73 Constitutional Reform Act 2005 s 7: the Lord Chief Justice is not responsible for the efficient disposal of business in the courts, and neither does he lead the court service.
74 Including the review of any such determination.
75 2008 Act s 2(2).
76 2008 Act s 2(3).
77 2008 Act ss 47 and 58.
78 2008 Act s 2(4).
79 Scottish Parliament, Stage 1 Report on the Judiciary and Courts (Scotland) Bill (n 65) para 62.
80 Scottish Parliament, Stage 1 Report on the Judiciary and Courts (Scotland) Bill (n 65) paras 63-65.
81 See Scottish Parliament, Stage 1 Report on the Judiciary and Courts (Scotland) Bill (n 65) para 66; and Scottish Parliament, *Official Report*, Justice Committee, col 8554 (14 May 2008).

the Parliament and it will be interesting to see what emerges now that the Act is in force, and what the Lord President, who favours encouragement to participate in training rather than formal compulsion,[82] will require of judges.

Although significant concerns were voiced in the Parliament about the administrative burden which these new functions would place on the Lord President,[83] a subsequent independent review concluded that, given the additional support and resources which would be available, the additional workload was manageable and effective.[84] Labour MSPs, in particular, were also concerned that transferring administrative control over court services from Scottish Ministers to the Lord President could compromise democratic accountability on matters such as the location of sheriff and justice of the peace courts,[85] which led to the Cabinet Secretary for Justice agreeing to a compromise on these issues.[86] The provision of sweeping new powers for the Lord President was, however, accepted on the basis that it would, as Lord Hamilton put it, "bring many benefits for the administration of justice in Scotland": it would enable him to speak on behalf of a unified judiciary, thereby helping it to "play a full and co-ordinated role in the development of proposals for improving the administration of justice".[87] The Cabinet Secretary for Justice reminded the Parliament that the Lord President and senior judges had sought the creation of a judicially led court service on the ground that if they were "to accept greater responsibility for the running of the system, they should have control over the administrative support in carrying out these responsibilities",[88] a view which was ultimately supported by MSPs.

Taken together, the Lord President's new powers and responsibilities constitute a significant attempt by the Parliament to modernise the governance and administration of the Scottish judiciary. While the Lord President has, of course, traditionally been viewed within the legal establishment as the *de facto* head of the judiciary and has wielded considerable informal power and influence, the unambiguous nature of his new statutory authority over all judges (and not just the Court of Session Bench) clarifies and centralises

82 Scottish Parliament, *Official Report*, Justice Committee, col 572 (11 March 2008). The relevant provisions came into force in April 2010.
83 Justice Committee, Stage 1 Report on the Judiciary and Courts (Scotland) Bill (n 65) para 52.
84 See *Independent Review of Impact of Judiciary and Courts (Scotland) Bill on Judicial Time Commitment*, 2 June 2008 ("the Osler Review") para 10.1. See for comment, Scottish Parliament, Judiciary and Courts (Scotland) Bill: Parliamentary Consideration Prior to Stage 3, SPICe briefing, 9 September 2008, 5.
85 Scottish Parliament, Stage 1 Report on the Judiciary and Courts (Scotland) Bill (n 65) para 209.
86 Scottish Parliament, *Official Report*, col 8582 (14 May 2008), as implemented in the 2008 Act ss 50-51, 57.
87 See Written Submission of the Lord President (n 72) 2-3,
88 Scottish Parliament, *Official Report*, col 8553 (14 May 2008).

the judicial management structure, without compromising judicial independence. It also sets out in broad terms the duties and powers of the Lord President, thereby providing a degree of formal transparency and accountability which was lacking. While these provisions are unlikely to make a major difference to the way in which judges perform their duties in court, they do make it clear to both judges and the public that the Lord President is responsible for the leadership of the judiciary and for the efficient disposal of business in the Scottish courts.[89]

(3) Judicial appointments

A further significant formalisation of provision under the Act is the establishment of the JAB as a statutory body.[90] In order to maintain the independence of the judiciary and public confidence in the judicial appointments process, the newly constituted JAB is an advisory non-departmental public body under statute[91] and, in performing its functions, it is not subject to the "direction or control of any member of the Scottish Executive or any other person".[92] A clear attempt has therefore been made to ensure that the JAB is politically independent,[93] although its pre-statutory composition is essentially unchanged.

The JAB is charged with recommending to members of the Scottish Executive individuals for appointment to judicial office in Scotland,[94] and advising members of the Executive on appointments.[95] Only those who have been recommended by the JAB can be nominated by the First Minister or Scottish Ministers.[96] Separate provision is, however, made for the appointment of the Lord President and Lord Justice-Clerk[97] under which special panels are established to make recommendations to the First Minister: regard

---

89 Note that provision is made for what should happen in the event that the office of Lord President or the Lord Justice-Clerk is vacant, or when the holders of either office are incapacitated or suspended: see 2008 Act ss 4-8. It repeals the Senior Judiciary (Vacancies and Incapacity) (Scotland) Act 2006 (asp 9).

90 2008 Act s 9, Sch 1 para1.

91 Policy Memorandum on the Judiciary and Courts (Scotland) Bill (n 49) paras 52, 53.

92 Including the Lord President: 2008 Act s 9(3).

93 Which corresponds with the *Latimer House Guidelines*: see *Commonwealth Principles* (n 9) at 17-18.

94 That is, judges of the Court of Session; the chairman of the Scottish Land Court; temporary judges (except where the person has held defined judicial office such as a judge of the European Court); sheriffs principal; sheriffs; part-time sheriffs; and other judicial offices specified by Scottish Ministers by order: see 2008 Act ss 9(2)(a) and 10. Special provision is made for temporary judges at s 22, and temporary sheriffs principal and part-time sheriffs at ss 24, 26-29.

95 2008 Act s 9(2)(b).

96 2008 Act s 11(1).

97 2008 Act ss 19, 20.

must be had to these recommendations when the First Minister decides who to nominate for office to the Prime Minister.[98]

There is also a statutory requirement[99] that selection for all judicial offices must be "solely on merit" and that a person may be appointed to these offices only if the JAB[100] is satisfied that the individual is "of good character". Although "merit" is not defined in the statute, and its meaning is not always agreed upon, it seems in this context to include the skills and abilities of applicants in the context of the criteria of the posts that are being applied for – it is therefore wider than purely professional skills and knowledge.[101] The test of good character is one that must be met by all applicants for judicial office, with merit being the sole criterion thereafter.[102] A specific statutory requirement is also placed upon the JAB to encourage diversity,[103] with the objective of ensuring that candidates for judicial office are drawn from as wide a pool as possible and that the judiciary is representative of Scottish society.[104] Importantly, however, the requirement to encourage diversity is subject to the pre-eminent criteria of merit and good character.[105]

During the passage of the Bill, a number of misgivings on the issue of diversity were expressed by Lord McCluskey, who argued that "if I am going to be operated on by a brain surgeon, I want the brain surgeon to be the best one – I do not want him operating because he is black, Jewish, Catholic or whatever ... Affirmative action has no place in the selection of brain surgeons or High Court judges".[106] Professor Alan Paterson countered, rightly, that the position of judges was not analogous to surgeons, as the judiciary was an "arm of government", which inferred "issues of institutional accountability as well as a need for an independent form of appointment which contains the necessary checks and balances required by the separation of powers".[107] Moreover, surgeons do not, unlike judges, necessarily need to demonstrate empathy and an understanding of the social and policy contexts and consequences of their actions: by way of example, it may be observed that women are unlikely to harbour doubts about the professional credentials of male

98   That is, under the Scotland Act 1998 s 95.
99   2008 Act, ss 12 and 20.
100 Or panel in the case of appointment to the posts of Lord President and Lord Justice-Clerk.
101 Explanatory Notes (n 64) 7.
102 Explanatory Notes (n 64) 8.
103 2008 Act s 14.
104 Explanatory Notes (n 64) 8.
105 *Prima facie* there is no requirement to consider diversity in respect of appointment to the offices of Lord President and Lord Justice-Clerk.
106 Scottish Parliament, *Official Report*, Justice Committee, col 633 (18 March 2008).
107 Scottish Parliament, Stage 1 Report on the Judiciary and Courts (Scotland) Bill (n 65) para 112.

as opposed to female surgeons, but they may have justifiable grounds for querying the ability of an overwhelmingly male judiciary to determine the extent of women's rights.[108] The establishment by the JAB of a Diversity Working Group and the view of the Parliament's Justice Committee that the Scottish Government should ensure that a "holistic" approach is taken to issues of diversity in judicial appointments[109] suggests that debate on this issue will continue.

The composition of the JAB is also of significance. The Act provides that it is to consist of three judicial members who are appointed by the Lord President, two legal members appointed by Scottish Ministers, and lay members appointed by Scottish Ministers:[110] the majority of the JAB is non-judicial and is selected by Scottish Ministers. No members of the JAB, however, whether judicial, legal or lay, can hold defined political office or be a civil servant.[111] For obvious reasons, the legal knowledge, skills and competence of candidates are assessed by the judicial and legal members only.[112]

In his written submission on the Bill, the Lord President had argued that the number of judicial members was inadequate.[113] Moreover, the number of lay members must be equal to the total number of judicial and legal members,[114] despite the Lord President making it clear that he was not persuaded that this was a "manifestation of any particularly compelling constitutional principle".[115] This would indeed appear to be so: the composition of judicial appointments commissions had also caused debate during the drafting of the *Latimer House Guidelines*, where provision advocating that they should have a majority of members drawn from the senior judiciary was replaced by a less prescriptive recommendation following comment from Commonwealth governments.[116] In any case, it would seem that an attempt has been made by the Parliament to ensure not only that those holding political office or in government service are excluded from membership, but also that the JAB is

---

108 For an excellent discussion of these issues, see K Malleson, "Justifying gender equality on the bench: why difference won't do" (2003) 11/1 *Feminist Legal Studies* 1.
109 Scottish Parliament, Stage 1 Report on the Judiciary and Courts (Scotland) Bill (n 65) paras 118-120.
110 2008 Act Sch 1 paras 2, 3. The judicial members are a Court of Session judge other than the Lord President or Lord Justice-Clerk, a sheriff principal, and a sheriff; and the two legal members are an advocate and a solicitor.
111 2008 Act Sch 1 para 5.
112 2008 Act s 13.
113 Written Submission of the Lord President (n 72) 3.
114 2008 Act Sch 1 para 4.
115 Written Submission of the Lord President (n 72) 3.
116 *Latimer House Guidelines* (n 9) para II.1: see also Lord Hope, "Judicial independence" (n 3) at 107.

not dominated by the judiciary or, more broadly, the legal "establishment".[117] Indeed, the composition of the JAB reflects the view of the Scottish Government that a judicial majority could be perceived as "almost a self-fulfilling ordinance",[118] a position which the Parliament appears to have accepted.[119] In light of the concerns which existed until recently about the lack of openness in the judicial appointments process and its domination by political and legal vested interests, this approach is not unreasonable.

Moreover, notwithstanding these reforms, it should be noted that the 2008 Act amends the pre-existing rules governing the legal qualifications for appointment to judicial office only slightly,[120] and the procedures for making recommendations for appointment to the offices of Lord President, Lord Justice-Clerk, judge of the Court of Session, sheriff principal and sheriff, which are provided by the Scotland Act, also remain in force.[121] The Prime Minister therefore still recommends candidates to the Monarch for appointment to the offices of Lord President and Lord Justice-Clerk following nomination by the First Minister.[122] The First Minister continues to recommend to the Monarch appointments as judge of the Court of Session, sheriff principal and sheriff.[123]

Accordingly, there is still political involvement in the judicial appointments process. As indicated earlier, however, an element of statutorily restricted involvement by senior ministers is justifiable as a means of conferring the seal of democratic approval on judicial appointees before they assume office. In this context, it was not unreasonable for the Cabinet Secretary for Justice to express the view that it would be "absurd" for the First Minister not to have a role in appointments to the posts of Lord President and Lord Justice-Clerk, although such appointments should not be "political".[124] By this, he presumably meant that the appropriate function of the First Minister is to symbolise the democratic sanction of judicial appointment, rather than to make a selection for office on political grounds. In the final analysis, what is crucial is that

---

117 A similar approach is taken in respect of membership of the panels which make recommendations for appointment to the offices of Lord President and Lord Justice-Clerk: see 2008 Act Sch 2 paras 1(1), (2) and 3.

118 Scottish Parliament, *Official Report*, Justice Committee, col 689 (25 March 2008).

119 Scottish Ministers may vary the number of judicial and legal members by order: 2008 Act Sch 1, 3(4).

120 Under 2008 Act s 21, previous provision is amended to allow solicitors with rights of audience of five years in either the Court of Session *or* the High Court of Justiciary to become Court of Session judges.

121 Scotland Act 1998 s 95.

122 Scotland Act 1998 s 95.

123 Scotland Act 1998 s 95.

124 Scottish Parliament, *Official Report*, Justice Committee, col 692 (25 March 2008).

the 2008 Act provides clearly that there is now an independent statutory body which advises on candidates for office, that the key decisions are not taken by the Lord Advocate or other Scottish ministers, and that judicial independence is not materially at risk.

(4) Judicial conduct, discipline and removal from office

The 2008 Act addresses the issue of judicial conduct and discipline which, as mentioned earlier, was an area which was criticised by the Scottish Government in the policy memorandum on the Bill.[125] Notwithstanding opposition from judges,[126] the Act makes some provision for judicial conduct and disciplinary procedures, while at the same time preserving the independence of the judiciary. Importantly, responsibility for these matters rests solely with the Lord President as the head of the Scottish judiciary: this may be contrasted with the position in England and Wales, where the Lord Chancellor (i.e. a member of the government) is involved in the promulgation of rules on judicial conduct under the Constitutional Reform Act.[127]

More specifically, the Lord President is given a discretionary power to make rules for the investigation and determination of judicial conduct and the subsequent review of such determinations.[128] Lord Hamilton had been opposed to the creation of a formalised complaints process of the sort which had originally been proposed in the Bill,[129] on the basis that the traditionally informal arrangements regarding Court of Session judges had, he felt, worked well.[130] He had also been concerned that a formal complaints procedure could significantly increase the number of complaints, given that most complaints were thought to be made by disappointed litigants, which would have implications for judicial time and resources.[131] If, however, such a process was to be established, he believed that the Lord President should have the power to make the rules, as was provided subsequently by the Act.

Interestingly, the Act also provides a list, which is not exhaustive, of provisions which the rules may contain.[132] These are unexceptional, and make no stipulation as to what unacceptable conduct may be, but they do suggest an expectation on the part of the Parliament that the Lord President should

---

125 Policy Memorandum (n 49).
126 For example, Lord Hamilton, Scottish Parliament, *Official Report*, col 579 (11 March 2008).
127 Constitutional Reform Act 2005 s 115. Harrison, "Judging the judges" (n47) at 433-434.
128 2008 Act s 28. Note that these rules have not, at the time of writing, been produced.
129 That is, at cl 26-32.
130 Written Submission from the Lord President (n 72) at 5.
131 Written Submission from the Lord President (n 72) at 5.
132 2008 Act s 28. Harrison, "Judging the judges" (n47) at 432-433.

create a detailed procedural structure, rather than simply a more formal version of the old system. Indeed, after hearing the views of bodies such as Victim Support Scotland and the Law Society of Scotland, and considering procedures in other jurisdictions, the Justice Committee stated that it was "imperative that there is a formal complaints process".[133] Despite an attempt to make some aspects of the complaints regime compulsory at Stage 2 of the legislative process,[134] the Act is careful not to require the Lord President to make particular rules, thereby respecting his independence and the *Latimer House Guidelines*, which recommend that judges should be responsible for developing their own code of conduct.[135] Notwithstanding this, some have questioned whether the Lord President has been given too much autonomy and whether the system is sufficiently robust.[136] Much will no doubt depend on the adequacy of the procedures themselves, but it is contended that the Act is justified in entrusting the matter to the Lord President and in excluding political involvement in order to give full effect to the separation of powers. In any case, if the procedures were to prove seriously inadequate, it remains possible for the Parliament to impose statutory provision.

In addition to informal sanctions,[137] the Act explicitly sets out three disciplinary sanctions which the Lord President alone may impose on a holder of judicial office in the event that an investigation has been carried out regarding individual conduct.[138] The Lord President may give formal advice, a formal warning, or a reprimand.[139] Clearly, the imposition of any disciplinary sanction by the Lord President would be a serious matter, and it is unlikely that these formal powers will be exercised often. In addition, if the Lord President considers it necessary "for the purpose of maintaining public confidence in the judiciary", he may suspend a judge for such time as he considers appropriate.[140] These provisions are a welcome development: previously, the absence of formal sanctions short of actual removal from office was an obvious *lacuna* in the system.

---

133 Scottish Parliament, Stage 1 Report on the Judiciary and Courts (Scotland) Bill (n 65) paras 182 and 155-159.

134 This was withdrawn subsequently: see Scottish Parliament, *Official Report*, Justice Committee, col 907 (10 June 2008).

135 *Latimer House Guidelines* (n 9) para V.1.

136 Harrison, "Judging the judges" (n 47) at 433-435.

137 2008 Act s 29 (3).

138 2008 Act s 29 (1). The Lord President may appoint an investigator to deal with complaints: see s 28(2)(f).

139 It is assumed that the sanctions are set out in ascending order of seriousness. For discussion, see Harrison, "Judging the judges" (n47) at 434-436.

140 2008 Act s 34.

The Act also makes provision for an independent Judicial Complaints Reviewer, ("the Reviewer")[141] whose function is to review the handling of investigations into judicial conduct,[142] to refer the case to the Lord President where the Reviewer considers that an investigation has not been carried out competently,[143] to prepare and publish reports for Scottish Ministers in respect of investigations and to make written representations to the Lord President about investigation procedures.[144] Importantly, primacy is again given to the Lord President as the head of the independent judiciary. Thus, the Reviewer may be appointed only with the consent of the Lord President[145] and there is extensive provision to ensure that the Reviewer is independent of political, ministerial or judicial interests.[146] The Reviewer has no power to review the substantive merits of any investigation, and is limited to consideration of procedural matters. His remit is restricted by comparison with that of the Judicial Ombudsman in England and Wales, who is empowered by the Constitutional Reform Act to set aside determinations which are unreliable:[147] the main justification for this was perhaps cost, as the Reviewer, who will operate within a smaller judicial system, will work part-time.[148] Indeed, it would seem that the function of the Reviewer is essentially that of providing a measure of independent oversight of the way in which complaints are dealt with procedurally, which the Lord President himself has acknowledged may be appropriate to ensure that the system "commands the necessary degree of public confidence".[149] As the Cabinet Secretary for Justice put it, the Reviewer can provide a degree of comfort to the general public that "matters will be dealt with" and that the system is not "simply about judges reviewing themselves to protect themselves".[150] Thus, in cases where the Reviewer feels that an investigation has not been carried out correctly under the rules and refers the case to the Lord President, the matter is then wholly in the hands of the Lord President, who has wide discretionary powers of disposal.[151]

The 2008 Act also revises the provision for the removal of Court of Session

---

141 2008 Act s 30. For critical analysis, see Harrison, "Judging the judges" (n47) at 436-442.

142 At the request of the complainant or the judicial office holder: 2008 Act s 30(2)(a).

143 That is, in terms of the rules provided for by 2008 Act s 28(1).

144 To which the Lord President must have regard: 2008 Act s 30(4).

145 2008 Act s 30(1).

146 2008 Act ss 30(5) and 31.

147 Constitutional Reform Act 2005 s 111(5). Harrison, "Judging the judges" (n47) at 436-437.

148 Scottish Parliament, Stage 1 Report on the Judiciary and Courts (Scotland) Bill (n 65) paras 172-177.

149 Written Submission of the Lord President (n 72) 5-6.

150 Scottish Parliament, Justice Committee, col 695 (25 March 2008).

151 2008 Act s 33.

judges[152] from office, an issue which is obviously central to the maintenance of judicial independence. Under the Scotland Act 1998 and transitory arrangements made under statutory instrument,[153] a tribunal could be established to advise the First Minister on whether to recommend to the Queen that a Court of Session judge was unfit for office on the grounds of inability, neglect of duty or misbehaviour, after the tribunal's report had been laid before the Scottish Parliament and approved by majority vote. The 2008 Act replaces the transitory subordinate legislation, which was concerned with subsidiary procedural issues, and provides that the First Minister must, when requested by the Lord President, and may, if the First Minister thinks fit, establish tribunals to determine whether the holders of defined judicial offices are unfit for office on the same grounds.[154] Given the importance of protecting the independence of the judiciary, the Act also imposes a number of exacting requirements to restrict the powers of the First Minister. Thus, the First Minister must, before establishing a tribunal, consult with the Lord President.[155] Crucially, the composition of the tribunal is also such as to ensure that judicial independence is not compromised. It must consist of two individuals who hold (or who have held) "high judicial office",[156] a senior solicitor or advocate, and one lay person.[157] It is also provided that at least one of the judicial members must be a member of the Judicial Committee of the Privy Council,[158] and at least one must be, or have been, a Court of Session judge.[159] Moreover, the First Minister's selection of tribunal members must be agreed by the Lord President,[160] and the tribunal must be chaired by a member of the Judicial Committee of the Privy Council,[161] who has the casting vote.[162] It is very difficult to envisage a tribunal of this nature ever bowing to political pressure from the First Minister. Moreover, s 95 of the Scotland Act continues to require that there should be majority approval by the Scottish

152 And the Chairman of the Scottish Land Court: see 2008 Act s 35: for temporary judges, see s 39.

153 Scotland Act 1998, s 95; Scotland Act 1998 (Transitory and Transitional Provisions) (Removal of Judges) Order 1999, SSI 1999/1017.

154 2008 Act s 35(1), (2). The relevant offices are Lord President, Lord Justice-Clerk, judge of the Court of Session, Chairman of the Scottish Land Court, and temporary judge.

155 2008 Act s 35(3). If it is the Lord President's fitness for office which is at issue, the Lord Justice-Clerk must be consulted.

156 As defined by the Constitutional Reform Act 2005 s 60.

157 2008 Act s 35(4).

158 2008 Act s 35(6).

159 2008 Act s 35(7).

160 2008 Act s 35(8): or the Lord Justice-Clerk if the Lord President's fitness for office is under consideration.

161 2008 Act s 35(9), (10).

162 2008 Act s 35(11).

Parliament of a motion to remove a Court of Session judge from office before the First Minister can make any such recommendation to the Queen.

Similar but suitably revised provision is made for the removal from office of sheriffs principal, sheriffs and part-time sheriffs on the same grounds of inability, neglect of duty or misbehaviour,[163] notwithstanding opposition from the Sheriffs' Association on the basis that the previous procedures for removal had, it felt, given sheriffs greater statutory protection.[164] Once again, however, the statutorily defined composition of the tribunal is clearly such as to preclude political interference with judicial independence,[165] and the Parliament's Justice Committee, while noting the sheriffs' position, was of the view that the new procedures provided appropriate safeguards.[166] Given the equivalent arrangements for Court of Session judges, this approach appears reasonable and justifiable. The Act also provides that tribunal procedures, powers of suspension and the authorisation of investigations into the fitness for office of justices of the peace should be made by the Court of Session under Acts of Sederunt,[167] rather than by Scottish Ministers, as was previously the case:[168] authority has therefore been transferred to the judiciary, again in accordance with the guiding principle of judicial independence.

(5) The Scottish Court Service

A further significant development provided for in the 2008 Act, which was touched on in earlier discussion, is the creation of a new Scottish Court Service ("SCS") to provide administrative support for the Scottish courts and judiciary.[169] Interestingly, while the SCS must agree a corporate plan with Scottish Ministers and may present advice, information and proposals to them,[170] the responsibility for its governance lies with the SCS itself, which is composed of seven members of the judiciary and six non-judicial members, supported by civil servants: the SCS is not part of the Scottish Government.[171]

---

163 2008 Act s 40. This replaces the Sheriff Courts (Scotland) Act 1971 s 12.
164 Sheriff Dickson, Scottish Parliament, *Official Report*, Justice Committee, cols 595-596 (11 March 2008).
165 That is, one member of the Judicial Committee of the Privy Council, either a sheriff principal or a sheriff, a senior advocate or solicitor and a lay person: 2008 Act s 40.
166 Scottish Parliament, Stage 1 Report on the Judiciary and Courts (Scotland) Bill (n 65) para 188.
167 2008 Act s 41.
168 That is, under the Criminal Proceedings etc (Reform) (Scotland) Act 2007 s 71.
169 2008 Act ss 60, 61.
170 2008 Act ss 65, 66.
171 But as part of the Scottish administration it must present an annual report to the Scottish Ministers and lay a copy before the Scottish Parliament: see 2008 Act s 67.

The judicial members, who must always be in the majority,[172] comprise the Lord President (who chairs the SCS), the Lord Justice-Clerk, a Court of Session judge, a sheriff principal, two sheriffs and a justice of the peace. The non-judicial members comprise an advocate, a solicitor, the chief executive of the service, and three lay persons: all members (other than the Lord Justice-Clerk and chief executive, who are *ex officio* members) are appointed by the Lord President.[173]

While the Lord President and sheriffs principal have traditionally exercised considerable authority in the management and administration of their courts, these provisions are nonetheless a remarkable and potentially controversial development in that they make the Lord President and senior members of the judiciary formally responsible for the strategic governance and managerial oversight of the courts. Although Scottish Ministers have the default power to carry out the functions of the SCS if it is putting the efficient and effective functioning of the courts at risk,[174] they have essentially been removed from responsibility for the administration of the courts, other than in relation to matters such as sheriff and justice of the peace court locations and boundaries, which, as mentioned earlier, were felt to involve issues of democratic accountability.

It is, of course, to be hoped that the new SCS will, as a result of the leadership and expertise of the Lord President and judicial members, improve the quality of service provided by the courts. Without overstating matters, however, there should be awareness of the potential for criticism of the Lord President and judiciary, in the event that the SCS is perceived to be failing in its duties by politicians or the public. Although day-to-day management of the service will be the responsibility of the chief executive, the Lord President will, inevitably, have to assume responsibility in the event of major controversy or failures. In this context, the Lord President may be required to explain or justify SCS policy, which could conflict with that of Scottish Ministers or majority opinion in the Scottish Parliament. Conceivably, the Lord President could be pressurised by the possible exercise of ministers' default powers or requests to appear before the Parliament.[175] Although the Lord President cannot be compelled formally to give evidence by the Parliament,[176] Lord Hamilton has indicated that he would be prepared to do

172 2008 Act Sch 3 2, (5), (6).
173 2008 Act Sch 3, 2(2), (3).
174 2008 Act s 70.
175 Judiciary and Courts (Scotland) Bill, Written Submission from Sir David Edward 2-3.
176 Scotland Act 1998 s 23(7).

so in the context of questions on the SCS.[177] Accordingly, there is at least the potential for controversy which could damage public confidence in the Lord President and judicial independence. Notwithstanding the duty on the First Minister and others to maintain the independence of the judiciary, particular care should therefore be taken by both the SCS and politicians to ensure that unnecessary conflict does not arise. In this context, it will be interesting to see how the new arrangements operate, if, for example, differences of opinion emerge between the judicially controlled SCS and the Scottish Government over the implementation of the recent recommendations of the Report of the Scottish Civil Courts Review, which was chaired by the Lord Justice-Clerk.

E. CONCLUSION

The concept of judicial independence is of profound constitutional signifi- cance in Scotland and throughout the UK. It is fundamental to the mainte- nance of the rule of law, and there is a deep-rooted constitutional convention of judicial independence in Scotland. There is also broad public confidence in the impartiality and competence of the judiciary. Despite this, the legal and constitutional arrangements which were in place until recently to maintain judicial independence in particular were a piecemeal and anachronistic accre- tion of statute, constitutional doctrine, custom and administrative measures. While there had been disquiet about the rules for appointing, disciplining and removing judges from office (which are central to the maintenance of judicial independence), it was not until significant reforms were introduced for the judiciary in the rest of the UK under the Constitutional Reform Act 2005 that it was recognised that comprehensive change was required in Scotland.

The passing by the Scottish Parliament of the Judiciary and Courts (Scotland) Act 2008 introduced major reforms which have as their guiding principle the maintenance and reinforcement of judicial independence in Scotland, while at the same time making appropriate provision for political and lay involvement in the key areas of judicial appointment, conduct and tenure, and the court service. This is an important and delicate balance to strike, and, for the most part, it is argued that the Parliament has been successful. The 2008 Act modernises and draws together provision for the Scottish judiciary. Although its schema was influenced initially by the UK Constitutional Reform Act, this does not detract from its importance. Indeed, given the ad hoc nature of the previous arrangements, it is one of

---

177   Lord President Hamilton, Scottish Parliament Justice Committee, col 570 (11 March 2008).

the most significant pieces of legislation for the Scottish judiciary since the Union with England Act 1707. While it may be argued that if provision for Scotland had been made by Westminster under the Constitutional Reform Act, the substantive outcome would perhaps not have been vastly different, the Scottish Parliament has crafted and passed complex and weighty legislation which is an important constitutional landmark for the Scottish judiciary, and a considerable improvement on what existed before. In the final analysis, the Parliament gave lengthy and detailed consideration to the specific needs of the Scottish judiciary in the devolved constitution and created bespoke and comprehensive statutory provision for it. This, surely, is exactly the sort of positive legislative achievement that was envisaged when the Parliament was created in 1998.

11 Criminal Law and Criminal Justice: An Exercise in Ad Hocery

Pamela R Ferguson[°]

A. INTRODUCTION
B. CRIMINAL PROCEDURE
C. SENTENCING POWERS
D. THE SUBSTANTIVE CRIMINAL LAW
E. THE PARLIAMENTARY PROCESS
F. CONCLUSIONS

A. INTRODUCTION

At the time of writing[1] the Scottish Parliament has passed 147 statutes, more than a third of which affect criminal procedure, sentencing, or the substantive criminal law.[2] Such is the extent of these changes that this chapter can do no more than highlight some of the main provisions and offer some critique.[3] Prior to the re-establishment of the Scottish Parliament, Scots criminal procedure had frequently been amended by legislation, and it is unsurprising that this has continued post-devolution. While many of the changes have been highly successful,[4] it may be suggested that we have moved further along the spectrum from a largely adversarial process to one which now bears a greater number of features of an inquisitorial system – often in the name of "managerial efficiency".[5] Whether or not one favours the changes that have

[°] Professor of Law, University of Dundee. I am indebted to Pete Duff and Robin White for helpful comments on an earlier version of this chapter.
1 January 2010.
2 This estimate includes statutes which do not contain any offence provisions as such, but empower the Scottish Ministers to make regulations which create offences. For a recent example, see the Climate Change (Scotland) Act 2009.
3 The law of evidence relating to criminal cases is considered in chapter 13 of this volume.
4 See J Chalmers et al, *An Evaluation of the High Court Reforms Arising from the Criminal Procedure (Amendment) (Scotland) Act 2004* (2007).
5 See P Duff, "Changing conceptions of the Scottish criminal trial: the duty to agree uncontroversial evidence", in A Duff et al (eds), *The Trial on Trial: Truth & Due Process* (2004) 29. This tendency is also apparent in the provisions of the Criminal Justice and Licensing (Scotland) Bill

been made to criminal procedure, these have at least been based largely on the recommendations of commissions, established by the Scottish Executive and chaired by senior members of the judiciary.[6] The same cannot be said for the substantive law, which has frequently been amended, and new offences created. The Westminster Parliament was often castigated for failing to find time for Scottish legislation, and there were hopes that devolution would lead to consolidation of the statutory criminal law, and possibly even codification of the common law.[7] Devolution has created the ideal opportunity for a re-assessment of our criminal law, but there is little evidence that this is being attempted in any systematic fashion. As a starting point, the Scottish Parliament should formulate principles of criminalisation. For instance, many would argue that the criminal sanction should be employed as a last resort, and that strict liability offences should be employed sparingly, with careful consideration being given to the provision of statutory defences. The extent of new offences, many of which impose strict liability, suggests that these are not principles to which the Parliament adheres.

B. CRIMINAL PROCEDURE

The Scottish Parliament has been particularly active here. District courts are gradually being replaced by justice of the peace courts,[8] and a variety of specialist courts have been established, focusing on domestic abuse,[9] youth offending[10] and drug abuse.[11] These courts were created to ensure that certain types of offender are dealt with expeditiously. More generally, the courts have been given powers to impose a range of orders designed to control future behaviour. These include orders for lifelong restriction (OLRs),[12]

---

relating to disclosure of evidence by the prosecution, and the requirement for the accused in solemn proceedings to provide a "defence statement" in advance of the trial.

6 See the Maclean Report (*Report of the Committee on Serious Violent and Sexual Offenders* (2000)); the Bonomy Report (*Review of the Practices and Procedure of the High Court of Justiciary* (2002)); the McInnes Report (*Report of the Summary Justice Review Committee* (2004)) and the Coulsfield Report (*Review of the Law and Practice of Disclosure in Criminal Proceedings* (2007)).

7 Although Scotland has no criminal code, there is an unofficial draft code: see E Clive et al, *A Draft Criminal Code for Scotland with Commentary* (2003), published under the auspices of the Scottish Law Commission.

8 Criminal Proceedings etc (Reform) (Scotland) Act 2007 (hereafter "the 2007 Act") Pt 4.

9 See Scottish Executive, *Evaluation of the Pilot Domestic Abuse Court* (2007).

10 See Scottish Executive, *Evaluation of the Airdrie and Hamilton Youth Court Pilots* (2006).

11 See Scottish Executive, *Establishing Drug Courts in Scotland: Early Experiences of the Pilot Drug Courts in Glasgow and Fife* (2003).

12 Criminal Justice (Scotland) Act 2003 (henceforth "the 2003 Act") s 1, which inserts ss 210B-210H into the Criminal Procedure (Scotland) Act 1995 (henceforth "the 1995 Act").

football banning orders (FBOs),[13] risk of sexual harm orders (RSHOs),[14] parenting orders (POs)[15] and greater power to impose antisocial behaviour orders (ASBOs).[16] Orders for lifelong restriction can be imposed on persons convicted of certain violent or sexual offences where the court is satisfied *on the balance of probabilities* that liberating such a person would "seriously endanger the lives, or physical or psychological well-being, of members of the public at large". Football banning orders prohibit those against whom they are granted from attending regulated football matches, and require them to report at a police station when certain matches are being held overseas.[17] The Scottish FBO has been described as "more draconian" than similar provisions enacted for England and Wales.[18] Orders for lifelong restriction and FBOs can be imposed as part of the sentencing process, but the latter can also be granted by a sheriff on the application of the police, without there having been a criminal conviction. Likewise, the police may apply for an RSHO where the person to whom the order relates has, on at least two occasions, engaged in sexually explicit conduct or communication with a child. Both RSHOs and ASBOs prohibit those against whom they are granted from "doing anything described in the order"[19] for a fixed period.[20] Controversially, sheriffs have been empowered to make ASBOs for persons as young as twelve,[21] and to make interim ASBOs pending a final decision.[22] Although RSHOs, ASBOs, POs and FBOs can each be created using civil court procedures, breaching their requirements without reasonable excuse is a criminal offence.[23] In the case of ASBOs and RSHOs, the maximum penalty is five years' imprisonment.[24] The increasing use of civil law orders enforced by criminal law sanctions to regulate a wide range of anti-social behaviour is regarded by

13 Police, Public Order and Criminal Justice (Scotland) Act 2006 (henceforth "the 2006 Act") s 51(2).
14 Protection of Children and Prevention of Sexual Offences (Scotland) Act 2005 (henceforth "the 2005 Protection Act") s 2.
15 Antisocial Behaviour etc (Scotland) Act 2004 (henceforth "the 2004 Act") s 102.
16 ASBOs were first introduced in Scotland by the Crime and Disorder Act 1998 s 19, but their ambit has been widened by the 2004 Act.
17 2006 Act s 53(1).
18 M James and G Pearson, "Football banning orders: analysing their use in court" (2006) 70 *J Crim L* 509 at 529.
19 2005 Protection Act s 2(7)(a) (RSHO); 2004 Act s 4(5) (ASBO). The 2005 Act is likely to be amended on enactment of the Criminal Justice and Licensing (Scotland) Bill, s 75 of which allows such an order to *require* the doing of certain things.
20 In the case of an RSHO the specified period is to be at least two years (2005 Protection Act s 2(7)(b)).
21 2004 Act s 4(1).
22 By the 2003 Act s 44 which amends the Crime and Disorder Act 1998 s 19.
23 2004 Act ss 9(1) and 107(1) (ASBO, PO); 2005 Protection Act s 7(1) (RSHO); 2006 Act s 68(1) (FBO).
24 2004 Act s 9(2)(b), and 2005 Protection Act s 7(4)(b), respectively.

many as an unwelcome development;[25] it circumvents many of the safeguards inherent in criminal procedure, such as its more stringent rules of evidence, which do not apply when such orders are imposed in civil courts. Breach of the order is tantamount to a strict liability offence – no *mens rea* of having done so intentionally or even recklessly need be established – and this can be for engaging in behaviour which would not otherwise be criminal. This raises issues as to the integrity of the criminal process.[26]

A concern with more effective management of cases is reflected in reforms of High Court procedure, designed to reduce "churning", whereby cases set down for trial were being repeatedly adjourned.[27] This led to the introduction of mandatory "preliminary hearings",[28] at which the Crown and the defence are encouraged to agree uncontroversial evidence. Scotland had long taken pride in the fact that the maximum period for which an accused person could be imprisoned prior to commencement of his or her trial was 110 days. If the prosecution did not start the trial before this time period elapsed, then the accused person had to be liberated and could not be tried thereafter. This has been changed, such that the limit is now 140 days.[29] These changes are intended to improve the efficiency of the criminal process, and few would doubt the value of this. It is, however, imperative that savings in time and money are not gained by sacrificing valuable aspects of criminal procedure, in terms of its overall fairness to those who stand accused of breaching the criminal law.

---

25 ASBOs, in particular, have been subject to a great deal of criticism, both here and in England. See, e.g., S Cracknell, "Antisocial behaviour orders" (2000) 22 *Journal of Social Welfare and Family Law* 108; R H Burke and R Morrill, "Anti-social behaviour orders: an infringement of the Human Rights Act 1998?" (2002) 11 *Nottingham LJ* 1; A Cleland and K Tisdall, "The challenge of antisocial behaviour: new relationships between the state, children and parents" (2005) 19 *International Journal of Law, Policy and the Family* 395; A Cleland, "The Antisocial Behaviour etc (Scotland) Act 2004: exposing the punitive fault line below the children's hearing system" (2005) 9 *Edin LR* 439; A Samuels, "Anti-social behaviour orders: their legal and jurisprudential significance" (2005) 69 *J Crim L* 223; A Ashworth, *Sentencing and Criminal Justice*, 4th edn (2005) ch 11.

26 In *Clingham v Royal Borough of Kensington and Chelsea; R (on behalf of McCann) v Crown Court of Manchester* [2003] 1 AC 787 the House of Lords confirmed that the creation of an ASBO under the Crime and Disorder Act 1998 was a civil law matter, but that the grounds for imposing an order required proof beyond reasonable doubt. The civil law rules of evidence continue to apply, however, such that there is no need for witnesses to testify, and hearsay evidence is admissible.

27 See the Bonomy Report para 4.4.

28 Criminal Procedure (Amendment) (Scotland) Act 2004 s 1, which inserts a new s 72 into the 1995 Act. See the Bonomy Report para 4.4.

29 Criminal Procedure (Amendment) (Scotland) Act 2004 s 5, which amends s 65(4) of the 1995 Act. Failure by the Crown to adhere to this timetable results in liberation of the accused, but the trial can nonetheless proceed thereafter. See also the 2007 Act s 11 which amends s 147 of the 1995 Act to allow a sheriff to extend the pre-trial forty-day detention period in summary cases, on cause shown.

Some reforms, for example in relation to bail,[30] were intended to ensure compliance with the requirements of the European Convention on Human Rights (ECHR). A court must now explain its reasoning if it decides not to impose a higher sentence where the accused has breached bail.[31] A move to greater transparency is also evident in the enactment of the Judiciary and Courts (Scotland) Act 2008, which put the Judicial Appointments Board for Scotland on a statutory footing, following criticism of the ad hoc nature of the Board when it was first established.[32] This also makes the Lord President/ Lord Justice-General the head of the judiciary, including the justice of the peace courts.

A detailed examination of changes made to police powers in the past ten years is beyond the scope of this chapter, but since these can impact on criminal procedure a few observations are in order. Even as the High Court has been narrowing the ambit of the crime of breach of the peace[33] to ensure that it is compatible with the ECHR,[34] legislation has increased police powers to deal with disorderly behaviour. A constable now has statutory authority to direct a group of individuals (defined as two or more people) in a public place to disperse, purely on the basis that there are "reasonable grounds for believing that [their] presence or behaviour … is causing or is likely to cause alarm or distress to any members of the public".[35] Thus, the officer can take pre-emptive action, rather than waiting for a breach of the peace to occur. A constable may prohibit such a group from returning for a period of up to twenty-four hours.[36] As with ASBOs, this restricts the liberty of the individual without prosecution, let alone conviction. Civil liberties have also been narrowed by the requirement that those planning to hold a procession must generally give the local authority twenty-eight days' notice of this (the notice period was formerly seven days).[37] The police have been given

---

30 See the 2007 Act Pt 1, which in large part codifies the common law on bail.

31 2007 Act s 3(1)(c), which amends s 27 of the 1995 Act. Earlier bail reforms were effected by the Bail, Judicial Appointments etc (Scotland) Act 2000 Pt 1; the Sexual Offences (Procedure and Evidence) (Scotland) Act 2002 s 5; the 2003 Act ss 48 and 66; and the Criminal Procedure (Amendment) (Scotland) Act 2004, Pts 2 and 3. Legislation has increasingly imposed a duty on courts to state their reasoning, particularly where a decision is not to impose a higher sentence where one would generally be expected; see also below in relation to sentencing for certain statutory aggravations.

32 See J Gilmour, "The Judicial Appointments Board – a misnomer" (2002) *JLSS*, 1 August 2002, at 25.

33 See, in particular, *Smith v Donnelly* 2002 JC 55; and *Harris v HM Advocate* [2009] HCJAC 80, 2009 SLT 1078.

34 In particular, art 7 (criminal offences to be clearly defined by law); art 10 (freedom of expression); and art 11 (freedom of assembly and association).

35 2004 Act s 21(1).

36 2004 Act s 21(3).

37 2006 Act s 70 which amends the Civic Government (Scotland) Act 1982 s 62.

greater authority to take finger- and palm-prints, as well as DNA samples, from certain categories of arrested persons,[38] and to test those arrested for a "relevant offence" for Class A drugs.[39] The relevant offences encompass a broad range; as well as misuse of drugs, they include many dishonesty offences (theft, robbery, fraud, reset, uttering a forged document, and embezzlement) and assault. It is an offence to refuse to comply with a drugs test.[40]

Further amendments to the Criminal Procedure (Scotland) Act 1995 have increased police powers in relation to suspects, witnesses and persons detained on suspicion of having committed an offence. Suspects and witnesses must now specify not only their name and address[41] but also their nationality, date of birth, and such details of their place of birth as the constable considers necessary to establish the person's identity.[42] Failure to provide this information without reasonable excuse is an offence. Those detained for questioning were obliged hitherto to provide only their names and addresses. This obligation has been increased to include details of nationality, and date and place of birth.[43] The police can now take a suspect's fingerprints for the limited purpose of verifying identity.[44] Refusal to co-operate is an offence. DNA samples taken from those detained on suspicion of having committed certain sexual or violent offences may be retained by the police for three years, so long as criminal proceedings have been instituted, even if the proceedings do not result in a guilty plea or conviction.[45] Again, these developments raise issues as to the appropriate balance between protecting the public from future offences, and safeguarding individuals' privacy and liberty. The European Court of Human Rights has declared unlawful the more extensive powers of retention provided in England.[46]

Victims of crime have been given a more active role.[47] Certain categories of victim are entitled to make a statement to the court, describing the impact

---

38 Primarily sex offenders: see the 2006 Act s 77, which inserts ss 19AA and 19AB into the 1995 Act.
39 That is, cocaine and diamorphine/heroin: 2006 Act s 84, which inserts ss 20A and 20B into the 1995 Act.
40 1995 Act s 20A(7).
41 1995 Act s 13.
42 2006 Act s 81(3), which inserts s 13(1A) into the 1995 Act.
43 2006 Act s 81(6), which inserts s 14(10) into the 1995 Act.
44 2006 Act s 82, which inserts s 13(1B) and (1C) into the 1995 Act. At the time of writing, these provisions are not yet in force.
45 2006 Act s 83, which inserts s 18A into the 1995 Act. The retention period can be extended for further two-year periods if a chief constable persuades a sheriff that there are reasonable grounds for so doing.
46 By the Criminal Justice and Police Act 2001: see *S and Marper v United Kingdom* [2008] ECHR 1581, (2009) 48 EHRR 50.
47 2003 Act Pt 2, based on the Scottish Executive's *Scottish Strategy for Victims* (2001).

of the crime, and such statements must be taken into account when the court is passing sentence.[48] The list of offences to which this applies has been extended to include most crimes involving personal violence or indecency, and also theft by housebreaking, fire-raising, and road traffic offences which involve fatalities.[49] Those who are victims of a prescribed offence[50] which has resulted in a sentence of imprisonment or detention for a period of at least eighteen months[51] are entitled to receive information about the convicted person, including details about that person's release, transfer, death in custody or escape,[52] and to make written representations to the Scottish Ministers concerning release.[53] Victims who are deemed to be especially vulnerable may be afforded special measures to facilitate the giving of their evidence in criminal trials.[54]

The crimes for which prosecutors can offer fixed penalties (commonly referred to as fiscal fines) have been extended, and the maximum penalty increased to £300.[55] Taking no action is now to be treated as acceptance of the offer of a fiscal fine.[56] Procurators fiscal can impose compensation orders (to a maximum of £5,000)[57] and "work orders" requiring the performance of unpaid work for between ten and fifty hours.[58] The tendency for alleged offences to be dealt with otherwise than by prosecution is apparent also in the increase in the range of offence categories for which the police may issue fixed penalties.[59] These include several statutory offences[60] as well as some

---

48 2003 Act s 14(2). The court can disregard any irrelevant aspects of a victim statement. See Scottish Executive Social Research, *An Evaluation of the Pilot Victim Statement Schemes in Scotland* (2007; available at *http://www.scotland.gov.uk/Publications/2007/03/27152727/0*); and J Chalmers et al, "Victim impact statements: can work, do work (for those who bother to make them)" [2007] *Crim LR* 360.

49 Victim Statements (Prescribed Offences) (No 2) (Scotland) Order 2009, SSI 2009/71.

50 Prescribed by virtue of the Victim Notification (Prescribed Offences) (Scotland) Order 2004, SSI 2004/411.

51 Victim Notification Scheme (Scotland) Order 2008 SSI 2008/185 art 2 amends the 2003 Act s 16(1)(a) to reduce the original minimum period of four years which triggers victims' rights to receive the specified information.

52 2003 Act s 16(1).

53 2003 Act s 17.

54 Vulnerable Witnesses (Scotland) Act 2004. These provisions are discussed in more detail by F P Davidson in chapter 13 of this volume.

55 2007 Act s 50(1); and the Criminal Procedure (Scotland) Act 1995 Fixed Penalty Order 2008, SSI 2008/108, which amends s 302 of the 1995 Act.

56 2007 Act s 50(1)(a)(iv) which inserts s 302(2)(ca) into the 1995 Act.

57 2007 Act s 50(2) which inserts s 302A into the 1995 Act.

58 2007 Act s 51 which inserts s 303ZA into the 1995 Act. At the time of writing, these provisions are in force in relation to only some parts of Scotland. See the Criminal Proceedings etc (Reform) (Scotland) Act 2007 (Commencement No 4) Order 2008, SSI 2008/192.

59 2004 Act s 129.

60 Disorderly conduct while drunk in licensed premises; refusing to leave such premises on being

common law ones.[61] The growth of alternatives to prosecution is a cause for concern;[62] it is a further example of the prosecution process being circumvented in order to process a greater number of cases more efficiently, with police and prosecutors increasingly exercising a judicial role.

C. SENTENCING POWERS

The general trend here has been the introduction of a greater range of sentencing options,[63] and the power to impose harsher sentences.[64] The maximum penalties in the sheriff courts have been increased to imprisonment for twelve months in summary procedure,[65] and five years in solemn cases.[66] In determining the appropriate sentence, a court must now take into account whether and at what stage an accused person pled guilty.[67] A judge who does not impose a lesser sentence for a plea of guilty tendered at an early stage must give reasons for this decision.[68] The provision of sentencing discounts for guilty pleas raises concerns as to whether such pleas can always be said to be voluntary; the possibility of greater punishment if convicted after trial offers a high incentive for pleading guilty.

---

requested to do so; being drunk and incapable, or while in charge of a child; consuming alcohol in a public place; persisting, to the annoyance of others, in playing musical instruments, singing, playing radios etc; urinating and defecating causing annoyance; vandalism. (The first two were substituted by the Licensing (Scotland) Act 2005 (Consequential Provisions) Order 2009, SSI 2009//248, Sch 1(1) para 10.)

61 That is, malicious mischief and breach of the peace (2004 Act s 128).

62 See R White, "Out of court and out of sight: how often are 'alternatives to prosecution' used?" (2008) 12 *Edin LR* 481.

63 See the discussion of OLRs, FBOs and so on, above; and s 14 of the Criminal Justice and Licensing (Scotland) Bill which will introduce, *inter alia*, "community payback orders", "unpaid work or other activity requirements", "programme requirements", "mental health treatment requirements", "drug treatment requirements", and "alcohol treatment requirements".

64 If enacted, ss 3-5 of the Criminal Justice and Licensing (Scotland) Bill will establish a Sentencing Council to promote consistency in sentencing practice by the promulgation of sentencing guidelines.

65 By the 2007 Act s 43(a), which amends s 5(2)(d) of the 1995 Act.

66 This was by statutory instrument: the Crime and Punishment (Scotland) Act 1997 (Commencement No 6 and Savings) Order 2004, SSI 2004/176 art 2 brought into force the Crime and Punishment (Scotland) Act 1997 s 13(1)(a), which amended s 3(3) of the 1995 Act. Although the sentencing powers of justice of the peace courts currently remain the same as those of the district courts, the Scottish Ministers have the power to amend this: see the 2007 Act s 46. Note also the shift in responsibility from the courts to the executive for the enforcement of fines, introduced by the 2007 Act s 55, which introduces s 226A into the 1995 Act. This was based on the recommendations of the McInnes Report at para 32.53.

67 Criminal Procedure (Amendment) (Scotland) Act 2004 s 20, which amended s 196 of the 1995 Act. (A similar requirement was recognised in *Du Plooy, Alderdice, Crooks and O'Neil v HM Advocate* 2003 SLT 1237.)

68 Criminal Procedure (Amendment) (Scotland) Act 2004 s 20(3).

The Scottish Parliament has empowered the courts to impose increased sentences for a number of specific aggravations, based on certain characteristics of the victim. For example, it is a statutory offence to assault, obstruct or hinder emergency workers such as police, fire-fighters and ambulance workers.[69] Courts must also take into account whether an offence was aggravated by prejudice based on the victim's religion,[70] disability,[71] sexual orientation or transgender identity.[72]

D. THE SUBSTANTIVE CRIMINAL LAW

It is difficult to determine the precise number of offences created by the Scottish Parliament, particularly since some provisions have re-enacted, amended or added to existing offences, rather than creating entirely new ones. A conservative estimate suggests that there are more than 400 offence provisions in statutes passed by the Scottish Parliament in the past ten years. There seems to be only two examples of *de*-criminalisation.[73] Some statutes regulate an activity in large part by proscription.[74] The Charities and Trustee Investment (Scotland) Act 2005 and the Housing (Scotland) Act 2006 each contain more than a dozen offences. There are thirty-five offences in the Sexual Offences (Scotland) Act 2009, and a similar number in the Animal Health and Welfare (Scotland) Act 2006. What conclusions can be drawn from the motley collection of new offences? Many Scottish provisions are enacted to ensure that the criminal law is the same north and south of the Border.[75] Other criminal law statutes paint a picture of Scotland as a largely

---

69 Emergency Workers (Scotland) Act 2005 s 1(1). See also the Fire (Scotland) Act 2005 s 39.
70 2003 Act s 74.
71 Offences (Aggravation by Prejudice) (Scotland) Act 2009 s 1.
72 Offences (Aggravation by Prejudice) (Scotland) Act 2009 s 2. At the time of writing, this is not in force.
73 Convention Rights (Compliance) (Scotland) Act 2001 s 10 repeals a provision which criminalises homosexual acts involving more than two people (this amends the Criminal Law (Consolidation) (Scotland) Act 1995 s 13). Crofting Reform etc. Act 2007 s 28 provides a new means of enforcing common grazings regulations, resulting in a breach of such regulations no longer being a criminal offence.
74 See, e.g., the Protection of Wild Mammals (Scotland) Act 2002; the Fur Farming (Prohibition) (Scotland) Act 2002; the Dog Fouling (Scotland) Act 2003; the Breastfeeding etc (Scotland) Act 2005; the Emergency Workers (Scotland) Act 2005; the Prohibition of Female Genital Mutilation (Scotland) Act 2005; the Prostitution (Public Places) (Scotland) Act 2007; and the Christmas Day and New Year's Day Trading (Scotland) Act 2007.
75 For example, the Fur Farming (Prohibition) (Scotland) Act 2002 (designed to deter fur farmers from relocating to Scotland as a result of the English ban – there were no fur farms in Scotland at the time of the passing of the legislation); the Prohibition of Female Genital Mutilation (Scotland) Act 2005; the Charities and Trustee Investment (Scotland) Act 2005; the Christmas Day and New Year's Day Trading (Scotland) Act 2007 (but note that the English legislation applies only to Christmas

rural nation concerned with land management[76] and animal welfare,[77] which is what one might expect in a country in which agriculture plays a prominent role.[78] Examination of criminal legislation also provides an indication of the types of problems perceived to be facing Scottish society, with measures designed to tackle the culture of alcohol misuse,[79] the carrying of knives and other potential weapons,[80] and the activities of paedophiles.[81] Children are also the focus of the vexed question of parental punishment; there is now no defence of reasonable chastisement if this involved shaking, hitting on the head or using an implement to strike a child.[82] This may not offer Scottish children sufficient protection from harm, and the legislation may well be challenged as being contrary to art 3 of the ECHR.[83]

One might imagine that the Land Reform (Scotland) Act 2003 would not impact on the criminal law, but in fact it contains a section headed "Ploughing"

Day); the Protection of Vulnerable Groups (Scotland) Act 2007; and the Offences (Aggravation by Prejudice) (Scotland) Act 2009. FBOs and ASBOs have their origins in English law.

76 See Land Reform (Scotland) Act 2003; Robin Rigg Offshore Wind Farm (Navigation and Fishing) (Scotland) Act 2003; and Nature Conservation (Scotland) Act 2004.

77 Protection of Wild Mammals (Scotland) Act 2002; Fur Farming (Prohibition) (Scotland) Act 2002; and Animal Health and Welfare (Scotland) Act 2006. The first of these (which banned hunting with dogs of wild mammals such as foxes) was challenged as being contrary to the ECHR art 1 Protocol 1, which states that individuals are entitled to peaceful enjoyment of their possessions. The vires of the statute was upheld by the courts: *Adams v Scottish Ministers* 2004 SC 665; and *Whaley and Friend v Lord Advocate* [2005] CSIH 69, 2006 SC 121. Friend's appeal to the House of Lords was refused: [2007] UKHL 53, 2007 SLT 1209.

78 There are several statutes involving fishing – see, e.g., Salmon Conservation (Scotland) Act 2001; Salmon and Freshwater Fisheries (Consolidation) (Scotland) Act 2003; and Aquaculture and Fisheries (Scotland) Act 2007. The 2003 Act contains more than thirty offences.

79 See the detailed provisions of the Licensing (Scotland) Act 2005 which, *inter alia*, regulates the sale of alcohol to children and young persons, and to persons who are already inebriated.

80 This is discussed in more detail, below. Knife dealers are further regulated by ss 58 and 59 of the 2007 Act. The 2006 Act s 75 amends the Criminal Justice Act 1988 s 141A to increase the age at which knives can be purchased to eighteen, unless the knife is for domestic use. It also makes clear that swords are included in the list of items to which this provision applies.

81 The concern with potential paedophiles is exemplified by several enactments. For example, the Criminal Justice (Scotland) Act 2003 s 19 increases the penalty for breach of s 52 of the Civic Government (Scotland) Act 1982 (relating to the taking, showing, distribution or possession of indecent photographs of children); the Protection of Children (Scotland) Act 2003 s 3 empowers the Scottish Ministers to establish a list of individuals who are considered unsuitable to work with children, and makes it a criminal offence for anyone on the list to work with children; the Protection of Children and Prevention of Sexual Offences (Scotland) Act 2005 introduces an offence colloquially referred to as the "grooming" of a child for sexual purposes (s 1). See also the Protection of Vulnerable Groups (Scotland) Act 2007 which prohibits certain individuals from working with children.

82 2003 Act s 51(3). Other forms of chastisement will be judged against various criteria, including the child's age, gender and state of health, the nature of any injuries sustained, the duration and frequency of the punishment, the reason for its administration, and so on (s 51(1)).

83 See H Keating, "Protecting or punishing children: physical punishment, human rights and English law reform" (2006) 26 *Legal Studies* 394.

which provides that a landowner who has ploughed or otherwise disturbed a path or right of way must reinstate it. Failure to do so within fourteen days is an offence.[84] Just as this provision applies only to landowners, other statutes criminalise the activities of certain categories of persons. These include traders,[85] the directors of diagnostic laboratories,[86] the operators of sunbed premises,[87] fish farmers and shellfish farmers.[88] Other provisions are of more general application,[89] such as the prohibition on smoking in "no-smoking" premises.[90] The Licensing (Scotland) Act 2005 is an example of a statute containing many offences which can only be committed by certain categories of people, such as those in the licensing trade, and others which apply to the wider public. These few examples illustrate that offence provisions are frequently found in unexpected locations, making it far from simple to keep abreast of developments in the criminal law.

Mention has already been made of the Sexual Offences (Scotland) Act 2009. This is the most important reform of the criminal common law enacted to date by the Scottish Parliament. A detailed description would require a chapter in itself, but key provisions include a more appropriate definition of the *actus reus* of rape: it expands the common law definition of penetration of the vagina to include anal or oral penile penetration.[91] It reforms the *mens rea* of the crime, such that it is rape if an accused had no reasonable belief that a victim was in fact consenting to the penetration.[92] There are now statutory offences of, *inter alia*, coercing a person into being present during a sexual activity,[93] or into looking at a sexual image,[94] indecent communications,[95] and

---

84 Land Reform (Scotland) Act 2003 s 23(3). There are several offence provisions in the Local Electoral Administration and Registration Services (Scotland) Act 2006 and the Planning etc (Scotland) Act 2006.
85 For example, the Christmas Day and New Year's Day Trading (Scotland) Act 2007 s 1, aimed at the occupiers or managers of large shops (see s 4).
86 Public Health etc (Scotland) Act 2008 s 17(1).
87 Public Health etc (Scotland) Act 2008 ss 95(1), 96(1) and (2), and 98(1).
88 Aquaculture and Fisheries (Scotland) Act 2007 s 2.
89 For example, the touting offence in the Glasgow Commonwealth Games Act 2008 s 17(1).
90 Smoking, Health and Social Care (Scotland) Act 2005 s 2. It is also an offence for the manager of premises to allow smoking in such premises (s 1). The Scottish Ministers have power to modify the offence of selling tobacco to under-age persons (s 9) and this has been used to increase the minimum permitted age to eighteen (Smoking, Health and Social Care (Scotland) Act 2005 (Variation of Age Limit for Sale of Tobacco etc and Consequential Modifications) Order, SSI 2007/437).
91 Sexual Offences (Scotland) Act 2009 (hereafter "the 2009 Act") s 1(1).
92 2009 Act s 1(1).
93 2009 Act s 5. See also s 22 where the complainer is a child aged twelve or younger, and s 32 where the complainer is an older child (aged thirteen to fifteen).
94 2009 Act s 6. See also ss 23 and s 33.
95 2009 Act s 7. See also ss 24 and 34.

voyeurism.[96] Several offences are restatements or reformulations of what had hitherto been common law crimes – "coercing a person into being present during a sexual activity"[97] or "communicating indecently"[98] could have been charged at common law as a breach of the peace. Nonetheless, this codification of the law on sexual offences is to be welcomed.[99] It may pave the way for enactment of a more substantial criminal code.

Further changes to the substantive law include the criminalisation of the clients or potential clients of prostitutes, in that soliciting or loitering in a "relevant place" in order to engage the services of a prostitute is now an offence.[100] This recognises the gender imbalance in criminalising the behaviour of prostitutes (most of whom are female) but not their clients. Many prostitutes are the victims of earlier sexual abuse and/or human trafficking, and the 2003 Act creates new offences of trafficking for the purposes of sexual exploitation.[101] This Act also gave effect in Scots law to the UK's obligations under the Organisation for Economic Co-operation and Development Convention on Combating Bribery of Foreign Public Officials 1997[102] by giving the crime of bribery extraterritorial effect.[103] Likewise, the fulfilment of international obligations was the motivation for the incorporation into domestic law of genocide, crimes against humanity, war crimes, and offences against the administration of justice of the International Criminal Court.[104]

As previously mentioned, some attempt at consolidation would be beneficial. For instance, the offences of having an offensive weapon[105] or article with a blade or sharp point[106] in a public place have been supplemented by a provision which makes it an offence to have such items in a prison.[107] Earlier amendments by the Westminster Parliament had applied these prohibitions to schools.[108] These various sections could usefully be amalgamated to create

96 2009 Act s 9. See also ss 26 and 36.
97 2009 Act s 5(1).
98 2009 Act s 7(1).
99 Albeit it is an incomplete codification – see further, below.
100 Prostitution (Public Places) (Scotland) Act 2007 s 1.
101 2003 Act s 22. This implements the European Council Framework Decision on Trafficking in Human Beings.
102 2003 Act s 68(1).
103 It has, however, been argued that Scots law has failed fully to comply with its international obligations: see P Arnell, "The crime of bribery in Scotland" (2009) *SLT* 1.
104 International Criminal Court (Scotland) Act 2001 ss 1 and 4. The equivalent legislation for the rest of the UK is the International Criminal Court Act 2001. Both Acts are designed to implement the UK's obligations under the Rome Statute of the International Criminal Court.
105 See the Criminal Law (Consolidation) (Scotland) Act 1995 s 47.
106 Criminal Law (Consolidation) (Scotland) Act 1995 (hereafter "the 1995 Consolidation Act") s 49.
107 1995 Consolidation Act s 49C, inserted by the Custodial Sentences and Weapons (Scotland) Act 2007 s 63.
108 1995 Consolidation Act s 49A, inserted by the Offensive Weapons Act 1996 s 4(3).

one offence. The defences also require attention; there seems little reason for providing a defence of "reasonable excuse" for offensive weapons in public places,[109] but requiring a "good reason" for offensive weapons or articles with a blade or sharp point in prisons[110] or in school premises,[111] and for articles with a blade or sharp point in public places.[112]

Specific offences have been enacted to govern situations which could already be prosecuted under the common law. Hence, s 1 of the Emergency Workers (Scotland) Act 2005 originally applied to assaulting, obstructing or hindering constables, members of a fire brigade or persons acting for the Scottish Ambulance Service Board. More recent amendments have added registered medical practitioners, nurses and midwives to this list.[113] It is a separate offence, in s 2 of that Act, to assault, obstruct or hinder certain other people who are responding to emergency circumstances. The relevant capacities for this section include prison officers; members of the crew of a vessel operated, *inter alia*, by the Royal National Lifeboat Institution; social workers; and mental health officers.[114] Registered medical practitioners, nurses and midwives had been included in this section in the original version of the Act, but were later removed,[115] presumably owing to their inclusion in s 1 instead. It is a separate offence to assault or impede a person who is assisting an emergency worker,[116] and yet another offence to assault or impede health workers in hospital premises.[117] Much of this could readily be dealt with by the common law crime of assault. The maximum penalty for this statutory assault was originally nine months' imprisonment,[118] which was higher than the sheriff courts' summary sentencing powers for common law assault. Once sentencing powers for common law offences in summary proceedings were increased to twelve months' imprisonment, the 2005 Act's sentencing provisions also required to be increased.[119] Now that the maximum penalty under the statute equates to that for common law crimes, the 2005 Act appears to be largely redundant. It is at best symbolic, emphasising to the public that assaulting emergency workers will not be

---

109   1995 Consolidation Act s 47(1).
110   1995 Consolidation Act s 49C(2).
111   1995 Consolidation Act s 49A(2).
112   1995 Consolidation Act s 49.
113   Emergency Workers (Scotland) Act 2005 (Modification) Order 2008, SSI 2008/37 art 2(b).
114   Emergency Workers (Scotland) Act 2005 s 2(3) (henceforth "the 2005 Workers Act").
115   By the Emergency Workers (Scotland) Act 2005 (Modification) Order 2008, SSI 2008/37 art 3.
116   2005 Workers Act s 3.
117   2005 Workers Act s 5. These are defined as registered medical practitioners, nurses and midwives.
118   2005 Workers Act s 6.
119   This was done by the 2007 Act s 44(4).

tolerated.[120] There are similar offences in the Fire (Scotland) Act 2005 and the Police (Scotland) Act 1967. Consolidation is required.

As we have already noted, other statutory aggravations relate to various forms of prejudice. Is such legislation desirable? It sends a strong message that as a society we deplore this form of abuse, and this in turn may lead to greater tolerance of others' differences. On the other hand, it is questionable whether it is in fact worse to be targeted because of one's sexual orientation, religion or race than for other reasons (for example, because of one's mode of dress).[121] It does, however, result in a proliferation of offences. As with the statutory offences of assaulting emergency services personnel, it would be preferable if these various aggravations based on prejudice could at least be consolidated in one statute. Another example of unnecessary criminalisation is the Breastfeeding etc (Scotland) Act 2005. Its preamble states that its objectives are "to make it an offence to prevent or stop a person in charge of a child who is otherwise permitted to be in a public place or licensed premises from feeding milk to that child in that place or on those premises; to make provision in relation to the promotion of breastfeeding; and for connected purposes". Its primary purpose was surely the second of these: to promote breastfeeding, which is a laudable aim. But the mechanism for achieving this – the creation of an offence coupled with the imposition of vicarious liability – is inappropriate. Scotland certainly has a low level of breastfeeding,[122] but a tendency of licensees to eject nursing mothers from their premises is surely not a major cause of this.[123]

Several statutes create specific crimes for behaviours which could be prosecuted at common law as fraud. For instance, it is an offence for a person falsely to pretend to be a fire services enforcement officer,[124] a wildlife inspector,[125] a social worker[126] or social service worker.[127] Other statutes provide offences of

120 The provisions on hindering and obstructing may be more useful; the Act specifies that "obstruction" does not require a physical element, and the provision of false information amounts to "hindering" (2005 Workers Act s 4).
121 This seems to have been the motivation behind the murder of Sophie Lancaster, who was dressed as a "goth" (see BBC News, 30 March 2008). I am indebted to Robin White for the example.
122 The Scottish NHS had set itself a target to increase the proportion of newborns exclusively breastfed at six to eight weeks from the 2006/7 figure of around 26% to nearly 33%. See http://www.isdscotland. org/isd/5939.html.
123 In fact, the rates seem to have decreased since the passing of the Act: see H Puttick, "Health fear as fewer mothers breastfeed their babies", The Herald, 15 May 2007.
124 Fire (Scotland) Act 2005 s 72(4)(b).
125 Nature Conservation (Scotland) Act 2004 Sch 6, para 17. This amends the Countryside and Rights of Way Act 2000.
126 Regulation of Care (Scotland) Act 2001 s 52(1)(a).
127 Regulation of Care (Scotland) Act 2001 s 52(1)(b).

making false statements in documents.[128] Some of these provisions are more extensive than common law fraud, since they criminalise reckless mis-statements.[129] Whether recklessness ought to be a sufficient *mens rea* is a moot point but, on the assumption that it should, a better means of achieving this would be to create a general (statutory) offence of fraud, with intention or recklessness as alternative forms of *mens rea*. This would avoid the creation of many separate offences.

E. THE PARLIAMENTARY PROCESS

In its first two sessions the Scottish Parliament passed seventy-seven "legislative consent motions",[130] thereby agreeing that a devolved matter could be dealt with by Westminster legislation.[131] Several of these related to criminal law matters.[132] One can see the logic in allowing the Westminster Parliament to legislate both for England and Wales, and Scotland. The process has been defended on the basis that

> there is a cross-border interest in issues such as immigration, organised crime and customs. Criminals who operate in the UK will be the first to look for gaps in co-operation, fault lines in legislation or loopholes in police powers ... Increasingly, crime has an international dimension.[133]

However, the use of legislative consent motions does make it yet more difficult to keep abreast of the law, since one has to consider enactments and amendments from both parliaments. For example, while most sexual offences will be found in the Sexual Offences (Scotland) Act 2009 once this is brought into force, for a complete picture one must take account not only of those common law and statutory offences which remain outwith the Act,[134] but also of the reform of homosexual offences enacted by the Westminster

---

128 See the Mental Health (Care and Treatment) (Scotland) Act 2003 s 318; and the Building (Scotland) Act 2003 ss 11(4) and 16(1).

129 Building (Scotland) Act 2003 s 16(1)(b). See also ss 19(4)(b), 20(1)(b), 34(2) and 37(4)(c).

130 From 1999 to 2003 (thirty-nine motions); 2003 to 2007 (thirty-eight motions).

131 There is a convention that the Westminster Parliament will not generally legislate with regard to devolved matters without the consent of the Scottish Parliament. Prior to 30 November 2005, the process by which the Scottish Parliament was asked to give its consent was referred to as a "Sewel motion" (*Hansard:* HL Deb 21 July 1998 vol 592, col 791).

132 See, e.g., Sexual Offences (Amendment) Act 2000; Tobacco Advertising and Promotion Act 2002; Anti-Terrorism, Crime and Security Act 2001; Sexual Offences Act 2003; Fireworks Act 2003; Serious Crime Act 2007.

133 Scottish Parliament, *Official Report*, col 14146 (2 February 2005), per Jeremy Purvis, Liberal Democrat MSP.

134 For example, a common law charge of sexual assault remains competent, and incest remains an offence by virtue of the 1995 Consolidation Act s 1(1).

Parliament.[135] When in opposition, the Scottish National Party was highly critical of the use of legislative consent motions.[136] Academic commentators have also questioned whether, in the words of Stephen Tierney, "this procedure is simply an efficient device in the management of interparliamentary relations, or an instance of Westminster encroaching upon the Scottish Parliament's autonomy".[137]

F. CONCLUSIONS

I have argued elsewhere that several common law crimes and defences require clarification by legislation, and that there are *lacunae* which ought to be filled by enactment of new offences.[138] As previously noted, the Sexual Offences (Scotland) Act 2009 represents Holyrood's greatest achievement to date. It should, however, be borne in mind that Parliament asked the Scottish Law Commission to recommend reform only because of public outcry resulting from an acquittal in a rape prosecution. The judge had been correct to order an acquittal; it was not rape where a woman offered no resistance to sexual intercourse, according to the common law definition which applied at that time. Yet academics had been critical of that same definition for many years.[139] It should not require a *cause célèbre* to instigate reform of the common law. Perhaps the greatest concern lies in the sheer difficulty in finding out what exactly the criminal law provides. This would be made far easier, and the possibility of overlapping or redundant provisions decreased, if the common law were to be codified, and existing statutory offences – or at least those in relatively obscure places – consolidated. Such a codifying and/or consoli-

135 Sexual Offences (Amendment) Act 2000 s 1(3). This reduced the age of consent from eighteen to sixteen by amending the 1995 Consolidation Act s 13.
136 See, e.g., Scottish Parliament, *Official Report*, col 227 (19 January 2000), per Roseanna Cunningham MSP. It should, however, be noted that the SNP administration has also made use of legislative consent motions. Recent examples include the Policing and Crime Act 2009; Bribery Bill 2009; and Crime and Security Bill 2009.
137 S Tierney, "Giving with one hand: Scottish devolution within a unitary state" (2007) *International Journal of Constitutional Law* 730 at 750. See also A Sinclair, "The Supreme Court: a separation of powers or a union of laws? Some further problems of Anglo–Scots legal relations" (2005) *Criminal Lawyer* 6 at 7; A Batey and A C Page, "Scotland's other Parliament: Westminster legislation about devolved matters in Scotland since devolution" (2002) *Public Law* 501; and P Arnell, "Muddy waters: legislative competence and the International Criminal Court in Scotland" (2002) 2 *Oxford University Commonwealth Law Journal* 281.
138 See P R Ferguson and C McDiarmid, *Scots Criminal Law: A Critical Analysis* (2009), especially ch 22.
139 For example, C H W Gane, *Sexual Offences* (1992); P R Ferguson, "Controversial aspects of the law of rape: an Anglo-Scottish comparison', in R Hunter (ed), *Justice and Crime: Essays in Honour of The Lord Emslie* (1993) 180.

dating measure might help to guard against the creation of offences for largely symbolic purposes, such as the proliferation of statutory aggravations. The issue confronting the Scottish Parliament was well expressed by Eric Clive:

> The question is not whether there will be legislative intervention in the substantive criminal law of Scotland. There will be. The question is whether it will be coherent or incoherent. Will the Scottish Parliament in twenty years' time have left a legacy of legislative chaos in this area or something of which it and Scotland could be proud?[140]

The answer to this after the first ten years, at least, is that there is more chaos than one would like, and less coherence than one might have hoped for.

---

140   E Clive, "Submission of a draft criminal code for Scotland to the Minister for Justice" (2003) 7 *Edin LR* 395 at 398.

12 Juvenile Offending: Welfare or Toughness

Claire McDiarmid[*]

* Senior Lecturer, Strathclyde Law School. The author would like to thank Kenneth Norrie and Elaine Sutherland for commenting on an earlier draft.

A. INTRODUCTION

The most striking point about offending by juveniles during the period of the Scottish Parliament's existence is the political capital which "dealing with the problem" is perceived to create. The past ten years have been a period in which the media have affirmed and reaffirmed the "problem" of out-of-control youth.[1] While this account has not gone unchallenged,[2] it can be said to have been dominant and it has given governments, both in Westminster and Holyrood, the opportunity to be seen to be taking a firm stance. Such "toughness" is often seen as the province of New Labour[3] – the follow-up to Tony Blair's 1997 election mantra that his party would be "tough on crime and tough on the causes of crime". Almost as soon as the party was first elected nationally, Jack Straw, the then Home Secretary, "unveiled the biggest crackdown on youth crime for fifty years".[4] It is interesting, therefore, that a similarly robust approach was taken in Scotland, given that, for the first eight years of its existence, the Holyrood Parliament was in the hands of a New Labour/Liberal Democrat coalition. The next chapter in the ongoing youth justice narrative is provided by the shift to an SNP-led administration in May 2007 when the rhetoric softens and a perspective which recognises the interests of young offenders themselves is reintroduced into the debate. These administrations will be identified by the titles they conferred on themselves: the "Scottish Executive" for the Labour/LibDem coalition and the "Scottish Government" for the period when the SNP has been in (minority) control.

As (a New Labour) First Minister, Jack McConnell was widely reported as having declared war on youth crime,[5] making it a flagship policy of his (coalition) Executive.[6] As a result, Scotland was undoubtedly affected by the currents of managerialism[7] and punitiveness which have been apparent in England and Wales.[8] A strident, negative rhetoric is discernible, which identifies the young as the cause of certain forms of blight in communities

1 See, e.g., K Loveys, "Yobs are running riot, say family of murdered father", *Daily Mail*, 3 October 2009; K Lowry, "Village's fears as neds set to return", *The Sun*, 24 May 2004; J Hamilton, "Teenage kicks push city's fire brigades to limit", *Evening News*, 9 April 2002, 7.
2 See, e.g., L Hancock, "Urban regeneneration, young people, crime and criminalisation", in B Goldson and J Muncie (eds), *Youth Crime and Justice* (2006) 172.
3 See, e.g, D A Green, "Public opinion versus public judgments about crime: correcting the 'comedy of errors'" (2006) 46 *Brit J Criminol* 131 especially 138.
4 K Maguire, "Blair to stand firm on single mum cuts", *The Mirror*, 28 November 1997, 6.
5 See, e.g., "Fresh war on young crooks", *Daily Record*, 29 January 2002, 17; L Adams and K Farquharson, "Crime and punishment", *Sunday Times*, 19 May 2002.
6 He was First Minister from 2001 to 2007.
7 L McAra, "Welfare in crisis? Key developments in Scottish youth justice", in J Muncie and B Goldson (eds), *Comparative Youth Justice* (2006) 127 at 133-134.
8 See, e.g., C Ball, "Youth justice? Half a century of responses to youth offending" (2004) *CrimLR* 167.

and promises "tough" responses.[9] Even relatively benign and diversionary
initiatives, such as the provision of restorative justice mechanisms for young
offenders, were "spun" in terms of their more potentially punitive attributes.
For example, a news release in January 2004 stated:

> Every local authority youth justice action team receives funding for restorative
> justice projects in their area. While individual projects vary, examples include:
> getting young offenders who have sprayed graffiti on school buildings to clean up
> their mess; getting young offenders who have destroyed gardens to be responsible
> for repairing the damage.[10]

It is, however, easy to "talk tough". Talk, as they say, is cheap. In its evaluation
of the Parliament's treatment of juvenile offending, then, this chapter will
consider, as far as it can, the relationship between this rhetoric of punitiveness and the legislative reality of the child's best interests. It will be argued
that punitiveness did not constitute the whole story and welfare was never
a spent force. Rather, through the children's hearings system and, indeed,
certain other initiatives, Scotland held to the welfare principle in addressing
most offending by young people:[11] that is, that meeting the child's needs is the
best way to deal with his or her misdeeds. The matter is important because,
as the Scottish Government discovered to its cost, in relation to class sizes
in primary schools, in any conflict between written but unlegislated policy
and statutory provisions, the latter will prevail.[12] To some extent, therefore,
the Scottish Parliament can say what it likes about youth justice. It will be
judged by its legislation and, to date, such legislation (or at least that which is
in force) amounts to a single provision on information for victims,[13] together
with certain aspects of the Anti-social Behaviour etc (Scotland) Act 2004
(specifically, dispersal orders, movement restriction conditions (or electronic
tagging), anti-social behaviour orders ("ASBOs") and parenting orders, all of
which are considered subsequently).[14] Primary legislation, then, is taken as
the clearest indication of the Parliament's actually having acted in relation to
juvenile offending; however, plainly, some important initiatives are implemented without the need for this. Both youth courts and fast-track hearings

---

9 See, e.g., D Mcdougall, "Teen crime a quarter of all offences", *The Scotsman*, 17 May 2002, 12;
  "McConnell tells thugs to beware", *Evening News* 22 May 2003, 2, both quoting Cathy Jamieson,
  the New Labour Education Minister (in 2002) and, subsequently, Justice Minister (in 2003).
10 "Extra funding for youth justice", 8 January 2004.
11 The option of prosecution in the (adult) courts continues to exist (under the Criminal Procedure
  Scotland Act 1995 s 42) currently for children aged eight and over (Criminal Procedure (Scotland)
  Act 1995 s 41) and usually in relation to commission of the gravest crimes. This age will be raised
  to twelve when the new S41A of the Criminal Procedure (Scotland) Act 1995 comes into force.
12 *East Lothian Council, Petitioner* 2008 SLT 921.
13 Criminal Justice (Scotland) Act 2003 s 53.
14 These are discussed below. See notes 95-140 and accompanying text.

fall into this category and will be considered subsequently.

It is also necessary to attempt to characterise the approach of the current Scottish Government which has proposals at the Bill stage in relation to children's hearings and a recently enacted statute, which is not yet in force, which contains provisions on the age of criminal responsibility and on child imprisonment.[15] It is a little frustrating that an administration which has been in power for almost three years must still be judged only on draft legislation and on provisions which are not yet in force. One reason for this is, almost certainly, that the SNP does not have an overall majority in the Scottish Parliament and this affects its ability to impose its ideology. Nonetheless, it may be taken from this slowness that it is exercising some caution in this area which, in itself, is welcome in that it tends to direct the political spotlight away from young offenders. The SNP administration has not completed much in relation to youth offending but it will be argued that its actions and its rhetoric are, at least, commensurable with each other.

B. EARLY SIGNS OF TENSION BETWEEN TOUGHNESS AND WELFARE

It is appropriate to start this evaluation at a point prior to the period under discussion, with Donald Dewar's 1997 Kilbrandon Child Care lecture.[16] In 1999, Dewar became New Labour's first First Minister but he had previously worked as a reporter to the children's panel, practising welfare in response to juvenile offending. His Kilbrandon speech provides a particular insight into the welfare/toughness dichotomy at a key point immediately before the realisation of the Scottish Parliament itself. In it, he noted "the pressures of the understandable public concern over crime and anti-social behaviour",[17] and that "[t]he argument for the short sharp shock, retribution and deterrence [was] always with us and a balance [had] to be struck".[18] Nonetheless, he still stated his belief that the Kilbrandon principles[19] "[held] good"[20] and "look[ed]

---

15 Children's Hearings (Scotland) Bill; Criminal Justice and Licensing (Scotland) Act ss 52 and 64.
16 Dewar, *Children's Hearings*, Third Kilbrandon Child Care Lecture (1998).
17 *Children's Hearings* (n 16) 2.
18 *Children's Hearings* (n 16) 2.
19 The "Kilbrandon Report" (*Children and Young Persons, Scotland* (Cmnd 2306, 1964)) set down the basic framework for the children's hearings system and particularly provided the rationale for the pre-eminence of the welfare principle. It is discussed more fully below (see notes 37-40, below, and accompanying text). The report's recommendations were enacted in the Social Work (Scotland) Act 1968 and continued in the Children (Scotland) Act 1995 which currently governs the operation of the system. The Children's Hearings (Scotland) Bill (discussed below – see notes 141-147 and accompanying text) also remains true to the Kilbrandon ethos.
20 Dewar, *Children's Hearings* (n 16) 2.

forward to the day when all [the] strands [of his lecture] [could] be brought together in a Scottish Parliament and [could] make some decision about how we buil[t] on the inheritance of the Kilbrandon Report and move[d] on".[21] Overall, his lecture demonstrates a recognition of the particular pressures arising from the "new punitiveness"[22] in criminal justice generally but along- side an expression of confidence in the Scottish bedrock of welfare. This is a reasonable statement of the position from which the Scottish Parliament started its foray into juvenile offending. It also begins to highlight the contra- dictions and definitional dilemmas inherent in youth justice more generally.

C. YOUTH JUSTICE AS A SOCIAL CONSTRUCTION AND THE CHILD/CRIMINAL PARADOX

(1) The question of definition

At one level, the extent of the juvenile offending "problem" is largely within government control. Herbert Packer has noted that "we can have as much or as little crime as we please, depending upon what we choose to count as criminal".[23] This relates to the concept of criminalisation generally – to the question of which behaviours are so unacceptable that a given society chooses to proscribe them. Juvenile offending, as a form of crime, is clearly governed by these fundamental, classificatory decisions but it brings with it its own definitional dilemmas. Barry Goldson and John Muncie have suggested that "youth justice systems are relative constructs subject to the varying impulses of policy-makers and the means by which the power to 'define' is exercised and applied".[24] In other words, the meaning to be attached to "youth justice" shifts, depending on the political agenda espoused by those with the power to delineate it at any given time.

(2) Exercising the power to define: "persistent offending"

An example of the application of this power is the approach taken by the Scottish Executive to persistent offending by juveniles. In December 2002, in introducing the roll-out of programmes for the reduction of such offending, Cathy Jamieson, the then Justice Minister, seems to be identifying herself with communities affected by crime rather than the young people who are

---

21 Dewar, *Children's Hearings* (n 16) 16.
22 J Pratt et al, "Introduction" to *The New Punitiveness: Trends, Theories, Perspectives* (2005), especially xii-xiii.
23 H Packer, *The Limits of the Criminal Sanction* (1969) 364.
24 B Goldson and J Muncie, "Critical anatomy: towards a principled youth justice", in Goldson and Muncie, *Youth Crime and Justice* (n 2) 203 at 203.

said to have committed such offences. She said: "Youth crime continues to be a major concern in our communities. There are a small number of young people across the country who persistently offend and cause misery for a large number of people."[25] The Executive's answer to this was the application of "managerialism", defined by Muncie and Hughes as being "characterised by increased emphasis on achieving results rather than administrative processes; the setting of explicit targets and performance indicators to enable the auditing of efficiency and effectiveness".[26] Thus, in 2001, the Scottish Executive stated its aim to reduce re-referrals on offence grounds to children's hearings by 10% by 2004[27] and, in 2002, to reduce persistent offending by juveniles by 10% by 2006.[28]

It should be noted at the outset that a welfare-based approach to juvenile crime, which seeks to effect change across the child's life by identifying and then meeting his or her needs, may not lend itself to overt managerialism of this nature in relation to only the one, highly specific, area of behaviour constituted by offending. Leaving this to one side, however, in order for the Executive's pledge to be meaningful, in any sense, it was necessary to define "persistence". The appropriate statistics are the province of the Scottish Children's Reporter Administration ("SCRA") and had generally been recorded by it in terms of children referred to the hearings system for having committed ten or more offences in any year.[29] However, in its Annual Report for 2003-2004, the measure was changed to five or more offending episodes within a six-month period.[30] This meant that direct comparison with previous years' figures was rendered impossible.[31] More importantly, following a freedom of information request by an SNP MSP, *The Herald* reported that "The Scottish Executive ha[d] interfered extensively and clashed with the children's panel quango over the extent of persistent youth offending, casting doubt on the reliability of its annual report".[32]

This change in the basis of calculation, effected partly through intervention by the Scottish Executive, reveals persistent youth offending as a further

---

25 "New programmes to tackle youth crime", Scottish Executive news release, 19 December 2002.
26 J Muncie and G Hughes, "Modes of youth governance: political rationalities, criminalization and resistance", in J Muncie et al (eds), *Youth Justice: Critical Readings* (2002) 5.
27 Scottish Executive, *Working Together for Scotland: A Programme for Government* (2001) s 2.4.
28 Part of the Scottish Executive's *Ten-Point Action Plan on Youth Justice*, published in 2002.
29 See SCRA, *Annual Report 2000-2001* 10; SCRA, *Annual Report 2001-2002* 12; SCRA, *Annual Report 2002-2003* 16.
30 SCRA, *Annual Report 2003-2004* 10 n 1 therein.
31 See C McDiarmid, "Welfare, offending and the Scottish children's hearings system" (2005) 27 *J Soc Wel &Fam L* 31 at 40.
32 D Fraser, "Documents reveal executive's clash with agency on youth crime", *The Herald*, 3 February 2005, 1.

facet of the youth justice construct, having content only as defined, manufactured and, in this instance, apparently manipulated, by the powerful.

(3) The singularity of youth crime

Overall, it might be appropriate to ask why "youth crime" is regarded as a social problem in its own right at all, separate from "crime" generally. Does it really matter to the victim if the assailant, or thief, is aged fourteen or forty-one? One answer is that it is marked by the coming together of two social issues which would otherwise be approached from diametrically opposed directions. On the one hand, there are children and young people who, as a group, might be characterised as vulnerable and in need of protection. On the other, there are criminals to whom the state's response is usually punitive. The two do not sit together comfortably, yet the "child-offender" personifies both simultaneously.[33] The difficulty with formulating government policy in respect of this group is that emphasis is always placed on one or other of the terms "youth" or "crime". Youth crime is, and ought to be, a social issue in its own right if that emphasis is placed on the status of its individual subject as a child or young person. Otherwise, it is simply a further manifestation of the general problem of crime. Indeed, the term "justice" itself, within "youth justice", carries the unspoken question "to whom?". The Kilbrandon Report[34] might be a blueprint for (social) justice to young people "in trouble", whether arising through their own offending behaviour or otherwise. The Scottish Executive showed a great deal of concern for communities adversely affected by youth crime,[35] the appropriate response to which, in its view, required firm action against the young. The term "justice" allows this ambiguity to go largely unexplored.

It is essentially at this level of whether to tilt the balance in favour of youth or crime – welfare or toughness – that the power to construct is apparent. For example, in its earliest review of the matter, in 2000,[36] the Scottish Executive proposed, *inter alia*, "a renaming of the children's hearings system: one option would be simply to drop the reference to children". Presumably another option, not canvassed, would have been to drop the reference to "hearings". On the one hand, then, a "children's system" would have been left; on the other, a "hearings system". In fact, no change has been made but

33 See C McDiarmid, *Childhood and Crime* (2007), especially 165-167; J Fionda, *Devils and Angels: Youth Policy and Crime* (2005).
34 See n 19.
35 Scottish Executive, *Scotland's Action Programme to Reduce Youth Crime* (2002) 2.
36 Scottish Executive, *Report of Advisory Group on Youth Crime* (2000) para 7.

the Executive's proposal can be characterised as an attempt to draw attention away from the status as children of those with whom the system is dealing. As in all areas of criminal justice, balance between the rights of the accused and the public interest is what is sought. In relation to children who offend, however, the commitment to welfare, which will now be examined, suggests that these two interests are not so dichotomised – that there is a public interest in treating children appropriately.

D. THE CENTRALITY OF WELFARE

Welfare – meeting the child's needs as the mechanism for, *inter alia*, resolving his or her offending behaviour – did not by chance become the basis of the Scottish response to juvenile crime. Rather, it was rolled out as a result of the reasoned and innovative recommendations contained in the Kilbrandon Report.[37] This, and the system it spawned, relates to all children "in trouble" but the Kilbrandon Committee gave specific consideration to the issue of juvenile offending. It said:

> Any answer to the question – what is the best machinery for the treatment of juvenile delinquency – must reflect the acceptance of certain broad principles as to what are considered to be its essential function, since function affects both procedure and constitution. What then is the essential function? The object must be to effect, so far as this can be achieved by public action, the reduction, and ideally the elimination, of delinquency. If public concern must always be for the effective treatment of delinquency, the appropriate treatment measures in any individual case can be decided only on an informed assessment of the individual child's actual needs.[38]

Thus, Kilbrandon's call to arms on welfare's behalf was unequivocal, and children's welfare throughout their childhoods remains today the "paramount consideration" of courts and children's hearings in taking decisions under Pt II of the Children (Scotland) Act 1995.[39] This goes beyond the standard set even by the UN Convention on the Rights of the Child (1989) ("CRC")[40] which requires only that the child's welfare should be "a primary consideration". When prosecuting children, even (adult) criminal courts are required to "have regard to the welfare of the child".[41] Welfare, then, supplied the

---

37 See n 19.

38 Kilbrandon Report para 12. See also paras 77-81 and 250.

39 Section 16(1), though this is slightly qualified by s 16(5) which empowers children's hearings to displace welfare in favour of public safety in any appropriate case. The Children's Hearings (Scotland) Bill provides that a slightly diluted form of the welfare principle would apply even in such a case. See n 144 and accompanying text.

40 Article 3(1).

41 Criminal Procedure (Scotland) Act 1995 s 50(6).

basic philosophical and legislative framework for dealing with children who offend, which was inherited by the Scottish Parliament when it came into existence in 1999. None of this framework has been repealed. Indeed, it has been suggested that "core institutions such as the children's hearings system became inextricably linked to a sense of Scottishness",[42] which might provide an ideological connection to a Scottish Nationalist agenda, though, so far, the Scottish Government's approach has been predicated on the system's efficacy.[43] Nonetheless, it is fair to say that the Scottish Executive indulged in sabre rattling towards welfare, from the early years of the new millennium, some of which will now be considered.

E. WELFARE: A PERCEIVED CREDIBILITY GAP?

Welfare has come to be perceived as a "soft" response to youth crime,[44] yet the breadth of the discretion which it confers is such that almost any intervention could be imposed on the child[45] if it could in some way be explicated as being in his or her best interests from, at two rather unlikely exemplifying extremes, "therapeutic" beatings[46] to unlimited McDonald's Happy Meals. Thus, whatever its aims, it is not necessarily perceived as benign. Roger Matthews has noted, for example, that "the pursuit of rehabilitative strategies can lead to more prolonged and intensive forms of regulation. In the attempt to do more good it is always possible … to do more harm".[47] Within welfare, however, punishment, *per se*, has no part to play, therefore welfare cannot fit all that comfortably into a social climate which is (apparently) characterised by its punitiveness.

The Scottish Executive seemed excessively sensitive to public opinion and, particularly, to any implication of not being "tough" in the youth justice context.[48] Public funding was, for example, withdrawn from an outward bound project, the Airborne Initiative in South Lanarkshire, after its portrayal in

---

42 McAra, "Welfare in crisis?" (n 7) at 130.

43 "Children's Hearings Bill", Scottish Government news release, 24 February 2010.

44 See, e.g., R Stevenson and R Brotchie, *Getting it Right for Every Child: Report on the Responses to the Phase 1 Consultation on the Review of the Children's Hearings System* (2004) para 5.6; K Skellington Orr et al, *An Assessment of the Support and Information for Victims of Youth Crime (SIVYC) Pilot Scheme* (2005) para 1.12.

45 Children (Scotland) Act 1995 s 70(3)(b).

46 A possible misuse of welfare suggested by Sanford J Fox in "The Scottish panels: an American viewpoint on children's right to punishment" (1975) 20 *JLSS* 78 at 79.

47 R Matthews, "The myth of punitiveness" (2005) 9 *Theoretical Criminology* 175 at 179.

48 See, e.g., I Loader, "Fall of the 'Platonic guardians': liberalism, criminology and political responses to crime in England and Wales" (2006) 46 *Brit J Criminol* 561, especially 578 on the Labour Party's response to crime generally.

a BBC documentary in 2004 which included footage of some participants drinking and taking drugs. The project had been set up by former members of the Airborne parachute regiment as a direct alternative to imprisonment for serious and persistent offenders, aged eighteen to twenty-five. As Joan Burnie in the *Daily Record* graphically explained the matter, *Chancers* (the documentary series) "was cynically pitched to make the punters think that their money was being wasted on the wasters, that it was a holiday camp for neds and an easy, peasy option to prison".[49] Despite this, the Executive's axe fell on the project, to almost universal condemnation. Nonetheless, the decision to terminate funding is indicative of the importance the Executive attached, especially then, to the perception of the populist will or public opinion,[50] yet it is unclear by what mechanism this was to be gauged. As Matthews has noted in relation to academic commentary, while "[t]he notion of public opinion is a central reference point in the punitiveness literature ... [it] has often been pointed out [that] there is always a danger that rather than report it, social scientists construct it".[51] There may also be a danger that politicians' insistence that there exists a bottom-up wave of public anger about youth crime, which can only be assuaged by tough responses similarly constructs, or at least reinvigorates, any such wave.

This, then, is a good example of the rather undiscerning application of perceived public opinion and of the assumption that it is opposed to "soft" responses.[52] Nonetheless, if the Executive's policy was driven by this perceived need to avoid "softness", then one deceptively easy solution might have been to remove offending as a ground for referral to the (welfare-based) children's hearings system altogether. For commentators at the time, the proposals for a youth court raised this spectre.

F. YOUTH COURTS: DISAPPLY THE WELFARE PRINCIPLE?

The youth courts pilot scheme (first in Hamilton and later extended to Airdrie) coincided with, or, indeed, caused, speculation in the Scottish press that the Scottish Executive had plans to remove offending by a child as a ground for referral to the children's hearings system as part of its "toughness"

---

49 "The fly in the ointment is that Airborne really worked", *Daily Record*, 27 February 2004, 11.
50 It should, nonetheless, be noted that the Scottish Executive gave lack of cost-effectiveness as its reason for the withdrawal of funding.
51 Matthews, "The myth of punitiveness" (n 47) at 191.
52 Other research suggests that the more informed the public is about particular crimes and the criminals who commit them, the less punitive its response. See B Chapman et al, *Improving Public Attitudes to the Criminal Justice System: The Impact of Information* (Home Office Research Study 245) (2002) at 30-32.

agenda.[53] At least one MSP voiced concern that youth courts might replace the children's hearings system.[54] Though this fear has proved groundless, this backdrop emphasises the importance of evaluating the youth court as a criminal justice mechanism for dealing specifically with individuals (aged sixteen and seventeen and, in some cases, fifteen)[55] who are categorised, certainly in terms of the CRC, as children.[56]

The youth court pilot project was said to form part of a ten-point action plan to tackle youth crime and disorder, agreed by the Scottish Cabinet in June 2002.[57] Laura Piacentini and Reece Waters have, however, noted that that "plan makes no mention of a youth court".[58] Indeed, the Scottish Executive had previously indicated that it would consider the children's hearings system's ability to deal with sixteen- and seventeen-year-olds.[59] The "toughness" rhetoric is apparent in the announcement of the pilot. Jack McConnell stated:

> [y]outh crime is a serious issue affecting our communities. It concerns the Scottish public and it concerns everyone in the Executive … this ten-point action plan will directly tackle that small but persistent group of young offenders whose behaviour so concerns and damages our communities.[60]

In announcing the opening of the Hamilton youth court in June 2003, Lesley McAra notes that Cathy Jamieson, then Minister for Justice, expressly stated: "punishment is a key part of the youth justice process".[61]

The Scottish Executive took the view that youth courts could be set up under existing legislation.[62] Accordingly, these courts operate as a microcosm of the sheriff court sitting in summary cases, with an exclusively youthful clientele, but with the same sentencing powers.[63] This suggests, first of all,

53 For a discussion, see McDiarmid, "Welfare, offending" (n 31) at 35.
54 Robert Brown, Liberal Democrat MSP. See H Macdonell, "Labour plans to jail parents splits coalition", *The Scotsman*, 20 May 2002, 10.
55 See G McIvor et al, *Evaluation of the Airdrie and Hamilton Youth Court Pilots* (2006) paras 1.2 and 1.3.
56 CRC art 1 and Age of Majority (Scotland) Act 1969 s 1.
57 The pilot youth courts themselves were introduced in Hamilton in June 2003 and in Airdrie in June 2004.
58 L Piacentini and R Waters, "The politicization of youth crime in Scotland and the rise of the 'Burberry Court'" (2006) 6 *Youth Justice* 43 at 44.
59 One of the recommendations in the Scottish Executive's *Report of the Advisory Group on Youth Crime* (n 36) was "a detailed examination of the feasibility of a bridging pilot scheme which would refer as many 16/17 year olds as possible to the Hearings system". See Piacentini and Waters, "The politicization of youth crime" (n 58) 44.
60 "Youth offenders on justice fast track", Scottish Executive news release, 27 June 2002.
61 McAra, "Welfare in crisis? (n 7) at 135.
62 F Popham et al, *Evaluation of the Hamilton Sheriff Youth Court Pilot 2003-2005* (2005) para 1.
63 McIvor et al, *Evaluation* (n 55) para 4.44. Criminal Procedure (Scotland) Act 1995 Pt XI sets down sentencing powers.

that the Executive's intention was that youth courts would be weighted towards the crime side of the "youth crime" equation. McAra has commented that the decision to adopt a court-based setting "serves to reinforce the more robust, punitive approach which has now been adopted towards persistent offenders".[64] Piacentini and Waters have expressed particular concerns about the youth courts' lack of recognition of international juvenile justice norms as set down in the CRC and the UN Standard Minimum Rules for the Administration of Juvenile Justice (1985) ("the Beijing Rules").[65]

On the face of it, then, youth courts appear to be an example of toughness rhetoric being made real. This is, however, not quite the whole story. First, it should be noted that, prior to the introduction of the courts, the only option for a sixteen- or seventeen-year-old who was not already on a supervision requirement imposed by a children's hearing and who was charged with a criminal offence was prosecution in the (adult) courts.[66] While youth courts are not fundamentally different from sheriff courts, one of their (few) unique youth-oriented elements is that there is some scope for intensive social work intervention with the young person during a deferred sentence or in addition to a community-based penalty such as probation.[67] "It should be noted that these services are not specific to the Youth Court: they can, for example, be accessed via the Children's Hearings System"[68] – which would only intervene if this was in the child's best interests. Second, some clients of the youth court did perceive certain advantages over the adult system in terms of "support and assistance from the appointed youth court social worker" and a perception of lesser punitiveness.[69] Overall, it would be wrong to characterise the youth courts as other than a "tough" response to juvenile crime in terms of the toughness/welfare dichotomy discussed above, yet these two points suggest at least a slightly paradoxical approach. Even this largely punitive measure is tempered a little by welfare considerations.

There are still only two youth courts in Scotland and the current SNP-led administration has approached the matter of their continued viability with some caution. A promised review, scheduled for spring 2009,[70] was finally made public in April 2010.[71] While the Report itself highlighted a number

---

64 McAra, "Welfare in crisis? (n 7) 135.
65 Piacentini and Waters, "The politicization of youth crime" (n 58), especially at 48 and 52-54.
66 Criminal Procedure (Scotland) Act 1995 s 42(1); Children (Scotland) Act 1995 s 93(2)(b).
67 Popham et al, *Evaluation* (n 62) paras 3.91-3.95.
68 Popham et al, *Evaluation* (n 62) para 3.91.
69 Piacentini and Waters, "The politicization of youth crime" (n 58) at 50.
70 Scottish Government, media briefing, 17 January 2008.
71 Community Justice Services, Scottish Government, *Review of the Hamilton & Airdrie Youth Courts Report* (web only publication) at *http://www.scotland.gov.uk/Publications/2009/12/09093018/0.*

of benefits, such as intensive social work interventions, it also found that
there had been no significant impact on reoffending rates and that the youth
court was not particularly cost-effective.[72] The Scottish Government also
undertook to "consider[…] further … a specialist [Youth] hearing for sixteen
and seventeen year olds",[73] a proposal of the Scottish Prisons Commission
which was concerned about the abruptness of the transition from (children's)
hearings to adult court at the age of sixteen.[74] Here, then, is some evidence
of the SNP moving with caution in this area and of a more conciliatory
approach to the issues which does not overtly range "communities" against
young offenders.

G. FAST-TRACK CHILDREN'S HEARINGS: A MISPLACED OBSESSION WITH PERSISTENT OFFENDING

The other central plank of the Scottish Executive's response to persistent
offending was the introduction of the fast-track children's hearing. Its aim
was "to improve practice and outcomes with respect to the ways that the
hearings system and associated services dealt with young people who persistently offend".[75] As the name suggests, one specific purpose was to shorten the
time between the child's commission of an offence and her or his appearance
at a children's hearing on that ground[76] and to reduce the time taken overall
as well as at each individual stage of decision-making.[77] To be eligible for
fast-tracking, a young person had to meet the criterion of having committed
five or more offences in a six-month period.[78] A further explicit aim was,
therefore, to reduce re-offending rates.[79]

Fast-track hearings might be said to have constituted paradigm examples
of the operation of the children's hearings system, in that they took place
relatively soon after the event constituting the ground for referral and they
were particularly well resourced (to meet their aim of "ensur[ing] that all
young people who persistently offend and who require an appropriate

---

72 Community Justice Services (n 71) paras 29, 49 and 51.
73 Scottish Government, *Protecting Scotland's Communities: Fair, Fast and Flexible Justice* (2008)
    20.
74 Scottish Prisons Commission, *Scotland's Choice* (2008) para 3.18.
75 M Hill et al, *Fast Track Children's Hearings Pilot: Final Report of the Evaluation of the Pilot*
    (abridged version) (2005) 1.
76 Hill et al, *Fast Track Children's Hearings Pilot* (n 75) 8.
77 Hill et al, *Fast Track Children's Hearings Pilot* (n 75) 1.
78 Reporters did have some discretion to refer others, for example on the basis of the commission of
    a serious offence: Hill et al, *Fast Track Children's Hearings Pilot* (n 75) 1.
79 Hill et al, *Fast Track Children's Hearings Pilot* (n 75) 1.

programme have access to one").[80] They won over the "hearts and minds of those engaged in implementing"[81] them but, crucially for an administration obsessed with bringing down youth offending rates, the reductions achieved here were less than those brought about in the control areas (where fast-tracking was not undertaken) used for the evaluation of the pilot.[82] Accordingly, the whole scheme was discontinued in 2005.

In this regard, it could be said that rhetoric won a pyrrhic victory. Fast-track hearings were initially spun as a robust (or "tough") response to persistent juvenile offending. When their impact on this issue was not instant and beneficial (at least by comparison with control groups) they could no longer serve that purpose. They were, therefore, scrapped. However, at some level, they met Kathleen Marshall's criticism that

> The Children's Hearings system is a pale reflection of what Kilbrandon envisaged because it is in effect a great idea that has never really been tried – never really been tested – because it has never been as fully resourced and empowered as it should have been in terms of access to services.[83]

These hearings were welcomed by those involved in their implementation and "[e]vidence from reporters and panel members indicated that social work assessments and action plans were better in fast track areas".[84] As a philosophical approach, welfare is holistic. Reducing offending behaviour is one of its aims but not the only one. Too much may have been expected of fast-track hearings too quickly.

H. PUBLIC OPINION: SHOULD DEEDS OUST NEEDS?

Despite the implementation of the youth court and fast-track pilots, toughness was, to some extent, still in search of a rationale. At about the same time as the inception of the Airdrie youth court, in an example of placing the cart (of pilot policy implementation) before the horse (of consultation), the Scottish Executive did, finally, seek to establish the views of the public as to whether, in general, children's hearings and, accordingly, the welfare principle, should continue to deal with offending by young people.

It raised the matter rather indirectly, buried as question 8 of its general consultation on, and review of, the children's hearings system *Getting it*

---

80 Hill et al, *Fast Track Children's Hearings Pilot* (n 75) 1.
81 Hill et al, *Fast Track Children's Hearings Pilot* (n 75) 28.
82 Hill et al, *Fast Track Children's Hearings Pilot* (n 75) 14.
83 *Children's Hearings and the Love that Binds: Reflections on Community, Discipline and Exile* (ninth Kilbrandon lecture) (2009) 37-38.
84 Hill et al, *Fast Track Children's Hearings Pilot* (n 75) at 26.

Right for Every Child, the first phase of which was conducted between April and July 2004. The question was "Is it still right that one generalist system should look at all types of cases?". Its existence certainly provided the opportunity for respondents to lobby for the separation of offending from other grounds for referral if they shared the sense that the system was "soft". Indeed, in stating its own view of the desirable objectives for the hearings system in the consultation pack, the Executive included, as the first two in its list, "deliver[ing] effective outcomes for children, brothers and sisters, families and *communities*" and "lead[ing] to: protected, educated, healthier children; *changed behaviour, safer communities*; and *reduced offending*".[85] Thus, the child's best interests were ranked alongside those of communities. The Executive's support for youth justice as justice for those affected by the crimes of young people is apparent here. Indeed, the prominence given to these points led "many respondents" to comment "that the way that the objectives were listed in the consultation pack seemed to imply placing the same weight on delivering outcomes for families and communities as on the needs of children. This was seen as contradicting the principles of a child-centred system".[86]

In the event, "strong support"[87] for the retention of a single system was identified. Only 5% and 4% of respondents thought that "reducing offending" and "protecting communities" respectively should be what the children's hearings system was trying to achieve, by contrast with 36% who saw "addressing children's needs" as a key aim in this context.[88] The consultation was open[89] and widely publicised. It was, thus, an indication that there was not the groundswell of public opinion in favour of punitiveness (or against welfare as a response to juvenile offending), on the basis of which the Scottish Executive had, hitherto, apparently been proceeding.

I. VICTIMS AND (OR OF?) THE CHILD'S WELFARE

One further area in which the rhetoric of toughness seems to conflict with the reality of welfare is in relation to the treatment of victims of youth crime. Victims generally have assumed a particular importance in criminal justice policy in many jurisdictions and the debate about the appropriateness of conferring

---

85 Stevenson and Brotchie, *Getting it Right* (n 44) para 2.2. Emphasis added.

86 Stevenson and Brotchie, *Getting it Right* (n 44) para 2.5.

87 Stevenson and Brotchie, *Getting it Right* (n 44) ii.

88 Stevenson and Brotchie, *Getting it Right* (n 44) para 2.13.

89 There were 732 respondents in total: 541 (75%) responses came from individuals – 70% of those individuals stated that they had had some involvement with the children's hearings system, 58% as panel members (Stevenson and Brotchie, *Getting it Right* (n 44) i).

on them actual rights of participation in the criminal process continues.[90] In November 2004, the then deputy Scottish Justice Minister, Hugh Henry, cast the issue as, at one level, victims against criminals, as follows:

> While the number of victims of crime is relatively small, the fear of crime in Scotland remains very real and we cannot underestimate the impact which this has. We are determined to better protect the majority of law-abiding, hardworking Scots from the law-breaking few who blight their lives and communities … [91]

In relation to youth crime, and in announcing measures to provide its victims with more information, he had previously said "For too long … the Children's Hearings system has not been able to respond to the legitimate concerns of victims. No longer".[92] This rhetoric might suggest, then, that any rights to be accorded to victims would reflect the "tough" approach and would weigh against the child-perpetrators of relevant offences. In fact, while an obligation is placed on the Principal Reporter to provide information (that is, the action taken by the reporter and the ultimate disposal of the case) to victims, any such disclosure has to accord with the child-offender's best interests.[93] Thus, the welfare principle still operates as a control. The SNP administration's only intervention here has been to roll out across Scotland the information scheme[94] but without amending the legislation or changing, in any way, the balance between the rights of victims and the rights of the child-offender. Welfare, then, retains its pre-eminence in this sphere.

It is now necessary to consider relevant aspects of a major piece of legislation which encompasses youth crime: the Anti-social Behaviour etc (Scotland) Act 2004.

J. THE ANTI-SOCIAL BEHAVIOUR ETC (SCOTLAND) ACT 2004: AN ASSAULT ON WELFARE?

In the period following the advent of the Scottish Parliament, the term "anti-social behaviour" became a buzz-phrase of the New Labour-led administrations both north and south of the Border.[95] The behaviours which the 2004

---

90 See, e.g., I Edwards, "An ambiguous participant: the crime victim and criminal justice decision-making" (2004) 44 *Brit J Criminology* 967.

91 "Scottish strategy for victims progress report", Scottish Executive news release, 29 November 2004.

92 "Support for crime victims", Scottish Executive news release, 29 September 2003.

93 Criminal Justice (Scotland) Act 2003 s 53.

94 "Support for victims of youth crime", Scottish Government news release, 24 September 2009. It was initially piloted in Forth Valley (see K Skellington Orr et al, *An Assessment* (n 44)).

95 See, e.g., M Clarke, "Blair blitz on yobs; anti-social behaviour is now the biggest issue declares premier", *Daily Mail*, 1 November 2002, 26.

Act was designed to address were not regarded, in themselves, as sufficiently serious to constitute criminal offences. At one level, then, it is inappropriate to include these provisions in a discussion of offending by juveniles. However, particularly in relation to young people, "crime and anti-social behaviour" are frequently run together as two aspects of the same issue. Indeed, anti-social behaviour is often presented as a problem connected directly to youth. For example, with reference to the introduction of the Executive's first proposals on such behaviour, Cathy Jamieson said:

> we would be kidding ourselves if we think that youth crime and anti-social behaviour present anything but real and pressing problems in communities across Scotland. We make no apology for putting the fight against youth crime and anti-social behaviour at the top of our list of priorities ... I believe in young people. I believe in prevention and intervention first and foremost. But a system without effective sanctions is no protection at all for our communities ...[96]

It is striking, then, that two of the Act's major innovations – the ASBO[97] and the dispersal order[98] – were not age-specific (they could be imposed on adults as well) yet were "spun" as solutions to the perceived "youth problem". The Act also made it possible for children's hearings to require a child to be electronically tagged,[99] and introduced parenting orders.[100]

All of these measures provoked alarm on behalf of commentators on juvenile justice in Scotland[101] who, rightly, viewed them as a stealthy assault on the welfare principle. They also clearly relate to youth crime, yet are presented as "only" anti-social behaviour. They may therefore receive less scrutiny than would a raft of measures which directly created new offences. This slightly subversive use of anti-social behaviour controls can be seen in the vagueness of its definition in the first place.[102] It arises where an individual either acts in a manner, or pursues a course of conduct, that causes or is likely to cause alarm or distress to at least one person not of his or her own household.[103] This definition could encapsulate many levels of undesirable behaviour[104] and

---

96 "£1 million for youth crime prevention", Scottish Executive news release, 25 June 2003.
97 Antisocial Behaviour etc (Scotland) Act 2004 s 4.
98 Antisocial Behaviour etc (Scotland) Act 2004 s 19.
99 Antisocial Behaviour etc (Scotland) Act 2004 s 135, inserting new subss (9)-(17) into the Children (Scotland) Act 1995 s 70.
100 Antisocial Behaviour etc (Scotland) Act 2004 Pt 9.
101 See, e.g., A Cleland, "The Antisocial Behaviour etc (Scotland) Act 2004: exposing the punitive fault line below the children's hearing system" (2005) 9 *Edin LR* 439.
102 See, e.g., A Ashworth, "Social control and 'anti-social behaviour': the subversion of human rights?" (2004) 120 *LQR* 263.
103 Antisocial Behaviour etc (Scotland) Act 2004 s 143(1).
104 For a discussion, see A Millie, "Antisocial behaviour, behavioural expectations and an urban aesthetic" (2008) 48 *Brit J Criminol* 379.

is therefore unhelpful as a basis for criminalisation, though, as will now be discussed, the measures contained in the 2004 Act do criminalise breaches.

(1) Dispersal orders: taking the streets away from the young

Turning first to dispersal orders, these allow the police to disperse groups of two or more individuals in areas which have been predetermined, by a senior police officer, to have been subject to anti-social behaviour and, on this basis, pre-designated as localities where the dispersal power will operate.[105] In relation to the young, dispersal orders are insidious because they take no account of the reasons, which may be benign and to do with, for example, personal safety,[106] for groups congregating. Dispersal orders have frequently been used against the young.[107] Failure to comply with an order to disperse constitutes a criminal offence, illustrating the way in which the 2004 Act indirectly criminalises those whose behaviour it deems anti-social.[108] Both rhetorically and in practice, then, such orders are tough, operating on behalf of communities against the young on the basis of the vague definition of anti-social behaviour discussed above.

(2) Parenting orders: misplaced criminal responsibility

Parenting orders are imposed on a parent by the court on the application of either the local authority (where the child has committed an offence or engaged in anti-social behaviour) or the Principal Reporter (on either of these grounds or because the order is "desirable in the interests of improving the welfare of the child").[109] Their effect is to require their recipient to comply with "such requirements as are specified" and to attend counselling or guidance sessions for a period of not more than three months.[110] Leaving to one side those imposed on the welfare ground, these orders take the fact that the child has been found to be responsible for criminal, or anti-social, behaviour and use that as a basis for imposing a particular form of state control over another person: her or his parent. While parents are, undoubtedly, "responsible" for their children, in various ways,[111] it is questionable whether

---

105 Antisocial Behaviour etc (Scotland) Act 2004 ss 19 and 21.
106 See Hancock, "Urban regeneneration" (n 2).
107 See A Crawford and S Lister, *The Use and Impact of Dispersal Orders: Sticking Plasters and Wake-up Calls* (2007).
108 Antisocial Behaviour etc (Scotland) Act 2004 s 22(2).
109 Antisocial Behaviour etc (Scotland) Act 2004 s 102.
110 Antisocial Behaviour etc (Scotland) Act 2004 s 103.
111 Children (Scotland) Act 1995 s 1, for example, imposes various parental responsibilities.

it is beneficial for the child's wrongdoing to operate in this way.[112] Young people should take appropriate responsibility for their own misdeeds because criminal responsibility is personal to the perpetrator. Parents can be held criminally liable, in certain circumstances, for their very poor parenting.[113] These orders, however, remove that direct link between personal behaviour and its consequences: criminal sanctions apply ultimately for non-compliance.[114]

It is, of course, possible, that some parents – and their children – might benefit from the instruction in parenting provided through such orders but the fact that they are compulsory and indirectly punitive militates against this. Indeed, they have been criticised for targeting the "poor and powerless" and not "parents who work in senior corporate positions that demand 100 hours a week and who are continually absent from the lives of their children".[115] In September 2008, the *Daily Mail* reported that "Not one Parenting Order [had] been granted in the three years since legislation was introduced by the previous Labour administration at Holyrood".[116] The then Children's Commissioner, Kathleen Marshall, suggested that this might have been "because those closest to the situation have felt they would not actually help children".[117]

Again, then, welfare permeates the debate. The 2004 Act includes the provision allowing application (by reporters) for such orders on welfare grounds. Even the Scottish Executive's own *Guidance on Parenting Orders*, issued in 2005, states that "They are not about punishing parents, but are about providing the help and support that parents need to change their behaviour".[118] The fact that no such order was granted throughout the period of New Labour control of the Scottish Parliament suggests that they simply do not fit with a (children's hearings) system which has only ever sought voluntary co-operation from parents. The Children's Hearings Bill seeks to integrate them slightly better into that system by giving hearings the power to ask the Principal Reporter to consider making an application for one where the panel members think this "might be appropriate",[119] a view which would,

---

112 See E E Sutherland, "Parenting Orders: a culturally-alien response of questionable efficacy" (2004) 49 *JR* 105

113 See, e.g., Children and Young Persons (Scotland) Act 1937 s 12 which criminalises, *inter alia*, neglect and ill-treatment.

114 R Waters and R Woodward, "Punishing 'poor parents': 'respect', 'responsibility' and parenting orders in Scotland" (2007) 7 *Youth Justice* 5 at 11.

115 Waters and Woodward, "Punishing 'poor parents'" (n 114) 7.

116 T Bugler, "Power to target parents of feral children 'have never been used'", *Daily Mail*, 22 September 2008, 4.

117 Bugler, "Power to target parents" (n 116).

118 Para 9.

119 Children's Hearings (Scotland) Bill s 125.

it can be assumed, be heavily permeated with welfare considerations.

(3) ASBOs: overtly anti-welfare?

Moving now to ASBOs, these orders raise major issues about criminalisation in that their effect is to impose prohibitions on their recipients or, in other words, to interdict them from certain actions.[120] It is a criminal offence to fail to comply with such a prohibition.[121] Thus, ASBOs effectively create bespoke and personalised criminal law but often in relation to matters so minor that their status as criminal offences in their own right could not be justified. This has been criticised generally.[122] It is especially insidious where the recipients are children, in relation to whom, as a group, particular issues as to the possession of criminal capacity at all may arise.[123]

The criteria for ASBOs are identical for juveniles and adults and apply where the individual concerned has engaged in anti-social behaviour, on the definition discussed above. The 2004 Act also requires, where a sheriff is considering imposing an ASBO on a child, that the advice of a children's hearing must first be obtained. The criterion which that hearing must apply is whether the ASBO is required to protect someone other than the child.[124] This is, therefore, the only circumstance in which a child may be referred to a children's hearing other than on welfare grounds.[125] More concerning, within the hearing itself, is the fact that "The remit seems so tightly drawn as to preclude a wide-ranging discussion of the child's circumstances. The emphasis is on protection of the public, not on the welfare of the child".[126] There is little scope to see them as other than "tough", though sheriffs imposing ASBOs on juveniles may (but do not have to) thereafter refer such young people to children's hearings[127] which, in these circumstances, will apply the welfare principle.

The Scottish Government has itself been highly critical of so-called "junior ASBOs" – those which are imposed on juveniles – on value-for-money grounds, announcing in June 2008 that "£7m of government funding

---

120 Antisocial Behaviour etc (Scotland) Act 2004 s 4(5).
121 Antisocial Behaviour etc (Scotland) Act 2004 s 9(1).
122 See A Ashworth, "Is the criminal law a lost cause?" (2000) 116 *LQR* 225.
123 This is the approach taken by the CRC art 40(3). For a full discussion of the child's criminal capacity, see McDiarmid, *Childhood and Crime* (n 33), especially ch 3.
124 Antisocial Behaviour etc (Scotland) Act 2004 s 4(4).
125 Though, in any appropriate case, welfare can be displaced in favour of public safety at the decision-making stage. See n 39.
126 Cleland, "The Antisocial Behaviour etc (Scotland) Act" (n 101) at 443.
127 Children (Scotland) Act 1995 s 52(2)(m), inserted by Antisocial Behaviour etc (Scotland) Act 2004 s 12.

had been spent on Asbos for under-16s since 2004. But only fourteen of the orders [had] ever been issued".[128] An Audit Scotland report the previous year had indicated that "The introduction of anti-social behaviour orders for twelve to fifteen-year-olds has created tensions with approaches to dealing with offending by young people through the children's hearings system".[129] Despite this, the government has made no move to amend the 2004 Act[130] so that ASBOs cease to be available for juveniles and the Children's Hearings Bill seems to assume their continued applicability.[131]

Overall, junior ASBOs subjugate the otherwise overarching principle of the child's best interests for purposes which may play well as part of the "toughness" rhetoric but which have little else to recommend them, though the power to refer "ASBOed" children to children's hearings slightly tempers the orders' punitiveness.

(4) Electronic tagging: a sheep in wolf's clothing?

Finally, it is necessary to consider electronic tagging, which can be fitted into a welfare framework only with difficulty. Indeed, the legislation calls such orders "movement restriction conditions",[132] and one of the Scottish Executive's purposes in allowing children's hearings to make such disposals was to make it clear that tougher approaches to persistent juvenile offending were available.[133] Yet this disposal can be made by a hearing only if one or other of the exacting grounds required for authorisation of the use of secure accommodation is met. Broadly, these require a pattern of absconding and the likelihood that the child will injure him- or herself or others.[134]

More importantly, a child who is tagged by a children's hearing must also be provided with intensive support and monitoring ("ISMS") in the form of a written plan itemising measures which will be taken to safeguard and promote his or her welfare in the immediate and the longer term.[135] Research carried out by the SCRA indicates that it is this intensive support package

128 BBC News website, "Junior Asbos 'cost £500,000 each'", 19 June 2008 (available at *http://news.bbc.co.uk/1/hi/scotland/7463474.stm*).
129 Audit Scotland, *Dealing with Offending by Young People: Performance Update* (2007) para 5. See also paras 40-44.
130 Section 4(2)(a).
131 Children's Hearings (Scotland) Bill s 126
132 Children (Scotland) Act 1995 s 70(9A)(b), as inserted by Antisocial Behaviour etc (Scotland) Act 2004 s 135(1) and (2).
133 See "Councils warned over tagging cash", BBC News website, 11 August 2005 (available at *http://news.bbc.co.uk/1/hi/scotland/4141714.stm*).
134 Children (Scotland) Act 1995 s 70(10).
135 Intensive Support and Monitoring (Scotland) Regulations 2008, SSI 2008/75 reg 4.

which has been particularly attractive to children's panel members.[136] Overall, the research seems to indicate a desire on the part of panel members (and reporters) to fit these measures into the welfare framework of the system itself rather than to "punish" persistent offenders, as may have been part of the rationale for their introduction.[137]

In England and Wales, Jo Phoenix has noted that "highlighting the welfare needs of young lawbreakers can, and does, render them *more* not *less* punishable".[138] This is on the basis that such needs are added into the overall "at riskiness" calculation which is carried out in assessment of young offenders so that the risk is not only a risk of offending. This then feeds into the notion that "welfare can be provided through youth (criminal) justice interventions".[139] The ISMS experience in Scotland, as documented in the SCRA research, gives some limited support for the view that this is not replicated in the Scottish context – or at least not within the children's hearings system. The predominance of the welfare principle has insulated it against use in such an openly repressive fashion.

Anti-social behaviour was the creation of the Scottish Executive but, while the current Scottish Government has been disparaging of certain aspects of it, it has made no move to repeal even these parts of the 2004 Act. In its own policy document on anti-social behaviour, it has, however, noted the need to "encourage more balanced, evidence-based reporting and counter negative stereotypes and the demonisation of young people in the media".[140] This fits with its overall less hostile approach to the young who do wrong; this approach will be considered below, starting with the Children's Hearings (Scotland) Bill.

K. THE SNP ADMINISTRATION: A SHIFT IN PERSPECTIVE

The Scottish Government withdrew its first draft of this Bill in the light of sustained criticism of its terms, especially from children's panel members.[141] Following a period of intensive consultation,[142] it published its revised Bill

---

136 SCRA, *Movement Restriction Conditions in the Children's Hearings System* (2007) at 6, 26-27, 30 and 32-33.

137 SCRA, *Movement Restriction Conditions*, especially at 6.

138 J Phoenix, "Beyond risk assessment: the return of repressive welfarism?", in M Barry and F McNeill (eds), *Youth Offending and Youth Justice* (2009) 113 at 114.

139 J Phoenix, "Beyond risk assessment" (n 133) at 128.

140 Scottish Government, *Promoting Positive Outcomes* vol 1 (2009) para 1.5(8).

141 S Naysmith, "Row as controversial Children's Bill put back to next year", *The Herald*, 28 August 2009, 26.

142 See, e.g., Scottish Government, *Children's Hearings Bill Newsletter*, issue 4, November 2009.

on 3 March 2010. This unusual process – withdrawal and re-issue – may be indicative, in itself, of the need for a high level of consensus where the government lacks an overall majority.

The Bill's terms are not a radical departure from those on children's hearings in the Children (Scotland) Act 1995 but, if anything, it bolsters the commitment to welfare which is (still) to be "the paramount consideration" where a children's hearing or court is "coming to a decision about a matter relating to a child" (under the Bill).[143] An innovation is that welfare is also to be "a primary consideration" even where the hearing decides that public protection requires a departure from the paramountcy principle.[144] Of course, the SNP's general approach to youth justice has been much more careful and less negative than its New Labour antecedents, so it is unsurprising that it should support welfare. The strength of its support is, however, a welcome revelation. It states that there are no alternative approaches to welfare in the Bill because "Putting the child at the centre of the Hearings system and promoting and supporting their rights and welfare are fundamental to the reforms and the proposed new arrangements".[145] Indeed, its opening statement on the policy underlying the Bill demonstrates its general support for the young. It says: "The Scottish Government is committed to improving outcomes for children and young people. We want our children to have the best start in life and to be ready to succeed."[146] Where offending behaviour is specifically considered in this policy memorandum, it is in the context of the benefits of commitment to the Kilbrandon principle that such behaviour is, like care and protection grounds, an indication of need on the part of the child.[147]

It is not possible to draw any clear conclusions from a Bill, which is, by definition, merely a draft of the legislation itself, though there is an indication here of the renewal of the importance of the interests of the young person both in policy and in legislation. Any disjunction between rhetoric and reality is not pronounced. The SNP administration, then, at least looks to be providing a less politicised space in which to apply its approach to juvenile offending.

Nonetheless, if primary legislation is the measure of action, then the discernible shift arising under the SNP is not quantitative but simply in this more restrained approach to the issues, which is also apparent, for example,

143 Section 24(2)
144 Section 25. For the current position, see n 39.
145 Scottish Government, *Children's Hearings (Scotland) Bill: Policy Memorandum* (2010) para 41.
146 *Policy Memorandum* (n 145) para 3.
147 *Policy Memorandum* (n 145) paras 12, 13, 327.

in the opening statement of its key policy document in this area, *Preventing Offending by Young People: A Framework for Action*.[148] It states: "The vast majority of young people in Scotland make a positive contribution to society and are valuable and valued members of their communities."[149] Thus, young people are situated within communities. The government is not clearly aligned with the latter against the former. Indeed, the SNP "reject[s] the polarisation of children's needs and community safety; [it] will champion both".[150] More concrete evidence of a lighter touch can be found in the release of money, which had been ring-fenced, specifically to address youth offending, by the previous administration, back into a general fund made available to local authorities.[151] The reduction of youth offending is a part only of the overarching aim of government to promote sustainable economic growth.[152] All of these measures might give rise to allegations of doing (too) little, yet perhaps they reflect the need for youth justice to escape the media glare for a period. To that extent, doing less is welcome.

In addition to the children's hearings Bill, there is newly enacted legislation which is not yet in force on the age of criminal responsibility[153] and to abolish "unruly certificates"[154] (which allowed the remand, to (adult) prison, of children aged fourteen and fifteen who were certified, by the court, to be "unruly or depraved").[155] The terms of the provisions on the age of criminal responsibility are open to criticism for their unnecessary complexity and because they may not, in fact, meet the government's stated intention of complying with international law in this area.[156] However, if these two sections are considered together, they play much more positively in that they place their weight on the "youth" side of the "youth crime" equation discussed above. The government has separately stated that it "is committed to ending for good"[157] the overtly tough practice of sending children to (adult) prison at all.

---

148 (2008).
149 *Preventing Offending by Young People: A Framework for Action* 2.
150 *Preventing Offending by Young People: A Framework for Action* 2.
151 *Preventing Offending by Young People: A Framework for Action* 5.
152 *Preventing Offending by Young People: A Framework for Action* 5.
153 Criminal Justice and Licensing (Scotland) Act 2010 s 52.
154 Criminal Justice and Licensing (Scotland) Act 2010 s 64.
155 Criminal Procedure (Scotland) Act 1995 s 51(1)(bb)(ii).
156 See C McDiarmid, "The age of criminal responsibility in Scots law" (2009) 379 *SCOLAG* 116; also E E Sutherland, "The age of reason or the reasons for an age? The age of criminal responsibility" (2002) *SLT (News)* 1.
157 Scottish Government (n 73) 22.

L. CONCLUSION

Of course, the terms in which the executive branch frames its approach to youth justice do matter. If, as the New Labour-led Scottish Executive did, it chooses to label youth crime a major "problem" and clearly to ally itself with the "communities" adversely affected by it, then, at least tacitly, it excludes the young – all of them or just those who offend – from those communities. As Alison Cleland and Kay Tisdall have pointed out, the "community" mobilised here is not one of warmth and support to which a young person belongs but a more vengeful construct which comes together to identify and then castigate wrongdoing.[158] In this regard, the SNP administration's more muted rhetoric is welcome. Individual young people commit offences; constant repetition of the seriousness of the "youth crime problem" has a tendency to taint all of the young.

Through both administrations, welfare has remained constant. The Executive talked tough but made no move to legislate it out of existence, even including it both as a brake on the provision of information to victims of youth crime and as a possible reason for the imposition of a parenting order. In an administration for which the assault on youth crime was such a key policy, even doing nothing against welfare can be cast as recognition of its value. The SNP is pursuing a more cautious approach generally. In its consideration of specialised hearings for sixteen- and seventeen-year-olds, and the shift in the presentation of its policies away from the community perspective towards the overarching value of young people, welfare can find a closer fit. Welfare is not a panacea but its abolition as the universal response to youth crime should not be on the basis of an untested perception of its softness.

"Youth justice" is a construct – its content being determined by those who set its agenda, at the top of which framework rests the executive branch of government. Its value lies in its recognition that the young should be treated differently – whether because of a lack of understanding of wrongdoing or because of a faith in their greater rehabilitative potential. Seeking to realise the potential of the young must be its core. The Scottish Parliament must deal with juvenile offending on this basis.

---

158 A Cleland and K Tisdall, "The challenge of anti-social behaviour: new relationships between the state, children and parents" (2005) 19 *Int JLPF* 395 at 416.

13 Evidence

Fraser P Davidson°

A. INTRODUCTION

Various chapters in this work will no doubt be able to allude to the root and branch reform of the law wrought by the Scottish Parliament, or to how certain areas of the law languished for many years in dire need of legislative reform but were unable to command parliamentary time prior to the advent

* Professor of Law, School of Law, University of Stirling

of the Scottish Parliament. This cannot be claimed in relation to the law of evidence. While much of this area of the law continues to be judge-made, statute has intruded on the law, often in radically important ways, from the middle of the nineteenth century onwards. While the Scottish Parliament has indeed passed measures of considerable significance for the law of evidence, these have tended to develop themes introduced by earlier measures, while probably the most important pieces of legislation were passed by the Westminster Parliament.

From the middle of the nineteenth century onwards, the Westminster Parliament passed measures which gradually abolished the manifold restrictions and prohibitions regarding the classes of individual who might give evidence. The story of the twentieth century perhaps tells how legislative intervention allowed courts to consider evidence which the common law had regarded as suspect or unworthy of attention. This might be best represented by the effective abolition of the rule against hearsay in civil cases through the Civil Evidence (Scotland) Act 1988, and the making of hearsay evidence admissible in criminal cases in situations where the maker of the statement was not available to testify as a witness as a result of the Criminal Justice (Scotland) Act 1995. It was the Westminster Parliament which abolished the requirement of corroboration in civil cases and the concept of proof by writ or oath, which first sought to regulate evidence relating to character and previous convictions in criminal cases, and which introduced rules regarding the taking of evidence on commission and the giving of evidence via video link. Most of the provisions regarding documentary evidence derive from that source and it was of course the Westminster Parliament which passed the Human Rights Act 1998. This gave effect to the European Convention on Human Rights, art 6 of which (guaranteeing the right to a fair trial) has had a considerable impact on all the legal systems of the UK.

B. THE ACHIEVEMENTS OF THE SCOTTISH PARLIAMENT

Although the Scots law of evidence had a strong statutory foundation prior to the creation of the Scottish Parliament, it should not be supposed that this body has failed to have an impact on this branch of the law. Several of its measures have affected aspects of the law of evidence, but two deserve specific scrutiny – the Sexual Offences (Procedure and Evidence) (Scotland) Act 2002 and the Vulnerable Witnesses (Scotland) Act 2004. A particular provision of the Criminal Justice and Licensing (Scotland) Bill 2009, currently before the Scottish Parliament, deserves to be addressed. Since the point of this work is to assess the achievements in the field, a detailed analysis of the relevant provisions, their strengths, weaknesses and implications will be sacrificed in favour of a broad description of their import, followed by an attempt to place them in context.

C. CRIMINAL JUSTICE AND LICENSING (SCOTLAND) BILL 2009 – THE COMPELLABILITY OF SPOUSES AND CIVIL PARTNERS

Historically, spouses have received special treatment as regards the giving of evidence – special treatment which was then extended to civil partners. However, s 63 of the Bill would substantially revise s 264 of the Criminal Procedure (Scotland) Act 1995 (hereafter the "1995 Act") in order to make it clear that a spouse or civil partner of an accused is both competent and compellable as a witness for the defence, the prosecution or a co-accused. This is subject to the qualification that if the spouse or civil partner is also a co-accused, he or she can rely on the ordinary privilege of a co-accused to decline to testify. The clause would also disapply any other rule of law which would prevent or restrict the giving of evidence by the spouse or civil partner of an accused.

The history of the development of law in this area is rather complex. The common law position was that the spouse of an accused was not competent for either prosecution or defence unless he or she was alleged to be the victim of the offence.[1] A number of individual statutes passed during the nineteenth century then made a spouse a competent witness for an accused in certain specific contexts. However, it was not until 1898 that a spouse became generally competent as a witness for an accused, it later being judicially established that competence also implied compellability.[2] Although the spouse of an accused was, over a large number of years, rendered competent as a witness for the prosecution in particular contexts, he or she did not become generally so until 1980. The same legislation rendered the spouse competent as a witness for a co-accused, he or she having not been competent for a co-accused prior to then. The Civil Partnership Act 2004 later dealt with the position of civil partners in the same way.

However, the relevant legislation[3] provided that "nothing in this section shall make the spouse of an accused a compellable witness for a co-accused or

---

1 *Muirhead v McIntosh* (1886) 13 R (J) 52.
2 See *Hunter v HM Advocate* 1984 JC 90, especially per Lord Justice-Clerk Wheatley at 93.
3 Latterly 1995 Act s 264(2)(a).

for the prosecutor in a case where such spouse would not be so compellable at common law". Someone with knowledge of the common law could work out that this meant that the spouse was compellable for the prosecution when he or she was the alleged victim of the offence, and was not compellable for a co-accused in any circumstances. The Civil Partnership Act 2004 was much more intelligible, s 130(2) stating that the accused's civil partner is not compellable for a co-accused or for the prosecutor. This, of course, created an anomaly. Obviously, the idea of a civil partner has been recognised for only a very few years. Previously, individuals who might now be the civil partner of an accused would have had no special status, and invariably would there-fore have been compellable. Following the passing of the 2004 Act, the civil partner of an accused was not compellable for the prosecution in *any* circum-stances, even those in which the accused's spouse would be compellable. It might be added that while in civil cases the common law position was that the spouse of a party was not competent as a witness, as a result of legislative intervention he or she has been entirely compellable for any party since 1853.

Even where a spouse or civil partner chose to testify, or indeed in the case of a spouse was compelled to testify, he or she could not be obliged to disclose any communication made between the spouses or partners during the marriage or civil partnership.[4] While it might seem logical that such a privilege should exist for the benefit of the accused,[5] the legislation was phrased to confer the benefit, and thus the right to waive the privilege, on the testifying spouse or civil partner, an interpretation which has been confirmed judicially.[6] By contrast, in civil proceedings the Evidence (Scotland) Act 1853 s 3 imposes an absolute embargo on disclosure of marital communi-cations. There would seem to be no logical justification for these radically different approaches. In England and Wales the corresponding provisions were repealed some years ago.[7]

The law in this area, then, despite having made significant advances, still featured areas of inconsistency and anomaly. Yet the biggest question remained the justification for the basic spousal privilege to refuse to testify. In 2006 the Scottish Executive issued a Consultation Paper on Proposals to Amend the Law on Compellability of Spousal Witnesses, which asked whether the rule allowing the spouse or civil partner of an accused person to refuse to testify should be abolished. The primary driver for reform was

4 See 1995 Act s 264(2)(b); and Civil Partnership Act 2004 s 130(3). The original provision was Criminal Evidence Act 1898 s 1(d).
5 See Burger CJ in *Trammel v US* 445 US 40 at 53 (1980).
6 See Lord Hill Watson in *HM Advocate v HD* 1953 JC 65 at 66.
7 See Civil Evidence Act 1968 s 16(3); and Police and Criminal Evidence Act 1984 s 80(9).

possibly the outcry caused by perceived abuses of the rule, as where an accused married the person who might have been the main witness for the prosecution, so that he or she could not be compelled to testify against him or her. However, other reasons the Consultation Paper advanced for reform included[8] the fact that the rule did not apply to cohabitees or to other family members of the accused, but the main reason was that the rule prevented courts accessing key evidence.[9]

The Scottish Executive had favoured simple repeal of s 264 of the 1995 Act and s 130 of the Civil Partnership Act 2004. That could have invited the difficulty that the courts might then have taken the view that the common law rules would have revived so that, while the civil partner of an accused would have been both competent and compellable in all circumstances, the spouse of an accused would have not been competent, far less compellable, except in a narrow range of cases. It is therefore appropriate that the Bill would recast s 264 in a form which makes it clear that the spouse or civil partner of an accused is both competent and compellable as a witness for the defence, the prosecution or a co-accused. Along with the repeal of s 130 of the Civil Partnership Act 2004, this means that spouses and civil partners are treated in the same way, that way being just like other witnesses. The Bill is also to be commended for taking the option of simply withdrawing the privilege of a spouse or civil partner of an accused to refuse to testify against him, the Consultation Paper having canvassed the option of adopting the model of s 80(2A)-(3) of the Police and Criminal Evidence Act 1984 in England and Wales so as to render a spouse or civil partner of an accused compellable only in relation to offences against children.[10] Assuming that the case for retention of the privilege does not stand up, it would have made little sense to have abolished it in only a restricted class of cases.

The Scottish Executive seemed to have been unaware that the simple repeal of ss 264 and 130 would also have abolished the privilege of a testifying spouse or civil partner to decline to reveal marital communications. Accordingly, the Consultation Paper put forward no case for such a step. However, it is certainly the case that no convincing rationale can be found for the existence of such a privilege, so that its removal by the Bill is undoubtedly a progressive step. Nonetheless, the removal of this privilege renders

8 At para 4.1.
9 At para 4.2.
10 While the Police and Criminal Evidence Act 1984 (PACE) makes a spouse or civil partner of an accused compellable only in relation to offences against children which involve personal violence or sexual abuse, the Scottish Executive saw no reason so to limit the extension of compellability: para 4.5.

the continuing existence of a not dissimilar privilege in civil proceedings all the more anomalous.

Given the symbolic importance of marital testimonial privileges, their abolition in criminal proceedings would be one of the greatest achievements of the Scottish Parliament in the law of evidence. Yet the story is really one of the continuation of a process started by the Westminster Parliament in the nineteenth century, and carried forward on an incremental basis over the intervening years. It is a process of removing indefensible barriers to the availability of evidence, a process which in the case of marital testimonial privileges remains to be completed.

D. VULNERABLE WITNESSES

Moving backwards in time, the next legislation to be considered is the Vulnerable Witnesses (Scotland) Act 2004 (hereafter the "2004 Act"). As its title suggests, the main thrust of the Act is to sanction the use of special measures for taking the evidence of vulnerable witnesses in legal proceedings. It also makes provision for preventing individuals charged with certain offences from conducting their own defence at any trial or witness statement proof where a child under the age of twelve is to testify, and from seeking personally to precognose such a child – a matter considered in the next section of this chapter. Further, it abolishes the competence test for witnesses. Other aspects of the Act are not directly related to its main theme – the creation of presumptions regarding certain types of identification evidence in criminal proceedings; the rendering admissible of expert psychological or psychiatric evidence regarding the behaviour of the complainer in certain types of offence; and the imposition of restrictions regarding evidence bearing on the character of witnesses in proceedings relating to the establishment of grounds of referral to children's hearings. While these further aspects are important in their way, they will not be addressed in the following evaluation of the Act.

(1) Competence test

Looking first at the competence test, s 24 of the 2004 Act indicates that the evidence of any witness in criminal or civil proceedings is not to be inadmissible solely because the witness does not understand the nature of his or her duty to give truthful evidence or the difference between truth and lies. Accordingly, the court is prohibited from taking any step to establish whether the witness understands such matters. The significance of the prohibition is that this was essentially how courts would establish whether children were competent to give evidence. There was no automatic age at which a child witness would automatically become competent. Very young children[11] could be held to be competent, but sometimes older children were not permitted to testify.[12] Everything turned on the trial judge's assessment of the child's competence, and in criminal cases if the judge allowed a child to testify without ascertaining its competence, a conviction which depended to any significant degree upon the child's evidence might be put at risk.[13] In more recent years, the steps which might require to be taken threatened to become ever more elaborate.[14] Matters could become even more complex if the court had regard to the evidence of others to help it decide on the competence of a particular child.[15] Given the increasing complexity of the exercise and the potential for inconsistency of approach,[16] it can be appreciated that it made sense simply to abolish any test of competency based on comprehension and instead permit all children to testify. The same argument could also be made in relation to those adult witnesses whose competence might be threatened because of problems of comprehension. It doubtless remains open for judges and juries who require to assess such evidence to take into account factors such as age and understanding in assessing the credibility of witnesses and the value of their evidence.

There is no doubt that this is a provision of considerable importance, which might indeed be seen to revolutionise the approach of the law in this area. Yet in another way it is simply another step in the process, begun by the Westminster Parliament, of removing the various impediments to particular classes of witnesses giving evidence.

(2) The giving of evidence by vulnerable witnesses

As indicated above, the 2004 Act allows special measures to be provided to assist vulnerable witnesses to give evidence. A vulnerable witness is either a person under the age of sixteen on the date of commencement of the proceedings ("a child witness")[17] or a person in relation to whom there is a significant risk that the quality (in terms of its completeness, coherence and accuracy)[18]

---

11 *Millar* (1870) 1 Coup 430: three year old permitted to testify.
12 *Robertson v Robertson* (1888) 15 R 1001: a child of seven.
13 *Kelly v Docherty* 1991 SLT 419.
14 See Lord Prosser in *R v Walker* 1999 SC 380 at 384.
15 See Lord Justice-Clerk Ross in *L v L* 1996 SLT 767 at 774.
16 Compare the approach of *P v HM Advocate* 1991 SCCR 933; and *R v Walker* (n 14).
17 Section 271(1)(a); and 2004 Act s 11(1)(a) in respect of civil proceedings.
18 Section 271(4); and 2004 Act s 11(4) in respect of civil proceedings.

of their evidence will be diminished by reason of mental disorder,[19] or fear or distress in connection with giving evidence at the trial.[20] In deciding whether a person falls into this latter category of vulnerable witness, the court must take into account:

- the nature and circumstances of the alleged offence or, in respect of civil proceedings, the nature and circumstances of the alleged matter to which the proceedings relate;[21]
- the nature of the evidence which the person is likely to give;[22]
- the relationship (if any) between the person and the accused or a party to civil proceedings;[23]
- the person's age and maturity;[24]
- any behaviour towards the person on the part of the accused (or a party to civil proceedings), or members of the family or associates of the accused (or a party), or any other person who is likely to be an accused or a party or a witness in the proceedings;[25]
- such other matters as appear to the court to be relevant,[26] including the person's social and cultural background and ethnic origins, sexual orientation, domestic and employment circumstances, religious beliefs or political opinions, and any physical disability or other physical impairment which the person has.

(3) Special measures

The special measures which may be used under the legislation are:[27]

- the taking of evidence on video by a commissioner appointed by the court;
- the use of a live television link;
- the use of a screen;
- the use of a supporter; and
- giving evidence in chief in the form of a prior statement.

A combination of such measures may also be authorised.

(a) Evidence on commission

In criminal proceedings an accused may not, except by leave of the court on special cause shown, be present in the room where such proceedings are taking place, but is entitled by such means as seem suitable to the court to watch and hear the proceedings.[28] The same is true of a party to civil proceedings, save

19 Within the meaning of Mental Health (Care and Treatment) (Scotland) Act 2003 s 328.
20 Section 271(1)(b); and 2004 Act s 11(1)(b) in respect of civil proceedings.
21 Section 271(2)(a); and 2004 Act s11(2)(a).
22 Section 271(2)(b); and 2004 Act s 11(2)(b) in respect of civil proceedings.
23 Section 271(2)(c); and 2004 Act s 11(2)(c).
24 Section 271(2)(d); and 2004 Act s 11(2)(d) in respect of civil proceedings.
25 Section 271(2)(e); and 2004 Act s 11(2)(e).
26 Section 271(2)(f); and 2004 Act s 11(2)(f) in respect of civil proceedings.
27 Section 271H; and 2004 Act s 18.
28 Section 271I(3).

that special cause need not be shown before the court may grant leave for him to be present.[29]

(b) Television link

This is the expedient which is usually resorted to when a child witness requires a special measure to give evidence, especially in cases involving physical or sexual abuse.[30]

(c) Screens

Where the special measure to be used is a screen, it shall be used to conceal the accused (or, in civil cases, the parties to the proceedings)[31] from the sight of the witness,[32] although the court must make arrangements to ensure that the accused is or the parties[33] are able to watch and hear the witness giving evidence.[34]

(d) Supporters

A supporter is a person nominated by or on behalf of the witness, who may be present alongside the witness to give support while the witness is giving evidence.[35] A person who is to give evidence at the trial may not act as the supporter at any time before giving evidence.[36] The supporter must not prompt or otherwise seek to influence the witness in the course of giving evidence.[37]

(e) Prior statement

A party citing a vulnerable witness may lodge in evidence a prior statement made by that witness, and that statement will be admissible as the whole or part of the witness's evidence in chief, without the witness being required to appear in court to adopt or otherwise speak to the statement.[38] Such a statement must be contained in a document but the term "document" is

---

29 See 2004 Act s 19(3).
30 See Scottish Executive, *Vital Voices: Helping Vulnerable Witnesses Give Evidence* (2002), para 4.9.
31 See 2004 Act s 21(1).
32 Section 271K(1).
33 See 2004 Act, s 21(2).
34 Section 271K(2).
35 Section 271L(1); and 2004 Act s 22(1) in civil cases.
36 Section 271L(2); and 2004 Act s 22(2) in civil cases.
37 Section 271L(3); and 2004 Act s 22(3) in civil cases.
38 Section 271M; and see Scottish Executive, *Vital Voices*, paras 4.11-4.15.

defined to include any form of recording, including audio or visual.[39] Thus
it is possible that a statement made in a video-recorded interview might be
tendered under this provision. There is, of course, no possibility of cross-
examination under this procedure. Since this is essentially a provision which
admits a form of hearsay evidence, there is no counterpart as regards civil
proceedings, given that hearsay is generally admissible in civil cases.

(4) Child witnesses

The legislation differentiates between child witnesses and other vulnerable witnesses in that a child witness is assumed to be entitled to the benefit
of one or more of the special measures described above for the purpose of
giving evidence.[40] So, if, in a criminal case, the party citing a child witness
seeks a standard special measure – that is, the use of a live television link
within the court building, the use of a screen, or the use of a supporter in
conjunction with either of these measures[41] – the court shall automatically
authorise the use of that measure.[42] If any other kind of special measure
is sought, the court should authorise the use of that measure only if satisfied that it is appropriate to do so.[43] In civil cases, there is no reference to
"standard" measures. However, the court must have regard to the measures
which the party citing a child witness considers appropriate, and if that party
seeks any of the measures which would be "standard" measures in a criminal
case, the court must assume this to be the most appropriate means of taking
the child's evidence.[44]

Where a child witness is to give evidence at, or for the purposes of, a trial
in respect of certain serious offences[45] and the child is aged under twelve on
the date of commencement of the proceedings,[46] the court shall not make an
order which has the effect of requiring the child to be present in the court-
room or any part of the court building in which the court-room is located for
the purpose of giving evidence, unless satisfied:

- where the child has expressed a wish to be so present, that this is appropriate;
- in any other case, that the taking of the evidence of the child without it being
  so present would give rise to a significant risk of prejudice to the fairness of the

39 Section 262(3).
40 Section 271A(1).
41 Section 271A(14).
42 Section 271A(5)(a)(i). In civil proceedings, 2004 Act s 12(3) indicates that if such measures are
    sought, the court must assume this to be the most appropriate means of taking the child's evidence.
43 Section 271A(5)(a)(ii).
44 2004 Act s 12(1)-(3).
45 See s 271B(2).
46 Section 271B(1).

trial or otherwise to the interests of justice, which risk significantly outweighs any risk of prejudice to the interests of the child witness if the order is made.[47]

(5) Other vulnerable witnesses

Other vulnerable witnesses cannot demand special measures as of right. Rather, a party citing such a witness can seek an order authorising the use of one or more of such special measures. The court may make such an order if satisfied that:

- the witness is indeed a vulnerable witness;
- the special measure(s) sought is or are the most appropriate for the purpose of taking the witness's evidence;
- it is appropriate to make the order, having regard to the possible effect on the witness if required to give evidence without the benefit of any special measure; and
- it is likely that the witness would be better able to give evidence with the benefit of a special measure.

A court is entitled to authorise the use of some other special measure if it is otherwise satisfied on the above matters, but is not satisfied that the special measure(s) sought are the most appropriate.[48]

(6) To what extent is the law altered?

To what extent do the measures introduced by the 2004 Act and outlined above represent a major change? It is certainly not the case that the law was entirely insensitive to the difficulties faced by vulnerable witnesses prior to the Act. Courts have always enjoyed, and continue to enjoy, power to make certain special arrangements for taking the evidence of any individual. Thus, when a young child gives evidence, he or she is often allowed to sit in the well of the court, beside solicitors and counsel, while they and sometimes the judge will remove wigs and gowns. The court may allow a relative to sit beside a child, and the judge may even decide to sit in the well of the court. The court may also allow any witness to give evidence from behind a screen, sometimes anonymously. And while a statutory power to clear the court where a child is called as a witness in any proceedings in relation to an offence against, or any conduct contrary to, decency or morality has existed since 1937,[49] the judge also has an inherent power to clear from the court-room all persons not having a direct involvement in the proceedings.[50] While

47 Section 271B(3).
48 Section 271C; and 2004 Act s 12(5)-(7).
49 In the form of Children and Young Persons (Scotland) Act 1937 s 45. The relevant provision is now in 1995 Act s 50(3).
50 See the Lord Justice-General's memorandum of 26 July 1990 on child witnesses.

it is sometimes assumed that the above powers operate only in regard to child witnesses, it has been confirmed judicially that this is not so.[51]

Nor does the 2004 Act represent the first statutory attempt to address the difficulties faced by vulnerable witnesses. Following the Scottish Law Commission Report on Evidence of Children and other Potentially Vulnerable Witnesses,[52] it was Westminster legislation which first authorised the court to allow child witnesses to give evidence via a live television link,[53] then to give evidence either on commission or in court but from behind a screen,[54] thereafter extending these special measures to witnesses suffering from mental impairment or disorder.[55]

The innovations of the 2004 Act are, then, to extend the range of special measures available to the court; to extend the definition of "vulnerable witness"; to create an effective right for child witnesses to demand certain types of special measures when giving evidence;[56] and, for the first time,[57] to establish in civil cases a regime for the affording protection to vulnerable witnesses which in large part mirrors that which operates in criminal proceedings. These are, of course, major reforms. It is difficult to overestimate the importance of the extension of the protection into the civil sphere. Equally, it is welcome that one does not need to be a child or to suffer from any degree of handicap in order to be a vulnerable witness in particular contexts. An ordinary individual may find it difficult to testify in the usual way where, for example, the offence in question is of a particularly horrific nature; they are testifying to a particularly traumatic incident; they are closely related to a party or the accused; they are elderly; their background makes the prospect of testifying in court distressing; they are a member of a minority group and likely to fear intimidation; or they have actually suffered harassment or intimidation. Yet the fact remains that the Act simply continues the reform of this area of the law instigated by the Westminster Parliament. Nor is the regime unique. Similar, and sometimes more far-reaching, protections may be found in legislation in England and elsewhere. Moreover, although the immediate

51 See the views of the court in *Hampson v HM Advocate* 2003 SLT 94 at paras 6-8, where the complainer in a rape case, who suffered from paranoid psychosis with secondary depression and obsessive compulsive disorder, was allowed to testify behind a screen.

52 Scot Law Com No 125, 1990. This in turn followed its Discussion Paper on the same subject (Scot Law Com DP No 75, 1988).

53 Law Reform (Miscellaneous Provisions) (Scotland) Act 1990 ss 56-59.

54 Prisoners and Criminal Proceedings (Scotland) Act 1993 ss 33-34.

55 Crime and Punishment (Scotland) Act 1997.

56 Whereas before the court always had to be persuaded that any special measures sought were appropriate: see *HM Advocate v Birkett* 1993 SLT 395.

57 Save that children might in certain circumstances give evidence by live video link in care proceedings – see AS (Child Care and Maintenance Rules) 1997, SI 1997/291 r 3.22.

inspiration of the 2004 Act was the Scottish Executive report *Vital Voices: Helping Vulnerable Witnesses Give Evidence* (2002), many of the reforms are foreshadowed in Scottish Law Commission Report No 125 and the Scottish Office consultation paper *Towards a Just Conclusion: Vulnerable and Intimidated Witnesses in Scottish Criminal and Civil Cases* (1998).

E. SEXUAL OFFENCES (PROCEDURE AND EVIDENCE) (SCOTLAND) ACT 2002

The final measure to be scrutinised is the 2002 Act. It imposes restrictions on the admissibility of evidence relating to the character of complainers in trials for such offences, and it provides for the disclosure of the previous sexual offences of the accused where such evidence is admitted.

(1) The character of complainers in sexual offence cases

As a result of amendments made by the 2002 Act in trials relating to most sexual offences,[58] s 274 of the 1995 Act now prohibits evidence or questioning which shows or tends to show that the complainer:

- is not of good character (whether in relation to sexual matters or otherwise);
- engaged in sexual behaviour not forming part of the subject matter of the charge; or
- has, at any time (other than shortly before, at the same time as, or shortly after the acts which form part of the subject matter of the charge), engaged in non-sexual behaviour such as might found the inference that the complainer is likely to have consented to those acts; or has at any time been subject to any such condition or predisposition as might found that inference; or
- is not a credible or reliable witness.

Nonetheless, a court may grant an application to admit otherwise prohibited evidence in terms of s 275. Any application must set out:[59]

- the evidence sought to be admitted or elicited;
- the nature of any questioning proposed;
- the issues at the trial to which that evidence is considered to be relevant;
- the reasons for that evidence being considered to be relevant to those issues;
- the inferences which the applicant proposes to submit to the court that it should draw from that evidence.

Before it can grant an application, the court must be satisfied that:

- the evidence or questioning will relate only to a specific occurrence or occurrences of sexual or other behaviour, or to specific facts, demonstrating

---

58 See s 288C.
59 Section 275(4).

the complainer's character, or any condition or predisposition to which the complainer is or has been subject;[60]

- such occurrence(s) or facts are relevant to issues falling to be proved by the prosecutor or the accused in the trial;[61] and
- the probative value of the evidence sought to be admitted or elicited is significant and likely to outweigh any risk of prejudice to the proper administration of justice arising from its being admitted or elicited.[62]

If the court does grant such an application, it may do so subject to conditions[63] and must state the items of evidence it is admitting or the lines of questioning it is allowing.[64] Thereafter, the court may at any time limit the extent of that evidence or questioning.[65]

(2) To what extent did the Act change the law?

At common law, a victim's sexual character was regarded as potentially relevant.[66] So it was competent to prove "that the woman said to have been attacked had yielded her person recently to the same man",[67] or that she was a person of reputed bad moral character,[68] or that she was an associate of prostitutes.[69] It was not until 1980 that the Scottish Law Commission in its *Memorandum*[70] *on the Law of Evidence* suggested that the reasoning behind the view that a woman's sexual morality reflected on her credibility related "to the moral standards of the nineteenth century", so that evidence of "bad" sexual character should no longer be admissible. This view was reiterated in its *Report on Evidence in Cases of Rape and other Sexual Offences*.[71] The law was duly changed by s 36 of the Law Reform (Miscellaneous Provisions) (Scotland) Act 1985, which added ss 141A and 141B (and ss 346A and 346B in summary cases) to the Criminal Procedure (Scotland) Act 1975, those provisions eventually becoming ss 274 and 275 of the 1995 Act.

The original version of s 274 stated that in trials relating to a wide range of sexual offences,[72] the court should not admit, or allow questioning designed

---

60 Section 275(1)(a) – as where psychiatric evidence is permitted to suggest that the complainer suffered from false memory syndrome: *HM Advocate v A* 2005 SLT 975.
61 Section 275(1)(b).
62 Section 275(1)(c).
63 Section 275(7).
64 Section 275(8).
65 Section 275(10).
66 See Lord Justice-Clerk Macdonald in *Dickie v HM Advocate* (1897) 24 R (J) 82 at 84.
67 Lord Justice-Clerk Macdonald in *Dickie v HM Advocate at 84*.
68 See Lord Justice-Clerk Inglis in *Reid* (1861) 4 Irv 124 at 129.
69 *Webster* (1847) Ark 269.
70 No 46 para Q.07.
71 1983, No 78: see especially ch 5.
72 See s 274(2).

to elicit, evidence tending to show that the complainer:

- was not of good character in relation to sexual matters;
- was a prostitute or an associate of prostitutes; or
- had at any time engaged with any person in sexual behaviour not forming part of the subject matter of the charge.

Nevertheless, s 275 permitted the defence to apply to the court to permit evidence or questioning which would otherwise offend against the prohibition, if:

- it was designed to explain or rebut evidence adduced otherwise than by or on behalf of the accused; or
- it related to sexual behaviour which took place on the same occasion as the behaviour with which the accused was charged, or was relevant to a defence of incrimination; or
- it would be contrary to the interests of justice to exclude it.

It can be seen that, as is hardly surprising, the content and structure of the present and former versions of ss 274-275 are rather similar. The reforms wrought in 2002 were driven by a number of concerns regarding the then existing legislation expressed by the Scottish Executive in its pre-legislative consultation document *Redressing the Balance* – that the exceptions in s 275 were so wide "as almost to render the basic prohibition ineffective",[73] that research showed both that the prohibition was often ignored in practice,[74] and that it was too easy for the defence to resort to subtle attacks on the complainer's general character which undermined her sexual character.[75] *Redressing the Balance*, therefore, proposed a slightly different approach, inspired by the Canadian Criminal Code, whereby the accused in sexual offence cases would be prohibited from leading evidence or engaging in questioning reflecting on the character of the complainer unless such evidence had clear probative value which was not outweighed by its prejudicial effect.

The prohibition now therefore targets any evidence directed at the character of the complainer, rather than merely her sexual character. It is also general, rather than being confined to the defence, in case the Crown inadvertently introduces such evidence which is then exploited by the defence.[76] Much more emphasis is placed on the court having to be convinced that there is a very good reason for admitting evidence which would otherwise fall foul of the prohibition; on the court knowing exactly what this evidence will consist of and what it is designed to achieve; and on the court exercising

73 Scottish Executive, *Redressing the Balance* para 97.
74 *Redressing the Balance* (n 73) para 99.
75 *Redressing the Balance* (n 73) para 104.
76 *Redressing the Balance* (n 73) paras 98, 123-128.

strict control of this evidence. Moreover, the court must be satisfied that the evidence is relevant to an issue in the trial, so that it should not be possible to raise matters relating to the lifestyle of the complainer so as to undermine her credibility. And even if the evidence is relevant, the court must still be persuaded that its value outweighs any prejudicial tendency it might have, having regard to the complainer's dignity and privacy.[77]

The 2002 Act, then, represents a significant advance in this area, addressing the limitations and inadequacies of the previous legislation. However, the important point for the purposes of the present discussion is the fact that there was such previous legislation. The relevant provisions of the 2002 Act simply revised the terms of ss 274-275 of the 1995 Act, even if the revision was radical in nature. Indeed, in part, that revision simply carries forward previous thinking on the issues, since the Scottish Law Commission *Report on Evidence in Cases of Rape and other Sexual Offences*[78] contained a draft Bill which would have prohibited evidence reflecting on character in general, as indeed would the original form of s 36 of the Law Reform (Miscellaneous Provisions) (Scotland) Act 1985.

(3) Disclosure of previous convictions of accused introducing character evidence

If an accused makes a successful application under s 275, and is permitted to lead evidence or ask questions which reflect upon the character of the complainer, then certain consequences follow. Ordinarily such a step would be regarded as impugning the character of the complainer and would allow the prosecutor to request the court to allow cross-examination of the accused as to his bad character or previous convictions,[79] and/or to allow the leading of evidence of the accused's bad character or previous convictions.[80] However, s 275A(1)[81] now directs that where the accused has made a successful application, the prosecutor shall forthwith place before the presiding judge any previous relevant conviction of the accused. A "relevant conviction" is defined as either a conviction for one of the offences referred to in s 274 or a conviction for any other offence where a substantial sexual element was present.[82] Any such conviction must then be laid before the jury, or in summary proceed-

---

77 See Lord Carloway in *Cumming v HM Advocate* 2003 SCCR 261 at 264D-F.
78 1983, No 78. And see paras 3.1-3.2.
79 Under 1995 Act s 266.
80 Under s 270.
81 Added by 2002 Act s 10.
82 Section 275A(10).

ings taken into consideration by the judge, unless the accused objects.[83] The grounds on which he may object are that:[84]

- where the conviction is not for one of the specified offences, it does not in fact have a substantial sexual element;
- that the conviction does not apply to him;[85]
- that its taking into consideration would be contrary to the interests of justice – but the court, unless the contrary is shown, shall presume that its taking into consideration is in the interests of justice.[86]

This is again a very significant reform. Under the usual legislative regime it is recognised that while evidence of an accused's character should generally be inadmissible, it would be unfair for an accused to be able to attack the character of the complainer without putting his own character at issue. Yet that regime operates on the basis that the prosecutor requires to apply to be permitted to lead such evidence. Most of the time, prosecutors would not trouble to make such applications.[87] By contrast, if someone accused of a sexual offence is allowed to lead evidence of the complainer's character (and, of course, he might not be), under s 275A(1) the prosecutor is now actually *obliged* to lay evidence of the accused's previous convictions for sexual offences before the court. Moreover, while the judge may be persuaded that taking such convictions into consideration would be contrary to the interests of justice, the thrust of the provision is that such convictions should ordinarily be laid before a jury.[88]

Yet while the importance of this provision may be acknowledged, it is simply a particular development of the legislative regime relating to evidence of an accused's character which was first established by the Westminster Parliament as long ago as 1898.

F. CONCLUSION

The Scottish Parliament has contributed significantly to the development of the Scots law of evidence, and one would not wish to downplay its achievements in that regard. Yet it has been shown above that evidence is one area in which the Westminster Parliament could not be accused of neglecting Scots law. If a need for legislative reform was identified, it was generally met.

---

83 Section 275A(2). See *Redressing the Balance* (n 73) paras 135-138.
84 1995 Act s 275A(4).
85 Or, in proceedings on indictment, that it is otherwise inadmissible.
86 Section 275A(7).
87 See *Redressing the Balance* (n 73) para 135.
88 But see Lord Hope in *DS v HM Advocate* 2007 SC (PC) 1, para 47.

Thus, while the measures introduced by the Scottish Parliament have been important, indeed quite radical in some cases, they have tended to continue the legislative development of particular areas of the law of evidence already begun by the Westminster Parliament. No real theme emerges from those measures. They have dealt with a series of different issues, each in a specific way. The Scots law of evidence continues to evolve along its own lines, in some respects similar to and in others different from the law of England, but that has long been the case, so that this owes nothing to the creation of the Scottish Parliament. Scotland might be said to have a mostly admirable, modern law of evidence with strong statutory foundations. Little regarding that foundation could be said to be distinctively Scottish, since most of the ideas underpinning the legislation are to be found in other legal systems, while over the years policy-makers have explicitly borrowed such ideas from England and elsewhere, and indeed improved upon them. Such an approach is, of course, entirely commendable and it is hoped that the Scottish Parliament continues to keep abreast of the most enlightened thinking on the subject in its ongoing development of our law of evidence.

Economy and Environment

14 Property Law: How the World Changed at Martinmas

*Robert Rennie**

* Professor of Conveyancing, University of Glasgow.

A. INTRODUCTION – UK LEGISLATION

The first statute which was relevant to conveyancing was passed in 1540.[1] A great deal of legislation was passed in the nineteenth century.[2] The Conveyancing (Scotland) Act 1874 (hereafter "the 1874 Act") remained the fundamental conveyancing statute until 1924.[3] A small number of issues were dealt with in 1938[4] but, apart from that, there was very little legislative activity until 1970.[5] Compulsory redemption and the prohibition of feuduties were introduced in 1974.[6] Finally, in 1979, land registration was introduced.[7] There were various other Acts between 1979 and 1995 which dealt with discrete areas of the law.[8] In 1988 the Scottish Law Commission delivered a report

1 Deeds Act 1540 (c 37).
2 The important statutes were the Titles to Land Consolidation (Scotland) Act 1868, and the Conveyancing (Scotland) Act 1874.
3 Conveyancing (Scotland) Act 1924.
4 Conveyancing Amendment (Scotland) Act 1938.
5 Conveyancing and Feudal Reform (Scotland) Act 1970.
6 Land Tenure Reform (Scotland) Act 1974.
7 Land Registration (Scotland) Act 1979.
8 Matrimonial Homes (Family Protection)(Scotland) Act 1981; Law Reform (Miscellaneous Provisions) (Scotland) Act 1985; Housing (Scotland) Act 1987; Property Misdescriptions Act 1991.

on the law relating to the execution of deeds to the Lord Advocate.[9] At this time Bills which related purely to Scotland and were non-contentious were generally introduced by private members whose right to introduce a Bill was decided by ballot. The Requirements of Writing (Scotland) Bill was to be so introduced but, unfortunately, the private member concerned failed to turn up and the Bill was lost. It says a great deal about the priority afforded by successive UK governments to purely Scottish Bills that the Act was not passed until 1995.[10] In 1997 there was further legislation to deal with the vexed question of supersession of missives.[11]

B. THE FEUDAL SYSTEM

Although there is evidence of a feudal charter being granted by Duncan II in 1094, it is generally accepted that the feudal system became established in Scotland during the reign of David I, which began in 1124. It began as a means of government and later evolved into a rudimentary system of private town planning. The Scottish Law Commission began looking at land tenure and property law in general as part of its Fourth Programme of Law Reform. The first discussion paper to be published related to the law of the tenement.[12] In July 1991 the Commission published a discussion paper on the abolition of the feudal system.[13] The main difficulty with abolition of the feudal system was not the abolition of the feudal structure as such but the existence of real burdens and conditions. The easy option was to abolish them altogether and leave proprietors with absolute ownership fettered only by planning laws and the like. A final report on feudal abolition was published by the Scottish Law Commission in 1999.[14] This was followed by a report on the law relating to real burdens.[15] The Scottish Law Commission also published a report on the law of the tenement in 1998.[16] By this time the new Scottish Parliament had been established and matters of property law and conveyancing were devolved to it. In many ways the Scottish Parliament had a golden opportunity because there was no legislative log jam. The result was the three pieces of legislation which radically altered property and land tenure law in Scotland

9 *Report on the Requirements of Writing* (Scot Law Com No 112, 1988).
10 Requirements of Writing (Scotland) Act 1995.
11 Contract (Scotland) Act 1997.
12 Discussion Paper No 91 (1990).
13 Discussion Paper No 93 (1991).
14 *Abolition of the Feudal System* (Scot Law Com No 168, 1999).
15 *Real Burdens* (Scot Law Com No 181, 2000).
16 *The Law of the Tenement* (Scot Law Com No 62, 1998).

which, for the most part, all came into force at the stroke of midnight on Martinmas (28 November) 2004.[17]

C. ABOLITION OF FEUDAL TENURE

The Abolition of Feudal Tenure etc (Scotland) Act 2000 received Royal Assent on 9 June 2000 and came into force on 28 November 2004 with the exception of certain provisions which came into force on or just after Royal Assent. These latter provisions had to come into effect immediately to prevent superiors exacting ransom payments in the run-up to abolition. It was always clear that abolition of the feudal structure itself would not present many technical or legal difficulties. The opening section of the 2000 Act is very clear and to the point. It provides:

> The feudal system of land tenure, that is to say the entire system whereby land is held by a vassal in perpetual tenure from a superior is, on the appointed day, abolished.

The Act is a well-drafted piece of legislation.

(1) Feuduties

Any remaining feuduties ceased to be real burdens[18] on the land and the former superior had a limited amount of time[19] in which to serve a notice requiring the compensatory payment. Thus, one of the pillars of the feudal system, the *reddendo*, was finally swept away.

(2) Real burdens

Real burdens enforceable by a superior, and a superior alone were extinguished, subject to certain temporary rights to re-allot or preserve.[20]

(3) Human rights

Apart from redemption payments in respect of feuduties, no compensation was payable, generally speaking, to feudal superiors despite the fact that they were being deprived of an ownership right in land. Limited compensation was payable if a burden had resulted in a reduced consideration. This might

---

17 Abolition of Feudal Tenure etc (Scotland) Act 2000; Title Conditions (Scotland) Act 2003; Tenements (Scotland) Act 2004 (hereafter "the 2000 Act", "the 2003 Act" and "the 2004 Act").

18 As did other ground burdens.

19 Two years from the appointed day.

20 2000 Act s 17(1)(a).

have had repercussions in human rights law.[21] The European Convention on Human Rights had been adopted into domestic law[22] and, significantly, the Scottish Parliament cannot pass a Bill which contravenes the Convention.[23] Care was therefore taken to ensure that the abolition legislation complied with the Convention. Feudal superiors were given the right to re-allot the right to enforce real burdens to other neighbouring land owned by them in the ordinary sense of ownership. In the case of pre-emptions and redemptions, superiors were also allowed to preserve these as personal rights not attached to any other land. In addition to this, conservation bodies, local authorities, health authorities and rural housing bodies were also allowed to preserve enforcement rights as personal real burdens which would not attach to any benefited or dominant land. These notices had to be served and registered before the appointed day. The take-up by feudal superiors was low.[24] In addition, feudal superiors were allowed to enter into preservation agreements with feuars before abolition, and if a feuar refused to enter such an agreement the superior had a limited right of appeal to the Lands Tribunal.[25]

(4) Facility and service burdens

It was clear that some feudal real burdens had very little to do with the feudal superior as such. These burdens, generally speaking, related to the maintenance of some common facility or service such as the maintenance of a mutual fence or obligations in relation to private lanes and water supplies. It was clear that these burdens should not be abolished simply because they were feudal in origin. Accordingly it was provided[26] that these burdens would remain enforceable by proprietors having right to make use of the facility or service.

(5) Anachronisms

One of the odd non-feudal tenures, the King's Kindly Tenants of Lochmaben, was abolished and converted into ownership.[27] Any existing entails were disentailed.[28] Baronies, dignities and offices attached to land were not completely

21 European Convention for the Protection of Human Rights and Fundamental Freedoms, Protocol 1 art 1.
22 Human Rights Act 1998; Scotland Act 1998.
23 Scotland Act 1998 s 29.
24 The total number of notices registered under the 2000 Act was 3,738, the vast majority under s 18.
25 2000 Act ss 19-21; only ten such agreements were registered.
26 2000 Act s 23, repealed by 2003 Act Sch 15 but re-enacted there in s 56.
27 2000 Act s 64.
28 2000 Act s 50.

abolished. While this may not seem an important matter, it did seem to me at the time odd. There was a measure of reform, however;[29] any jurisdiction or conveyancing privilege incidental to a barony ceased to exist on the appointed day, but the dignity of baron remained. It was also provided that where a barony title ceased to exist as a feudal estate, but the dignity remained, the dignity would not attach to the land.[30] Effectively, what the reform meant in practice was that baronies could no longer change hands by virtue of a disposition of land, usually the rump of an old estate which could be said to form the *caput* or hearthstone of the barony.[31] The Act makes no provision for a document of transfer in relation to the remaining dignity of baron, although it does provide that the dignity is "incorporeal heritable property".[32] Large amounts of money do change hands for baronies but there is now no official register to which reference can be made to check ownership.[33] Just why baronies were not simply abolished is not clear to me, although it may simply have been because people had already paid large sums of money for them and questions of compensation and human rights compatibility might have arisen.

(6) Cleansing the Register of feudal burdens

So far as existing title sheets for registered properties are concerned, the effects of feudal abolition have still to be seen. The Keeper has no obligation to cleanse the Register of extinct burdens.[34] She will have to cleanse the Register if a request is made in an application for registration or rectification on the expiry of ten years from the appointed day.[35] This is unfortunate and might be said to be a weakness in the legislation. People, even lawyers, tend to make the assumption that whatever is in the title sheet must be valid and enforceable. There will also be difficult decisions for the Keeper to take, particularly having regard to the possible existence of third-party rights.[36]

One of the awkward results of feudal abolition where the feudal superior's right to enforce a real burden is extinguished but third parties have separate enforcement rights is how to construe real burdens which make specific

---

29 2000 Act s 63.
30 2000 Act s 63(2).
31 See *Spencer Thomas of Buquhollie v Newell* 1992 SLT 973.
32 2000 Act s 63(3).
33 There is an unofficial register.
34 2000 Act s 46(1).
35 Abolition of Feudal Tenure etc (Scotland) Act 2000 (Prescribed Periods) Order 2004, SSI 2004/478.
36 Under 2003 Act ss 52 and 53.

reference to the feudal superior. Examples are prohibitions of certain activities without the superior's consent or a requirement that plans and so on must be approved by a superior before construction can proceed. The legislation,[37] as amended by the 2003 Act, provides that feudal terms are simply to be ignored.

Where the burden survives and title to enforce is vest in a number of co-proprietors, however, obtaining consent to a particular activity is bound to be problematic. It has now been held that there will be certain circumstances where no-one's approval will be required despite the terms of the real burden.[38] Unfortunately, circumstances in which the burden will be held to be completely extinguished are not clear. In the *At Homes Nationwide Ltd* case, feudal superiors retained a right to vet and approve new owners in a private sheltered housing complex. If, post-feudal abolition, approval had to be obtained from every existing proprietor in the sheltered housing complex, it would probably have proved impossible, or at least impractical, to buy and sell such properties. However, the Lands Tribunal did uphold the simple prohibition on occupation of such units by people other than those who were infirm or over a certain age.

(7) Remaining contractual liability

Real burdens in a feudal writ were always enforceable by a feudal superior as a matter of personal contract, even as against successor vassals who entered with the superior. Quite apart from feudal principles relating to investiture, real burdens were always contractually enforceable as between the original parties to the feudal grant or indeed the original parties to a disposition containing burdens.[39] In terms of the feudal abolition legislation,[40] nothing in the Act affects any contractual right (other than the right to feu duty) as between the parties to the grant or as between one of them and a person to whom any such right is assigned. Effectively what this means is that where a feudal writ is granted prior to the appointed day, then the real burdens will still be enforceable by the original superior against the original vassal or feuar as a matter of personal contract. However, the section goes further than this and envisages the possibility that the former superior might assign these personal rights to another party, post-abolition. This provision is to be contrasted with the provision for non-feudal real burdens contained in the

---

37 2000 Act s 73.
38 See *At Homes Nationwide Ltd v Morris* 2007 GWD 31-535; *Smith v Prior* 2007 GWD 30-523.
39 *Scottish Co-operative Wholesale Society v Finnie* 1937 SC 835.
40 2000 Act s 75(1).

2003 Act[41] where it is provided that incidental liability to which a constitutive deed gives rise as respects prospective real burdens ends when the deed is registered and the real burden has become effective. In other words, so far as non-feudal real burdens are concerned, they are either personal obligations or real burdens but cannot be both. The difficulty surrounding feudal real burdens and contractual liability relates to the possibility of assignation of the right of enforcement. There will, I suppose, be few cases where there is a specific assignation of the right to enforce in a disposition of a superiority title but there is, of course, an assignation of writs clause. What is clear, however, is that once the feuar post-abolition transfers title, personal liability has gone.[42]

D. LEASEHOLD REFORM – CASUALTIES

Because the feudal system was not abolished in Scotland until 2004, there was no need for a system of leasehold tenure. However, long leases were granted in certain areas of Scotland. Leases of 999 years were sometimes granted instead of feus, where, for example, the land was originally held on burgage tenure. Long leases were also granted as an alternative to feus, where the estate was entailed.[43]

(1) Leasehold casualties

Long leases provided for a ground rent. This did not usually pose any problems, even although the ground rents were so small they were hardly ever collected. In any event, the right to arrears prescribed in five years and an irritancy could always be purged by payment of the arrears. Many long leases, however, also contained an obligation on the tenant to pay a one-off payment, known as a casualty, on the occurrence of certain events. One of these events was the assignation of the lease to a new tenant. Where the casualty payment was simply a multiplier of the ground rent, there was no great problem. However some casualties provided that the single payment should be of the "yearly market rent" at the time of the entry of the assignee. This resulted in some purchasers of houses held on long leasehold titles being faced with enormous bills worked out on a yearly market rental, not just for the land but for the land and the house or other buildings erected thereon. The (then) Scottish Executive moved quickly and referred the matter to the

41 2003 Act s 61.
42 K G C Reid, *The Abolition of Feudal Tenure in Scotland* para 1.22.
43 The right to feu from an entailed estate was not granted until 1914: Entail (Scotland) Act 1914 s 4.

Scottish Law Commission. The result was the Leasehold Casualties (Scotland) Act 2001. This is a good example of the Scottish Parliament moving to deal with an anomaly in Scottish property law and moreover an anomaly which was having a significant negative effect in the property market. The 2001 Act provides for nominal compensation in respect of the extinction of the casualties, based on a multiplier of the ground rent.[44] There is also provision to the effect that irritancy provisions in certain leases are void.[45] Where casualties have not been paid in the past, it is provided that the obligation does not transmit on assignation or other transfer to a new tenant.[46]

(2) Conversion of long leases

The Abolition of Feudal Tenure etc (Scotland) Act 2000 contains a provision prohibiting the grant of leases in excess of 175 years.[47] In any event, for some time, it has not been possible to create leases of domestic property in excess of twenty years.[48] Any wholesale reform of the land tenure structure in Scotland would be lacking if the question of existing long leasehold titles were ignored. Accordingly, on 21 December, 2006, the Scottish Law Commission issued a report on the conversion of long leases to an ownership title.[49] The Scottish Government is to initiate a consultation process in 2010 which is likely to result in legislation at some point. The structure of the Bill[50] is much the same as the structure of the 2000 Act. The tenant does not need to serve any notice on the landlord; conversion is automatic unless the tenant opts out. Conversion will not extinguish a heritable security over the tenant's interest and leasehold conditions may in certain circumstances become real burdens on the new ownership title. What is extinguished is the landlord's ownership title. As with feudal abolition, there is no suggestion that compensation will be payable for the loss of the ownership title.

E. MORTGAGE RIGHTS – DEBTOR PROTECTION

I suppose it would be generally accepted that in good economic times there is less sympathy for those who are in debt because it is largely assumed to be their own fault. On the other hand, in times of recession, it is accepted that

44 Leasehold Casualties Act (Scotland) 2001 ss 2-4.
45 2001 Act ss 5 and 6.
46 2001 Act s 7.
47 2000 Act s 67.
48 Land Tenure Reform (Scotland) 1974 s 8.
49 *Conversion of Long Leases* (Scot Law Com No 204, 2006).
50 As framed by the Scottish Law Commission.

people may end up in debt or facing repossession through no fault of their own, but simply because they are no longer employed. Property law legislation is, generally speaking, a technical matter, although there are always socio-economic undertones. Before the current recession, legislation was put in place to give further protection to home owners, and indeed their families, where there was a threatened repossession.[51] The Home Owner and Debtor Protection (Scotland) Act 2010 will place even greater procedural restrictions on the rights of heritable creditors to repossess. Under the Mortgage Rights (Scotland) Act 2001, calling-up notices, default notices and the like have to be served not just on the proprietor but also on the debtor (where he or she is a different person) and on any non-entitled spouse of the debtor. The notice must also be served on any person living with the debtor and other parties. These parties then have the right to ask the sheriff to delay the proceedings. The Mortgage Rights (Scotland) Act applies only to residential property, as will any new legislation. At the moment, about 95% of repossession actions are undefended. Under the new legislation it will not be competent to raise proceedings unless preliminary steps have been taken. Moreover, there will have to be a hearing, even if the debtor does not defend. The court can take into account, among other things, the reason for the arrears in payment. There may be a good reason, such as the loss of employment. Undoubtedly there will be difficult decisions for sheriffs in such genuine hardship cases. There is always bound to be a tension between pure property rights, such as the rights of a heritable creditor to realise a security for a debt, and considerations of social fairness; and the correct balance, it seems to me, will depend on the underlying economic conditions from time to time.

F. REAL BURDENS AND SERVITUDES

The Title Conditions (Scotland) Act 2003 received Royal Assent on 3 April 2003 and came into force on 28 November 2004, with the exception of certain provisions which came into force on or just after Royal Assent. It would, I think, be accepted that this Act was by far the most difficult to draft. Abolition of the feudal structure was achieved essentially in one sweeping section.[52] One of the main questions which had to be considered by the Scottish Law Commission and the Scottish Government was whether real burdens had a place in a non-feudal system of land tenure. As a matter of policy, it was eventually decided that real burdens should remain a feature of

---

51   Mortgage Rights (Scotland) Act 2001.
52   Abolition of Feudal Tenure etc (Scotland) Act s 1.

the new system. However, framing a coherent framework for real burdens in a non-feudal context proved to be a difficult task. The question was whether neighbouring proprietors should have the right to enforce real burdens against other neighbours.

There were, I suppose, always two ways of approaching the problem. On the one hand, one could adopt a pragmatic approach and simply provide that all properties within a certain radius of a property subject to a real burden would be entitled to enforce that burden. This, of course, would make some sense in as much as adjoining proprietors are the ones who are most likely to be affected by breach of a real burden, say, not to use property for a trade, business or profession. The second approach was a technical one which would involve the enactment of the existing common law rules modified so far as necessary to take account of a non-feudal system of land ownership. The second approach was the one adopted by the Scottish Government.

(1) The existing common law

It is, I think, fair to say that few people (including lawyers) fully understood the principles of the common law in relation to real burdens. In many ways the practice of solicitors, where there was a suggestion that a real burden had been contravened, was simply to obtain a letter of consent from "the superior". However, in many cases, the real burdens were not feudal real burdens but were created in dispositions or deeds of conditions by builders. Moreover, there was a tendency to insert obligations of all kinds into titles, without regard for the common law rules relating to the creation of real burdens.[53] Many of the cases relating to real burdens were fact-specific and thus not always to be regarded as precedents. Nowhere, however, was confusion more rife than in the case of third-party enforcement rights held by co-feuars or co-disponees. There were common law rules in relation to this matter[54] but they were cumbersome and not always easy to interpret.

(2) Common law enacted

Part 1 of the 2003 Act effectively enacts the common law and redefines real burdens in relation to creation, enforceability and interpretation. Most of the Act is retrospective, applying to existing as well as new real burdens.[55] The genesis of the Act is, of course, the extensive report by the Scottish Law

---

53 See R Rennie, "The reality of real burdens" 1998 SLT (News) 149.
54 The rules in *Hislop v MacRitchie's Trustees* (1881) 8 R (HL) 95.
55 2003 Act s 119(10).

Commission on real burdens.[56] There is a clear definition of a real burden in s 1 and the basic common law is not altered. A real burden is an encumbrance on land constituted in favour of the owner of other land in that person's capacity as owner of that other land. Thus the praedial rule remains, and indeed is reinforced. The Lands Tribunal has already interpreted this section, holding in some cases that a purported real burden was personal only and did not bind singular successors.[57] There are restrictions on the content of real burdens. The common law principle that a real burden cannot be illegal, contrary to public policy, in unreasonable restraint of trade or repugnant with ownership is preserved.[58] One of the main achievements of the legislation is to clarify who will actually have enforcement rights in respect of new real burdens. Not only must only burdened and benefited properties be identified in the deed creating the real burden[59] but the real burden itself must be registered in the titles to both properties.[60] Part 1 also contains a much-needed clarification of the law relating to real burdens for the payment of maintenance charges. It had always been a principle of the common law that where a real burden consisted in an obligation to pay money, then the amount had to be specific and not simply a proportion or percentage.[61] That rule (if it ever was a rule) is now reversed.[62] As before, a person has a right to enforce a real burden if he has both title and interest to enforce.[63] Generally speaking, the party who will enforce will be the owner of the benefited property but the Act extends enforcement rights to other parties such as the holder of a real right of lease or proper liferent, or a non entitled spouse. Prior to the Scottish Law Commission report there was considerable discussion over the question of interest to enforce, and how (if at all) it was to be defined. All the pre-2004 cases were, of course, fact-specific and, frankly, they cannot be reconciled.[64] Consultees were divided on the issue of whether or not a statutory definition of interest to enforce was necessary. It was felt, however, that some definition would be better than none. The definition has proved controversial. In terms of the 2003 Act,[65] a person has interest to enforce if breach of a real

56 *Real Burdens* (n15).
57 *Faely v Clark* 2006 GWD 28-626; *Halladale (Shaftsbury) Ltd* unreported, 20 June 2005 (Lands Tr).
58 2003 Act s 3(6); see *Sheltered Housing Management Ltd v Jack* 2007 GWD 32-553.
59 2003 Act s 4(2)(c).
60 2003 Act s 4(5).
61 *David Watson Property Management v Woolwich Equitable Building Society* 1992 SLT 430.
62 2003 Act s 5.
63 2003 Act s 8(1).
64 See the discussion in R Rennie, "Interest to enforce real burdens", in R Rennie (ed), *The Promised Land: Property Law Reform* ch 1.
65 2003 Act s 8(3).

burden is causing or will cause material detriment to the value or enjoyment of the benefited property. At first glance the definition seems innocuous and to encapsulate the common law. However, it does focus on the effect of the breach of a real burden rather than the nature of the real burden and its relationship to the benefited property. It appears as though the statutory test for interest to enforce is higher than the common law test.[66] As far as enforceability against the burdened property is concerned, action can be taken not just against the owner but also against a tenant or any other person having use of the burdened property.[67]

At common law, liability in respect of breach of a real burden did not end with ownership of the burdened property, and that principle has continued under the 2003 Act.[68] However, this continuing liability was mitigated by a requirement to register a notice of potential liability.[69] There are also very useful provisions in relation to shared liability and the splitting of the benefited and burdened properties.[70]

(3) Interpretation of real burdens

There is a two-line provision in the 2003 Act[71] which radically changes the common law. Prior to 2004, a real burden was construed strictly against the party who was trying to enforce the same.[72] Real burdens are now to be construed simply in the same manner as other deeds relating to land intended to be registered.

(4) Extinction of real burdens

Conveyancing practice has for some time been bedevilled by technical arguments in relation to such mundane things as house extensions which were technically in breach of some ancient real burden prohibiting alteration. The common law of acquiescence based on personal bar did operate but many purchasers' solicitors did not wish to rely on it and therefore insisted on retrospective waivers and letters of consent from superiors and other parties. The new provisions[73] are therefore greatly to be welcomed. As before, a real burden can be extinguished or modified by the grant of a discharge by the

66 See *Barker v Lewis* 2007 SLT (Sh Ct) 48; 2008 SLT (Sh Ct) 17.
67 2003 Act s 9.
68 2003 Act s 10.
69 2003 Act s 10A.
70 2003 Act ss 11-13.
71 2003 Act s 14.
72 See, e.g., *Lothian Regional Council v Rennie* 1991 SLT 465.
73 2003 Act ss 15-24.

party with title to enforce.[74] However, there is now statutory acquiescence and indeed a five-year prescription. The statutory acquiescence[75] will apply where material expenditure has taken place in relation to an activity which is in breach of a real burden and the party entitled to enforce has not objected within a period of twelve weeks following substantial completion of the activity. Moreover, a real burden is extinguished to the extent of a particular breach where no enforcement action has been taken within a five-year period of the breach or five years from the appointed day.[76] In the case of burdens which are at least 100 years old, there is a new statutory termination procedure[77] which can be resorted to where it is desired to remove ancient or indeed inappropriate burdens.

(5) Community burdens

The notion that a real burden may affect all the properties in an estate is not new. Part 2 of the 2003 Act, however, sets out a statutory code. A community burden is a real burden imposed under a common scheme on two or more properties where each property is both a benefited and a burdened property in relation to the burden. Typically, in a modern estate, there will be a deed of conditions granted by the developer, setting out real burdens which apply to all the properties on the estate. The estate becomes a community and all owners can enforce the burdens against each other. In the pre-2004 law, however, unless such mutual enforcement rights were expressly created, they would only arise if there was a mutual scheme and even then would not arise if there was a factor, such as a superior's right to waive conditions, which was inconsistent with mutual enforcement.

Thus, where it was stated that the burdens could be waived or modified by a single party such as a superior, then, unless the mutual enforcement rights were expressly granted, they did not exist.[78] The 2003 Act contains provisions in relation to community burdens and the power of a majority of proprietors to appoint a manager and indeed to instruct common maintenance.[79] There were always going to be problems in relation to the grant of a waiver or a discharge of a community burden, but these problems do not relate to the provisions of the 2003 Act; they were always with us, although

74 2003 Act s 15.
75 2003 Act s 16.
76 28 November 2004.
77 2003 Act ss 21-24.
78 *Turner v Hamilton* (1890) 17 R 494.
79 2003 Act ss 26-31.

they were ignored. Thus, where co-feuars had third-party enforcement rights against each other, strictly speaking, a waiver would have been required from the superior and all the co-feuars with an interest. The provisions of the 2003 Act in relation to variation and discharge are therefore an improvement on the existing common law and should not be criticised as some sort of added complication. A majority of owners in a community can grant a deed of variation or discharge subject, of course, to the rights of the minority to take the matter to the Lands Tribunal.[80] It is obvious that the prospect of walking round an estate of 100 houses with a view to collecting the signatures of a majority is not appealing. Accordingly, there is an alternative method of obtaining a waiver or discharge simply by obtaining the consent of the owners of adjacent units.[81] An adjacent unit is any unit which is at some point within four metres of the unit for which a consent or variation or discharge is sought.[82] It is then up to the other proprietors, having received intimation, to attempt to preserve the community burden by bringing the matter to the Lands Tribunal.[83] This is an intensely practical, and in my view entirely sensible, provision, and of course it is consistent with the definition of interest to enforce which requires there to be material detriment to the value or enjoyment of a benefited property.[84]

(6) Personal real burdens

The statutory definition of a real burden is clear: it is an encumbrance on land, enforceable by a proprietor of other land by virtue of that party's ownership of that other land.[85] It does seem rather odd, therefore, that the 2003 Act should introduce a new species of burden known as a personal real burden which is only real or praedial at the burdened end, but can be enforced by a party by virtue of that party's particular status rather than that party's ownership of any land. Personal real burdens are introduced in Pt 3 of the 2003 Act, although they did also feature in the 2000 Act where certain feudal burdens could be preserved as personal real burdens.[86] I regard the notion of a personal real burden as a contradiction in terms. Essentially, personal real burdens can be created by public bodies such as Scottish Ministers, local authori-

80 2003 Act ss 32-34.
81 2003 Act s 35.
82 2003 Act s 32.
83 2003 Act s 37.
84 2003 Act s 8(3).
85 2003 Act s 1(1).
86 See *Teague Developments Ltd v City of Edinburgh Council*, unreported, 27 February 2008 (Lands Tr).

ties, conservation bodies and the Crown.[87] The personal real burdens are conservation burdens, rural housing burdens, maritime burdens, economic development burdens and healthcare burdens, and the main thrust of the provisions is to restrict land to a particular use. Thus, if the National Trust for Scotland wishes to convey ancient property subject to a real burden that it will never be altered, extended or added to, a personal real burden can be inserted in the disposition and this will be enforceable by the National Trust for Scotland as a body quite irrespective of whether it owns any land in the vicinity.[88] Similarly, a special type of pre-emption can be created by a rural housing body such as a local authority or housing association when it sells property in a rural area. Essentially, if the disponee wishes to sell on, there is a statutory pre-emption so that the property can, if necessary, be brought back into the rural social housing stock.[89] The Crown can create burdens over the sea bed or foreshore for the benefit of the public and these burdens will be enforceable by the Crown as such.[90] Perhaps the most innovative burden is the economic development burden, although the scope of this is not clear.[91] Essentially, this type of burden can be created by a local authority or by the Scottish Ministers. If land is sold for a particular development (such as a factory), then it will be possible to restrict the use or alternatively to provide that some form of uplift payment will be made to Scottish Ministers or the local authority if a new planning use (such as housing) is contemplated in the future.[92] The definition of such a burden, however, is simply that it be for the purpose of promoting economic development, and it would appear as though the development need not be on the burdened land. A healthcare burden can be created in favour of the Scottish Ministers for the purpose of promoting the provision for healthcare. Again, the healthcare burden may comprise an obligation to pay a sum of money.[93] Since there is no benefited property where a personal real burden is created, the holder of the personal real burden is presumed to have an interest to enforce.[94]

87 2003 Act Pt 3 ss 38-48; there has not been a great take-up. Unofficial statistics suggest that less
    than 5% of deeds which create real burdens create personal real burdens.
88 2003 Act ss 38-42.
89 2003 Act s 43.
90 2003 Act s 44.
91 2003 Act s 45.
92 2003 Act s 45.
93 2003 Act s 46.
94 2003 Act s 47.

(7) Pre-2004 real burdens – transitional provisions

One of the difficulties with the pre-2004 law was that it was in many cases extremely difficult, if not impossible, to come to a view on who had title to enforce. This was especially the case where the burdens were created in non-feudal deeds. Where burdens were created in a disposition, they were enforceable as between the original granter and grantee purely as a matter of contract.[95] In a properly drawn disposition there would have been a statement to the effect that the burdens would be enforceable by the granter and the granter's successors in the ownership of identified land. However, that rule was honoured in the breach rather than the observance. In some cases, it might be implied that the successors of the granter in the rump of a landed estate would have title to enforce as against the disponee and the successors of the disponee.[96] Similarly with third-party rights of enforcement: while these could be expressly created in favour of co-feuars or co-disponees, they also arose by implication.[97] The 2003 Act contains a very stark provision whereby all rights of enforcement which arise by implication are extinguished.[98] However, a party who thinks that he or she may have such an implied right of enforcement may register a notice to that effect within ten years from the appointed day.[99] Such a notice must be intimated to the proprietors of the burdened property and may be objected to, in which case the matter is referred to the Lands Tribunal. Very few of these notices have been registered and, accordingly, in 2014 a great many burdens created in dispositions will be extinguished. Many feudal real burdens have, of course, already been extinguished.[100] The Keeper does not have a duty to cleanse the register of extinct burdens until the tenth anniversary of the appointed day.[101]

(8) Existing third-party rights – new enforcers

Given the abolition of implied rights of enforcement, it was necessary to preserve expressly enforcement rights for co-proprietors against each other in relation to existing burdens which were in effect community burdens. Section 52 of the 2003 Act enacts the common law of third-party rights as

---

95 *Scottish Co-operative Wholesale Society v Finnie* 1937 SC 835.
96 See *J A MacTaggart & Co v Harrower* (1906) 8 F 1101; *Botanic Gardens Picture House Ltd v Adamson* 1924 SC 549.
97 *Hislop v MacRitchie's Trustees* (1881) 8 R (HL) 95.
98 2003 Act s 49(1).
99 2003 Act ss 49(2) and 50.
100 2000 Act s 17.
101 2003 Act s 51.

set out in *Hislop v MacRitchie's Trustees*.[102] Essentially, for a third-party disponee or former vassal to have third-party rights of enforcement, the real burden must have been imposed under a common scheme, and there must be nothing in the deed or deeds to the contrary (such as a reservation of a right to vary or waive real burdens expressly reserved to a superior or one other party).[103] This section has been criticised because there is no definition of common scheme, however the phrase itself is well defined in the existing common law. If there is a problem with this section then, as Professor Reid has pointed out, there was the same problem with the common law, and the policy, at least initially, was not to increase the number of people who would have enforcement rights.[104] When the Bill left the Scottish Law Commission there was no s 53. Indeed, the views of the Scottish Law Commission were that enforcement rights should be restricted to proprietors of properties within a four-metre radius of the burdened property. Putting aside the question of interest to enforce, that would have restricted the number of people on a residential estate who had title to enforce where the burdens were created in a deed of conditions. For some reason which is not clear, the then Scottish Executive took the view that there should be no restriction on existing enforcement rights, possibly fearing a challenge under art 1 of Protocol 1 of the European Convention on Human Rights. As Professor Reid points out,[105] the chances of such a challenge were, frankly, remote. However, the Scottish Executive went further and introduced an additional section[106] which has added to the number of people who have enforcement rights. I suspect that most members of the public would have assumed that one of the main reasons for having all the legislation was to abolish a system whereby some parties could hold other parties to ransom over technical breaches of real burdens. Section 53 is badly drafted and has already been amended once. By introducing the concept of "related properties", the number of potential enforcers has been increased. Moreover, neither section is made subject to the other, which has resulted in uncertainty. Given that the point of legislation is to remove the uncertainty of the common law, it would have to be said that ss 52 and 53 of the 2003 Act have not achieved this certainty and indeed have probably created more uncertainty. As Professor Reid points out, however, if one accepts that the standard of material detri-

---

102 (1881) 8 R (HL) 95.
103 See *Turner v Hamilton* (1890) 17 R 494.
104 See K G C Reid, "New Enforcers for Old Burdens", in R Rennie (ed), *The Promised Land: Property Law Reform* para 3-18.
105 See Reid, "New enforcers for old burdens" (n 104) para 3-13.
106 2003 Act s 53.

ment which one must achieve before there is an interest to enforce is high, few parties with title to enforce outwith the original four-metre radius will have an interest.[107]

(9) Sheltered housing

Special provisions are enacted in respect of private sheltered housing complexes, and burdens are divided between core burdens and non-core burdens. Core burdens are burdens which regulate the use, maintenance, reinstatement or management of a facility or service, designed to make the service suitable for elderly or infirm people. A two-thirds majority is required to change these burdens in a sheltered housing development.

(10) Facility and service burdens

The 2000 Act contained a provision[108] whereby feudal real burdens which regulated the use of a facility or a service used by a number of proprietors were expressly preserved without the need for a re-allotment or preservation notice. This provision is repeated in the 2003 Act.[109] Facility and service burdens are enforceable by the owners of those properties which benefit from the facility or service and all these properties are also subject to these burdens. Obvious examples are common bin stores, common paths and rights for pipes etc. A provision of this type is fundamental to a system of land ownership where real burdens have a positive as well as a negative effect.

(11) Duties of the Keeper

As I have already indicated, the Keeper has no duty to cleanse the registers until 2014. However, it is also provided[110] that the Keeper must then enter into the title sheet of the burdened property a statement that the burden subsists by virtue of any of ss 52-56 of the Act or s 60 of the 2000 Act.[111] If the Keeper has sufficient information, she must also enter that statement on the title sheet of the benefited property with a description of the burdened property. One must assume that in many cases identifying the benefited property or properties will be a difficult task.

---

107 See Reid, "New enforcers for old burdens" (n 104) para 3-17; Rennie, "Interest to enforce real burdens" (n 64) ch 1.
108 2000 Act s 23.
109 2003 Act s 56.
110 2003 Act s 58.
111 Preserved Crown right to maritime burdens.

(12) Personal contractual liability

The 2000 Act provided[112] that extinction of a feudal real burden had no effect on any incidental personal contractual liability. However, the 2003 Act provides[113] that such incidental contractual liability which arises from the constitutive deed ends when the deed has been registered and the real burden has become effective. Accordingly, a burden is either a real burden or it may be a contractual burden but it cannot be both at the same time. It is frankly not clear why there should be any difference between feudal and non-feudal burdens. The preservation of personal contractual liability can pose problems for public bodies such as local authorities. Even where there is local government re-organisation, the new successor authority, generally speaking, stands in the shoes of the preceding authority for all purposes including personal contractual liability.

(13) Manager burdens

One of the many criticisms of the pre-2004 regime for real burdens was that it allowed developers and superiors to impose management structures on estates, and in many cases restricted the right to appoint managers or factors to the superior or developer, at least in the first instance. There was particular disquiet in sheltered housing complexes where the supervisory care element was closely tied to the original developer. New provisions are introduced in the 2003 Act.[114] Key to the new provisions is the overriding power to dismiss and appoint a manager.[115]

(14) Development management schemes

Although the thrust of the 2003 Act, like the common law, is to provide a framework for real burdens, it was thought appropriate to allow parties to adopt a statutory management scheme. Accordingly, Pt 6 of the 2003 Act[116] sets out the procedure by which such a scheme can be adopted. The statutory provisions, however, were not brought into force until 1 June 2009.[117] In many ways a scheme of this type resembles a deed of conditions because it is regis-tered by the owner of the land before any development takes place. Essen-

---

112 2000 Act s 75.
113 2003 Act s 61.
114 2003 Act ss 63-66: for examples of how these provisions may operate, see Rennie, *Land Tenure in Scotland* (2004) para 6-32.
115 2003 Act s 64.
116 2003 Act ss 71-74.
117 Title Conditions (Scotland) Act 2003 (Development Management Scheme) Order 2009, SSI 2009/729.

tially, it is a set of rules contained in the statutory instrument.[118] Although the statutory provisions do not state that the rules of the scheme are real burdens, many of the sections of the 2003 Act are applied to the rules.[119] The rules provide for an owners' association for management purposes. It remains to be seen whether this statutory scheme will be taken up to any great extent.

(15) Servitudes

Part 7 of the 2003 Act deals with servitudes. There is no enactment of the common law as a whole, but there are certain very useful amendments. In the first place, it is now provided that a deed is not effective to create a positive servitude unless registered against both benefited and burdened properties. However, it is no longer an objection to the validity of such a servitude that at the time when the deed was registered the same person owned both benefited and burdened properties. The servitude is simply suspended until there is a severance. This deals with the vexed question of whether or not it is possible to create servitudes in a deed of conditions applicable to a whole estate before any of these units is actually severed from the estate. There is also provision in relation to the so-called "closed list". New servitudes are now possible but they cannot be repugnant with ownership.[120] A free-standing servitude of parking is therefore a possibility[121] but presumably a servitude of exclusive use of a parking space to the complete exclusion of the owner would be repugnant with ownership.[122] One of the victims of the closed list theory was a servitude to lead an electricity wire over someone else's land.[123] It is now provided[124] that a right to lead a pipe, cable, wire or other such enclosed unit over or under land for any purpose may be constituted as a positive servitude. Moreover, this provision is retrospective, whereas the other provisions in relation to servitudes are not, so although a servitude of signage may now be competent, one which was purported to be created before 28 November 2004 is not.[125] Negative servitudes such as a servitude of light or prospect are, after the appointed day, incompetent[126] and will have to be created as negative real burdens. Existing negative servitudes simply become negative

118 The statutory instrument was made under s 104 of the Scotland Act 1998.
119 2003 Act s 72.
120 2003 Act s 76.
121 See *Moncrieff v Jamieson* 2007 SLT 989.
122 But see *Holms v Ashford Estates Ltd* 2009 SLT 389.
123 *Neill v Scobbie* 1993 GWD 8-572.
124 2003 Act s 77.
125 *Romano v Standard Commercial Property Services Ltd* 2008 SLT 859.
126 2003 Act s 79.

real burdens or converted servitudes.[127] However, these converted servitudes are extinguished on the expiry of ten years unless specifically preserved by registered notice, except where the negative servitude has actually been registered against the burdened property or appears in the title sheet of that property prior to the appointed day. Similarly, rights of entry or rights to make certain uses of the burdened property which are framed as real burdens in deeds are now properly regarded as positive servitudes.[128]

(16) Pre-emptions and reversions

Part 8 of the 2003 Act[129] deals with pre-emption and reversion. The practice of solicitors in relation to pre-emptions has usually been to ask the holders of a pre-emption whether or not they wish to exercise the right. The previous statutory provisions, however, actually required a formal offer to be made to the holder of the pre-emption. The new provisions allow for an undertaking to be granted not to exercise the pre-emption[130] in addition to the old method of actually making an offer to sell. In relation to reversions, feudal reversions will usually have been extinguished. Of more significance is the abolition of the statutory reversion under the School Sites Act 1841.[131]

In certain circumstances compensation will be payable by the local authority when a school or school house ceases to be used for educational purposes. Similarly, the right to petition under s 7 of the Entail Sites Act 1840 is abolished on the automatic disentail of entailed land.

(17) The jurisdiction of the Lands Tribunal

The 2003 Act has expanded the jurisdiction of the Lands Tribunal. Previously, the Tribunal's only jurisdiction related to burdens which were clearly real burdens as such. Under the new provisions[132] the Tribunal can decide, for example, that a burden is not enforceable simply because it does not qualify as a real burden. Moreover, in addition to its original jurisdiction to discharge or vary real burdens, most disputes relating to the preservation, re-allotment or extinction of real burdens can be referred to the Tribunal.[133]

127 2003 Act s 80.
128 2003 Act s 81.
129 Sections 82-89.
130 Section 83.
131 For the difficulties caused, see *Hamilton v Grampian Regional Council* 1995 GWD 8-443; 1996 GWD 5-227.
132 2003 Act Pt 9 ss 90-104.
133 See *Brown v Richardson* 2007 GWD 28-490; *Council for Music in Hospitals v Trustees for Richard Gerald Associates* 2008 SLT (Lands Tr) 17 and 44.

The Tribunal retains the power to award compensation, although this is a power which has been used sparingly and is likely to be used only where the loss is substantial.[134] One of the major reforms is that the Tribunal can now consider and grant unopposed applications without the need for a full hearing.[135] However, this reform does not apply to applications to vary or discharge servitudes.[136] Under the previous legislation[137] there were only three factors which the Tribunal could consider in deciding whether or not to vary or discharge a real burden. The 2003 Act sets out no fewer than ten factors to which the Tribunal is to have regard. There is also the general principle that the Tribunal must consider the reasonableness of an application in general terms.[138] The Tribunal has tended to focus on factor (f), namely the purpose of the title condition, before looking at other factors. However, the general trend appears to be to grant most applications to vary or discharge.[139] There is another significant change in the way in which the Tribunal operates, and that relates to expenses.[140] The Tribunal may, in determining an application, make such order as to expenses as it thinks fit, but is to have regard in particular to the extent to which the application, or any opposition to the application, is successful. Accordingly, those who wish to oppose an application to discharge a real burden, or indeed those who wish to preserve an ancient burden to frustrate development, must weigh up the economic consequences of losing. The Tribunal has not been slow to award expenses.[141]

(18) Real burdens and statutory acquisition

There has always been a view that the compulsory acquisition of land by way of either a statutory conveyance or a general vesting declaration extinguishes existing real burdens and servitudes, because restrictions on land are themselves inconsistent with the notion of compulsory acquisition for statutory purposes.[142] The 2003 Act contains a provision which confirms this view.[143] Moreover, where land is acquired by agreement, but could have

---

134 See *George Wimpey East Scotland Ltd v Fleming* 2006 SLT (Lands Tr) 59.
135 2003 Act s 97.
136 See *Ventureline Ltd*, unreported, 2 August 2006 (Lands Tr).
137 Conveyancing and Feudal Reform (Scotland) Act 1970.
138 2003 Act s 98.
139 For a comprehensive table of cases decided since the coming into force of the 2003 Act, see K G C Reid and G Gretton, *Conveyancing* 2009 (2010) 187.
140 2003 Act s 103.
141 See *Regan v Mullen* 2006 GWD 25-56; *Smith v Prior* 2007 GWD 30-523; *Jensen v Tyler* 2008 SLT (Lands Tr) 39; *Sheltered Housing Management v Jack* 2008 SLT 1058.
142 *Town Council of Oban v Callander and Oban Railway* (1892) 19 R 912.
143 2003 Act s 106.

been acquired by compulsory purchase, any burden or servitude will also be extinguished, although in this case the acquiring authority must notify the owner of the benefited property or the holder of a personal real burden or an owners' association or the holder of a servitude. These parties can make an application to the Lands Tribunal to renew the burden within twenty-one days.[144]

G. TENEMENTS

(1) Common law and the new regime

The Tenements (Scotland) Act 2004[145] received Royal Assent on 22 October 2004, and the main provisions came into effect on 28 November 2004. The existing common law of the tenement, which applied where the titles were silent, was based on the law of common interest. In many cases, of course, particularly in the west of Scotland, the titles of individual tenement or flatted properties made certain core parts of the tenement common property and imposed maintenance obligations on all the proprietors by way of real burdens. The law of common property, however, does not provide a management system. Indeed, the general rule is that no one common owner can carry out work on the common property without the consent of the others unless it is an essential repair.[146] While up to this point the 2004 Act was the last property-related Act to be passed by the Scottish Parliament, the project on the law of the tenement had been the first large scale property law project undertaken by the Scottish Law Commission back in 1990.[147]

Many European and indeed American jurisdictions have a complete statutory code for flatted properties, containing detailed provisions for maintenance and management. One of the questions which faced the Scottish Law Commission at the outset was whether to alter the existing common law of the tenement, especially in relation to maintenance and repair, where existing titles were silent or deficient, or to suggest a complete statutory scheme which would apply to all tenements or blocks of flats no matter when they were erected and which would replace all existing title conditions. There is no doubt that the latter option would have been radical and also might have raised human rights issues. Moreover, it would be fair to say that in Scotland,

---

144 2003 Act s 107.
145 Hereafter "the 2004 Act".
146 See *Rafique v Amin* 1997 SLT 1385; *Thomas Dagg & Sons Ltd v Dickensian Property Co Ltd* 2005 GWD 6-84.
147 Discussion Paper No 91 (1990); Report 1998 (Scot Law Com No 162).

and indeed in the United Kingdom, lawyers and legislators have shied away from wholesale statutory schemes. Accordingly, the 2004 Act was framed as a fall-back scheme where the titles are silent.[148]

(2) Ownership in tenements

Sections 1-3 of the 2004 Act deal with boundaries and pertinents and simply enact the existing common law of property which applies where the titles are silent. As before, a top flat extends to and includes the roof[149] and the bottom flat extends to and includes the solum under that flat.[150] The words "extends to" necessarily imply that the air space between the ceiling of the top flat and the roof belong to the top flat, and that any basement and foundations belong to the bottom flat. So far as air space above the roof is concerned, the common law position is confirmed, namely that ownership of air space attaches to ownership of the solum.[151] One of the main difficulties in relation to ownership related to dormer windows which had been projected from the roof in circumstances where the roof was not common. Although ownership of the top flat served by the dormer included ownership of the roof, it did not include ownership of the triangle of air space outwith a pitched roof taken up by the dormer. That air space was owned by whoever owned the solum. In a neatly drafted provision, ownership of that triangle of air space is now given to the owner of the roof.[152] It must, of course, be borne in mind at all times that these statutory provisions, like the previous common law, apply only where the titles are silent.

(3) Pertinents

The common law of the tenement is altered to a certain extent by the provisions in the 2004 Act relating to pertinents.[153] Certain parts of a tenement are, in the absence of provisions in the title, made common property. These parts include closes, lifts, paths, fire escapes, rhones, pipes, flues and so on where these items serve more than one flat.

---

148 For a detailed commentary on the 2004 Act, see K G C Reid and G Gretton, *Conveyancing 2004* (2005) 121-150 and D B Reid, "The Tenements (Scotland) Act 2004", in Rennie (ed), *The Promised Land: Property Law Reform* ch 6.
149 2004 Act s 2(3).
150 2004 Act s 2(4).
151 2004 Act s 2(6).
152 2004 Act s 2(7).
153 2004 Act s 3.

(4) Maintenance and management

The 2004 Act provides a Tenement Management Scheme.[154] Given the fact that no attempt was made to alter the rules of common law ownership, the question which arose was whether or not it would be possible to alter the general rules of common interest relating to maintenance, repair, support and shelter effectively imposing obligations to maintain parts of the tenement which were in exclusive ownership of proprietors. The novel approach which was taken was to designate certain core parts of a tenement as "scheme property" without actually altering ownership. Any part of the tenement that is already common to two or more owners is scheme property, as is any such part the maintenance of which is made the responsibility of two or more owners by a burden in the title. Apart from these rather obvious examples, various other parts of the tenement are scheme property, namely the ground, foundations, external walls, roof (including any supporting structure), the part of any mutual gable pertaining to the tenement and any other wall, beam or column that is load bearing. Individual parts of scheme property which serve only one flat, such as a door or window, are not scheme property. Rule 2 of the statutory Tenement Management Scheme sets out a procedure for making decisions including voting procedures, and r 3 sets out the matters on which scheme decisions may be made. Rule 4 provides for liability and apportionment of costs and r 5 for re-distribution of shares where, for example, recovery cannot be made from one particular owner because he or she has been sequestrated or cannot be traced. Rule 6 deals with procedural irregularities and r 7 contains provisions allowing emergency work to be carried out and charged back. The scheme binds all owners where it applies but applies only where there are no provisions in the title.

(5) Support and shelter

Although the existing rules of common interest as they applied to tenements are abolished,[155] there are new statutory provisions which provide for a positive obligation to provide support and shelter and prohibit interference with support or shelter.[156]

(6) Liability for arrears

One of the vexed questions which arose during the Bill's progress through the Scottish Parliament was the liability of successive owners for arrears

154   2004 Act ss 4-6 and Sch 1.
155   2004 Act s 7.
156   2004 Act ss 8-10.

of common charges owed by predecessors in title. The basic provision had been that successors would become liable. However, an extra provision[157] was added during the Bill's passage to provide that liability would not transmit unless a notice of potential liability for costs was registered at least fourteen days before the acquisition date. The acquisition date is defined as the date on which the new owner "acquired right to the flat". "Acquiring right" is a difficult concept. The most sensible date would be the date of conclusion of missives for the purchase but it is clear that missives do not give any right to the property itself.[158] There has been criticism of the practice of registering protective notices of some factors.

(7) Access, insurance and services

The 2004 Act contains very useful and practical provisions which provide that all owners will have access to other flats for maintenance purposes.[159] The Act also imposes a duty on each owner to keep in force some contract of insurance against prescribed risks which may be by way of common policy.[160] There is a new statutory right to lead any pipe, cable, or other equipment through any part of the tenement in terms of procedures prescribed by Scottish Ministers.[161]

(8) Demolition and abandonment of tenements

Demolition of a tenement building has never altered the ownership position and the 2004 Act preserves that principle.[162] Accordingly, when a tenement of four storeys is demolished, the original owners of the flats still own the slices of air space which were formerly taken up by these flats. This can, of course, cause considerable problems for the disposal of the vacant site, especially where some of the original flat owners cannot be traced. There are provisions in the 2004 Act for the apportionment of the cost of demolishing a tenement among the proprietors.[163] Generally speaking, there will be equal sharing unless there are large discrepancies in the sizes of flats in which case floor area will be relevant. Where a tenement building has been demolished and two or more flats are owned by different persons, then the statutory provision for disposal applies.[164] Basically, any owner of a former flat can apply to

157 2004 Act s 12.
158 *Burnett's Trustee v Grainger* 2004 SLT 513.
159 2004 Act s 17.
160 2004 Act s 18.
161 2004 Act s 19.
162 2004 Act s 20.
163 2004 Act s 21.
164 2004 Act s 22.

the court for the power to sell.[165] The net sale proceeds are divided equally unless there is a large-scale discrepancy in floor areas. There is an alternative provision facilitating sale where a tenement building has been abandoned because of its poor condition.[166] The benefit of these provisions is that they allow a sale without the need to trace all the last flat owners and any purchaser will receive a good title.

H. THE LEGISLATIVE ACHIEVEMENT

It is easy, of course, especially with the benefit of hindsight, to pick holes in technical provisions. Lawyers, in particular, are good at doing this. However, the real test of any legislation is whether or not it results in an improvement on what went before. I think the answer to that question in relation to the property law legislation is an unqualified "yes". The existing common law relating to real burdens, in particular, was badly understood even by lawyers and, frankly, rarely applied in practice, especially where third-party rights of enforcement were involved.

(1) Feudal abolition

The abolition of the feudal system was achieved with remarkable ease in legislative terms. There were no human rights challenges even although an ownership interest (the superiority) was extinguished without compensation. No-one can question the benefits to be obtained by the abolition of feudal tenure and the Act is for the most part well drafted and easy to interpret and implement. All existing feu duties were swept away and feudal burdens extinguished subject to rights of re-allotment and preservation. Questions have been raised over the prohibition of leases of over 175 years. There is no such prohibition in England but there is, of course, a proliferation of leasehold tenure there which is presumably something to be discouraged in Scotland. The question does arise as to whether investment in Scotland may be hampered by this restriction. My own view is that personal real burdens[167] are not a concept which should feature in a non-feudal system of land tenure. It is unfortunate, I suppose, that the parties who can hold personal real burdens are public bodies, the Scottish Ministers, local authorities, conservation bodies, housing authorities, the Crown, and healthcare authorities. It could be said, therefore, that, in some respects, public bodies are the

---

165 2004 Act s 22(3) and Sch 3.
166 2004 Act s 24.
167 Which can also be created by certain parties post-feudal abolition.

new superiors. However, mercifully, use of personal real burdens has not been extensive. I think it might have been preferable simply to extinguish all rights to enforce burdens where they were enforceable purely by a superior, whether on a contractual basis or otherwise, or at least to have made it clear that the contractual rights applied only as between the original superior and original vassal, with no right to assign. Taken as a whole, the Abolition of Feudal Tenure etc (Scotland) Act is a successful piece of legislation and a significant achievement of the Scottish Parliament.

(2) Real burdens

The 2003 Act provides for the most part a firm statutory framework in a post-feudal era. There will always be those who believe that there should be no private rights to control the use of other people's land and that such controls should be left to local authorities or other public bodies. Equally, however, there has always been a body of opinion which is against any notion of "absolute" ownership. The rules in relation to the creation of post-appointed day real burdens are clear and are already working well. If there is a difficulty with the 2003 Act, it relates to the treatment of pre-2004 real burdens and in particular third-party rights of enforcement. The new provisions for community burdens are clear so far as title to enforce is concerned: all units within a community are both burdened and benefited properties. So far as existing burdens are concerned, s 52 of the 2003 Act simply re-states the existing common law. There was always going to be a difficult policy decision to be made, given that the existing common law was complicated, especially in relation to title to enforce. If one accepted that co-proprietors should be able to enforce existing real burdens, even feudal ones, then the only question was whether or not to restrict the class of enforcers to those in the immediate vicinity of the burdened property. Hence the four-metre proposal was the one which was eventually put forward by the Scottish Law Commission. Such a rule, criticised by some as "cheap and cheerful", would have provided a degree of certainty, although such neighbouring proprietors would still have required to show an interest to enforce. There were concerns within the Justice Department that restricting enforcement rights would involve depriving other co-proprietors of a title to enforce which they would have had at common law. There were fears that this might render the statutory provisions open to challenge as a breach of the human right on ownership of property. If, however, one examines this critically, it is unlikely that there would have been such a breach because more distant proprietors would not have had an interest to enforce even if they had a title. Unfortunately, s 53 has resulted in further confusion. That section did not appear in the Scottish Law Commission version of the Bill and there can be no doubt that in so far as title to enforce at least is concerned, its effect could be to increase the number of parties who can enforce existing pre-2004 real burdens. It is difficult to see the justification for the introduction of a new category of enforcer, namely the owner of a "related" property, especially since s 53 still requires the real burdens to be imposed under a common scheme. Could a property be "related" if it was not part of a common scheme, where, for example, all the properties were covered by a single deed of conditions? Unfortunately, it has to be said that the combined effect of ss 52 and 53 has been to create considerable uncertainty. However, as Professor Reid has pointed out,[168] the fact that the "material detriment" test for interest to enforce appears to be a high one may deprive the majority of proprietors, even ones living in close proximity to the burdened property, of any enforcement rights at all.[169] With the abolition of the feudal system, the primary enforcement right of a feudal superior vanished. So far as pre-2004 burdens are concerned, the law is somewhat uncertain because the combined effect of the statutory provisions cannot be said to have produced a clear set of rules relating to enforcement. It may, however, turn out to be the case that real burdens will in general terms be less enforceable than they were, if only because of their requirement to show a very substantial degree of interest.

(3) Long leases

There are now two prohibitions of leases in place.[170] There has always been a fear in Scotland of the proliferation of leasehold title. The suggestion is that the feudal system could simply be re-created by the grant of long leases. That certainly is what happened in England after Edward I prohibited sub-infeudation. A lease, of course, is a consensual document; there is no requirement for a prospective tenant to accept such a title. So far as commercial developments are concerned, there may also be economic arguments in favour of longer leases. On balance, my own view is that there is no need for there to be two limits. I would be in favour of a single limit for all leases of 175 years and the removal of the prohibition of 20 years for domestic leases. It seems to me that an upper limit is necessary, particularly in view of the impending legislation for the conversion of long leases into ordinary ownership.

---

168   Reid, "New enforcers for old burdens" (n 104) para 3-3.17.
169   See *Barker v Lewis* 2007 SLT (Sh Ct) 48; 2008 SLT (Sh Ct) 17.
170   Twenty years for domestic property and 175 years generally.

(4) Tenements

The criticism of the common law was that it did not provide for an effective management structure and indeed allowed sensible and in many cases necessary repairs to be blocked by one proprietor. There is no doubt that the statutory provisions, combined with existing title provisions, do provide a far better system for management and maintenance of tenements than the old common law. The problem, of course, with a fall-back scheme like this is that one has to look first at the real burdens in the title and then come to a view on whether or not there are any gaps before resorting to the tenement management scheme. The titles, for example, may in fact provide a very basic management scheme providing that decisions will be taken at a meeting. That is probably going to be enough to displace the more detailed provisions of rr 2 and 3 of the statutory Tenement Management Scheme. The statutory scheme does not apply where the scheme in the title is too simple or is difficult to operate. The attractions of having a one scheme for all become more apparent when one has to consider how the provisions of individual titles actually work (or not). In the west of Scotland, factors or property managers were and are common, although that could not be said for all tenement titles in the east of Scotland. It used to be the case that lawyers and estate agents were the least popular members of society, with factors and property managers close behind. Presumably, bankers now head the unpopularity stakes. I suspect that Scottish people in general do not take kindly to being managed or, put simply, told what must be done. A leak from the roof of a tenement is not something which is likely to worry a ground-floor proprietor despite the fact that the roof is the covering for the whole tenement. One can see that there might have been a benefit in having a complete statutory code for the maintenance and management of tenement property which superseded all existing title provisions and applied to all tenements whenever erected. Of course, drawing up such a scheme would be difficult and the scheme would have to be very general. It is obvious that the more general a statutory scheme is, the less effective it will be in individual cases. For this reason a balance was struck between a fully statutory scheme and leaving the law much as it was.

(5) The legislative achievement

The Acts of 2000, 2003 and 2004 are a considerable legislative achievement. Much of the credit, of course, must go to the Scottish Law Commission and in particular to Professor Kenneth Reid who was the lead commissioner on the various projects. Perhaps the most important fact was that the Scottish Parliament recognised the value to society of non-contentious property law reform. The legislation itself is, of course, highly technical, especially the 2003 Act. Those of us who appeared to give evidence before the Justice Committee of the day were, however, impressed by the relevance of the questions we were asked in relation to the provisions of the Bills. Indeed, I think it is fair to say that the MSPs who were involved did appreciate both the scope and the significance of the legislation.

15 Business

David Cabrelli[*]

A. INTRODUCTION

In March 1999, the same year that the Scottish Parliament was re-established, the then Scottish Office commissioned a report entitled *Pathfinders to the Parliament: A Business Agenda for the Scottish Parliament*.[1] The report was divided on the basis of key sectors of the Scottish economy and each of the groups was convened by key business individuals operating within those sectors. Each group made suggestions for policy and legislative initiatives. The majority of the issues raised could be classified as policy issues which fell within the remit of the then Scottish Executive. Others entailed legislative proposals:

> There is also a strong view that the Scottish Parliament should not put Scottish business at a disadvantage by adopting financial or regulatory policies which put additional burdens on Scottish business and make them less competitive in the global market ... the Drinks and Hospitality Pathfinder Group recommends the modernisation of Scottish licensing laws to bring them into line with European neighbours and also to meet the expectations of both domestic consumers and visitors to Scotland.

Remarkably, since 1999, there have been very few Acts of the Scottish Parliament ("ASPs") introducing reforms to the law of Scotland which can be categorised as falling squarely within the compass of business law or commercial

---

* Lecturer in Commercial Law, University of Edinburgh.
1 Available from *http://www.scotland.gov.uk/library/documents-w8/pttp-00.htm* (last accessed 3 March 2010).

law. The opportunities for reform may, in part, have been constrained by the terms of the Scotland Act 1998 which limit the powers of the Scottish Parliament in relation to business law or commercial law, but equally the distinct lack of business law reform is not for want of suggestions from the Scottish Law Commission.[2] Indeed, the most likely candidate for an ASP which can be categorised as an attempt at commercial law reform is the Bankruptcy and Diligence Reform (Scotland) etc Act 2007 ("BAD Act"). In particular, Pt 2 of the BAD Act included provisions designed to reform the law relating to the registration, creation and alteration of floating charges. However, Pt 2 is not yet in force and the remainder of it is not wholly related to commercial law since it primarily reforms the law of personal insolvency, debt, debt enforcement and diligence. Furthermore, another ASP, namely the Licensing (Scotland) Act 2005, which applies to the sale of alcohol from premises, undoubtedly impinges upon the activities of sundry Scottish businesses. However, its scope of application is not restricted to sales of alcohol by businesses and it is of equal importance in the context of non-commercial and charitable spheres of activity. With that in mind, this chapter will focus on the recently enacted Arbitration (Scotland) Act 2010 ("the Act") whose remit is to reform the main out-of-court mechanism for the resolution of commercial law disputes. The principal aim of the Act is particularly aspirational, namely to encourage the use of arbitration domestically and attract international arbitration business to Scotland.[3] The Act was passed by the Scottish Parliament on 18 November 2009, received Royal Assent on 5 January 2010 and came into force on 7 June 2010.

B. THE DEFICIENCIES IN THE PRE-ACT SCOTS LAW OF ARBITRATION

Prior to the coming into force of the Act, the sources of the Scottish law of arbitration were scattered far and wide, ranging from the common law to legislation (such as the Arbitration (Scotland) Act 1894 and the Administration of Justice (Scotland) Act 1972) and the Institutional writers.[4] It had been well recognised for a number of years that the law of arbitration in Scotland possessed a number of imperfections. Nine deficiencies in particular were

2 For example, *Report on Partnership Law* (Scot Law Com No 192, 2003), among others.
3 Scottish Parliament Policy Memorandum on the Arbitration (Scotland) Bill, 30 January 2009, paras 28 and 42 (*http://www.scottish.parliament.uk/s3/bills/19-Arbitration/b19s3-introd-pm.pdf*) (last accessed 3 March 2010).
4 F Davidson, *Arbitration* (2000) 4-5; The Rt Hon Lord Hope of Craighead, "Arbitration", in *The Laws of Scotland: Stair Memorial Encyclopaedia*, Reissue (1999) paras 1-4.

identified by the Scottish branch of the Chartered Institute of Arbitrators ("CIArb") in a letter submitted to the Scottish Parliament's Economy, Energy and Tourism Committee,[5] as follows:

1. the lack of an inherent power in Scots law for an arbiter to award damages or expenses;
2. the lack of clarity concerning:
   (a) the immunity of an arbiter from suit;
   (b) the severability of an arbitration agreement from the underlying commercial contract;
   (c) the ability of a party or his agent to be appointed sole arbiter;
3. the fact that the internationally accepted principle that an arbiter can determine his or her own jurisdiction (*kompetenz-kompetenz*) was expressly rejected in Scotland;[6]
4. the absence of a legal presumption in Scots law to the effect that an arbiter may make a part (partial) or interim award;
5. the position regarding the privacy or confidentiality of arbitration was particularly unclear;
6. the applicability of court rules of evidence was uncertain; and
7. the Stated Case Procedure included in s 3 of the Administration of Justice (Scotland) Act 1972, which enabled an appeal to be made from the arbiter's decision on a point of law, was perceived to be an anachronism[7] and one which had been expressly rejected in England by the Arbitration Act 1996.

The most serious defect in the common law of arbitration was the lack of a common law implied power on the part of an arbiter to award damages[8] or simple or compound interest[9] unless expressly sanctioned by the arbitration agreement. Moreover, there was a tendency for disputes processed through the arbitration procedure in Scotland to become bogged down by inefficiencies, expenses and delays because of the adoption of the rigid and somewhat mechanistic formalities of the Scottish court system of written pleadings, a development duly noted and criticised by Lord President Hope in *ERDC*

---

5 A version of that written submission is available as an article by H Dundas, "The Arbitration (Scotland) Bill 2008" *Winter 2009 CIArb Newsletter* 6, 7.
6 This can be contrasted with art 16(1) of the UNCITRAL Model Law on International Commercial Arbitration adopted by the United Nations Commission on International Trade Law on 21 June 1985 ("UNCITRAL Model Law") which was adopted into Scots law in 1991 by virtue of s 66 of, and Sch 7 to, the Law Reform (Miscellaneous Provisions) (Scotland) Act 1990; see F Davidson, *International Commercial Arbitration: Scotland and the UNCITRAL Model Law* (1991) ch 5.
7 Indeed, in *ERDC Construction Ltd v H M Love & Co (No 2)* 1996 SC 523 at 528 Lord President Hope was critical of the frequency with which it was resorted to.
8 *Aberdeen Railway Co v Blaikie Bros* (1853) 15 D (HL) 20.
9 *John G McGregor (Contractors) Ltd v Grampian Regional Council* 1991 SLT 136 at 137L per Lord Dunpark. However, an arbiter has an implied power to award expenses in terms of the common law, on which see The Rt Hon Lord Hope of Craighead, "Arbitration" (n 4) para 52; *Pollich v Heatley* 1910 SC 469 at 482 per LP Dunedin; and *Grampian Regional Council v John McGregor (Contractors) Ltd* 1994 SLT 133.

Construction Ltd v H M Love & Co (No 2).[10] Rules 23, 24 and 27 of the Scottish Arbitration Rules ("SA Rules") which are set out in Sch 1 to the Act specifically instruct the arbitral tribunal[11] and the parties in dispute to avoid unnecessary expenses and delay, as well as enabling them to determine their own procedure and rules of evidence (which may deviate from the formal rules of evidence and the system of written pleadings applicable in proceedings brought in the Scottish courts). The intention behind these provisions in the SA Rules is to confront and overcome the difficulties identified by Lord President Hope in *ERDC Construction*. Moreover, a great number of the SA Rules and the main body of the Act address each of the nine deficiencies identified by the CIArb above. For example, SA Rules rr 44A, 45 and 46 provide an arbitrator with an implicit power to award damages, interest and/ or expenses, and rr 73-75 direct that an arbitral tribunal and arbitrators are immune from liability in respect of their conduct of the arbitration proceedings. Furthermore, r 5 stipulates that a person may be appointed as a sole arbitrator and the doctrine of separability is enshrined in law in s 5 of the Act. Moreover, r 19 incorporates the principle of *kompetenz-kompetenz* into Scots law and rr 50-52 enable an arbitrator to make a partial or interim award. Rule 26 clarifies the position with regard to the privacy or confidentiality of arbitral proceedings. Rules 45-46 shed light on the role of the courts in procuring evidence and witnesses to attend arbitral proceedings and enable them to make orders on the application of the parties or the arbitral tribunal. Moreover, r 27 provides the arbitral tribunal with the power to determine the procedure to be followed in the arbitration, including issues such as admissibility, relevance, materiality and the weight of any evidence. Finally, s 3 of the Administration of Justice (Scotland) Act 1972 is repealed.[12] However, that is not to say that there is no locus for the court to be involved in proceedings prior to the production of an award, since r 41 enables the Outer House (on an application by any party) to determine any point of Scots law arising in the arbitration.

This chapter will not attempt to comment on the entirety of the provisions in the Act. Instead, the focus will be on the particular provisions which the writer views as deserving of particular discussion and analysis.

---

10 1996 SC 523 at 528.
11 The Act introduces some terminological changes. For example, a reference to an "arbitrator" will replace all references to an arbiter, and where there is more than one arbitrator involved in proceedings, this is referred to as an "arbitral tribunal".
12 Section 27 of, and Sch 2 to, the Act.

C. THE OBJECTIVES OF THE ACT AND THE UNDERPINNING PRINCIPLES

The primary objective of the Act is to modernise the Scottish law of arbitration so that it conforms with international best practice. This is achieved through a combination of reform and statutory codification. The explanatory notes to the Arbitration (Scotland) Bill noted that its content had been:

> drawn from the UNCITRAL Model Law, the UK Arbitration Act 1996,[13] from the work done in a draft Bill for Scotland developed by a working group chaired by Lord Dervaird in 2002 and from consultation comments by parties interested in the promotion of arbitration in Scotland.[14]

Thus, the Act represents the product and culmination of a long gestation period, where particular consideration and thought were given to the optimal model of arbitration law for a competitive economy in light of varied sources. Section 1 of the Act itemises the founding principles which underpin the Act, and directs as follows:

- the object of arbitration is to resolve disputes fairly, impartially and without unnecessary delay or expense,
- parties should be free to agree how to resolve disputes subject only to such safeguards as are necessary in the public interest, and
- the court should not intervene in an arbitration except as provided by the Act.

As Davidson has argued, it is unlikely that these three principles will be prioritised in terms of a hierarchy.[15] Instead, they are best thought of as precepts which will act as an aid to interpreting the main body of the Act and the SA Rules.[16] Of particular interest, however, is the deployment of the word "should" rather than "shall" in the third principle above. This is indicative of a continuing and sustained role for the court superintendence of disputes which have been submitted to arbitration. Indeed, in the case of *Vale Do Rio Doce Navegacao SA v Shanghai Bao Steel Ocean Shipping Co Ltd*,[17] Thomas J in the High Court in England ruled that the wording of s 32 of the Arbitration Act 1996 (which is in similar terms to the third founding principle above) ought to be construed in a fashion which limited the role of the courts but did not completely exclude it.[18] This undoubtedly will be the position in terms

---

13 Only ss 89-91 of the Arbitration Act 1996 (which deal with consumer arbitration) extend to Scotland.

14 See *http://www.scottish.parliament.uk/s3/bills/19-Arbitration/b19s3-introd-en.pdf* (last accessed 3 March 2010) at para 7 on p 2.

15 F Davidson, "Some thoughts on the draft Arbitration Bill" (2009) *JBL* 44 at 48.

16 Section 1 of the Act.

17 [2000] 2 All ER (Comm) 70.

18 [2000] 2 All ER (Comm) 70 at 84h-j.

of the regime introduced by the Act, since the SA Rules specifically envisage residual scope for court intervention on a conditional basis.[19]

Section 4 of the Act defines an arbitration agreement as "an agreement to submit a present or future dispute to arbitration (including any agreement which provides for arbitration in accordance with arbitration provisions contained in a separate document)". To that extent, the Scots law of arbitration promulgated by the Act is unusual or, at best, unique, since all international conventions insist that the submission to arbitration is embodied in written form as a matter of formal validity.[20] Nevertheless, where an agreement to arbitrate is made orally and not recorded in writing, for obvious reasons, issues of evidential weight will often coalesce in a manner which disables the party seeking to rely on that agreement. To that extent, a degree of caution should be struck in relation to this particular Scottish innovation.

Dealing with one of the deficiencies in the law of arbitration in Scotland duly highlighted by CIArb, s 5 of the Act directs that the agreement to submit to arbitration is separable and distinct from any underlying commercial agreement. On balance, while it is not clear cut, it is more probable than not that the provisions in the sections of the Act will be treated as inderogable. For that reason, it has been argued persuasively that the separability principle cannot be ousted by the agreement of the parties.[21] Thus, the law would appear to have been harmonised with English law as promulgated in s 7 of the Arbitration Act 1996.[22] However, s 5 of the Act differs in its terms from s 7 of the Arbitration Act 1996 in so far as there is nothing in the wording of the former to suggest that the parties may modify or disapply the separability principle in Scots law by agreement. The implication of s 5 of the Act is that the voidness, voidability or unenforceability of the latter will not operate to affect or invalidate the former. However, s 5 of the Act fails to clarify the legal status of the arbitration agreement where the parties never purported to conclude the main agreement which included the arbitration clause. In such a case, the question is whether the arbitration clause in the agreement (which never reached the stage of a legally binding contract, i.e. it did not exist) is nevertheless effective for the purposes of resolving disputes which arise between the parties. The alternative approach is that since the underlying contract is treated *non est factum*, the doctrine of separability performs

19 See SA Rules rr 41-42 and 67-69.
20 See A Redfern and M Hunter, *Law and Practice of International Commercial Arbitration*, 4th edn (2004) 159-162.
21 F Davidson, "Some thoughts on the draft Arbitration Bill" (n 15) at 52.
22 See also *Fiona Trust & Holding Corp v Privalov* [2007] 4 All ER 951.

insufficient labour to allow the arbitration agreement to survive.[23] Indeed, the latter is the position in English law, despite the ostensibly wide language in which s 7 of the Arbitration Act 1996 is couched.[24] It should be noted that the doctrine of separability is distinct from the question of jurisdictional competence of the arbitral tribunal which is covered by SA Rules rr 19 and 20, but the two issues are undoubtedly linked in that each exercises a sphere of influence over the other.

D. THE SA RULES

Section 6 of the Act directs that the SA Rules set out in Sch 1 are to govern "every arbitration seated in Scotland". The SA Rules consist of mandatory and default rules. Naturally, the former are inderogable[25] and the latter may be amended or disapplied by the parties in a commercial agreement, an arbitration agreement or some other agreement concluded before or after the arbitration has commenced.[26] However, the default rules cannot be equated to implied terms of the arbitration agreement since they are not drawn in language which is suitable to attract such status. Instead, they are best conceptualised as default statutory rules.[27] The SA Rules consist of 80 rules and represent a comprehensive code of arbitration. Each of the SA Rules is marked with an "M" or a "D" indicating whether it is mandatory or default in nature.

Part 1 of the SA Rules consists of eighteen rules and addresses the commencement and constitution of the arbitral tribunal. Issues such as the submission of a commercial dispute to arbitration in terms of an arbitration or other agreement, appointment of the arbitral tribunal and arbitrator, disclosure of conflicts of interest and the numbers, status, eligibility, removal, resignation and dismissal of arbitrators and arbitral tribunals are all covered.

In Pt 2 of the SA Rules, the focus shifts to the jurisdiction of the arbitral tribunal. Rules 19 and 20, which are both mandatory, seek to clarify the position with regard to the doctrine of *kompetenz-kompetenz*. In terms of rr 19 and 20, an arbitral tribunal is empowered to rule on its own jurisdictional competence in the following terms:

---

23 See Redfern and Hunter, *Law and Practice of International Commercial Arbitration* (n 20) 302-303; and the discussion in Davidson, *Arbitration* (n 4) 197-198.
24 *Fiona Trust & Holding Corp v Privalov* (n 22) 951 at 959c-e, especially at para 17 per Lord Hoffmann.
25 Section 8 of the Act.
26 Section 9 of the Act.
27 The legal implications of this distinction are addressed by Davidson in "Some thoughts on the draft Arbitration Bill" (n 15) at 45-46.

> The tribunal *may* rule on (a) whether there is a valid arbitration agreement, (b) whether the tribunal is properly constituted, and (c) what matters have been submitted to arbitration in accordance with the arbitration agreement. Any party *may* object to the tribunal on the ground that the tribunal does not have, or has exceeded, its jurisdiction in relation to any matter ...[28]

To that extent, rr 19 and 20 repeal the Scots common law position that the court had the sole authority to determine the jurisdictional competence of the arbitrator[29] and the law has been harmonised in accordance with the UNCITRAL Model Law and English law.[30] However, the difficulty with the above wording, and in particular the dual exercise of the word "may", is that it would appear to have failed to address directly one of the issues in arbitration law which perennially proves to generate complications, namely the existence or non-existence of *concurrent* control on the part of the courts. That is to say, whether the doctrine of *kompetenz-kompetenz* operates in an enabling fashion in the sense that the contracting party seeking to resist the jurisdiction of the arbitral tribunal has the *right* to raise that matter with the arbitrator or whether it means that any objection *must* be raised with the arbitrator.[31] The latter model is referred to as the negative effect of the doctrine of *kompetenz-kompetenz* and is consistent with a regime which entails non-concurrent control. On the face of the wording of SA Rules rr 19 and 20, on balance, the process of statutory interpretation would indicate that these provisions are enabling rather than compulsory, particularly when one considers that they mirror art 16(1) of the UNCITRAL Model Law which commentators have classified as a concurrent control regime.[32] This suggests that the correct interpretation of SA Rules rr 19 and 20 is such that the contracting party seeking to challenge the tribunal's jurisdiction is entitled to bypass the arbitral tribunal and proceed directly to the court with a jurisdictional challenge. Indeed, the text of r 22, which is a default rule permitting the parties to refer a jurisdictional objection direct to the court on certain conditions adumbrated in r 23, suggests that this indeed is the parliamentary intention. In English law, s 32 of the Arbitration Act 1996 and the case of *J T Mackley & Co Ltd v Gosport Marina Ltd*[33] demonstrate that the court will enjoy concurrent jurisdiction with the arbitral tribunal in respect of questions

---

28 Writer's annotations in italics.
29 *Caledonian Railway Co v Greenock and Wemyss Bay Railway Co* (1872) 10 M 892 at 898 per Lord Kinloch; and F Davidson, *Arbitration* (n 4) 187-189.
30 Article 16(1) of the UNCITRAL Model Law; and s 30(1) of the Arbitration Act 1996.
31 F Bachand, "Kompetenz-Kompetenz, Canadian Style" (2009) 25(3) *Arbitration International* 431 at 432.
32 Redfern and Hunter, *Law and Practice of International Commercial Arbitration* (n 20) 305.
33 [2002] EWHC 1315 (TCC).

concerning the jurisdictional competence of the latter, particularly when the issues involved are of general importance concerning the validity of a notice referring a dispute to arbitration. To that extent, it would appear that Scots law will be brought into line with English law, duly adopting a concurrent control regime.

Where the arbitral tribunal has pronounced on its own jurisdictional competence pursuant to an objection raised by a contracting party, r 21 (which is mandatory) provides that either party may apply to the Outer House of the Court of Session for judicial review of the decision of the tribunal on the jurisdictional matter within fourteen days of the arbitral tribunal's decision. There are two particular issues concerning r 21 which are deserving of comment. First, r 21(2) directs that "the tribunal may continue with the arbitration pending determination of the appeal". A literal interpretation of that provision suggests that the scope for an application to be made to the Outer House is limited – that is, it is restricted to the situation where the tribunal rejects a party's objection to its jurisdictional competence. There-fore, where the arbitral tribunal has declined jurisdiction over the dispute, the literal reading would appear to support the view that there is no machinery for a party to judicially review that negative jurisdictional ruling. However, it ought to be noted that r 21 is reflective of art 16(3) of the UNCITRAL Model Law. Commenting on the operation of art 16(3) of the UNCITRAL Model Law in Scotland, Davidson drew support from the observations of the Dervaird Committee[34] (on the correct interpretation of art 16(3)) for the contention that an application for judicial review would be competent on a negative jurisdictional finding.[35] Nevertheless, whether the Scottish courts will elect to adopt a purposive interpretation of r 21 where a negative ruling on jurisdiction is rendered by a tribunal is not wholly free from doubt at this stage. Secondly, the guidance in r 21 on the standard of scrutiny which the Court of Session must apply to this judicial review process is particularly sparse. It is unclear whether the Court of Session's scope of inquiry is limited to an assessment of the perversity or rationality of the tribunal's finding or whether it is intended to be more intrusive to the extent that it enjoins the court to scrutinise the tribunal's rationalisation of the law or a combination of fact and law. It is suggested that this omission is particularly unfortunate since it is an issue which is crucial to the operation of r 21 and one which the courts undoubtedly will be required to address.

34 *Joint Consultative Document with the Departmental Advisory Committee: The UNCITRAL Model Law on International Commercial Arbitration* (1987) 57.
35 F Davidson, *Arbitration* (n 4) 200-201.

Part 3 of the SA Rules governs the duties of the arbitral tribunal and the parties to the arbitration. Here, SA Rules rr 24 and 25 direct that the tribunal and the parties are under an obligation to ensure the arbitration is conducted without unnecessary delay and expense. Moreover, the arbitral tribunal must treat the parties fairly and be impartial and independent. Rule 27 provides that proceedings may be conducted in private. Subject to a number of exceptions, r 26 directs that if the parties, the arbitral tribunal or a third party discloses confidential information relating to the arbitration, this will amount to an actionable wrong as a breach of an obligation of confidence. The definition of "confidential information" in r 26(4) is restricted to non-public information relating to the arbitral dispute, the arbitral proceedings, the arbitral award or any civil proceedings relating to the arbitration in respect of which an order has been granted by a court under s 15 of the Act.[36] This would appear to be sufficiently wide to encompass the parties' pleadings and submissions, witness statements and transcripts of the evidence.[37] This can be contrasted with Australian law where the implied obligation of confidentiality is limited to documents which have been produced pursuant to an order of the tribunal.[38] One of the most important exceptions to the embargo on the release of confidential information is the ability of the parties, the arbitral tribunal or a third party to divulge confidential information in order to "enable any public body or office-holder to perform public functions properly" in terms of r 21(1)(c)(iii). The position of the courts was a particular source of concern in the debates in the Scottish Parliament concerning the Bill, and this wording appears to be sufficient to grant to the courts an immunity from suit.[39] It should be noted that r 26 is a default rule. Therefore, as advocated by Davidson, Scots law does not recognise an implied obligation of confidentiality of arbitral disputes and proceedings, "but rather [leaves it to] the parties to deal with the matter by agreement if they so choose",[40] failing which r 26 will impose a statutory requirement of limited confidentiality. A final point to note is that, where r 26 applies, the arbitral tribunal would appear to have no jurisdiction to rule on claims of breach of confidentiality and the matter

---

36 This is a court order which sanctions the non-disclosure of the identity of any party pursuant to the arbitration in any report of the court proceedings.

37 For example, see the English case of *Hassneh Insurance Co of Israel v Mew* [1993] 2 Lloyd's Rep 243 at 250 per Colman J.

38 *Esso Australia Resources Ltd v Plowman* (1995) 128 ALR 391.

39 See the motion on Stage 1 of the Arbitration (Scotland) Bill at *http://www.scottish.parliament. uk/business/officialReports/meetingsParliament/or-09/sor0625-02.htm#Col18954* (last accessed 3 March 2010) and in particular the points raised by Iain Smith MSP, Lewis McDonald MSP, Gavin Brown MSP and Wendy Alexander MSP at cols 18960, 18963, 18966 and 18969.

40 F Davidson, *Arbitration* (n 4) 212.

is exclusively reserved to the courts. The basis for such an assertion is the presence of the words "actionable as a breach of an obligation of confidence" in r 26(1) which suggests the absence of any role for the tribunal in such matters. This can be contrasted with the views of Thomas LJ in the Court of Appeal in *Emmott v Michael Wilson & Partners*[41] where it was suggested that the arbitral tribunal in which the relevant documents have been produced or generated should determine the issue of breach of confidentiality, rather than the courts.[42]

The regulation of arbitral proceedings, including the procedure and rules of evidence applicable, are governed by Pt 4 of the SA Rules which comprises rr 28-40. These rules relate to the evidential issues and matters of procedure and are default rules and subject to modification. Of much more significance are the mechanisms in Pts 5 and 8 of the SA Rules which enable referrals to be made to the courts on various grounds. Rules 41 and 42 direct that any party to the arbitral proceedings may refer a point of Scots law arising in the arbitration to the Outer House of the Court of Session at any point during the arbitration proceedings. The Outer House may determine that point of law if the parties are in agreement or the tribunal has consented and the court is satisfied that its involvement would entail a substantial saving in expenses and there is a good reason why the issue should be determined by it. Therefore, this provision introduces a limited role for judicial supervision or involvement in the arbitration proceedings. On the face of matters, there might appear to be a danger that court involvement in matters during the course of the arbitration proceedings will inevitably lead to court interference, duly usurping the role of the arbitral tribunal.[43] However, since the parties or the arbitral tribunal must agree to the involvement of the court in terms of r 41, there is limited scope for the courts to be obstructive. Rather bizarrely, while the point of law is being decided by the Outer House, the tribunal has the right to continue with the arbitral proceedings in earnest. No further appeal to the Inner House of the Court of Session or the UK Supreme Court is competent.

Essentially, SA Rules rr 67-69 provide for three mechanisms which enable the parties to challenge an arbitral award once it has been made, namely a jurisdictional challenge, a challenge based on "serious irregularity" in the arbitral tribunal's award and a challenge on the ground that the arbitral

41 [2008] EWCA Civ 184; [2008] 2 All ER (Comm) 193 at 219a-c.
42 S Crookenden, "Who should decide arbitration confidentiality issues?" (2009) 25 *Arbitration International* 603.
43 Redfern and Hunter, *Law and Practice of International Commercial Arbitration* (n 20) 393.

tribunal erred on a point of law. It is noteworthy that the right of appeal is to the Outer House, rather than the Inner House of the Court of Session, a matter which was criticised by the Faculty of Advocates in its written evidence to the Economy, Energy and Tourism Committee of the Scottish Parliament.[44] Rules 67-69 mirror the English procedures for challenge in ss 67-69 of the Arbitration Act 1996. Therefore, it is opined that English case law interpreting the aforementioned sections will be particularly instructive.

The first ground for challenge is based on the lack of jurisdiction of the arbitral tribunal – that is, it entails an assault on the substantive jurisdiction of the arbitral tribunal, for example under an underlying commercial contract or arbitration agreement. It is a mandatory provision and so may not be ousted by the agreement of the parties. Meanwhile, the second basis for a challenge is "serious irregularity" in terms of SA Rules r 68(1). The scope of what is understood by "serious irregularity" is drawn in r 68(2) and covers a myriad of factors which might cause or will cause substantial injustice to the party challenging the arbitral award. Examples of "serious irregularity" include the arbitral tribunal failing to conduct the arbitration in accordance with the agreement, the SA Rules or any other procedure agreed by the parties. Moreover, uncertainty or ambiguity as to the effect of an arbitral award or its effect is specified as a form of serious irregularity. It is also provided that where the tribunal has not treated the parties fairly, acts impartially, outwith its powers (other than exceeding its jurisdiction) or fails to deal with each of the issues put to it, this will amount to "serious irregularity". As for what is meant by a tribunal "acting outwith its powers", the decision of the House of Lords in the English case of *Lesotho Highlands Development Authority v Impregilo spA*[45] is extremely likely to be particularly persuasive. Section 69(2)(b) of the Arbitration Act 1996 stipulates that "serious irregularity" will arise where the arbitral tribunal exceeds its powers. The House of Lords ruled that where a decision of an arbitral tribunal amounts to an error of law, this of itself will not represent an excess of power. Thus, a clear demarcation line was drawn between the "excess of power" ground of "serious irregularity" and a legal error appeal. Since SA Rules rr 68 and 69 craft the same distinction, it is likely that *Lesotho Highlands* will be followed by a Scottish court in the context of a challenge of an arbitral award under the Act.

The third mechanism for challenging the award of an arbitral tribunal is drawn in r 69 and is referred to as a "legal error appeal" – that is, the

---

44 See para 28 at p 6 of the following website: *http://www.scottish.parliament.uk/s3/committees/eet/ inquiries/arbitration/FaculofAdvocates_SupEvid.pdf* (last accessed 3 March 2010).
45 [2006] 1 AC 221.

arbitrator has made an error of Scots law. It should be stressed that this is a default rule. One reason which militates in favour of default status is that the regimes in the Act and the Arbitration Act 1996 are unusual in so far as other modern arbitration regimes do not provide for a right of appeal on a point of law, thus respecting the need for a final, binding resolution of commercial disputes.[46] The danger is that the right of appeal to a court is deployed by an aggrieved party as a delaying tactic or as a means of avoiding the making of a payment under the arbitral award.[47] A separate point to emphasise is that r 69 amounts to the functional equivalent of s 3 of the Administration of Justice (Scotland) Act 1972. However, both are distinctive in as much as the former may be invoked after the final arbitral award has been issued, whereas an appeal could be made under the latter procedure only prior to the finalisation of the award.[48] Another difference between the two is that, unlike the procedure under s 3 of the Administration of Justice (Scotland) Act 1972, an appeal on the ground of error of law is not as of right if the other parties to the arbitration proceedings object. Instead, in such circumstances, leave must be sought from the Outer House.

E. CONCLUSION

While there is much of merit in the Act, the likely benefits which might flow from its introduction into Scots law should not be overstated. Speaking in the chamber of the Scottish Parliament at the Stage 3 proceedings which considered the Bill, Jim Mather MSP, the Minister for Business and Enterprise, rather optimistically opined that "more international arbitration work will be attracted to Scotland and we will see a renaissance of Scottish arbitration"[49] as a result of the reforms introduced by the Act. Indeed, the principal strength of the Act was linked to the advantages which would accrue to Scotland's economic performance by having a modern and effective procedure for the speedy determination of commercial disputes.[50] While being genuinely admirable, a note of caution should be struck to the effect that

---

46 Davidson, "Some thoughts on the draft Arbitration Bill" (n 15) at 64-65; and Redfern and Hunter, *Law and Practice of International Commercial Arbitration* (n 20) 500.

47 Redfern and Hunter, *Law and Practice of International Commercial Arbitration* (n 20) 501.

48 *Fairlie Yacht Slip Ltd v Lumsden* 1977 SLT (Notes) 41 at 42 per LP Emslie.

49 Scottish Parliament, *Official Report*, col 21270 (18 November 2009): *http://www.scottish. parliament.uk/business/officialReports/meetingsParliament/or-09/sor1118-02.htm#Col21260* (accessed 3 March 2010).

50 See the discussion in the Stage 1 Report of the Economy, Energy and Tourism Committee of the Scottish Parliament EE/S3/09/R5, SP Paper 302 at paras 23-34: *http://www.scottish.parliament. uk/S3/committees/eet/reports-09/eer09-05-00.htm* (accessed 3 March 2010).

such pronouncements and objectives are purely aspirational. The erection of a statutory framework which contains an arbitration code which is perceived to reflect the optimum of modern practice does not mean that such goals will be necessarily fulfilled. This point is reinforced by the fact that comprehensive arbitration codes exist and existed prior to the passing of the Act in Scotland, and commercial parties continue to be free to adopt them should they so wish.[51] To that extent, only time will tell whether the Act is a success or its frequency of application is as disappointing as that of the UNCITRAL Model Law applicable to international commercial arbitrations conducted in Scotland. On this note, the writer would end with one particular observation. During the passage of the Act through the Scottish Parliament, evidence given by the Scottish Council for International Arbitration and the Law Society of Scotland cautioned against the repeal of the UNCITRAL Model Law, expressing the point that the merits of such a measure were not wholly clear.[52] The writer would agree with these sentiments and suggest that the repeal of the UNCITRAL Model Law in Scots law was not an inevitable consequence of the introduction of a novel code of arbitration into domestic law. Indeed, it is wholly possible that the two could happily co-exist, with the former being the code of choice for the purposes of international commercial arbitrations and the latter applicable in the case of domestic commercial arbitrations. To that extent, notwithstanding the historically insignificant engagement of the UNCITRAL Model Law in Scotland, there is the real possibility that the decision to repeal it might prove to have been premature and result in a diminution, rather than an increase, in the quantity and frequency of international commercial arbitrations conducted in Scotland.

51 For example, the Scottish Arbitration Code 2007 produced by the Scottish Branch of CIArb: *http://www.scottish-arbitrators.org/z_pdf/scottish_arbitration_code_2007.pdf* (accessed 3 March 2010).

52 See the discussion in the Stage 1 Report of the Economy, Energy and Tourism Committee of the Scottish Parliament EE/S3/09/R5, SP Paper 302 at paras 52-60: *http://www.scottish.parliament. uk/S3/committees/eet/reports-09/eer09-05-00.htm* (accessed 3 March 2010).

16 Environment and Sustainable Development

Colin T Reid°

A. SUSTAINABLE DEVELOPMENT AND ENVIRONMENT
B. CONSTRAINTS
C. SUSTAINABLE DEVELOPMENT
(1) Procedure
(2) Pervasive
(3) Specific
D. ENVIRONMENT
(1) National Parks
(2) Nature conservation
(3) Environmental assessment
(4) Water
E. CLIMATE CHANGE
F. CONCLUSION

A considerable amount of the legislation passed by the Scottish Parliament can be seen as falling within the general area of environment and sustainable development, but providing an assessment of it is not straightforward. In the first place there are difficulties over the scope of what should be covered. Not only do environmental concerns and those relating to sustainable development have a significantly different, and sometimes conflicting, focus, but the limits of both of these concepts are uncertain.

A second key element is the need to take account of the extent to which there are significant constraints on the Scottish Parliament's ability to go its own way on many issues. This arises both because some significant matters are reserved for Westminster (for example, the taxes which are a key mechanism in reducing greenhouse gas emissions) and because so much environmental policy is determined at European Union level. A consequence of the latter point is that much significant legislative activity takes the form of

° Professor of Environmental Law, University of Dundee. I am grateful to my colleagues Andrea Ross (School of Law) and Sarah Hendry (UNESCO Centre for Water Law, Policy and Science) for their helpful comments on a draft of this chapter.

subordinate legislation utilising the wide powers conferred by the European Communities Act 1972, rather than requiring parliamentary legislation.

After considering these preliminary issues in more detail, this chapter will consider the role of sustainable development both within the parliamentary procedures and in the substantive content of legislation, as a pervasive issue and where specific substantive rules are imposed. The main areas where the Scottish Parliament has acted on environmental topics will then be examined, followed by consideration of the Climate Change (Scotland) Act 2009, which is a significant measure for both ideas. The chapter ends with an assessment of the Parliament's contribution in this field.

A. SUSTAINABLE DEVELOPMENT AND ENVIRONMENT

The term "sustainable development" does not have a precise and universally accepted meaning[1] – indeed, that is one of its attractions in political rhetoric – but must be distinguished from purely environmental concerns. That the environment is just one element to be taken into account is integral to the concept, whatever approach is taken. This is reflected in Scottish policy which has viewed sustainable development as an attempt to reconcile economic development and environmental protection,[2] as the means of assessing economic, social and environmental consequences of human activity,[3] or as based on a more multi-faceted approach where "living within environmental limits" is one of five principles on which policy is based.[4] Indeed, there has been concern that the environmental element within sustainable development is too easily outweighed by the competing elements.[5]

In the Scottish legislative context, the position is not altogether consistent, but the balance is clearly in favour of a recognition of the distinction between protecting the environment and promoting sustainable development. Perhaps most significantly, the Environmental Assessment (Scotland) Act 2005 preserves an examination of the environmental consequences of

---

1 "It is a pity that the issue which everyone on the planet will have to tackle at some point has acquired this impenetrable title. It is even more problematic that no definition exists which can be understood by everyone and built into their lives": Scottish Office, *Down to Earth – A Scottish Perspective on Sustainable Development* (1999) 4.

2 *Sustainable Development: The UK Strategy* (Cm 2426, 1994) 32.

3 Scottish Office, *Down to Earth* (n 1).

4 Scottish Executive, *Choosing our Future: Scotland's Sustainable Development Strategy* (2005) 7-9; the other principles are "ensuring a strong, healthy and just society", "achieving a sustainable economy", "promoting good governance" and "using sound science responsibly".

5 A Ross, "Is the environment getting squeezed out of sustainable development?" [2003] *PL* 249.

plans, policies and strategies as a distinct process,[6] as opposed to submerging it in a broader sustainability appraisal.[7] The two ideas are also kept apart in the Transport (Scotland) Act 2005 which expressly requires regional transport strategies to show how transport will be operated "to be consistent with the principle of sustainable development and to conserve and enhance the environment".[8] Within the Parliament the distinction has also been emphasised – for example, during committee sessions on the Nature Conservation (Scotland) Act 2004 the Minister stressed that the conservation measures were only part of the sustainable development strategy and should keep their distinct focus.[9] The current Scottish Government's frequent references to "sustainable economic growth" as an overriding policy goal had raised concern that the economic element was predominating, but more recently this has been balanced by slightly clearer statements that "living within environmental limits" is an inherent part of that concept.[10] It will therefore be necessary to consider the Scottish Parliament's legislation in relation to both sustainable development and the environment.

B. CONSTRAINTS

The extent to which the Scottish Parliament has been able to shape the law in this area is significantly constrained by external limits, under the devolution

6 Although the position is slightly muddied by the requirement when determining the likely significance for the environment of a plan to have regard to "the relevance of the plan or programme for the integration of environmental considerations in particular with a view to promoting sustainable development" (Environmental Assessment (Scotland) Act 2005 Sch 2 para 1).

7 Sustainability appraisals are used in England and Wales under, e.g., Planning and Compulsory Purchase Act 2004 ss 5, 19, 23; Planning Act 2008 ss 5-6; and Marine and Coastal Access Act 2009 Sch 5 para 7.

8 Transport (Scotland) Act 2005 s 5(2); see also Water Environment and Water Services (Scotland) Act 2003 s 2(4), (5).

9 "We have to take a view of sustainable development. We are all aware – the committee is particularly aware – that sustainable development has various component parts. If we try to turn every bill into a sustainable development strategy, we will have missed the point. The bill is about nature conservation and it will play an important part in our overall sustainable development strategy. However, it does not pretend that it is the sustainable development strategy": Ross Finnie (Minister for Environment and Rural Development), Scottish Parliament, *Official Report*, Environment and Rural Development Committee, col 529 (26 November 2003).

10 In the *Scottish Planning Policy* (2010), sustainable economic growth remains the "overarching purpose of the Scottish Government" (para 33) but this is seen as requiring development that "protects and enhances the quality of the natural and built environment as an asset for that growth" (para 33) and although sustainable development is still defined in terms of "integrat[ing] economic, social and environmental objectives" (para 35), "living within environmental limits" is the first of the guiding principles that is mentioned (para 35). These formulations in the final Policy are, however, less "environmental" than those suggested in *Scottish Planning Policy – Proposed Changes Consultation* (2009) para 10.

settlement, and as a consequence of membership of the European Union. At the domestic level, although "the environment" has always been identified as one of the areas within devolved competence,[11] the limits of that competence can significantly hinder the Parliament's freedom of action.[12] In a straightforward way, the geographical limits to the Parliament's powers have been a major issue in relation to the reform of policy and law on marine matters, resulting in a new legal framework split between the Marine and Coastal Access Act 2009 passed at Westminster (which directly confers certain responsibilities on Scottish Ministers)[13] and the Marine (Scotland) Act 2010 passed at Holyrood shortly thereafter.

The range of reserved matters also limits the Parliament's powers, more so than those of the Scottish Ministers since on several points decision-making power has been transferred to Scottish Ministers by executive devolution, for example in relation to consents for electricity generation[14] and the renewables obligation.[15] This issue has perhaps been most clearly demonstrated in relation to climate change, where it is the Westminster Parliament that controls the key fiscal measures designed to lower greenhouse gas emissions.[16] Similarly, taking a holistic approach to the control of waste and the emissions it produces is precluded since one key lever, the landfill tax, is a matter for Westminster,[17] while other possible measures may also trespass onto the reserved areas of competition, consumer protection or product standards.

The extent to which EU law dominates environmental matters is a further limitation on what the Scottish Parliament can do. It is EU law that dictates the key features of the law in Scotland across a wide range of environmental matters and most of this law is made not by the Scottish Parliament but by means of subordinate legislation authorised by the European Communities

11 For example, in the White Paper before the 1997 referendum; *Scotland's Parliament* (Cm 3658, 1997) 6.

12 See generally C T Reid, "Devolution and the environment", in A Ross (ed), *Environment and Regulation*, Hume Papers on Public Policy, vol 8 no 2 (2000).

13 For example, Marine and Coastal Access Act 2009 s 116, in relation to marine conservation zones, to be called marine protected areas off Scotland to match the terminology in the Marine (Scotland) Act 2010.

14 Scotland Act 1998 (Transfer of Functions to Scottish Ministers etc) Order 1999, SI 1999/1750 art 2, Sch 1.

15 The complexity of the legislative arrangements is amply demonstrated by the fact that the footnote reciting the statutory basis for the Scottish Ministers making the Renewables Obligation (Scotland) Order 2007, SSI 2007/267 runs to almost 300 words.

16 Notably the Climate Change Levy under the Finance Act 2000 and the CRC Energy Efficiency Scheme being introduced under the Climate Change Act 2008.

17 Finance Act 1996 Pt III. The Calman Commission has recommended that this tax be devolved to the Scottish authorities: Commission on Scottish Devolution, *Serving Scotland Better: Scotland and the United Kingdom in the 21st Century* (2009) recommendation 3.2.

Act 1972.[18] The Scottish Parliament does not have the power to rewrite much of the law on pollution control, water quality and waste, and a host of other environmental topics where the EU has been active. In two notable examples, however, the Parliament has used primary legislation in areas where south of the Border the usual practice of employing subordinate legislation has been followed.[19]

The first of these is the Water Environment and Water Services (Scotland) Act 2003. Implementing the Water Framework Directive[20] required the introduction of river basin management planning and major measures in relation to water pollution and abstraction. Whereas in England and Wales water law had been significantly reformed during the 1980s and 1990s,[21] there had been no reworking of the law in Scotland, which was to be found in a fragmented patchwork of much amended statutes dating back several decades or more. Accordingly, while subordinate legislation was used south of the Border to make the minimum changes necessary to implement the Directive,[22] the opportunity was taken to reorganise and reformulate the law in Scotland, making a new start with a comprehensive and coherent set of rules. Tidying up the law in a way that stretched well beyond the terms of the Directive required parliamentary intervention.

The second example is the Environmental Assessment (Scotland) Act 2005. Here the choice of parliamentary legislation reflected a political decision to go beyond the terms of the relevant European legislation and to apply the discipline of environmental assessment to a wider range of activities. Under the Strategic Environmental Assessment Directive[23] the requirement to carry out an assessment was extended from certain categories of individual projects[24] to apply also to the approval of certain plans or programmes. In Scotland it was decided that this requirement should apply beyond the scope of the Directive. Initially regulations were made to ensure the timeous implementation of what the Directive formally requires,[25] but

---

18 The extent to which such legislation is made at Whitehall even in devolved matters is explored in A Ross et al, "The implementation of EU environmental law in Scotland" (2009) 13 *Edin LR* 224.

19 The same is true to some extent in relation to the Flood Risk Management (Scotland) Act 2009, in part implementing the Floods Directive (Directive 2007/60 OJ 2007 L288/27), although parliamentary legislation on this subject has followed for England and Wales as well (Flood and Water Management Bill Act 2010).

20 Directive 2000/60 OJ 2000 L327/1.

21 W Howarth and D McGillivray, *Water Pollution and Water Quality Law* (2001) 97-108.

22 Water Environment (Water Framework Directive) (England and Wales) Regulations 2003, SI 2003/3242.

23 Directive 2001/42 OJ 2001 L197/30.

24 Under Directive 85/337 OJ 1985 L175/40, as amended by Directive 97/11 OJ 1997 L73/5.

25 Environmental Assessment of Plans and Programmes (Scotland) Regulations 2004, SSI 2004/258.

then the 2005 Act rendered all plans, programmes and strategies – not just those in the categories listed in the Directive – prepared by Scottish public bodies and office-holders subject to an environmental assessment.[26] Parliamentary legislation was required since this involved going further than merely implementing the Directive and therefore doing more than can be achieved by delegated legislation under the European Communities Act 1972.

C. SUSTAINABLE DEVELOPMENT

Unlike the legislation governing the National Assembly for Wales,[27] the Scotland Act 1998 makes no reference to sustainable development, but the concept has featured in the Parliament's work in three ways. First, some consideration of the impact for sustainable development is included in the legislative process; secondly, a broad obligation to have regard to sustainability has been imposed in many contexts; and thirdly, the concept lies at the core of a few specific measures.

(1) Procedure

The Standing Orders of the Parliament require most Bills to be accompanied by a Policy Memorandum that, among other things, sets out "an assessment of the effects, if any, of the Bill on ... sustainable development".[28] This is potentially a strong tool for ensuring that the full implications of proposed legislation are considered across the whole range of elements covered by the concept. However, a study of the first five years of the Parliament by Ross concluded that these memoranda "reveal[ed] no significant pattern and overall, the quality has remained variable", with "minimal effect on the subsequent parliamentary debates".[29] An examination of the memoranda for the Bills that became Acts during 2008 and 2009 reveals the same picture.

The recent memoranda continue to show a remarkable lack of consistency in phrasing, focus and depth. On some occasions there is just a simple

26 Environmental Assessment (Scotland) Act 2005 ss 4-10; there are some exceptions.
27 Government of Wales Act 1998 s 121 requiring the Assembly to set out how it would exercise its functions so as to promote sustainable development, now replaced by Government of Wales Act 2006 s 79 requiring the ministers to make a sustainable development scheme.
28 Scottish Parliament, Standing Orders (3rd edn 4th rev, June 2009) orders 9.3(3), (3A); Executive Bills must be accompanied by such a memorandum, Committee and Member's Bills may be accompanied by one, but Budget Bills are exempt (SO 9.16(2)).
29 A Ross, "Sustainable development in Scotland post devolution" (2006) 8 Env LR 6 at 20.

statement that there will be no,[30] or no direct,[31] or no negative,[32] impact on sustainable development, often a somewhat surprising conclusion given the range of social, economic and environmental factors included within sustainable development. Where more is said, on a few occasions there is reference to the wider policy context;[33] on others the focus is on the operational activities that will flow from the matters dealt with in the Bill;[34] and only occasionally is there substantial consideration of a range of sustainability issues.[35] Legislation has even proceeded where the memorandum has noted adverse environmental consequences, with little by way of counter-argument on other grounds.[36] The memoranda appear not to be fulfilling their potential as a means of ensuring consistent and thorough regard for sustainable development in the legislative work of the Parliament.

(2) Pervasive

The idea of sustainability first appeared in legislation in 1991[37] and since then has become an increasingly common feature in a wide range of statutes.[38] It is used in several ways, usually as either a general aim or as something to which consideration must be given, rather than in defining specific, enforceable obligations. The form of words used is very variable, but the general position remains fairly consistent, with attention to sustainable development being legally required but very rarely as a dominant consideration.

---

30 Policy Memorandum (para 38) on the Health Boards (Membership and Elections) (Scotland) Act 2009, which surely is relevant to governance and social justice issues.

31 Policy Memorandum (para 31) for the Convention Rights Proceedings (Amendment) (Scotland) Act 2009, which again surely has some relevance to social justice.

32 Policy Memorandum (para 178) for the Sexual Offences (Scotland) Act 2009, where the absence of negative effects is only part of the story and there is a contrast with the Memorandum (para 25) on the Offences (Aggravation by Prejudice) (Scotland) Act 2009 where the social benefits of tackling crime are mentioned.

33 For example, the Policy Memorandum (para 49) for the Scottish Register of Tartans Act 2008 expressly refers to the indicators in the Scottish Government's template for assessing the sustainable impact of policies, and the Policy Memorandum for the Flood Risk Management (Scotland) Act 2009 (paras 182-187) refers to the government's five Strategic Objectives.

34 For example, the Policy Memorandum for the Judiciary and Courts (Scotland) Act 2008 (para 149) refers to the Scottish Courts Service carrying out their [sic] functions with due regard to energy efficiency and sustainable travel plans; similarly the Memorandum for the Glasgow Commonwealth Games Act 2008 (para 81) notes that although the Bill will have no impact on sustainable development, the Games will, and it then outlines steps being taken to deal with this.

35 For example, Policy Memoranda for the Climate Change (Scotland) Act 2009 (paras 179-188) and Flood Risk Management (Scotland) Act 2009 (paras 182-187).

36 Policy Memorandum (paras 62-67) for the Abolition of Bridge Tolls (Scotland) Act 2008.

37 Natural Heritage (Scotland) Act 1991 s 1(1).

38 See generally A Ross, "Why legislate for sustainable development? An examination of sustainable development provisions in UK and Scottish statutes" (2008) 20 JEL 35.

A rare example of the concept being given predominance is in relation to aspects of the town and country planning legislation, where the sole objective expressly stated for development planning functions is that these must be exercised "with the objective of contributing to the achievement of sustainable development".[39] More commonly, the concept appears among other objectives or in a subordinate role. The aims of the National Parks in Scotland include promoting sustainable use of natural resources and sustainable economic and social development of the local communities,[40] and the flood risk management plans prepared by the Scottish Environment Protection Agency must identify measures to achieve certain objectives "in a way which it considers is most sustainable".[41] Where the provisions take the form of more direct duties, these are usually either very weakly phrased or subject to a qualification. Thus, the Scottish Further and Higher Education Funding Council is obliged to "have regard to the desirability of the achieving of sustainable development",[42] while the water legislation places the apparently more robust duty on authorities to "act in the way best calculated to contribute to the achievement of sustainable development", but only "so far as is consistent with the purposes of the relevant enactment or designated function in question".[43] Local authorities must secure best value "in a way which contributes to the achievement of sustainable development",[44] and the Climate Change (Scotland) Act 2009, discussed separately below, contains further examples.

Such provisions offer clear recognition of the significance of sustainable development, but there are major doubts over their effect and enforceability.[45] On the one hand, the presence of such provisions is important since it allows public authorities to shape their decisions and actions with regard to sustainable development in a way which would be unlawful if this was not listed as a consideration that was relevant to their activities. Similarly, it means that they cannot completely ignore the consequences of their actions

---

39 Town and Country Planning (Scotland) Act 1997 s 3E (added by Planning etc (Scotland) Act 2006 s 2).
40 National Parks (Scotland) Act 2000 s 1.
41 Flood Risk Management (Scotland) Act 2009 s 27(4).
42 Further and Higher Education (Scotland) Act 2005 s 20.
43 Water Environment and Water Services (Scotland) Act 2003 s 2(4); similar phrasing is used in the Water Industry (Scotland) Act 2002 s 51.
44 Local Government in Scotland Act 2003 s 1(5).
45 See S Hendry, "Worth the paper that it's written on? An analysis of statutory duty in modern environmental law" [2005] *JPL* 1145; C T Reid and I R Roberts, "Nature conservation duties: More appearance than substance" (2005) 17 *ELM* 162; A Ross, "Why legislate for sustainable development? An examination of sustainable development provisions in UK and Scottish statutes" (2008) 20 *JEL* 35 at 60-65; C T Reid, *Nature Conservation Law*, 3rd edn (2009) 63-64.

from this perspective. On the other hand, it is very unlikely indeed that such duties could ever be directly enforced by the courts,[46] even if the obstacle could be overcome of identifying someone to whom the duty is owed in a manner to establish title and interest to sue. A complete failure to pay any heed to the statutorily listed considerations might provide the basis for challenging the legality of any action (or failure to act) or decision, but given the scope for argument over exactly what sustainable development requires, the wide discretion granted to public authorities and the presence of other, often conflicting, considerations, it will only be in the most extreme of cases that an authority will be held to have acted unlawfully for failing to take heed of sustainability.

(3) Specific

Whereas the previous section has shown that there are several examples of sustainable development featuring in broad duties, specific examples using the concept in a more substantive way are harder to find. This is largely because of the difficulty of defining the concept and because it is in a sense the sum of a variety of different elements. Thus all sorts of measures dealing with economic, social and environmental matters can accurately be labelled as contributing to sustainable development, even though the term is not expressly used and each is limited to a narrow focus. Thus in terms of delivering sustainable development, almost every piece of legislation could be seen as having a greater or lesser role, whether positive or negative. The environmental statutes discussed below are obvious examples, as are measures discussed elsewhere in this book, such as the Planning etc (Scotland) Act 2006 and the legislation on anti-social behaviour, transport and governance issues affecting local government and health bodies.

The one example where sustainable development explicitly has a central role is in relation to the community right to buy under Pt 2 of the Land Reform (Scotland) Act 2003.[47] This legislation creates a mechanism for those living in an area to acquire a right of pre-emption to allow land to be taken into community ownership when it is offered for sale by the existing landowner, and sustainable development is an essential element at several stages. To begin with, a community wishing to make use of the right to buy must incor-

---

46 See the comments on the use and effect of similar broad duties by Maurice Kay LJ in R (Friends of the Earth) v Secretary of State for Energy and Climate Change [2009] EWCA Civ 810 at paras 17-20.

47 A Pillai, "Sustainable rural communities? A legal perspective on the community right to buy" (2010) 27 Land Use Policy 898.

porate a community body and apply to be entered on the register of community interests in land. Before ministers can register the interest they must be satisfied that "the main purpose of the body is consistent with furthering the achievement of sustainable development" and that acquisition of the land by the community body "is compatible with furthering the achievement of sustainable development".[48] If and when the land eventually comes to be sold, ministers can activate the community body's right to buy only if they are satisfied at that stage that "what the community body proposes to do with the land is compatible with furthering the achievement of sustainable development".[49] Sustainable development is similarly a significant consideration in the crofting community right to buy under Pt 3 of the 2003 Act.[50]

These provisions give sustainable development a key role, but given the absence of any statutory definition, or consensus on a precise meaning, their impact is rather uncertain. The relevant guidance does little to crystallise the position, defining sustainable development as an "an integrated long-term approach to economic, social and environmental issues" but making it clear that "the Act does not require that every element of any planned development be compatible with the achievement of sustainable development, but that the application *as a whole* should be compatible with furthering sustainable development".[51] Ministers therefore have wide discretion in what they will accept as furthering the statutory purpose.[52]

D. ENVIRONMENT

Attempting to analyse the environmental legislation of the Scottish Parliament again raises difficulties over the scope of what should be covered. In terms of direct impacts on the quality of the local environment, measures such as the Dog Fouling (Scotland) Act 2003 are as important as any of the legislation with grander environmental ambitions. In similar vein, the Robin Rigg Offshore Wind Farm (Navigation and Fishing) (Scotland) Act 2003, authorising the construction of a substantial wind farm in the Solway Firth, makes a localised but nevertheless important contribution to tackling the global environmental threats more comprehensively addressed in the Climate Change (Scotland) Act 2009, considered separately below. Moreover, in

48 Land Reform (Scotland) Act 2003 ss 34(4), 38(1).
49 Land Reform (Scotland) Act 2003 s 51(3).
50 Land Reform (Scotland) Act 2003 ss 71(4), 73(5), 74(1), 77(3).
51 Scottish Government, *Part 2 of the Land Reform (Scotland) Act 2003: Community Right to Buy - Guidance* (2009) paras 46-50. There is also the issue of the relationship between the guidance here and the differently phrased guidance in planning policy (see n 10 above).
52 Pillai, "Sustainable rural communities?" (n 47).

placing the focus on parliamentary activity, rather than including areas such as waste where the environmental legislating is done predominantly through delegated legislation, it should not be forgotten that such areas do still give rise to occasional parliamentary provisions, such as new rules on the preparation of integrated waste management plans.[53] The environmental element is also more or less strong in a range of measures falling more obviously under other chapters of this book, particularly in relation to the built environment,[54] fisheries,[55] rural development[56] and animal protection.[57]

For the purposes of this section four topics will be covered: National Parks, nature conservation, environmental assessment, and water. There is no common inspiration behind these, nor any strong linking theme, other than that they are areas, unlike so many others, where parliamentary rather than subordinate legislation has played a major role. Together they do show a generally increasing regard for the environment (and sustainable development) across the whole of the Parliament's activities, but usually through incremental change rather than major innovations.

(1) National Parks

The National Parks (Scotland) Act 2000 was the first statute with a significant environmental dimension passed by the Scottish Parliament, but it can hardly be claimed as a product of devolution. Discussion of National Parks in Scotland had never wholly died down after the decision in the late 1940s[58] not to introduce legislation equivalent to that allowing for parks to be established in England and Wales.[59] The starting point of the process that led to the 2000 Act, however, can be viewed as the recommendation in 1991 by the Countryside Commission for Scotland that certain mountain areas be given National Park status.[60] This was followed by the establishment of further working parties and partnerships and the newly elected Labour government announced in 1997 its intention to legislate for National Parks. By the time

---

53 Local Government in Scotland Act 2003 s 34.

54 Planning etc (Scotland) Act 2006.

55 For example, Salmon Conservation (Scotland) Act 2001, Salmon and Freshwater Fisheries (Consolidation) (Scotland) Act 2003, Aquaculture and Fisheries (Scotland) Act 2007.

56 For example, Agricultural Holdings (Scotland) Act 2003 s 18(4) which allows certain conservation activities to fall within the definition of "good husbandry".

57 For example, Fur Farming (Prohibition) (Scotland) Act 2002, Protection of Wild Mammals (Scotland) Act 2002.

58 *National Parks and the Conservation of Scotland* (Cmd 7235, 1947).

59 Taking effect as the National Parks and Access to the Countryside Act 1949.

60 *Brief History of National Parks Proposals* on Scottish Natural Heritage's website at *http://www. snh.org.uk/strategy/natparks/sr-npc02g.asp*.

such legislation was prepared, the Scottish Parliament had been created and was in a position to make it into law.

Although National Parks are not a distinctive idea,[61] the Scottish parks are distinctly different from those south of the Border in several ways,[62] most notably in the inclusion of a number of directly elected members on the National Park authority.[63] This reflects a determination on the part of the Scottish Parliament[64] that there should be a strong local voice in the running of the parks, which should not be in the hands of outside "experts". The same concern is shown in the provisions of the Nature Conservation (Scotland) Act 2004 which require broad notification and consultation before certain powers can be exercised (see below). Another major difference is the longer list of National Park aims in Scotland, including references to sustainable use of natural resources and to promoting sustainable economic and social development of the area's communities.[65] Such provisions show the emergence of sustainability as an important concept in law and policy, and as such are perhaps as much a matter of the date of the legislation as of any truly distinctive approach,[66] although they repeat the strong regard for the fate of those living in areas affected.

(2) Nature conservation

The reforms to nature conservation law again trace their origins to before the advent of devolution, but their final shape was very much the product of the new government and Parliament. After discussions earlier in the decade, in 1998 consultation papers on reform of the system of Sites of Special Scientific Interest (SSSIs) were published separately for Scotland[67] and for England and Wales,[68] where the proposals proceeded fairly rapidly to legislation.[69] In Scotland legislative attention turned first to the National Parks, and by the

---

61 At times political sensitivity to the fact that Scotland was one of the few countries without any areas labelled as National Parks seemed to play as significant a role in the debate as any clear idea of what such parks would add to the existing catalogue of designations.

62 C T Reid, *Nature Conservation Law* (n 45) 240-254.

63 National Parks (Scotland) Act 2000, Sch 1 para 3.

64 The provision for directly elected members was added only at Stage 3 of the parliamentary process.

65 National Parks (Scotland) Act 2000 s 1.

66 Although the recasting of the aims of the National Parks in England and Wales in 1995 did not adopt such language; National Parks and Access to the Countryside Act 1949 s 5(1), as amended by Environment Act 1995 s 61.

67 Scottish Office, *People and Nature: A New Approach to SSSI Designation in Scotland* (1998).

68 Department of the Environment, Transport and the Regions, *Sites of Special Scientific Interest: Better Protection and Management* (1998).

69 Countryside and Rights of Way Act 2000; further minor changes were made by the Natural Environment and Rural Communities Act 2006.

time the Nature Conservation (Scotland) Act 2004 came to be passed, the opportunity had been taken for a wider reform of the law. The law follows the same broad pattern of the previous legal framework,[70] but four features can be identified for comment.

First, the protection of nature is given considerably enhanced priority, with the system of SSSIs significantly strengthened so that the occupiers of land can now be stopped from carrying out damaging operations and ordered to manage their land in particular ways. The actions of statutory undertakers and visitors are also more directly controlled.[71] The legislation additionally extends the protection given to individual plants, birds and animals by penalising reckless as well as intentional conduct that causes them harm or disturbs them.[72] The first element is shared with the reforms in England and Wales but the general extension to include reckless activities is distinctively Scottish.

A second feature, noted above, is that although conservation may still have priority, the Scottish legislation pays heed to the impact of nature conservation measures on the people who live in the areas most affected (usually rural, often remote and too often weak in economic development). The very titles of the consultation papers in 1998 revealed this as a policy difference that was present within Great Britain even before devolution,[73] and it is now reflected in the legislation which requires designation of SSSIs and certain other steps[74] to be notified to a wide range of people, not just the owner and occupier but also community councils and community bodies registered under the Land Reform (Scotland) Act 2003, and to a wide range of statutory authorities and undertakers, all of whom have the opportunity to make representations.[75] Such measures are a response to the size of the areas likely to be designated and the significance of their natural resources for the local economy and to the concern that the emphasis on wildlife tended to ignore the fact that the local communities were also "endangered".

The third feature is the presence of a very generally phrased duty on public bodies and office-holders to exercise their functions to further the conservation of biodiversity.[76] As noted above in relation to sustainable development, such general duties are becoming increasingly common in legisla-

70 For detailed analysis, see Reid, *Nature Conservation Law* (n 45); C T Reid, "Nature conservation law", in F McManus (ed), *Environmental Law in Scotland* (2010).
71 Nature Conservation (Scotland) Act 2004 ss 3-22, 29-37.
72 For example, Nature Conservation (Scotland) Act 2004 Sch 6 paras 2, 8 and 11, amending Wildlife and Countryside Act 1981 ss 1, 9 and 13.
73 See n 67 and 68 above.
74 Nature Conservation (Scotland) Act 2004 ss 3, 29, Sch 3.
75 Nature Conservation (Scotland) Act 2004 s 48(2).
76 Nature Conservation (Scotland) Act 2004 s 1.

tion but their implementation and enforcement remain problematic. Here, two elements help to give more substance to the duty: the specification of the Scottish Biodiversity Strategy to give more concrete form to the notion of biodiversity, and the obligation on Scottish Ministers to report to the Parliament every three years on the implementation of the strategy.[77] Such measures mean that although the uncertainties over direct legal enforcement may remain, there is at least some mechanism, centred on the Parliament, for keeping an eye on what is being done and for ensuring that the obligation does not become a dead-letter. A similar approach is used in relation to climate change, as discussed below.

Finally, the 2004 Act sends mixed messages in relation to the state of the statute book itself. On the positive side, there has been some tidying up and consolidation of provisions. The legislation for Natural Heritage Areas, which was overtaken by developments in relation to National Parks, has been repealed without any such area ever being designated.[78] The new law on SSSIs is set out fully in the 2004 Act rather than through amendments to previous rules. The opportunity was taken to apply a single set of rules for the main controls on SSSIs designated under domestic law and on European Sites designated in compliance with EU conservation law and previously (and still in England and Wales) subject to a separate but broadly parallel regime.[79] On the other hand, many changes to the law on species protection have made by piecemeal, "cut-and-paste" amendments to the Wildlife and Countryside Act 1981, which now exists in two quite differently amended forms for Scotland and for England and Wales, and there has been no consolidation of the rules for species protected under domestic law[80] and under EU law.[81] Opportunities have been missed to simplify the law and make it easier for everyone to understand and apply.

(3) Environmental assessment

The Environmental Assessment (Scotland) Act 2005 demonstrates what is perhaps likely to be the most common pattern for environmental legislation, in that it stems from a combination of distinctive domestic policy choices with

---

77 Nature Conservation (Scotland) Act 2004 s 2.
78 Nature Conservation (Scotland) Act 2004 Sch 7 para 8, repealing Natural Heritage (Scotland) Act 1991 s 6.
79 Conservation (Natural Habitats, etc) (Scotland) Regulations 2004, SSI 2004/475 reg 9.
80 Wildlife and Countryside Act 1981 Pt I, as much amended.
81 Conservation (Natural Habitats, etc) Regulations 1994, SI 1994/2716, as much amended. The confusing overlap between the 1981 Act and the 1994 Regulations which meant that some species were covered by two similar but not identical sets of rules has been removed; Conservation (Natural Habitats, etc) Amendment (Scotland) Regulations 2007, SSI 2007/80 reg 29.

external initiatives that both demand some action and provide constraints on what can be done. There are likely to be comparatively few matters where environmental concerns within Scotland alone are sufficient to generate the impetus for legislative action,[82] and fewer where the Scottish legislators have a completely free hand in view of the need for the law in Scotland to work with measures at international, European or UK levels.

Here the external pressure came from the Directive on strategic environmental assessment,[83] which extended the process of environmental impact assessment from the approval of particular projects to include the approval of official plans and programmes that fall within certain categories. The internal element was the desire, embodied in the coalition agreement reached after the 2003 Scottish Parliament election, that "the full environmental impacts of all new strategies, programmes and plans developed by the public sector" should be properly considered.[84] Implementation of the Directive could have been done by delegated legislation alone, and this is what was done in relation to the plans and programmes on the part of the UK authorities,[85] and initially in Scotland to ensure timeous implementation as far as the Directive required.[86] The 2005 Act was then passed to apply the process (with very limited exceptions) to all plans, programmes and strategies developed by a wide range of public bodies in Scotland.[87]

Given that the Act serves to implement the Directive for those plans and programmes within the latter's terms, it is inevitable (as well as being sensible in any case) that the details of the assessment procedure follow those laid down in the Directive, so that the innovation in the Act is in its scope rather than in the mechanisms that it uses. The Act is thus a good example of both the scope for but legal and political constraints on the Scottish Parliament's environmental initiative.

(4) Water

Water law is the area of environmental law where the Scottish Parliament has been the most active, passing the Water Industry (Scotland) Act 2002, Water Environment and Water Services (Scotland) Act 2003, Water Services etc

82 Nature conservation is perhaps an exception where further significant changes are proposed, largely progressing with unfinished business from earlier reforms rather than in response to any external developments; Scottish Government, *Wildlife and Natural Environment Bill: Consultation Document* (2009).

83 Directive 2001/42 OJ 2001 L197/30.

84 Scottish Government, *A Partnership for a Better Scotland: Partnership Agreement* (2003) 48.

85 Environmental Assessment of Plans and Programmes Regulations 2004, SI 2004/1633.

86 Environmental Assessment of Plans and Programmes (Scotland) Regulations 2004, SSI 2004/258.

87 Environmental Assessment (Scotland) Act 2005 ss 4-6.

(Scotland) Act 2005, and the Flood Risk Management (Scotland) Act 2009. There have been a number of internal and external drivers behind these measures, several linked to infrastructure investment[88] rather than environmental concerns. Again, the need to implement EU law, in the form of the Water Framework and Floods Directives,[89] has proved a catalyst for legislation, but in each case the opportunity has been taken to rework existing law which was felt to be unfit for the challenges of today's world, both physically (as shown by serious floods in recent years) and legally. In relation to both water pollution and flooding, not only did the existing law fail to contain many of the elements required by the new EU legislation, but it was to be found scattered between several statutes of different dates and overlain by multiple layers of amendment. The time was ripe for a reformulation of the law and the presence of the Scottish Parliament enabled this to take place, whereas previously Scottish provisions had just been a minimal "add-on" to legislation concentrating on the position in England and Wales.[90]

In structural terms, the legislation that has emerged is not wholly consistent. The Water Environment and Water Services (Scotland) Act 2003 devotes sixteen sections to the process of river basin management planning, dealing with some aspects in considerable detail, yet in relation to the whole area of controls on water pollution, abstraction and works affecting watercourses the Act contents itself with conferring a broad regulation-making power, so that the detailed rules are to be found in the subsequent Water Environment (Controlled Activities) (Scotland) Regulations 2005.[91] Subordinate legislation thus continues to play a very important role despite the legislative activity in the Parliament itself.

In terms of substance, three general points can be made. The first is to note the move to a more holistic and long-term approach to water resources. This is shown in the role played by river basin management plans[92] and flood risk assessments, maps and plans,[93] all of which require a "joined-up" approach to the influences on and impact of the water environment. Similarly, the concept of "the water environment" as meaning "all surface water, ground-

---

88 S Hendry, "Water resources and water pollution", in F McManus (ed), *Environmental Law in Scotland* (2007) paras 6.136-6.138.
89 Directives 2000/60 OJ 2000 L327/1; and 2007/60 OJ 2007 L288/27.
90 For example, the insertion for Scotland of substantial new provisions on water pollution into the Control of Pollution Act 1974 by Sch 23 to the Water Act 1989 and Sch 16 to the Environment Act 1995.
91 SSI 2005/348.
92 Water Environment and Water Services (Scotland) Act 2003 ss 4-19.
93 Flood Risk Management (Scotland) Act 2009 ss 7-48.

water and wetlands"[94] and the definition of its protection being phrased in terms of aquatic ecosystems[95] reveal the approach being taken. Not unconnected, a second observation is the use of the language of sustainability in several places. Under the Water Environment and Water Services (Scotland) Act 2003 protecting the water environment includes "promoting sustainable water use based on the long-term protection of available water resources",[96] and there is a duty to promote sustainable flood management and to "act in the way best calculated to contribute to the achievement of sustainable development",[97] while the fact that regard must be had for the social and economic impact of the water-related functions again embodies an approach based on the more holistic approach inherent in sustainable development.[98] The Flood Risk Management (Scotland) Act 2009 also makes frequent use of sustainability, requiring authorities to "act in the way best calculated to manage flood risk in a sustainable way", to "promote sustainable flood risk management", and again to "act in the way best calculated to contribute to the achievement of sustainable development".[99]

The third point is the imposition of general duties such as those just mentioned. It is becoming increasingly common for legislation to impose general duties on public authorities, particularly in relation to sustainable development as noted above, but also with different emphasis. Thus the 2009 Act additionally requires authorities to "exercise their flood risk related functions with a view to reducing overall flood risk and, in particular, [to] exercise their functions ... so as to secure compliance with the [Floods] Directive";[100] the 2003 Act requires authorities to act so as to secure compliance with the Water Framework Directive and "so far as practicable, adopt an integrated approach by co-operating with each other with a view to co-ordinating the exercise of their respective functions".[101] This technique is far from restricted to the water legislation, but is particularly noticeable here.

94 Water Environment and Water Services (Scotland) Act 2003 s 3(2).
95 Water Environment and Water Services (Scotland) Act 2003 s 1(2), following the Water Framework Directive.
96 Water Environment and Water Services (Scotland) Act 2003 s 1(2).
97 Water Environment and Water Services (Scotland) Act 2003 s 2(4).
98 Water Environment and Water Services (Scotland) Act 2003 s 2(4).
99 Flood Risk Management (Scotland) Act 2009 s 1(2).
100 Flood Risk Management (Scotland) Act 2009 s 1(1).
101 Water Environment and Water Services (Scotland) Act 2003 s 2(1)-(4).

E. CLIMATE CHANGE

The Climate Change (Scotland) Act 2009 illustrates many of the points made in the preceding sections. Although it has been repeatedly claimed by the Government to be "world-leading legislation"[102] there is not much that is truly innovative in the Act other than the legal status of certain targets. The claim is based more on the ambition of its targets than on the establishment of clear mechanisms and procedures for achieving them. On the other hand, if the Act does indeed lead to changes on the scale needed to meet the targets for reductions in greenhouse gas emissions, then it will be responsible for a major transformation in Scotland's economy.

As in so many of the examples mentioned, the push to legislate has not been of wholly Scottish origins. The need to respond to climate change, a need itself prompted by developments (actual or hoped for) at international level, required action. In view of the devolution arrangements, this had to take place at both UK and Scottish levels, with the Scottish measures being developed alongside but following the UK legislation, the Climate Change Act 2008. The same sort of parallel development has also been seen in relation to marine matters. Dealing with the complex consequences of devolution was a major factor in the development of policy leading to the Marine and Coastal Access Act 2009, which confers additional powers on the Scottish Ministers[103] and was followed by the Marine (Scotland) Act 2010.

The area of climate change also illustrates strongly the constraints on legislative action in Scotland, since many of the key measures that can be introduced to tackle greenhouse gas emissions lie beyond the competence of the Scottish Parliament. In particular, the large-scale emissions trading regime which is central to efforts to reduce emissions is a matter of EU law,[104] while the UK authorities control allowance and trading schemes within the UK[105] and the tax measures that have sought to shift behaviour in recent years.[106] There is very limited scope to introduce new fiscal measures[107] and those that do exist – for example fuel duty and the landfill tax – are outwith the control

---

102 For example, at *http://www.scotland.gov.uk/Topics/Environment/climatechange/scotlands-action*.
103 For example, in relation to Marine Conservation Zones; Marine and Coastal Access Act 2009 s116(5).
104 EU Emissions Trading Scheme; see generally *http://ec.europa.eu/environment/climat/emission/index_en.htm*.
105 For example, the Carbon Reduction Commitment Energy Efficiency Scheme being introduced in 2010; CRC Energy Efficiency Scheme Order 2010, SI 2010/768; Department of Energy and Climate Change, *CRC Energy Efficiency Scheme User Guide* (2010).
106 For example, Climate Change Levy; Finance Act 2000 s 30 and Sch 6.
107 Unless these take the form of "local taxes to fund local authority expenditure": Scotland Act 1998 Sch 5 Pt II A1.

of the Scottish Parliament. Even initiatives on matters such as advertising and labelling of goods will fall within the area of reserved matters in relation to consumer protection.[108]

Despite these constraints, there were still tasks for Scottish legislation to accomplish. Most notably it was appropriate for the Scottish Parliament to determine the nature and extent of any duties to be imposed on the Scottish Ministers and other public authorities in Scotland and to amend or authorise other legislation within the scope of devolved powers where necessary to contribute to reducing greenhouse gas emissions. In keeping with the trend of earlier legislation, it is no surprise that the Climate Change (Scotland) Act 2009 also makes reference to sustainability. There is a general obligation on Ministers to take into account the need to exercise their functions in a way that contributes to the achievement of sustainable development,[109] and on public authorities to act in a way they consider most sustainable.[110] More specifically, a strategy on sustainable land use must be prepared,[111] while the range of factors – scientific, economic, social and environmental – to be considered in the setting of targets reflects the broad and integrated approach required by sustainable development.[112]

Another feature that the Act shares with other environmental legislation is the extent to which further detail is to come in the form of delegated legislation. The Act provides for regulations to be made in relation to a wide range of activities where legislative intervention may be desirable to change behaviour, for example in the preparation of waste prevention and management plans, the provision of recycling facilities and the use of recyclate, or to ensure reporting on performance.[113] In some areas it is unlikely that regulations will ever be made, for example in relation to a charge for the supply of carrier bags, where a direct attempt to introduce this has already been rejected[114] and the hope is that the voluntary measures being adopted by retailers will achieve the reduction sought in the number of bags used.[115] The existence of a clear power for governmental intervention if adequate progress is not

108 Scotland Act 1998 Sch 5 Pt II C7.
109 Climate Change (Scotland) Act 2009 s 92; this obligation also applies to the Advisory Body designated under the Act.
110 Climate Change (Scotland) Act 2009 s 44.
111 Climate Change (Scotland) Act 2009 s 57.
112 Climate Change (Scotland) Act 2009 ss 2(5), 4(4).
113 Climate Change (Scotland) Act 2009 ss 46, 78-82.
114 Environment and Rural Development Committee, *Stage 1 Report on the Environmental Levy on Plastic Bags (Scotland) Bill* (13th Report, 2005) and *Supplementary Stage 1 Report on the Environmental Levy on Plastic Bags (Scotland) Bill* (12th Report, 2006).
115 Policy Memorandum for the Climate Change (Scotland) Act 2009 paras 156-160.

made may act as an incentive on those concerned to ensure that voluntary measures do indeed achieve what is expected. Somewhat unusually, though, a number of these provisions expressly state that the Ministers must make the regulations contemplated,[116] confirming the prominent role for duties under the Act but still leaving the detail of the law to be settled later and outside Parliament.

As just noted, a major element in the 2009 Act is the imposition of a large number of duties on the Scottish Ministers and other public bodies. The main duties on Ministers in relation to the greenhouse gas reduction targets are set in uncompromising terms:

> The Scottish Ministers must ensure that the net Scottish emissions account for the year 2050 is at least 80% lower than the baseline.[117]

The stark phrasing placing an absolute obligation to achieve these targets contrasts with the more familiar language of duties to "have regard to" certain factors or "to further" certain objectives. No sanction is provided if the Ministers fail to carry out the duty but there is a detailed scheme of reporting to the Parliament and the public, supported by monitoring, advice and reports from an advisory body, whose views must be responded to; all of these matters are in turn provided for through the imposition of duties on those concerned.[118] Enforcement therefore relies on publicity and political pressures, but the ultimate consequences of a failure to fulfil the legal duty remain unclear.

Other duties abound in the 2009 Act. The Scottish Ministers are obliged to give guidance on climate change duties; to prepare a land use strategy and plans for promoting energy efficiency and renewable heat; to ensure good energy performance of government properties;[119] to give guidance to Scottish Water requiring it to promote water conservation and water efficiency;[120] and to make regulations on the assessment and energy performance of buildings and in relation to easing planning restrictions on micro-generation.[121] The Advisory Body designated under the Act is required to produce reports and

---

116 For example, in relation to the assessment of energy performance and emissions of buildings: Climate Change (Scotland) Act 2009 ss 63-64,

117 Climate Change (Scotland) Act 2009 s 1(1); similar phrasing is used in relation to the interim target for 2020 (s 2(1)). The "baseline" is the aggregate amount of net Scottish emissions of the various gases covered, measured in 1990 (for carbon dioxide, methane and nitrous oxide) and 1995 (for hydrofluorocarbons, perfluorocarbons and sulphur hexafluoride): Climate Change (Scotland) Act 2009 s 11.

118 Climate Change (Scotland) Act 2009 Pts 2-3.

119 Climate Change (Scotland) Act 2009 s 75, here qualified as a duty "so far as is reasonably practicable".

120 Climate Change (Scotland) Act 2009 s 74, adding Water Industry (Scotland) Act 2002 s 56(1)(aa).

121 Climate Change (Scotland) Act 2009 ss 45, 57, 60-64, 70-71.

advice;[122] public bodies are subject to a duty to exercise their functions in the way best calculated to deliver the greenhouse gas emission targets;[123] and local authorities are bound to establish a scheme for council tax reductions where energy efficiency improvements have been made to dwellings.[124] The number of duties being imposed is impressive; the attention paid to exactly how and by whom they can be enforced less so.

F. CONCLUSION

The Scottish Parliament[125] has devoted considerable time to matters relating to the environment and sustainable development. Pursuing sustainable development is a legal consideration in many contexts, the law on water has been transformed, there have been major changes to nature conservation laws and both the challenging obligations to reduce greenhouse gas emissions and the application of environmental impact assessment to almost all public plans and strategies have the potential to bring about significant shifts in Scotland's attitudes to and impact on the environment. Generally these measures do show an increasing regard for the environment (and sustainable development) across the whole of the Parliament's activities,[126] yet looking around us we do not see evidence of a fundamental alteration. Although proportional representation has allowed the Green Party to have a presence in the Scottish Parliament in a way inconceivable at Westminster,[127] "green" thinking has not predominated.

The overall impression therefore is of an approach much closer to "business as usual" than to one that truly respects environmental limits. This reflects the common preference of governments for "weak" over "strong" sustainability, that is for concepts of sustainable development that continue to place the emphasis on development (albeit with greater environmental awareness) as opposed to regarding ecological sustainability and the need to live within

---

122 Climate Change (Scotland) Act 2009 ss 27-28.
123 Climate Change (Scotland) Act 2009 s 44.
124 Climate Change (Scotland) Act 2009 s 65, adding Local Government Finance Act 1992 s 80A.
125 Like its pre-Union predecessor; see C T Reid, "Environmental legislation of the Scottish Parliament", in H MacQueen (ed), *Stair Society Miscellany VI* (2009) 63-73.
126 Exceptions can be pointed out, such as the Abolition of Bridge Tolls (Scotland) Act 2008 which was expected to increase greenhouse gas emissions, but this can be seen as rectifying an anomaly within a policy that is generally trying to move towards more environmentally-friendly transport system.
127 The Green Party has had one MSP in the first Parliament, seven in the second and two in the third.

the environmental limits of our world[128] as truly overriding considerations.[129] Despite the constraints noted above, a truly sustainability-minded Parliament could have set about radically transforming the environmental impact of life in Scotland.

Looking in more detail at the areas where the Parliament has chosen to legislate, there is little sign of a distinct environmental agenda. Initially, the main measures, such as in relation to National Parks and nature conservation, were the culmination of processes set in motion before devolution, and the other major statutes have been prompted by, or at least developed in parallel with, external developments – primarily EU initiatives. The constraints on the Parliament's powers to some extent make this inevitable, yet more initiative could have been shown. On the other hand, the opportunity has been seized to add a Scottish twist, for example the extra breadth of strategic environmental assessment and the more demanding climate change targets, and to ensure that areas of law in desperate need of reform, such as water, have been tackled.

In terms of content, the pervasive presence of sustainable development is a noteworthy feature, yet there must be doubts over how much difference it really makes. There is no statutory definition of sustainable development, nor even reference to an official strategy or policy as is done for biodiversity, and the uncertainty over the concept's meaning and application further weakens what are usually fairly slight obligations to have regard to sustainability. The varied quality and focus of the comments on sustainable development in the policy memoranda preceding Bills and the contents of the legislation also suggest at most an inconsistent and weak commitment to "weak sustainability" rather than a true embracing of "strong sustainability" or any real commitment to ecological sustainability. The potential for the memoranda to make a significant difference – even in raising awareness among legislators, if not in actually shaping policy – is not being realised.

In terms of legislative techniques, a key feature has been the prevalence of duties being imposed on ministers and public authorities. As discussed above, many of these are weakly phrased, but the Climate Change (Scotland) Act 2009 does impose apparently absolute duties on the Scottish Ministers. Many duties are imposed, but the consequences of failing to fulfil them are not

128 See, e.g., *Living Planet Report 2008* produced by WWF International, the Zoological Society of London and the Global Footprint Network (available at *http://assets.panda.org/downloads/living_planet_report_2008.pdf*).

129 E Heumayer, *Weak versus Strong Sustainability: Exploring the limits of two opposing paradigms*, 2nd edn (2003); A Ross, "Modern Interpretations of Sustainable Development" (2009) 36 *Journal of Law and Society* 32.

set out clearly, although in some cases reporting requirements do provide at least some mechanisms for monitoring progress and for accountability, albeit political rather than legal. This is a development not limited to Scotland or to environmental legislation,[130] and marks a distinct change in our constitutional arrangements, the full impact and implications of which remain to be seen.

In terms of legislative style, there is little else distinctive about the drafting in this area. There have been several bright points where very messy areas of the statute book have been tidied up. Examples where the law has been comprehensively restated, rather than just amended leaving a complicated jigsaw of provisions, include the recasting of the law on water (albeit split between statute and regulations) and of the rules on SSSIs, whose application to European Sites is a further benefit in terms of simplification and consistency.[131] Other small but appreciated steps include the repeal of the never-used provisions on Natural Heritage Areas and the restoration of a sound statutory footing for National Scenic Areas.[132] Nevertheless, there remains far too much piecemeal legislation with cut-and-paste amendments continuing to fragment the statute book and make the law difficult for anyone to work with, even with the benefit of the commercial and (slowly improving) official statutory databases. Delegated legislation continues to play a major, often the major, role in setting out the law, not just in detail but in terms of the key provisions in many areas such as waste and water pollution.

A fuller picture of the impact of the Scottish Parliament on the state of our environment can be gained only by taking into account a much wider range of measures, including significant ones discussed in other chapters of this book, and there are more measures underway[133] or promised.[134] The

---

130 For example, the opening sections in both the Fiscal Responsibility Act 2010 and Child Poverty Act 2010 from Westminste impose clear duties on ministers in very different contexts; see also n 46 above.

131 The consolidation of many statutes into the Salmon and Freshwater Fisheries (Consolidation) (Scotland) Act 2003 can also be mentioned.

132 National Scenic Areas (NSAs) were first provided for by the Town and Country Planning (Scotland) Act 1972 s 262C, which was added by the Housing and Planning Act 1986 Sch 11 para 38. By virtue of the Natural Heritage (Scotland) Act 1991 s 6(8), (9) and Sch 11, s 262C of the 1972 Act was partly repealed and the remainder amended so as to apply to Natural Heritage Areas, but its provisions continued to have effect unaltered in so far as they applied to areas which had already been designated as NSAs. When the planning legislation was consolidated, s 262C was in turn replaced by s 264 of the Town and Country Planning (Scotland) Act 1997, which referred exclusively to Natural Heritage Areas, but again the original provisions of s 262C were saved and continued to apply to existing NSAs (Planning (Consequential Provisions) (Scotland) Act 1997 Sch 3 para 11). Section 264 of the 1997 Act was repealed by the Nature Conservation (Scotland) Act 2004 Sch 7 and NSAs are now authorised by s 263A of the 1997 Act, added by the Planning etc (Scotland) Act 2006 s 50.

133 Marine (Scotland) Act 2010, awaiting Royal Assent as this text is submitted.

134 Scottish Government, *Wildlife and Natural Environment Bill: Consultation Document* (2009).

overall contribution is undoubtedly positive, but the change has been incremental rather than dramatic and there has been no transformation of our law or society on the scale that some would argue is required if we are to seek ecological sustainability and to live within the limits of our natural resources. Given the constitutional limits on its competence, there is only so much that the Scottish Parliament itself can do, but undoubtedly it could have done more.

17 Transport

Ann Faulds and Trudi Craggs[*]

A. INTRODUCTION

Transport is an essential part of any society. Transport systems support economic growth and meet expectations for travel and communication in an increasingly mobile society. Despite its importance, investment in transport infrastructure was limited during the twentieth century – a situation aggravated by unprecedented growth in private car use throughout the UK and elsewhere. The last UK Conservative government introduced a range of measures that altered the balance between subsidised public services and market-driven private services. Competition became a key driver in government policy and the deregulation of bus services transformed the lynchpin of the public transport system.

There has also been an increasing awareness of the environmental costs of travel and the need to address environmental impacts of travel and transport systems. The damaging effects of road congestion on economic activity and growth and of vehicle emissions on climate change were being increasingly

[*] Ann Faulds and Trudi Craggs are partners in Dundas & Wilson, CS, LLP, Solicitors.

recognised at the same time as vehicle use became increasingly essential to people's everyday lives.

These were the transport issues and challenges facing the new Scottish Parliament – challenges which had to be addressed in the context of national and local government structures, the legal framework for transport and the environment, and the availability of funding to support investment. In dealing with these challenges, the Scottish Parliament has taken into account the key drivers of infrastructure investment, environmental mitigation and social inclusion.

B. POLICY CONTEXT AND POLITICAL RISKS

It may be helpful to consider briefly the policy context for the Scottish Parliament's approach to these transport challenges and the political risks inherent in transport investment decisions.

Transport is provided for the pursuance of wider goals: to allow the movement of people and goods for economic and social activities within a spatial framework of locations where these activities are based. These beneficial effects of transport can be counterbalanced by damaging secondary effects such as congestion and pollution. The benefits may be distributed unevenly, leaving groups in the population excluded from access to these activities, or bearing the burden of the indirect negative effects of the transport system. Transport needs to evolve in response to changes in the economy, wealth, demography, technology and social demands. Car ownership in Scotland grew by 25% during the decade to 2008. Transport policy aims to address these challenges now and in the future while maintaining a favourable environment for economic growth and social justice. The key to reconciliation of these often potentially conflicting aims is the adoption of the principle of "sustainable development".

The political context for the formulation and implementation of transport policy is also important. It is generally recognised that transport policy and planning requires a long-term view and commitment to funding. It can take many years to secure the benefits of a transport policy and transport projects certainly take many years to plan, procure and deliver. This long-term requirement is often at odds with the short-term nature of our political systems and administration. The political risk in every major transport project is well known and it is one of the risks that is extremely difficult, if not impossible, to manage out. A recent example of managing political risk was seen in the Edinburgh Tram project. A significant amount of public money had been invested in that project when it found itself at risk of cancellation by the new SNP Government. The Scottish Parliament then voted to continue to support the project, although the consequences of this remain to be seen. The Edinburgh Airport Link was, however, postponed. Likewise, the recent decision to cancel the Glasgow Airport Rail Link triggered some bitter political exchanges between the Scottish Government and the local authority, leaving a general impression that the project had become a political football for reasons quite detached from national or local transport policy. The oft-debated consequences of "political short term-ism" raise fundamental questions about our political structures and the expectations of society that create an environment in which politicians are reluctant to vote for longer-term goals.

Another aspect of the impact of politics on transport planning and projects is the artificial transport boundaries created by current local authority areas. Before 1996, regional councils carried out the functions and duties for roads and transport, as well as strategic planning. This enabled the regional tier of government to focus on wider strategic issues, largely avoiding any potentially adverse effects of political parochialism. The establishment of smaller unitary authorities in 1996 narrowed the local political focus on transport and its challenges. The first attempt by the Scottish Parliament to address the resulting need for a regional transport focus was contained in the Transport (Scotland) Act 2001 (hereafter "the 2001 Act"), which empowered Scottish Ministers to require specified public bodies to prepare joint transport strategies.[1] It is no coincidence that some of the new unitary local authorities created voluntary regional transport partnerships, whose remit and scope mirrored the former jurisdictions of the regional councils.

Joint transport strategies were subsequently replaced by the arrangements put in place by the Transport (Scotland) Act 2005 (hereafter "the 2005 Act") for the establishment of regional transport partnerships,[2] which are considered further below. These new statutory regional transport authorities were placed under a duty to prepare regional transport strategies.[3] However, as transport policy and projects require funding, the risk of local self-interest undermining regional objectives remains. Indeed this risk was greatly increased by the introduction of the Single Outcome Agreement and the consequential removal of ring-fencing of budgets. The Single Outcome Agreement centres on the relationship between national and local government, leaving the

1 2001 Act s 1.
2 2005 Act s 1.
3 2005 Act s 5(1).

regional tier reliant on decisions taken by local politicians. Risks to regional transport policy and projects can now be managed only by local politicians themselves.

C. STATUTORY FRAMEWORK FOR MAKING POLICY

Since devolution, new structures for national, regional and local transport policy-making have been introduced, together with a range of new powers. Scottish transport policy is now set out in three tiers: the national transport strategy, regional transport strategies and local transport strategies.

(1) The national transport strategy

The first national transport strategy (NTS) was published in December 2006. It followed the enactment of the Transport (Scotland) Act 2001 and the Transport (Scotland) Act 2005. The NTS sets out the strategic agenda and identifies three strategic outcomes to be the focus of transport policy over a twenty-year period. These strategic outcomes[4] are:

- to improve journey times and connections, to tackle congestion and the lack of integration and connections in transport which impact on our high-level objectives for economic growth, social inclusion, integration and safety;
- to reduce emissions, to tackle the issues of climate change, air quality and health improvement which impact on our high-level objective for protecting the environment and improving health; and
- to improve quality, accessibility and affordability, to give people a choice of transport where availability means better quality transport services and value for money or an alternative to the car.

A number of commitments are identified relating to each strategic outcome but specific targets are not incorporated in the NTS. All measures requiring Scottish Government approval and funding have to be appraised using Scottish transport appraisal guidance (STAG).[5] STAG sets out a common framework for assessing the implications of transport intervention in relation to economic, environment, social justice and wider policy objectives. It is a useful planning tool for transport projects and initiatives.

(2) Regional transport strategy

The Transport (Scotland) Act 2005 established a new tier of transport authority with the creation of regional transport partnerships (RTP). These

---

4 *Scotland's National Transport Strategy* para 10.
5 See *http://www.scot-tag.org.uk* for details of STAG process. Note that the Scottish Executive changed its name to the Scottish Government in September 2007, although formally it is still designated as the "Scottish Executive" under the Scotland Act 1998.

bodies are made up of councillors from the councils whose area, or any part of the area, falls within the region covered by the RTP and other members who are appointed by Scottish Ministers. Voting restrictions are imposed to the effect that councillor members may vote on all matters but other members may vote only on matters that the RTP determines appropriate.[6] Weightings are also applied to councillor votes to ensure that the minimum voting capacity of councillor members is not less than two-thirds of the whole membership of the RTP. It follows that decisions of the RTP will reflect the views of its constituent councils.

The RTPs were placed under a duty to prepare a regional transport strategy (RTS) for their area and to have their RTS approved by Scottish Ministers. The 2005 Act sets out a range of matters[7] for which the RTS must make provision when assessing regional transport needs. These matters include demographic and land use changes, what can be done taking account of cost, funding and practicability; the transport needs of remote or sparsely populated areas; and the need for efficient transport links between heavily populated places. The RTS must also address how transport can be provided, developed, improved and operated to enhance social and economic well-being; to promote public safety; to be consistent with the principle of sustainable development; to conserve and enhance the environment; to promote social inclusion; to encourage equal opportunities; to facilitate access to health services; and to integrate with transport elsewhere. The RTS proposals must be prioritised and the document must state how the RTP's functions will be exercised to fulfil its strategy. The RTS must also specify other functions that are necessary to fulfil the strategy and should therefore be conferred upon the RTP.

The first round of RTSs was submitted to Scottish Ministers in April 2007. Each RTS took into account ministerial guidance[8] centred on national aims and objectives for transport and on the Scottish Executive's overall policy goals.

The RTS should set out a ten- to fifteen-year strategy to be reviewed, revised and refreshed every four years in line with the local government electoral cycle. It should contain an investment plan, covering the first five to ten years of the strategy, setting out a programme of capital investment required for successful implementation of the RTS. The investment is to be updated whenever considered appropriate by the RTP. A three-year plan to

---

6 2005 Act s 1(2)(e).

7 2005 Act s 5(2).

8 Scottish Executive, *Scotland's Transport Future: Guidance on Regional Transport Strategies* (March 2006).

implement the RTS is to be prepared and updated annually to reflect central and local government planning and funding cycles. The business plan should include both revenue and capital spending and borrowing. Finally, an annual progress report should be prepared by the RTP.

One criticism of the legal framework for RTPs is that they were not given any statutory functions, other than the preparation of the RTS, at the outset. The approach of the 2005 Act was to establish the RTP and have it prepare the RTS. The RTS would tease out what had to be done and how best it could be delivered. That exercise would identify whether or not there was a need for Scottish Ministers to transfer any statutory function currently held by a local authority to the RTP, or if there was a need for the local authority and the RTP to carry out the statutory function concurrently. Unsurprisingly, no statutory functions have been transferred to an RTP[9] so far. If local authorities were reluctant to transfer or share their statutory functions during a period of sustained economic growth, it is extremely unlikely that they will do so in a period of public-sector cutbacks.

Another issue is that, as a consequence of the operation of the Single Outcome Agreement between the Scottish Government and local government, the entire non-national transport budget is allocated to local authorities, without any ring-fencing for transport or local/regional transport projects or initiatives. The practical effect was to remove the capital budgets of RTPs. All RTS projects and initiatives now require direct funding from the constituent authorities. This creates the risk of local priorities and projects (both transport and non-transport) taking precedence over regional issues – the same risk that RTPs were presumably designed to help to manage.

The failure to transfer any statutory functions to RTPs, together with the practical implications of local authorities controlling the RTP capital budget, if any, has the overall effect of negating Chap 1 of Pt 1 of the 2005 Act. If all the RTPs will now do is to prepare a RTS, which is effectively a joint transport strategy,[10] then the Scottish Parliament may well wish to ask itself how it can secure the aims and objectives of Chap 1 of Pt 1 of the 2005 Act. How do we manage the political risks of short-term, parochial decision-making for strategic transport matters? The recent "expenses" press coverage about the Strathclyde Partnership for Transport (SPT) has focused political attention on RTPs. The structures, governance and policy tools are in place, but it

9 Strathclyde Partnership for Transport (SPT) is in a different position as statutory successor to the Strathclyde Passenger Transport Authority, the only PTA in Scotland. SPT therefore continues to operate SPT rail and underground services.
10 2001 Act s 1.

needs political will at both national and local levels of government to secure the benefits of regional transport planning in Scotland.

D. RAISING REVENUE

After a prolonged period of under-investment in transport infrastructure, the economic growth experienced during the decade from 1997 created the opportunity to bring forward major transport projects in Scotland and elsewhere in the UK. Significant sums of public money were invested in roads, bridges, light rail, heavy rail and other projects. Funding was, and is, the key constraint. Whatever the outcome of the current debate on the Scottish Futures Trust, it is clear that that there is no easy solution to this problem, which can only be exacerbated by the recent economic crisis and its impact on future public expenditure. One solution put forward by governments was to spend on public infrastructure projects to stimulate their economies. However, outcomes and solutions for transport investment in Scotland remain uncertain.

In promoting the 2001 Act, two proposals were considered with a view to raising revenue that would be hypothecated for transport investment. One was the introduction of workplace parking levies, which was considered but rejected by the Scottish Executive. They were, however, introduced in England. The other was one of the most controversial transport initiatives in recent times: road user charging, commonly known as "congestion charging". The power to make a road user charging scheme was introduced in the 2001 Act.[11] From the outset, a sense of hesitancy on the part of politicians was clear. The option of imposing a charging scheme on any part of the trunk road network was omitted.

The legal requirements for a road user charging scheme are directly linked to the charging authority's local transport strategy. A scheme can be made only if the charging authority has a local transport strategy and the scheme appears desirable for the purpose of directly or indirectly facilitating the achievement of the policies in its strategy.[12] However, the legal requirement is supplemented by Scottish Government guidance on integrated transport initiatives. As a matter of policy, the Scottish Government imposed a pre-condition requiring the charging authority to demonstrate "clear public support".[13] There is no guidance on what would demonstrate clear public

11 2001 Act s 49.
12 2001 Act s 49(3).
13 Approval in Principle letter from Scottish Ministers to the City of Edinburgh Council, dated 18
    December 2002.

support, leaving it to local politicians to take the first tough decision before the charging order would go anywhere near a minister.

In 2004, the City of Edinburgh Council bravely promoted a charging scheme in support of its integrated transport initiative, which involved a significant investment in trams, roads, public transport, park and ride and other projects. Unlike the equivalent scheme in London, the Edinburgh proposal was the subject of a public inquiry and a local referendum. Although the public inquiry endorsed the scheme, in the face of opposition from neighbouring local authorities, the referendum was not successful and the scheme was abandoned. There was, however, no legal requirement to hold a referendum. It was a political decision to do so. Evidence submitted to the inquiry confirmed that over 40% of Edinburgh residents had no access to a private car. In theory, those people should have benefited from the charging scheme as they would have enjoyed the benefits of increased investment in public transport without having to pay the charge.

The ramifications of the Edinburgh experience probably mean that no political party will risk taking forward what is seen to be a deeply unpopular charge. And yet the road network remains a vital economic resource, with increasing demands for investment and maintenance – and even salt supplies during bad weather. Politically, it may remain easier to manage demand for road space by queuing rather than charging. If that is the case, Pt 3 of the 2001 Act may also be redundant, especially in the context of current government policy to abolish tolls on the Forth and Tay Bridges.[14]

One of the overlooked provisions of the 2001 Act was the creation of joint boards for the management and maintenance of certain bridges.[15] This provision introduced the legal framework to establish the Forth Estuary Transport Authority (FETA). An important effect was to widen the scope of the powers and functions of the bridge authority to enable it to invest in transport infrastructure approaching the bridge. This allowed FETA to invest in the construction of the M90 link road.

E. ENVIRONMENTAL MITIGATION

Addressing the environmental impacts and costs of travel and transport will remain a high priority for policy-makers in the foreseeable future. Scotland faces ambitious targets to reduce emissions and to tackle climate change. In 2004 the transport sector contributed 22% of Scottish carbon emissions, with

14 Abolition of Bridge Tolls (Scotland) Act 2008.
15 2001 Act s 69.

86% of this coming from road transport.[16] The 2001 Act and the 2005 Act each contributed to the legal framework designed to provide tools for this purpose: some have been more effective than others.

The main tool to help manage environmental impacts by reducing car use may have been the power to make a road user charging scheme. However, for reasons already considered, no scheme has been implemented in Scotland and there appears to be no political will to create new schemes.

One of the more successful legal provisions is the introduction of quality partnership schemes in relation to bus services under the 2001 Act.[17] This enables a local transport authority to make a quality partnership scheme to cover all or part of its area if it is satisfied that the scheme will implement its general policies, improve the quality of local bus services, or reduce or limit traffic congestion, noise or air pollution. These schemes appear to be relatively popular with bus operators, perhaps because a partnership is to be preferred to the risk of a quality contract scheme.[18] Under the quality contract scheme, the local transport authority determines what local services should be provided in the area and the standards to which they should be provided.[19] This is a much more onerous scheme which involves a tendering process. However, the less onerous quality partnership scheme provides a useful mechanism for the local transport authority to work with bus operators to secure important environmental improvements. To date, these schemes have only been done on a voluntary basis.

F. SOCIAL INCLUSION

The flagship Scottish Government policy to address social inclusion is the travel concession schemes which can be made at either a local level (as envisaged in the Transport (Scotland) Act 2001[20]) or at a national level (as envisaged by the Transport (Scotland) Act 2005[21]).

A national concessionary travel scheme was introduced on 1 April 2006.[22] This allows anyone aged sixty or over and many disabled people who live in Scotland to travel free on any local bus and scheduled long-distance coach services around Scotland, at all times of the day. This is the only scheme which

16 Scottish Government, *National Transport Strategy* (December 2006) 15-16.
17 2001 Act s 3.
18 2001 Act s 13.
19 2001 Act s 13(5).
20 2001 Act s 68.
21 2005 Act s 40.
22 National Bus Travel Concession Scheme for Older and Disabled Persons (Scotland) Order 2006, SSI 2006/117.

has been made under the powers set out in the 2005 Act, although there is also a young person concessionary scheme in place. Both these schemes should enable the older and younger sections of society, who may not have access to a car, to have the same access to services as those who have a car.

The 2001 Act envisages that a scheme could be promoted by a single local transport authority or by two or more local transport authorities where there is a joint scheme. Similarly to the national scheme, such a scheme would provide concessionary travel for "eligible persons travelling on eligible services on eligible journeys".[23] Section 68(4) outlines the elements which must be included in the local scheme. These include: the rate of the concession, when the concession is available, how the operators will be reimbursed by the local transport authority, and how the scheme will be enforced.

So a local scheme could be tailored to a particular group in society to encourage social inclusion. The scheme could be applied to more than just bus services, depending on the transport services within any local transport authority, and so could be used to ensure that all modes of public transport are treated in the same way so as to maintain competition. For example, in Edinburgh, a local travel concession scheme could include the tram, once operational, and could allow anyone aged 60 or over to travel free on the tram at all times of the day. This would ensure that the tram service is treated in the same way as bus services under the national concessionary travel scheme. However, there has already been debate as to whether such a scheme should really be an extension to the national scheme, funded by central government, rather than a local scheme funded by the local transport authority. How this will be dealt with remains to be seen.

To date, no local travel concession schemes have been made and, given recent public-sector cutbacks, it is unlikely that any schemes will be forthcoming in the near future.

G. INFRASTRUCTURE INVESTMENT

As well as public Acts of the Scottish Parliament dealing with the policy context and addressing issues such as raising revenue, environmental mitigation and social inclusion, the Scottish Parliament has also considered and passed various Private Bills to aid the delivery of new or improved infrastructure after a period of under-investment.

Prior to the establishment of the Scottish Parliament and the Scotland Act 1998 ("the Scotland Act"), most private legislation affecting Scotland

23 2001 Act s 68(1).

was promoted under the Private Legislation Procedure (Scotland) Act 1936.
The Scotland Act amended the 1936 Act[24] so that the Scottish Parliament
could consider Private Bills dealing solely with devolved matters. It may not,
however, always be clear that a Bill which, when introduced, deals solely with
devolved matters will continue to do so.[25]

The Private Bill procedure adopted by the Scottish Parliament allows
parties known as "promoters" to introduce Bills to obtain particular powers
or benefits in excess of, or in conflict with, the general law. Ten Private Bills[26]
have been passed by the Scottish Parliament; seven of these relate to transport projects.[27]

The first transport Bill was the Stirling-Alloa-Kincardine Railway and
Linked Improvements Bill. It was described as having "historic importance",[28]
as "[F]or the first time, the Parliament is considering the delivery of a major
new rail project".[29]

However, despite initial optimism that the Private Bills process was the
way forward for obtaining consent for transport schemes, the Stirling-Alloa-
Kincardine Railway is the only one to be constructed and operating successfully. Two schemes are currently under construction (the Edinburgh tram
project and the Airdrie-Bathgate Railway) and one is currently being
procured (the Waverley railway line). Two schemes have been shelved (the
Edinburgh Airport Rail Link and the Glasgow Airport Rail Link) because of
lack of funding.

Given the track record of delivering transport projects in Scotland, the
Scottish Parliament may wish to ask itself why the Private Bill process has not
ensured that all of the transport projects have been delivered. Has the Private
Bill process been a success or has it fallen short of what it was intended to do?
Is there a "missing link" between authorising a project and funding it? How

24 Paragraph 5 of Sch 8 to the Scotland Act 1998.
25 For example at the final stage of the Edinburgh Tram (Line One) Bill, amendments to introduce
   a speed limit for the tram were proposed. However, as the setting of speed limits had not been
   devolved to the Scottish Parliament, such an amendment was deemed to be outwith its competence.
26 The Stirling-Alloa-Kincardine Railway and Linked Improvements Bill and the Robin Rigg
   Offshore Wind Farm (Navigation and Fishing) (Scotland) Bill were introduced in Session 1 of
   the Scottish Parliament but fell. They were carried over and re-introduced during Session 2.
27 These are the Stirling-Alloa-Kincardine Railway and Linked Improvements Bill, the Edinburgh
   Tram (Line One) Bill, the Edinburgh Tram (Line Two) Bill, the Waverley Railway (Scotland) Bill,
   the Glasgow Airport Rail Link Bill, the Edinburgh Airport Rail Link Bill and the Airdrie-Bathgate
   Railway and Linked Improvements Bill.
28 Scottish Parliament, *Official Report*, Stirling-Alloa-Kincardine Railway and Linked Improvements Bill Committee, col 4245 (11 December 2003).
29 Scottish Parliament, *Official Report*, Stirling-Alloa-Kincardine Railway and Linked Improvements Bill Committee, col 4242 (11 December 2003).

can funding be guaranteed to ensure that projects are delivered? Should there be a role for the Scottish Parliament following the passing of a Bill to monitor progress and to ensure that the will of the Parliament is adhered to?

H. THE PRIVATE BILL PROCESS

Consenting processes are often criticised for taking too long, particularly when compared with processes elsewhere in Europe. The passage of the Stirling-Alloa-Kincardine Railway and Linked Improvements Bill took almost fourteen months from introduction to receiving Royal Assent, which is perhaps not excessive. However, it took some twenty-six months for the two Edinburgh tram Bills to receive Royal Assent and the Waverley Railway (Scotland) Bill took almost three years from introduction to receiving Royal Assent.

It was clear from the outset, during the consideration of the Stirling-Alloa-Kincardine Railway and Linked Improvements Bill, that there were concerns in the Parliament about the Private Bills procedure: it was noted that "we must think about whether using an antediluvian process that is a hangover from the Victorian days – indeed it is a hangover from Westminster – is the best way of delivering major rail infrastructure projects ... "[30]

By the end of the consideration of the Stirling-Alloa-Kincardine Railway and Linked Improvements Bill, the Procedures Committee had been tasked with reviewing the procedure in response to the criticisms from both the committee considering the Bill and other MSPs. The Procedures Committee agreed to undertake a fundamental review of the procedure by taking a two-strand approach: it would consider longer-term options for removing from the Scottish Parliament some or all of the responsibility for scrutinising Private Bills, and also shorter-term priority improvements to the current procedures, given that Bills were still being promoted and required to be considered. The Procedures Committee heard evidence from various parties including the Scottish Executive, promoters, parliamentary agents and consultees.[31]

As a result of this, the Procedures Committee recommended that primary legislation be promoted by the Scottish Executive based on the Transport and

---

30 Scottish Parliament, *Official Report*, Stirling-Alloa-Kincardine Railway and Linked Improvements Bill Committee, col 4249 (11 December 2003).

31 Scottish Parliament, *Official Report*, Procedures Committee, col 682 (9 November 2004); Scottish Parliament, *Official Report*, Procedures Committee, col 708 (23 November 2004); Scottish Parliament, *Official Report*, Procedures Committee, col 730 (7 December 2004); and Scottish Parliament, *Official Report*, Procedures Committee, col 789 (1 February 2005).

Works order model in England, but with additional parliamentary scrutiny to ensure that there was still some accountability in the process. It considered that the main advantage of moving to a statutory process, as opposed to a purely parliamentary process, was that the detailed scrutiny would be carried out by persons appointed for that purpose rather than by MSPs, who may not have the relevant qualifications and experience. It was thought that by having a dedicated person to scrutinise Private Bills, the process would be quicker and more efficient, allowing more Bills to be taken forward and considered.[32] It was, however, recognised that it would take some time to bring forward the necessary legislation and that the Bills which were already being considered would not benefit from any change to the process.[33]

Consequently, in September 2005, the Procedures Committee was asked to consider a proposal which would allow independent assessors from the Inquiry Reporters Unit to hear and consider objections during the first phase of the consideration stage.[34] In essence, the assessor would provide a report for the committee to consider and to decide how to proceed. The primary benefit of this approach was that it would again reduce the burden on MSPs in dealing with complex and technical matters. It would also allow this part of the process to be dealt with more efficiently as it would allow evidence to be taken on four days each week rather than on one day. While not convinced that the introduction of the use of assessors would save much time for the last three Bills to be introduced, the Committee considered that it was a useful option albeit that the statutory solution was more satisfactory.[35]

Assessors were used for both the Edinburgh Airport Rail Link and the Glasgow Airport Rail Link. They took twelve and ten months respectively from introduction to being passed, a considerably shorter period when compared with the Edinburgh tram Bills. Similarly, the Airdrie-Bathgate Railway and Linked Improvement Bill took ten months. Clearly, this was an improvement to the process.

The longer-term solution was to introduce primary legislation to provide an alternative to the Private Bill process and this resulted in the Transport and Works (Scotland) Act 2007. This Act allows Scottish Ministers to make orders to authorise transport developments instead of these projects requiring Private Bills.[36] The aim was to make the process quicker, more proportionate

32 Scottish Parliament, Procedures Committee Report, 4th Report 2005 paras 31-34.
33 Scottish Parliament, Procedures Committee Report (n 32) paras 35, 118.
34 Paper (PR/S2/05/11/5) for Procedures Committee meeting on 27 September; Scottish Parliament, *Official Report*, Procedures Committee, col 1133 (27 September 2005).
35 Scottish Parliament, Procedures Committee Report, 1st Report 2006 paras 31, 34.
36 Explanatory Notes to the Transport and Works (Scotland) Act 2007 para 4.

and to make the Scottish Ministers rather than the Scottish Parliament the decision-making body where appropriate. In certain circumstances, however, the order must be approved by the Scottish Parliament: that is, where the order relates to a national development; where the order would amend a private Act of the Scottish Parliament; or where Scottish Ministers direct that the order should be approved by the Scottish Parliament.[37]

The 2007 Act sets out the procedure for making an order. Similarly to the Private Bills process, the 2007 Act outlines the procedure for making an application;[38] the procedure for making an objection or representation to the order;[39] what powers and consents can be sought under an order;[40] when an inquiry would be held;[41] and the making of the order itself.[42]

To date, only one order has been promoted using the new legislation.[43] Interestingly, however, since the Transport and Works (Scotland) Act 2007 came into force, a new "hybrid" procedure has been introduced,[44] which is being used for the Replacement Forth Crossing Bill. A Hybrid Bill "is a Public Bill introduced by a member of the Scottish Executive which adversely affects a particular interest of an individual or body in a manner different to the private interests of other individuals or bodies of the same category or class".[45] To ensure that the process is both robust and transparent, it is based on the Private Bill procedure, which has been adapted. It will be interesting to see how the hybrid process works, as this is the first time it has been used.

It is clear that the Scottish Parliament has learnt lessons from the passage of the various Private Bills and has tried to adapt the parliamentary process where possible, given the difficulties of requiring changes to be made, or of passing new primary legislation. That said, the 2007 Act, which is the alternative to the Private Bill process for works schemes, is untried and so it is not yet possible to compare the two processes or to assess whether the 2007 Act is fit for purpose and is a better alternative. This remains to be seen.

37 Transport and Works (Scotland) Act 2007 (hereafter "the 2007 Act") s 13.
38 2007 Act s 4.
39 2007 Act s 8.
40 2007 Act ss 14-15.
41 2007 Act s 9.
42 2007 Act ss 11-13.
43 Network Rail (Waverley Steps) Order, which was submitted on 11 February 2009.
44 Scottish Parliament, *Official Report*. 25 June 2009; Parliamentary Standing Orders Chapter 9C.
45 Standing Order 9C.1.1.

I. FINANCIAL SCRUTINY

The robustness of the assessment by the Private Bills Committees of the financial implications of transport projects must be questioned given that, to date, all of the schemes authorised by private Acts of the Scottish Parliament are now predicting out-turn costs in excess of the estimate of costs presented to the relevant committee. The costs associated with the Stirling-Alloa-Kincardine Railway escalated considerably during construction. As mentioned above, both the Edinburgh Airport Rail Link and the Glasgow Airport Rail Link were cancelled because of the fact that costs had increased significantly after the Bills were passed. The mounting costs of the Edinburgh tram project have been well documented in the press. So, could the Scottish Parliament have done anything to prevent this?

At the preliminary stage the Private Bill Committee must produce a report on whether to recommend to the Scottish Parliament that, first, the general principles of the Bill should be agreed to; and, secondly, that the Bill should proceed as a Private Bill. The consideration of these matters has in all of the Bills focused on the STAG appraisal, which tests the project against five key areas and also includes a cost/benefit appraisal for the project.

The STAG process was introduced to assess road schemes which were funded by the Scottish Government. However, the process has not been adapted for other types of transport schemes and not all benefits can be captured and measured as part of the appraisal process.

Significantly, the STAG appraisal is not an accompanying document as defined in the standing orders for the Private Bill process and thus it is questionable as to whether it even has a role in the Private Bills process. What is, however, an accompanying document is the estimate of expense and funding statement.[46] This sets out the estimated total cost of the project, and includes a detailed breakdown of each element of the project as well as details of the sources of funding for the project. It also sets out an estimate of the timescales of when the costs would be incurred and the funding required. The margin of uncertainties in relation to any aspect of the estimate should also be detailed.

In addition, where a Private Bill requires a payment from the Scottish Consolidated Fund or would have an impact on that fund, then the Scottish Parliament must agree to that expenditure by passing a financial resolution.[47] It is not clear, however, what the financial resolution is intended to do. As we have seen in relation to the Glasgow Airport Rail Link, it does not mean that

46 Standing Order 9A.2.3.
47 Standing Order 9A.14.

the funding is secure or available when required. Spending is determined annually as part of the Government's budget. Even if it did secure funding, it is doubtful that any reliance could be placed on the cost estimates provided to the Scottish Parliament, given the example of the actual out-turn costs for the Stirling-Alloa-Kincardine railway.

The flaw appears to be that the Private Bill process simply authorises the project. It gives powers to the promoter, but it is up to the promoter to decide whether to exercise those powers. The promoter, of course, has a commercial interest. If there is a public need for the infrastructure project, then it is assumed that it would be promoted and funded by central government.

So while it is for the promoter to decide whether to use the powers it has been given, it is for the Scottish Government to decide whether to fund the project, based on the STAG appraisal and subsequent business cases provided by the promoter to secure the necessary funding. Other than annual approval of the budget, the Scottish Parliament has very little control over how the money is actually spent and which schemes are funded. This was recognised by the Procedures Committee when reviewing the Private Bill process, which commented that "we need to have a process in which the Parliament can scrutinise fully the financial implications of private bills".[48]

Even if there was a process, however, MSPs cannot be expected to assess the financial viability of a project as part of the authorisation process. Furthermore, it is arguable that the funding of a scheme is not relevant when considering whether to grant authorisation to construct. That is perhaps a matter for a later stage and/or for others. That said, there would be a lack of realism if funding was not considered at the authorisation stage. Indeed, promoters and the Scottish Parliament could be criticised for wasting public time and money by considering schemes through the Private Bill process which are later found to be unaffordable and thus will never be delivered. But is the scrutiny through the Private Bill process adequate?

In the Waverley Railway (Scotland) Bill it was clear that cost control and over-runs were something for the promoter to manage – the Bill Committee stated that:

> It is for the promoter to ensure that, should the project proceed, costs are strictly adhered to and for the Scottish Executive, to satisfy itself as principal funder, that the promoter is managing the project in the most efficient and cost effective way… The Committee takes no further view on any of these issues, accepting they are post-Bill permission matters between the promoter and the Scottish Executive.[49]

48 Scottish Parliament, *Official Report*, Procedures Committee, col 913.
49 Waverley Railway (Scotland) Bill Committee, Preliminary Stage Report para 181.

Concerns about cost over-runs were also raised in relation to the Edinburgh tram Bills. During the parliamentary process, both committees placed considerable reliance on the STAG Appraisal and the cost/benefit analysis when considering the general principles of the Bills. In relation to the Edinburgh Tram (Line One) Bill, there was an additional evidence-taking session after the consideration stage on the general principles, focusing on the cost of the project.[50] It is clear that the committees were concerned about cost certainty and funding. Phasing was considered by the committees, but no amendments were made to the Bills to reflect any concerns in relation to funding.[51] Moreover, it is not clear whether such an amendment would even be competent.

So are cost control and funding post-Bill permission matters? Is that an abdication of the Scottish Parliament's responsibility and accountability or are these correctly matters for others? Should there be such a separation? In the planning system, the ability to fund and deliver a development for which planning permission is being sought is not a material consideration which should be taken in to account when considering whether to grant planning permission.

A Private Bill, however, does more than give permission to construct. It may also give permission to acquire land. So perhaps it is more apt to compare the Private Bill process with the compulsory purchase process under planning legislation. In the latter process, it is usual to demonstrate financial viability and deliverability. This begs the question of whether separating the consideration and responsibility for funding and cost control between the Scottish Parliament and the Scottish Government in the Private Bill process results in it being less effective than it could be.

As indicated above, the Stirling-Alloa-Kincardine Railway project is the only transport project to date which has been constructed and is operational. There were concerns at the preliminary stage about the benefits of the scheme and about its costs. The final cost of the scheme is more than twice the estimate provided to the Scottish Parliament and the railway was opened significantly later than predicted. That said, in its first year passenger numbers were well over double those forecast,[52] and it may therefore be argued that the project has been a success story.

In the final analysis, it is doubtful whether the Scottish Parliament could have done more to prevent or to manage the increased cost and delays. But,

50 Scottish Parliament, Edinburgh Tram (Line One) Bill Committee meeting, 7 February 2006.
51 Marshalled List of Amendments for Consideration Stage.
52 Transport Scotland Annual Report 2008/09, Chief Executive's Introduction p 2.

worryingly, will all of the projects authorised by Private Bills suffer a similar fate of increased construction costs and delays? Only time will tell, although the Edinburgh tram project is already reported to be significantly over budget and may be delayed by up to four years.

J. PUBLIC PERCEPTION

One of the aims of the Private Bill process was to ensure that the schemes were robustly scrutinised, given that, if passed, they would affect the interests and rights of private individuals. This aim was apparent from the first Bill when the Stirling-Alloa-Kincardine Railway and Linked Improvements Bill Committee was directed to give the Bill "fair cautious and objective"[53] consideration.

Generally, the Bills have followed model clauses used in Bills promoted at Westminster or orders promoted under the Transport and Works Act 1992. However, the Scottish Parliament should be commended for trying to ensure that plain English was used in the drafting of Bills so that they were clearly understood by all. It also questioned some of the model provisions in Bills and orders south of the Border, in particular the use of protective provisions. Some thought that this was the Scottish Parliament stamping its authority on the process, and striving to be different from Westminster. But, by questioning the drafting, the Parliament ensured that Bills were more concise and arguably more effective.

Very few amendments were made to the Stirling-Alloa-Kincardine Railway and Linked Improvements Bill during the consideration stage and no amendments were made during the final-stage debate prior to the Bill being passed. This, with hindsight, is perhaps not surprising, given the Parliament's inexperience of dealing with Private Bills.

When the Edinburgh tram Bills were considered, however, there were amendments to link the obligations in the Bills to their environmental statements, their codes of construction practice and their noise and vibration policies. At that time, the Environmental Statement was an accompanying document, but there was no clear link between the provisions of the Bills and the commitments within the statement: there was nothing which obliged the promoter to comply with its environmental statement and the Bills were amended accordingly. Similarly, the code of construction practice and the noise and vibration policy were prepared to address objections to the Bills,

---

53 Scottish Parliament, *Official Report*, Stirling-Alloa-Kincardine Railway and Linked Improvements Bill Committee, col 114 (10 November 2003).

but, as originally drafted, there was no obligation on the promoter to comply with these documents. Again, to ensure that the promoter was obliged to carry out the commitments it had made to the committee, the Bills were amended.

This approach has been adopted in every subsequent Bill and must surely have been welcomed by objectors. The Scottish Parliament clearly perceived a gap, and through amendments has sought to ensure that there is sufficient protection for objectors. Given that accompanying commitments have been made by promoters and relied upon by the Parliament's committees, such an approach should cause no difficulty to prudent promoters but will give considerable comfort to objectors. Some of the Bills went further and provided for the appointment of an officer to monitor and ensure compliance with the environmental commitments.[54]

When it came to the Waverley Railway (Scotland) Act, the Bill Committee also introduced a section with more far-reaching consequences for the delivery of the project. During the preliminary stage, there were clearly two conflicting views on the need to have a station at Stow. However, the Committee weighed up both sides and concluded that there was merit in investigating it further. The promoter did carry out further investigation, but it was apparent to the committee that the promoter still did not intend to build a station at Stow.

Siding with the objectors, the committee wanted to ensure that station would be provided given that the local community perceived a need. Thus, s 1(3) was inserted – it is commonly referred to as the "Mastermind Clause", so-called because of the late Magnus Magnusson's catch phrase in the TV programme *Mastermind*: "I've started so I'll finish". In the case of the Waverley (Scotland) Act, it means that once the authorised works are started, they must be finished. The intention of the clause was to ensure that all of the works and stations, including the one at Stow, were constructed. But could it frustrate the delivery of the project? And were the funding implications adequately considered?

What is apparent is that the committees on the various Bills clearly listened to the objectors and tried to ensure that there was a balance between authorising a scheme for the greater benefit while protecting individual interests. The Scottish Parliament should be commended for dealing with objections and for forcing amendments where necessary to ensure that promoters complied with commitments and undertakings they had given the committee.

54 Waverley Railway (Scotland) Act 2006 s 48; Glasgow Airport Rail Link Act 2007 s 46; Edinburgh Airport Rail Link 2007 s 51; Airdrie-Bathgate Railway and Linked Improvements Act 2007 s 47.

K. CONCLUSION

Has the first decade of law making by the Scottish Parliament been a success when it comes to transport? It is argued that the statutory context for transport policy-making and many of the transport policies introduced by the Transport (Scotland) Act 2001 and the Transport (Scotland) Act 2005 have been successful in helping the Scottish Government to achieve sustainable growth and have contributed towards achieving environmental targets and social inclusion.

The introduction of RTPs should have been a success, allowing, among other things, transport solutions to be considered from a regional perspective in order to promote sustainable development, conserve and enhance the environment and promote social inclusion. The absence of statutory functions and latterly funding has perhaps undermined the role of RTPs, although there may now be an opportunity to reconsider their role within the new world of public spending constraints.

The Scottish Parliament is clearly prepared to consider radical solutions to raising revenue to fund transport projects, having passed the Transport (Scotland) Act 2001 which introduced the powers to set up road user charging schemes. Its willingness to do so may be important in the future.

The Private Bill process has allowed promoters to bring forward transport schemes. After years of under-investment, a significant number of Bills have been promoted and this has been a learning process for the Scottish Parliament, promoters and objectors. The Scottish Parliament has shown that it is proactive and not afraid to change the way it carries out its business. It reviewed and changed its procedures to ensure that they were fit for purpose, efficient and proportionate. This has led to the introduction of the assessor process within the Private Bills process, the Hybrid Bill process, and the passing of the Transport and Works (Scotland) Act 2007. While not all of the schemes to date have been delivered, the Scottish Parliament has sought to balance the interests of the promoter and the objector within its remit.

Inevitably, funding is one of the key constraints which have frustrated the delivery of some of the projects, and political risk is another. These will no doubt continue to hamper the ability to deliver transport projects. But we have seen a raft of significant public and private legislation passed by the Scottish Parliament during its first decade, dealing with transport policy, revenue raising, environmental mitigation, social inclusion and infrastructure investment. It remains to be seen, however, whether the legislation delivers what the Scottish Parliament intended it to do.

Index

References to authors are those discussed in the text. References to footnotes are indicated by 'n' after the page number.

special measures, 257–60; *see also* vulnerable witness
STAG, 344, 355
Standards Commission for Scotland, 133
Stirling-Alloa-Kincardine Railway, 351, 352, 355, 356, 357, 358
Stow railway station, 359
Strathclyde Partnership for Transport, 346
Strathclyde Passenger Transport Authority, 346n
Straw, J, 226
Strengthening Judicial Independence in a Modern Scotland, 191
STV (single transferable vote), 136–7
sustainable development
  community right to buy, 325–6
  crofting, 326
  environment and, 319
  flood risk, 321n, 324
  flood risk management, 333
  local authorities, 324, 325
  meaning, 318
  national parks, 324
  overview of Scottish Parliament influence, 337–40
  pervasive, 323–5
  policy memoranda, 322–3, 338
  procedure, 322–3
  Scottish policy, 318
  specific examples, 325–6
  sustainable economic growth, 319
  town and country planning, 324
  water environment, 324, 333
sustainable land use strategy, 335

tainted blood, 46, 52
tartan
  definition, 86
  Scottish Register of Tartans, 86
Tay Bridge tolls, 348
television link, 258, 261; *see also* vulnerable witness
Tenement Management Scheme, 296, 301
tenements
  abandonment, 298
  access, 297
  acquiring right, 297
  air space, 295
  boundaries, 295
  common law, 294
  demolition, 297–8

dormer windows, 295
insurance, 297
liability for arrears, 296–7
maintenance and repair, 294–5, 296, 301
notice of potential liability for costs, 297
ownership, 295
pertinents, 295
services, 297
solum 295
support and shelter, 296
Tierney, S, 223
time-bar provision, 46–9
Tisdall, K, 249
town and country planning, 324
transport
  abolition of bridge tolls, 348
  alternative to Private Bill process, 353–4
  bridges, management and maintenance, 348
  congestion charging, 347
  development costs, escalation of, 355
  Edinburgh Airport link, 343
  Edinburgh Tram project, 342–3, 350
  environmental mitigation, 348–9
  financial resolution, 355–6
  financial scrutiny, 355–8
  financial viability of project, 356
  Forth Crossing replacement, 354
  Forth Estuary Transport Authority, 348
  generally, 341–2
  Glasgow Airport Rail Link, 343
  hybrid procedure, 354
  infrastructure investment, 350–2
  integrated transport initiatives, 347–8
  joint transport strategies, 343, 346
  local travel concession scheme, 350
  'Mastermind Clause', 359
  national transport strategy, 344
  orders to authorise developments, 353–4
  overview of Scottish Parliament influence, 360–1
  policy context, 342–4
  Private Bill procedure, 351–2; *see also* Private Bill
  public perception, 358–60
  quality contract scheme, 349